THE STRUGGLE FOR SOCIAL SUSTAINABILITY

Moral Conflicts in Global Social Policy

Edited by
Christopher Deeming

D1612594

P

First published in Great Britain in 2022 by

Policy Press, an imprint of
Bristol University Press
University of Bristol
1-9 Old Park Hill
Bristol
BS2 8BB
UK
t: +44 (0)117 374 6645
e: bup-info@bristol.ac.uk

Details of international sales and distribution partners are available at
policy.bristoluniversitypress.co.uk

British Library Cataloguing in Publication Data
A catalogue record for this book is available from the British Library

ISBN 978-1-4473-5610-3 hardcover
ISBN 978-1-4473-5611-0 paperback
ISBN 978-1-4473-5613-4 ePub
ISBN 978-1-4473-5612-7 ePdf

The right of Christopher Deeming to be identified as editor of this work has been asserted by
him in accordance with the Copyright, Designs and Patents Act 1988.

Cover design: Robin Hawes
Front cover image: shutterstock_29669362

Bristol University Press and Policy Press use environmentally responsible
print partners.

Printed in Great Britain by CMP, Poole

Contents

List of boxes, figures and tables

Boxes

Figures

Tables

List of boxes, figures and tables

List of abbreviations

AIPs	anti-immigrant parties
B4IG	Business for Inclusive Growth Initiative
BAME	black, Asian and minority ethnic
BEPS	base erosion and profit shifting
BIEN	Basic Income Earth Network
BLM	Black Lives Matter
BRIICS	Brazil, Russia, India, Indonesia, China and South Africa
CAP	collective action problem
CAT	Committee Against Torture
CAT	Convention Against Torture and Other Cruel, Inhuman or Degrading Treatment or Punishment
CCTs	Conditional Cash Transfers
CDD	community-driven development
CED	Committee on Enforced Disappearances
CEDAW	Committee on the Elimination of Discrimination Against Women
CEDAW	Convention on the Elimination of All Forms of Discrimination Against Women
CERD	Committee on Economic, Social and Cultural Rights
CHD	coronary heart disease
CMEPSP	Commission on the Measurement of Economic Performance and Social Progress
CMW	Committee on Migrant Workers
CO_2	carbon dioxide
CoE	Council of Europe
COP	Conference of the Parties
CRC	Committee on the Rights of the Child
CRPD	Committee on the Rights of Persons with Disabilities
CRPD	Convention on the Rights of Persons with Disabilities
CSD	Centre for Sustainable Development
CSDH	Commission on the Social Determinants of Health
CSR51	Convention relating to the Status of Refugees
DDR	Disability and Development Report
EC	European Commission
ECA	United Nations Economic Commission for Africa
ECEC	Early Childhood Education and Care

ECLAC	United Nations Economic Commission for Latin America and the Caribbean (CEPAL in Spanish and Portuguese)
EMRIP	Expert Mechanism on the Rights of Indigenous Peoples
ERA	Economic Report on Africa
ESCAP	United Nations Economic and Social Commission for Asia and the Pacific
ESS	European Social Survey
ESSAP	Economic and Social Survey of Asia and the Pacific
EU	European Union
FSDR	Financing for Sustainable Development Report
FSSBG	Framework for Strong, Sustainable and Balanced Growth
FSSD	Framework for Strategic Sustainable Development
G20	Group of Twenty is an international forum for the governments and central bank governors from 19 countries and the EU
G77	Group of 77 at the United Nations is a coalition of 134 developing countries
GDP	Gross Domestic Product
GEP	Global Economic Prospects
GNH	Gross National Happiness
GNP	gross national product
GPI	Genuine Progress Indicator
GRD	Global Resources Dividend
GSG	global social governance
Habitat	United Nations Conference on Human Settlements
HDI	Human Development Index
HDR	Human Development Report (UNDP flagship report)
HLE	healthy life expectancy
HLEG	High Level Expert Group on the Measurement of Economic and Social Progress
HRC	Human Rights Committee
ICCPR	International Covenant on Civil and Political Rights
ICED	International Conference for Ecological Sustainability
ICERD	International Convention on the Elimination of All Forms of Racial Discrimination
ICESCR	International Covenant on Economic, Social and Cultural Rights
ICMW	International Convention on the Protection of the Rights of All Migrant Workers and Members of Their Families
ICPPED	International Convention for the Protection of All Persons from Enforced Disappearance

IG	inclusive growth
IGF	Inclusive Growth Framework
IGI	Inclusive Growth Initiative
IHE	Institute for Health Equity
ILO	International Labour Organization
IMF	International Monetary Fund
IOM	International Organization for Migration
IPBES	Intergovernmental Science-Policy Platform on Biodiversity and Ecosystem Services
IPCC	Intergovernmental Panel on Climate Change
IPSP	International Panel on Social Progress
ISEW	Index of Sustainable Economic Welfare
IUCN	International Union for Conservation of Nature
IWS	international welfare state
IYOP	International Year of Older Persons
LE	life expectancy
LGBTQI+	lesbian, gay, bisexual, transgender, queer, intersex and others
MAP	Mutual Assessment Process
MCP	multiculturalism policies
MDGs	Millennium Development Goals
MEW	Measure of Economic Welfare
MIPAA	Madrid International Plan of Action on Ageing
NAEC	New Approaches to Economic Challenges
NDA	New Dynamics of Ageing
NGOs	non-governmental organisations
NIEO	new international economic order
NPF	National Performance Framework
NSF	Natural Step Framework
OECD	Organisation for Economic Co-operation and Development
OHCHR	Office of the United Nations High Commissioner for Human Rights
OSCE	Organization for Security and Co-operation in Europe
PAYG	Pay-As-You-Go
PHM	People's Health Movement
PI	participation income
PWW	Progress of the World's Women (UN Women's flagship report)
RCTs	randomized controlled trials
RWSS	Report on the World Social Situation (flagship report of the UN, now WSR)

SD	sustainable development
SDGs	Sustainable Development Goals
SDSN	Sustainable Development Solutions Network
SI	Social Investment
SOWIP	State of the World's Indigenous Peoples
SPF	Social Protection Floor
SPLC	Southern Poverty Law Center
SRVAW	Special Rapporteur on Violence against Women
SSF	Stiglitz–Sen–Fitoussi Commission
SWB	subjective wellbeing
TDR	Trade and Development Report
UBI	Universal Basic Income
UBS	Universal Basic Services
UCTs	Unconditional Cash Transfers
UDHR	Universal Declaration of Human Rights
UHC	universal health coverage
UN	United Nations
UNCED	United Nations Conference on Environment and Development
UNCHE	United Nations Conference on the Human Environment
UNCRC	United Nations Convention on the Rights of the Child
UN DESA	United Nations Department of Economic and Social Affairs
UNDP	United Nations Development Programme
UNEP	United Nations Environment Programme
UNESCO	United Nations Educational, Scientific and Cultural Organisation
UNFCCC	United Nations Framework Convention on Climate Change
UNGA	United Nations General Assembly
UNHCR	United Nations High Commissioner for Refugees
UNHRC	United Nations Human Rights Council
UNIATF	United Nations Inter-agency Task Force on Financing for Development
UNICEF	United Nations Children's Fund
UNODC	United Nations Office on Drugs and Crime
UNRISD	United Nations Research Institute for Social Development
UN SDSN	United Nations Sustainable Development Solutions Network
UN Women	United Nations Entity for Gender Equality and the Empowerment of Women

VDPA	Vienna Declaration and Programme of Action
WBG	World Bank Group
WCAR	World Conference Against Racism, Racial Discrimination
WCED	World Commission on Environment and Development
WCS	World Conservation Strategy
WCSDG	World Commission on the Social Dimension of Globalization
WDR	World Development Report (World Bank flagship report)
WEF	World Economic Forum
WESP	World Economic Situation and Prospects (UN flagship publication on trends in the global economy)
WFP	World Food Programme
WHO	World Health Organization
WHR	World Happiness Report
WHR	World Health Report (WHO's leading publication)
WMO	World Meteorological Organization
WRD	World Report on Disability (World Bank/WHO report)
WSPR	World Social Protection Report (ILO flagship report)
WSR	World Social Report (UN flagship publication by UN DESA, previously Report on the World Social Situation)
WSSD	World Summit for Social Development
WTO	World Trade Organization
WWF	World Wide Fund for Nature
WYR	World Youth Report (flagship publication of UN DESA)

Notes on contributors

Bradley W. Bateman is Professor of Economics and the President at Randolph College in Virginia. Works include *Capitalist Revolutionary: John Maynard Keynes* (Harvard University Press, 2011, with Roger Backhouse), *Keeping Faith, Losing Faith: Religious Belief and Political Economy* (Duke University Press, 2009, with Spencer Banzhof), *The Cambridge Companion to Keynes* (Cambridge University Press, 2006, with Roger Backhouse), and *Keynes's Uncertain Revolution* (University of Michigan Press, 1996). His work on the religious influences on American economics has appeared in many journals, including the *Journal of Economic Perspectives*, *History of Political Economy*, and the *Journal of the History of Economic Thought*.

Jean-Michel Bonvin is Professor of Socioeconomics and Sociology at the University of Geneva. His research interests include welfare reforms and theories of justice, especially the capability approach. He was Principal Investigator on the Overcoming Vulnerability: Life Course Perspectives (NCCR-LIVES) and EU projects such as Re-InVEST (2015–19) and SoCIEtY (2013–15). He is the Director of the Centre for the Study of Capabilities (CESCAP). Works include *Empowering Young People in Disempowering Times* (Edward Elgar, 2018, with Hans-Uwe Otto, Valerie Egdell and Roland Atzmüller), and *Amartya Sen: Une politique de la liberté* (Michalon, 2008, with Nicolas Farvaque).

Iris Borowy is Distinguished Professor at the University of Shanghai and Director of the Center for the History of Global Development. Her research interests focus on the history of international health, international organizations, sustainable development and the global history of waste. Recent works include *History of the Future of Economic Growth: Historical Roots of Current Debates on Sustainable Degrowth* (Routledge, 2017, with Matthias Schmelzer) and *Defining Sustainable Development for Our Common Future: A history of the World Commission on Environment and Development (Brundtland Commission)* (Routledge, 2014).

John Clarke is an Emeritus Professor of Social Policy at the UK's Open University and currently holds a Leverhulme Emeritus Fellowship to support his current work on the turbulent times marked by the rise of nationalist, populist and authoritarian politics. Recent publications include *Critical Dialogues: Thinking Together in Turbulent Times*, based on a series of conversations with people who have helped him to think (Policy Press, 2019), *Making Policy Move: Towards a Politics of Translation and Assemblage* (Policy Press, 2015, with Dave Bainton, Noémi Lendvai and Paul Stubbs).

Gary Craig is Visiting Professor at the Law School, University of Newcastle upon Tyne. He specializes in issues to do with 'race' and ethnicity, modern slavery and social justice. Recent works include *Global Social Justice* (Edward Elgar, 2019), *The Modern Slavery Agenda* (Policy Press, 2019) and *Understanding 'Race' and Ethnicity* (Policy Press, 2019). He is Trustee of three Third Sector organizations including the Tutu UK Foundation.

Christopher Deeming is in the School of Social Work and Social Policy at the University of Strathclyde. Recent works include *Minimum Income Standards and Reference Budgets: International and Comparative Policy Perspectives* (Policy Press, 2020) and *Reframing Global Social Policy* (Policy Press, 2018, co-edited with Paul Smyth).

Danny Dorling is a Professor who works in the School of Geography and the Environment at the University of Oxford. Recent works include *Slowdown: The End of the Great Acceleration – and Why It's Good for the Planet, the Economy, and Our Lives* (Yale University Press, 2020), and *Finntopia: What We Can Learn from the World's Happiest Country* (Agenda, 2020, with Annika Koljonen). He is a patron of the road crash charity RoadPeace (www.roadpeace.org).

Tony Fitzpatrick taught in several British universities for twenty-five years. In addition to numerous journal articles and book chapters, his most recent books are *How to Live Well: Epicurus as a Guide to Contemporary Social Reform* (Edward Elgar, 2018), *A Green History of the Welfare State* (Routledge, 2017), *International Handbook on Social Policy and the Environment* (Edward Elgar, 2014), *Climate Change and Poverty* (Policy Press, 2014).

Jane Jenson is Professor Emerita in the Department of Political Science, Université de Montréal and a fellow of the Royal Society of Canada since 1979. Her research focuses on comparative social policy in Europe and the Americas, with particular attention to the narratives surrounding the social investment perspective, and including the consequences for gender relations and women's status. A recent book is *Reassembling Motherhood: Procreation and Care in a Globalized*

World (Colombia University Press, 2017, co-edited with Yasmine Ergas and Sonya Michel).

Edward A. Koning is Associate Professor of Political Science at the University of Guelph, Ontario, Canada. Most of his research investigates the politics of immigration in Western democracies. Recent work includes *Immigration and the Politics of Welfare Exclusion* (University of Toronto Press, 2019), and articles in leading academic journals *Comparative European Politics*, *Comparative Political Studies*, *Ethnic and Racial Studies* and *Journal of Public Policy* on anti-immigrant politics, institutionalist theory, public opinion on immigration, and citizenship policy.

Francesco Laruffa is Research Fellow at the University of Geneva, where he worked for the EU-funded project Rebuilding an Inclusive, Value based Europe of Solidarity and Trust through Social Investments (Re-InVEST), rethinking social investment from a capability perspective. In Geneva, he is also a member of the Overcoming Vulnerabilities – Life Course Perspectives (NCCR-LIVES) and the Centre for the Study of Capabilities (CESCAP). His research interests include the normative dimension of welfare reform, theories of social justice, neoliberalism and critical theory.

Kate Pickett is Professor of Epidemiology; Deputy Director, Centre for Future Health; Associate Director, Leverhulme Centre for Anthropocene Biodiversity, all at the University of York. She was UK NIHR Career Scientist from 2007 to 2012, a fellow of the RSA and a fellow of the UK Faculty of Public Health. She is co-author, with Richard Wilkinson, of the best-selling and award-winning *The Spirit Level* (Penguin, 2010) and *The Inner Level* (Penguin, 2019). She is also co-founder and chair of the Equality Trust (www.equalitytrust.org.uk), global ambassador for the Wellbeing Economy Alliance and member of the Club of Rome.

Alan Walker is Professor of Social Policy and Social Gerontology at the University of Sheffield. He has been researching and has published extensively on aspects of ageing and social policy for more than 40 years and has also directed several major national and European research programmes and projects including Mobilising the potential of active ageing in Europe (MOPACT) (www.mopact.group.shef.ac.uk) and the New Dynamics of Ageing Programme. Recent works include *The*

New Dynamics of Ageing (Volume 1 and 2, Policy Press, 2018) and *The New Science of Ageing* (Policy Press, 2014).

Richard Wilkinson is Professor Emeritus of Social Epidemiology, University of Nottingham; Honorary Professor at University College London; Honorary Visiting Professor, University of York, and medallist of the Australian Society for Medical Research. He is co-author, with Kate Pickett, of the best-selling and award-winning *The Spirit Level* (Allen Lane, 2009) and *The Inner Level* (Allen Lane, 2018). He is also co-founder and patron of the Equality Trust, and global ambassador for the Wellbeing Economy Alliance (https://wellbeingeconomy.org).

Fiona Williams is Emeritus Professor of Social Policy at the University of Leeds and Honorary Professor in the Social Policy Research Centre at the University of New South Wales. Her research broadly covers gender, 'race' and migration in social policy theory, analysis and praxis. Her writing also focuses on care and the ethics of care. Recent work includes 'Care: Intersections of Scales, Inequalities, and Crises' (*Current Sociology*, 2018), and a new book *Social Policy: A Critical and Intersectional Analysis* (Polity, 2021).

Acknowledgements

The idea for this book originated from the L5418 Global Social Policy: Global Challenges developed at the University of Strathclyde, Glasgow. The book is for all those who seek to make this world a better place to live in. Sincere gratitude to all those who have commentated on the proposal and earlier drafts. A special thanks to everyone at Policy Press for their help with this volume, especially Laura Vickers-Rendall, Amelia Watts-Jones and Millie Prekop.

The editor and publisher wish to thank the following for permissions to reproduce materials and copyright materials:

- A PRECARIAT CHARTER: FROM DENIZENS TO CITIZENS by Guy Standing, London: Bloomsbury Academic, an imprint of Bloomsbury Publishing Plc, Copyright © 2014.
- Cambridge University Press material is reproduced here with permission from CUP.
- INEQUALITY: WHAT CAN BE DONE? By Anthony Atkinson, Cambridge, Mass.: Harvard University Press, Copyright © 2015 by the President and Fellows of Harvard College.
- Organisation for Economic Co-operation and Development material is reproduced here with permission from the OECD.
- SEVENTEEN CONTRADICTIONS AND THE END OF CAPITALISM By David Harvey, London: Profile Books, Copyright © 2017.
- The Equality Trust website material reproduced here is Creative Commons.
- The Political Quarterly material is reproduced here with permission from Wiley & Sons.
- World Health Organization material is reproduced here with permission from the WHO.
- United Nations material is reproduced and reprinted here with permission from the UN.

Preface

While the idea of 'sustainability' appears to be a relatively recent addition to the discursive field of social policy, it is also true that the 'social' of social policy has long been interested in issues to do with sustainability, relating to core principles of social justice, equality, welfare and wellbeing, for example, and the possibilities of democracy and being able to live in a safe environment with respect for the natural world. Yet we need a lot more work on sustainability in social policy that reflects and engenders the present struggle for sustainability, and exposes the socio-political and moral conflicts as well as the global governance debates and dilemmas facing the whole of humanity in our globalized world. It is now widely accepted that for a society to be considered sustainable, it must address environmental, ecological, economic and social concerns. Work on sustainable welfare is growing and the trend is sure to continue, complementing more longstanding concerns and debates in this field about the nature of 'warfare states', 'welfare states', 'patriarchal welfare states' and 'workfare states'.

It is also true that the 'social' of social policy, as a field of study, has arguably not received the critical attention it deserves – a gap that this timely volume aims to fill as the coronavirus pandemic has plunged the world into a crisis like no other. The global social crisis runs deep, as we shall see. The effects of global warming, the global 'climate and environmental emergency', the 'migration crisis', global financial crisis and the latest global health and economic crisis still unfolding reveal the extent of our highly interconnected world, and the scale of the post-national political challenges, nationalism and populism and the withdrawals from international commitments. Global institutions are severely challenged and are struggling to cope with the ongoing adverse social consequences of these crises, but there is hope, for global social policy development and for (transnational) solidarity, in grassroots struggle and the growing number of networks and coalitions mobilizing for change. The 2020s needs to usher in a decade of ambitious action to accelerate socially sustainable solutions to all the world's biggest challenges and deliver the Sustainable Development Goals (SDGs) by 2030.

In this volume, then, the idea of the social and that of 'social policy' is critically examined and reappraised, along with the notion of an increasingly globalising or globalised form of social policy, signified by international agreements, global goals and targets for humankind, all of which is increasingly geared towards the idea of 'social sustainability' itself. This reappraisal is not without problems or challenges, as this timely new volume serves to illustrate, because it is forcing us to critically reconsider and rethink age-old ideas, debates and perspectives in order to try and arrive at a better understanding of what the social of social policy may mean in and for the age of social sustainability.

Christopher Deeming
Glasgow
March 2021

1

The 'social' in the age of sustainability

Christopher Deeming

Introduction

COVID-19 is a human tragedy, but it has also created a generational opportunity, as UN Secretary-General António Guterres (2020) has observed. An opportunity to build back a more equal and sustainable world. New and emerging socially inclusive models and global policy frameworks are being formulated by policy makers to address the pressing global challenges of the 21st century, such as rising social inequality, extreme poverty and the climate emergency, that focus on important aspects of the *social* of social policy, are the subject of this volume. This introductory chapter provides a critical introduction to the idea of the 'social', and considers how notions of the social are now guiding the development of global social policy for the age of sustainability. The chapter also introduces the different contributions to the evolving debate on the social of social policy and the social dimensions of sustainability that this volume brings together for critical examination and reflection.

Social sustainability

The 'social' is now becoming more integrated in global social policy debates around sustainability (Koch and Oksana, 2016; Gough, 2017). Often, however, we find conceptions of the 'social' are less than well-defined in ascendant discourses of sustainability (Dillard et al, 2008; Vallance et al, 2011). Certainly, the United Nations 2030 Agenda for Sustainable Development (UNGA, 2015), and the associated 17 Sustainable Development Goals (SDGs, Box 1.1) with their 169 targets adopted by member states of the UN in September 2015, underlines a global commitment to 'achieving sustainable development in its three dimensions, economic, social and environmental in a balanced and integrated manner' (UNGA, 2015, 2020; UN, 2019a, 2019b). This is

Box 1.1: Global goals: from the MDGs to the SDGs

The 8 Millennium Development Goals (MDGs)	The 17 Sustainable Development Goals (SDGs) to Transform Our World
1. Eradicate extreme poverty and hunger	1. No poverty
2. Achieve universal primary education	2. Zero hunger
3. Promote gender equality and empower women	3. Ensure good health and well-being
4. Reduce child mortality	4. Ensure quality education
5. Improve maternal health	5. Achieve gender equality
6. Combat HIV/AIDS, malaria and other diseases	6. Ensure clean water and sanitation
7. Ensure environmental sustainability	7. Ensure affordable and clean energy
8. Develop a global partnership for development	8. Promote decent work and economic growth
	9. Build resilient infrastructure
	10. Reduced inequality within and among countries
	11. Make cities and communities sustainable
	12. Ensure sustainable consumption and production
	13. Climate action
	14. Conserve life below water
	15. Protect life on land
	16. Peace and justice strong institutions
	17. Partnerships to achieve the Goals

Note: For the MDGs see www.un.org/millenniumgoals/; for the SDGs see www.un.org/sustainabledevelopment/sustainable-development-goals/
Source: Adapted from UN UNGA (2015: 14).
(Reproduced with the permission of the United Nations.)

a major achievement, global social policy in the making (Gore, 2015; Fukuda-Parr and Muchhala, 2020). The SDGs are global goals, which build on the experience and successes of the international development goals, the Millennium Development Goals (MDGs, Box 1.1) agreed at the UN Millennium Summit in 2000 (UNGA, 2000), and also the recommendations and targets, eradicate poverty, support full employment, achieve equity, equality and protect human rights, found in the report *A Fair Globalization* of the World Commission on the Social Dimension of Globalization (WCSDG) (ILO, 2004), and the Copenhagen Declaration on Social Development adopted at the

World Summit for Social Development (WSSD) in 1995. All 193 UN member states have pledged to achieve the 17 SDGs by 2030, relating to global social problems of extreme poverty, inequality, climate change, environmental degradation, peace and justice as well as the promotion of healthy lives. Here we find the social, the ecological and the economic are understood to be interconnected, in order to address the global challenges that humanity now faces.

Agenda 2030 aims to mobilise global efforts to transform our world. The scale and ambition of this universal policy agenda and the political commitment has never been seen before, endorsed by 193 countries (UN member states), formulated and supported by the international and global institutions and organizations like the World Bank (2020a) and International Monetary Fund (IMF, 2020), the Organisation for Economic Co-operation and Development (OECD, 2019) and world-regional social policy actors. The European Union (EU), for example, was one of the leading forces behind the 2030 Agenda and is fully committed to its implementation. The SDGs thus act as a compass, guiding regional sustainability strategies, reviews and monitoring (for example, ECLAC, 2018; EC, 2019; ECA, 2018; ESCAP, 2019). The long-term development goals are helping to unite policy actors at all levels and across all regions.

In this age, then, we find growing interest in the *social* dimensions of sustainability. Importantly, we find ideas and contested conceptions of 'the social' (which have a long history in the social sciences), now taking centre stage in international and globalizing social policy debates, the focus of this volume. The notion of 'social sustainability' can be found at the *intersections* (a key theme of this volume) of the environment and the ecological, the economic and the social. As such, this new and emerging political agenda invites us to think about the 'social' in social + policy, and the emergent field of study − global + social + policy − as well as the related social and ethical dimensions of social sustainability, equity, equality, justice and cohesion, as the influential Nobel Laureate Amartya Sen (2013) reminds us.

Global policy perspectives and policy paradigms have been (slowly) shifting to encompass important elements of the social, particularly evident in the work of international institutions, regional actors and agencies in the United Nations system like the IMF.[1] The emerging new *social* spending strategy now taking shape at the IMF is perhaps testimony to this shift. The IMF, for example, is now a leading advocate of social investments in public health, public education, social assistance and safety nets and other key aspects of social infrastructure development.[2] The IMF is also promoting sustained economic growth, and 'inclusive growth', in order to meet the 2030 SDGs. Full and productive employment (SDG 8) it is claimed will help set the world free of extreme poverty (SDG 1) and social inequality (Goals 5 and 10) (IMF, 2019). This policy positioning by the IMF and many of the other international institutions is perhaps unremarkable in some ways, being the conventional wisdom, as global social policy is 'framed' (Bøås and McNeill, 2004) and 'reframed' (Deeming and Smyth, 2018). However, in other ways this does seem significant if we recall that the IMF and World Bank were the strong advocates of neoliberal policy prescriptions on the global stage during the 1980s and 1990s. As we find throughout the volume, international institutions and organizations established in the post-war era are constantly under pressure, involved in their own legitimation struggles and contests, increasingly in the realm of global governance and social movements, formations and coalitions for change involved in local, national and global politics and the dynamics of contention (see also O'Brien et al, 2000; Frey et al, 2014; Dingwerth et al, 2019; Tilly et al, 2019).

In the age of sustainability, the 'social' is facing multiple challenges and crises, however. In global social policy, Agenda 2030 is heavily contested and progress on the SDGs is slow, uneven and patchy, even before COVID-19 and the economic crises (World Bank Group (WBG) flagship reports Global Economic Prospects (GEP) consider the enormous global shock delivered by COVID-19, leading to steep recessions in many countries, World Bank, 2020b, 2021). Many of the SDGs are either 'gender-sparse' or 'gender-blind', for example (Razavi, 2016, 2019; UN Women, 2018). Despite the global commitment to gender equality, women still form the majority of the world's poorest people (Fredman, 2016). Persisting high levels of violence against women, economic exclusion and other systemic inequalities are of deep concern, revealing the lack of political commitment to address gender equality according to the United Nations Entity for Gender Equality and the Empowerment of Women (UN Women, 2019, 2020). Governance and institutional failings, underinvestment and underfunding concerns amid a slowing of the global economy and the climate emergency, all pre-date the pandemic (Sachs et al, 2018; Dalby et al, 2019; IPBES, 2019; IPCC, 2019; UNIATF, 2019; UN, 2020a).[3] COVID-19 could now set sustainable development and progress on the SDGs back years and even decades, global poverty is on the increase for the first time in decades (dire warnings are found in the latest editions of the UN flagship reports, Financing for Sustainable Development Report (FSDR) (UNIATF, 2020), World Economic Situation and

Prospects (WESP) (UN 2020a, 2021), and UNCTAD's (2020a, 2020b, 2020c) Trade and Development Report (TDR)).

Global social crisis

The global crisis runs deep.[4] The effects of global warming, the climate emergency, the global financial crisis and the latest global health crises and global economic shock still unfolding reveal the extent of our highly interconnected world, and the scale of the post-national political commitment from global institutions and societies needed to address them. They are all world issues, global problems and global challenges and multiple crises. They have all exposed social crises at every level, with many health and social protection systems and institutions severely challenged and struggling to cope in the age of extreme global inequality and poverty. The COVID-19 pandemic (with the new buzzwords 'social distancing' and 'self-isolation') is once again exposing the deep divides that exist within and between nations, but also the way risk is governed in an era of international financial liberalization. While the World Bank and IMF have made further loans available to the poorest countries grappling with the spread of the virus, it is clear they are prioritizing fiscal objectives and market-driven solutions rather than public health (Kentikelenis et al, 2020). The international financial institutions preferring to suspend debt payments on loans and grants, rather than cancelling them altogether in order to abolish debt burdens (Hickel, 2017; Oldekop et al, 2020).[5] The rich nations stand accused of being complicit in a 'climate debt trap' with their loans to developing countries for 'loss and damage' caused by climate change, and many argue that the polluters (the rich nations) should have to pay for the damage they have caused.[6]

The coronavirus crisis has had devastating health and socioeconomic impacts, it has exposed weaknesses, divisions and inequities in health and social protection systems around the world, and it has exacerbated health and social inequalities both within and between countries (UN, 2020b; WEF, in 2020).[7] Perhaps the crisis will help to restore 'universalism' and universal health coverage (UHC), moving towards a fairer world post-COVID-19 with more inclusive and sustainable economies (OECD, 2020). Universal healthcare systems are vital for promoting global public health security, a global priority objective of the World Health Organization (WHO), the global health agency of the UN. The inclusion of UHC in the SDGs (Target 3.8) is rooted in the right to health. Social protection systems are in crisis in many parts of the world, where universal social protection is far from a reality, and safety nets are simply not available to catch people if they fall into poverty. The global health crisis reinforces the need for stronger universal social protection floors in developing and developed countries alike, to protect all members of society, and has re-energized the global debate on unconditional basic income: 'basic income' or 'Universal Basic Income' (UBI) (Downes and Lansley, 2018). Moreover, the health and social crisis has further exposed many fictions, myths and lies: that free markets can deliver healthcare for all; that unpaid care work is not work; that we live in a post-racist world; that we are all in the same boat (Williams, 2021). Across every sphere, the impacts of COVID-19 are exacerbated for women and girls, the poorest and the most vulnerable in society and the developing countries (UN, 2020b; WBG, 2020). The world faces a "catastrophic moral failure" because of unequal COVID-19 vaccine policies, the Director-General of the WHO has warned. The price of this failure will be paid with lives and livelihoods in the world's poorest countries.[8]

We are likely to see significant changes in how society works as a result of COVID-19.[9] Already, we find that the crisis is transformatory in many ways. There is major governmental intervention at levels unprecedented in peacetime. Politicians and political parties are (mostly) united behind the raft of emergency packages, budgets and fiscal stimulus. Strong welfare states are once again the best automatic stabilizers in times of crisis, as unemployment soars, and new safety nets and aid packages have been designed and extended to help protect businesses and the self-employed in some contexts. Universal healthcare systems are the most powerful of policy instruments in a health crisis. Each night a grateful public in many countries like France, Italy, Spain, Portugal, the Netherlands, and the UK, paid tribute to the carers and frontline workers dealing with the coronavirus pandemic ('clap for carers'), a positive affirmation and display of social solidarity, and growing understanding of 'social value' created not by market forces but by society as a whole.[10]

The 'social' of social policy

Theorising 'the social' has a rich history in the social sciences, although notions and conceptions of the social are not always precisely defined.[11] The term 'social policy' has also itself received a lot of critical scrutiny over the years yet there is no standard definition. Interest in exploring the 'comparative' and 'global' dimensions of the social of social policy continues to grow, as does work uncovering the origins of social policy with the framing of the 'social question' that demanded 'social reform' and 'social policy' and 'social rights' of citizenship as a growing response to the privations of the 19th century (Kaufmann, 2013).[12]

In all of this endeavour we find the search for a better understanding of the social, the social sphere and social life (of the state and of civil society), and we learn more about the conceptual challenges associated with drawing clear distinctions between the economic and the political realm, or the 'public', private, market and familial spheres; these are familiar distinctions and complex institutions that have long interested moral philosophers and social theorists alike, from Adam Smith ([1759] 2009) and Hegel ([1821] 1967) to Jürgen Habermas ([1962] 1989), Daniel Bell ([1977] 1996), Axel Honneth (1995a) and Carole Pateman (1988) for example.[13] What does the 'social' mean in social policy debates, shaped by culture and history, and what does or might it increasingly mean in a transnational context in the work of the international organizations, the United Nations (UN) and International Labour Organization (ILO) for example (Emmerij et al, 2001; Bellucci and Weiss, 2020), and from a global social policy perspective (see also recent discussions of the social question(s) in global times by Bogalska-Martin and Matteudi, 2018; Breman et al, 2019; Faist, 2019; Leisering, 2021).

In this volume, then, we hold the idea of the 'social' in social policy up to fresh scrutiny. In so doing, we build on earlier works, along with some of our work, that has critically discussed the nature of the 'social' in social welfare (Clarke, 1996, 2007; Lewis et al, 2000; and Clarke writing in Chapter 2) and in social policy (Corbett and Walker, 2017; Williams, 2021; and Walker, Chapter 8, and Williams, Chapter 11 in this volume), and with the 'active' turn in social policy (Mahon, 2014; Deeming, 2016; Bonoli, 2018). Further insightful works have critically examined the new and emerging conceptions of the 'social' influencing the development of social policy, influential ideas about 'social investment' (Jenson, 2010a; Laruffa, 2018) and 'inclusive growth' (Jenson, 2015a, 2015b); also ideas about 'social exclusion' (Béland, 2007; Winlow and Hall, 2013), 'social inclusion' (Dujon et al, 2013), and the growing body of work discussing 'social inequality', 'social wellbeing' and 'social progress' (Wilkinson and Pickett, 2009, 2018 and Chapter 14 in this volume; Deeming, 2013 and Chapters 13 and 15), ideas about 'social capital' (Smith and Kulynych, 2002; Bebbington et al, 2004; McNeill, 2004; Ferragina and Arrigoni, 2017), 'social solidarity' (Stjernø, 2005; Barbier, 2013) and 'social cohesion' (Jenson, 2010b and Chapter 11 in this volume), along with conceptions of 'social justice' and 'global social justice' (Vosko, 2002; Craig, 2018 and Chapter 12 in this volume), 'ecosocial' perspectives (Fitzpatrick, 2001 and Chapter 6 in this volume; Koch and Fritz, 2014), 'social innovation' (Jenson, 2015c; Ayob et al, 2016) and 'social entrepreneurship' (Jenson, 2018), to name just some of the recent works critically exploring conceptions of the social of social policy.

Important work also continues to uncover the structured nature of inequality on a global scale; the gendered and ethno-racial structure of inequality (Razavi and Hassim, 2006; Taylor and Mahon, 2019; UN DESA, 2020; UN Women, 2020; Williams, 2021), and the many barriers to inclusion that people with disabilities and indigenous people face (who are at a disadvantage regarding most SDGs) according to UN and WHO flagship reports like the World Report on Disability (WDR) (WHO, 2011), Disability and Development Report (DDR) (UN DESA, 2019a), State of the World's Indigenous Peoples (SOWIP) (UN DESA, 2019b), and the World Social Report (WSR) examining global inequality (UN DESA, 2020). The so-called social questions relating to 'race' and 'women' signified gendered-ethno-racial divisions and struggle in patriarchal societies, within the context of structural and systemic racism (Pateman, 1988; Pilbeam, 2000; Fassin and Fassin, 2006; Wacquant, 2006, 2014). The Me Too (or #MeToo) women's empowerment movement has become a worldwide phenomenon, in the global struggle against violence against women. Male intimate partner violence and sexual violence is a major public health problem and a violation of women's human rights (WHO, 2013, 2014, 2017). While the Black Lives Matter (BLM) movement, established in 2013 in the USA, has grown into the largest black-led social movement advocating racial justice since the 1960s (Garza, 2020). It is now a global network calling for radical, sustainable solutions that affirm the prosperity of Black lives (Tilly et al, 2019).[14]

Social resilience and political struggle are becoming more evident on a global scale, in opposition to the lack of respect for basic human rights and key freedoms to equality, fair treatment and dignity as set out in foundational international human rights documents. These include the 30 Articles of the Universal Declaration of Human Rights (UDHR, Box 1.2), and the international agreements, treaties and conventions emerging out of conflict and social struggle, such as the International Convention on the Elimination of All Forms of Racial Discrimination (ICERD, in 1965), the International Covenant on Economic, Social and Cultural Rights (ICESCR, in 1966), the Convention on the Elimination of All Forms of Discrimination against Women (CEDAW, in 1979), UN Committee on the Rights of the Child (UNCRC, in 1989), and the Convention on the Rights of

---

Box 1.2: The 30 rights and freedoms set out in the Universal Declaration of Human Rights (UDHR)

The 30 rights and freedoms were adopted and proclaimed by the United Nations General Assembly (UNGA) on 10 December 1948

Article 1. Innate freedom and equality

Article 2. Ban on discrimination

Article 3. Right to life

Article 4. Ban on slavery

Article 5. Ban on torture

Article 6. Right to recognition as a person before the law

Article 7. Equality before the law

Article 8. Right to effective judiciary

Article 9. Ban on arbitrary detention

Article 10. Right to public hearing

Article 11. Right to the presumption of innocence

Article 12. Right to privacy

Article 13. Right to freedom of movement

Article 14. Right to asylum

Article 15. Right to a nationality

Article 16. Right to marriage and family

Article 17. Right to own property

Article 18. Right to freedom of thought and religion

Article 19. Right to freedom of opinion and expression

Article 20. Right to freedom of assembly and association

Article 21. Right to take part in government

Article 22. Right to social security

Article 23. Right to work

Article 24. Right to rest and leisure

Article 25. Right to an adequate standard of living

Article 26. Right to education

Article 27. Right to participate in cultural life

Article 28. Right to a social and international order

Article 29. Duties and limitations

Article 30. Salvatory clause

Source: United Nations: www.un.org/en/universal-declaration-human-rights/ (Reproduced with the permission of the United Nations.)

Persons with Disabilities (CRPD, in 2008). The core international human rights instruments and associated UN human rights monitoring bodies are shown in Box 1.3.

Intersectionality has become the watchword in the media, while academic work in this field continues to facilitate a deeper understanding of advantage and disadvantage as praxis and for the possibilities of politics and policy, human rights, equal rights and anti-discrimination (Collins, 2007; Collins and Bilge, 2020; Williams, 2021).[15] 'Race', class and gender as citizenship categories disadvantage many groups in society, and yet age straddles all of these categories.

Box 1.3: Core international human rights instruments

Acronym	Full name	Date adopted	UN monitoring bodies
CSR51	The 1951 Refugee Convention	28 July 1951	UNHCR
ICERD	International Convention on the Elimination of All Forms of Racial Discrimination	21 Dec 1965	CERD
ICCPR	International Covenant on Civil and Political Rights	16 Dec 1966	HRC
ICESCR	International Covenant on Economic, Social and Cultural Rights	16 Dec 1966	CESCR
CEDAW	Convention on the Elimination of All Forms of Discrimination against Women	18 Dec 1979	CEDAW
CAT	Convention against Torture and Other Cruel, Inhuman or Degrading Treatment or Punishment	10 Dec 1984	CAT
UNCRC	Convention on the Rights of the Child	20 Nov 1989	UNCRC
ICMW	International Convention on the Protection of the Rights of All Migrant Workers and Members of Their Families	18 Dec 1990	CMW
DEVAW	Declaration on the Elimination of Violence Against Women	20 Dec 1993	SRVAW
CRPD	Convention on the Rights of Persons with Disabilities	13 Dec 2006	CRPD
ICPPED	International Convention for the Protection of All Persons from Enforced Disappearance	20 Dec 2006	CED
UNDRIP	Declaration on the Rights of Indigenous Persons	13 Sept 2007	EMRIP

Source: Adapted from UN Office of the High Commissioner for Human Rights (OHCHR): www.ohchr.org/EN/ProfessionalInterest/Pages/CoreInstruments.aspx (Reproduced with the permission of the United Nations.)

Young people's experiences of social problems are more intensified, young people around the world know that jobs for teenagers and young people are scarce (unacceptably high numbers of young people experience poor education, employment outcomes and poverty: UN DESA, 2019c).[16]

Finally, there is a lack of a critical scrutiny over the social – or conceptions of the social – in the arguments of international institutions and regional bodies, who are in the business of constructing and promoting new and alternative ideas and visions for social policy (Jolly et al, 2009; Mahon, 2010, 2015, 2019; Jenson, 2010a, 2017; Béland and Petersen, 2014; Deeming and Smyth, 2018).[17] It is certainly true that there has been a discernible trend towards a common language of the 'social', 'inclusion', inclusiveness' and 'sustainability' in global social policy discourses and the policy instruments of global social governance (a common conceptual grammar, it would seem), accompanied by a growing trend towards greater collaboration and cooperation amongst international institutions and policy networks and epistemic communities, and the formulation if not the fulfilment of the SDGs arguably represents an unprecedented shared common motivation and global social policy objective. Needless to say, this does not mean long-standing academic and global policy debates have now finally been settled or are diminishing. The extent to which global and regional social policy is still caught up in the 'neoliberal' era of market generating inequality, for example, or whether we have now entered an era after neoliberalism, is an issue that is receiving much scholarly attention (Gore, 2000, 2015; Craig and Porter, 2005; Rodrik, 2006; Clarke, 2007, also writing in Chapter 2; Kaasch and Deacon, 2008; Jenson, 2010a; Mahon, 2010, 2011, 2013; Babb, 2013; Deeming and Smyth, 2018).

What is clear, however, is that international organizations like the World Bank have certainly been shifting their policy positions, as is evident in recent political discourses. The World Bank's reframing of global social policy is well captured in its annual flagship publication, the World Development Report (WDR). In 1996 it was claimed that virtually all solutions to social problems were to be solved by markets, the 1996 WDR strongly advocating the move away from 'plan' (state) to 'market' (World Bank, 1996). A year later, the tone had changed and the talk was now about bringing the state back in again, about 'rethinking the state' and the importance of 'good government' (World Bank, 1997). More recently, we find the demand for a more effective investment state, with the Bank championing 'public investment' in human capital, universal education, and vocational training and health services in order to promote social and economic wellbeing (World

Bank, 2006). Past mistakes and policy shortcomings are also openly acknowledged, notably the overly aggressive market-making policies deployed in many parts of the developing world, due in no small part to the Bank's 'structural adjustment' loans of the 1980s and 1990s (World Bank, 2005: 17, 93; 2007: 138).

Ideological battles continue to rage between global social policy actors, however, and also within them (Deacon, 2005; Kaasch and Deacon, 2008; Kaasch, 2013). Contestation and struggle in global policy making is well documented, policy positions continue to evolve and adapt, policy instruments and policy processes are complex, social policy remains largely the responsibility of nation states and national governments; there are also transfer and cultural effects and lived experiences and human voices that are all too often overlooked or excluded in policy-making processes (Narayan et al, 2000a, 2000b; Narayan and Petesch, 2002; Weiss et al, 2005; Evans and McBride, 2017). In the realm of ideation, then, international institutions and the experts that serve them diffuse their evidence and their ideas, and they define the social questions that influence and shape global, regional and domestic policy agendas. Their ideas often serve as policy blueprints, while their policy prescriptions on national social policy constitute powerful ideological weapons that seek to convince policy makers, interest groups and the population at large that change is necessary, or even desirable (Deacon et al, 1997; Béland and Orenstein, 2013; Stone, 2020).

It is clear we are in need of such fundamental reflections on the 'social' of social policy in global political discourses, and considered work interpreting social struggle and contestation, which often represents moral conflict and symbolic struggle. The claims being raised in fierce and complicated struggle usually centre on the social. Social justice demands due recognition and respect for differences as well as fair distribution, as Honneth ([1992] 1995b) and Fraser and Honneth (2003) maintain, and such demands and struggles are increasing under conditions of economic globalization and increasing inequality and stratification in society (Dean, 1996; Narayan et al, 2000b; Williams, 2000; Hobson, 2003; Weiss et al, 2005; Banting and Kymlicka, 2006; Lister, 2008; Yuval-Davis, 2011; Faist, 2015). All of this is forcing scholars to reconsider the 'social' and the possibilities of politics and social policy for sustaining the social in an increasingly complicated, globalized and challenging world.

The chapters in this book approach the social from multiple angles, rooted in history and culture studies, economics and political science, social politics, sociology and social epidemiology, written by scholars working within and across these different disciplines. The volume as a whole helps us to think more critically about important moral and political aspects of the 'social' and especially of the notion of 'social policy', increasingly conceived in global forms, 'global social policy', signified by international agreements, and the global goals and targets now directed towards the sustainability challenges facing humankind.[18]

This is important work for sure, revealing many different ideas and conceptions of 'the social' (that is, 'the socials': 'social cohesion', 'social justice', 'social wellbeing', 'social sustainability', 'social progress' and so on) in the arguments of international institutions, epistemic communities and domestic policy makers. Often these concepts, or quasi-concepts, are not clearly defined in policy documents, this volume is testament to that. As such they appear fuzzy, lacking in precision, but in many ways this is precisely what makes quasi-concepts particularly useful for policy-making purposes, in practical policy terms across space and time, as Jenson (2018) argues.

The volume then engages with the contested conceptions of 'the social' focusing on ideas about 'social justice', 'social cohesion' and 'social progress' in a global context. It is the critical engagement with these key social science concepts, or quasi-concepts, along with the pressing 'social questions' (to do changing world population, ageing societies, mass migration, and so on) and the global challenges of the 21st century (to do with social inequality, social wellbeing, social sustainability) that are of profound interest to the contributors and readers of this volume alike. Each contribution draws our attention to the inherent complexity of thinking about 'the social', not only the varying conceptions or dimensions of the 'social', but also in terms of thinking about scale and multiscalar approaches (that is, global, world-regional, national, local or interpersonal scales). In summary, each chapter forces us to think very carefully about the meaning of the 'social', and the different conceptualizations of the 'social' of social policy.

Outline of the volume

Neoliberalism, in many variants, involved a sustained attack on ideas, institutions and formations of the 'social', as John Clarke contends in Chapter 2. Indeed, the neoliberal period closing out the 20th century was often considered to mark the 'death of the social'. There is some obvious truth in this, evident in the ideologies of Thatcherism and Reaganism for example, and in the attack on social rights and the social sphere ('there is no such thing as society. There are individual men and women and there are families', claimed Margaret Thatcher in 1987), and in the neoliberal policy prescriptions of the World

Bank and IMF during the dominant 'Washington Consensus' era. Yet political and cultural formations of the social continued to exist alongside the dominant neoliberal tendency of global capitalism. While some commentators are now suggesting that we are moving beyond neoliberalism, or that global social policy is being reframed as ideas and discourse evolve (Deeming and Smyth, 2018), Clarke cautions us to be wary. We are living in and against a neoliberal global order. Dominant neoliberal ideas and legacies persist. John Clarke helps us to navigate the complex terrain, going beyond simple binaries, dichotomies and periodization. The important point here is to recognize the shape-shifting processes of neoliberalization on the one hand, but also alternative ways of thinking and organizing the social on the other.

Economics, it seems, often in the pursuit of a market society, has never really had an easy relationship or a happy coexistence with the 'social'. Nevertheless, economists have sought to embed the economy in society, as Bradley Bateman reminds us in Chapter 3. The enduring relevance of key economic ideas is the subject of Bateman's chapter, as he considers how the pressing social and economic questions of the day (the social questions, concerning rights and representation, diversity and difference) have been cast and recast, and the responses to these questions from the discipline of economics. Ultimately, economics is used to argue for and against social policies. Two clear nexuses between economic theory and social policy thus arise. The libertarian focus of much mainstream economic theory does not often lend itself to recommending solutions to social policy questions, whereas Keynesian economic theory does. The nexus between the social and economic is particularly intuitive when it comes to the issue of climate change, the question of sustainable development now facing humanity. If societies are to successfully address climate change, it will require immense levels of investment. New infrastructure is required to generate clean energy (SDG 7), while green energy is not the only industry where the fight against climate change can create jobs. Nor do investments have to be made to help fight climate change in order to be effective at providing more and better paid jobs; that is, investment in infrastructure, housing and homes, schools and hospitals creates jobs, and can help mitigate inequality, increase inclusion and cohesion. The possibility for the state to improve people's lives by creating more sustainable, resilient and inclusive societies is as relevant today as it was in the 'heyday' of Keynesian economics.

The question and limits of neoliberalism theme continues in Chapter 4. Here Jean-Michel Bonvin and Francesco Laruffa consider the 'social' investment perspective (focused on human capital formation) taking hold in global social policy discourses and the policy proposals advocated by international institutions like the OECD, the World Bank and the IMF, as well as regional actors like the EU and the European Commission (EC) and UN Regional Commissions like the Economic Commission for Latin America and the Caribbean (ECLAC). With this growing worldwide development they also sense the growing economization and de-politicization of the social. That is the loss of the social, with the focus on maximizing gross domestic product (GDP) and the employment rate, for example. Amartya Sen's Capability Approach, however, may provide a way out of such neoliberalizing policy processes. Given the central importance of democratic deliberation in this approach, Bonvin and Laruffa argue that *social* policy should be framed as an *enabling* factor of democracy in order to better promote equality in terms of both processes and outcomes. After all, the 'good society' will require flourishing democratic debates and public action to successfully promote inclusive societies for sustainable development, to challenge and undo established patterns of social inequality within and among nations.

The issue of the 'social' in 'sustainable development' is the subject of Chapter 5 by Iris Borowy. Much neglected in academic and policy-making circles, the 'social' dimension was certainly considered to be a central component of sustainable development at the UN from the 1980s, inextricably linked to economic and environmental concerns. If sustainable development is about meeting the needs of the present without compromising the ability of future generations to meet their own needs, then this poses a number of major challenges. Leaving aside the vexing issue of predicting future 'needs', there are clear tensions here in the social dimensions of sustainable development and related policy instruments, the SDGs. There are, on the one hand, clear tensions and trade-offs between the present pro-growth bias being promoted by the international institutions in an effort to end poverty (SDG 1) and reduce inequality within and between countries (SDG 10), while on the other hand the pursuit of endless economic growth is clearly incompatible with an environmentally sustainable world (represented by SDG 12, ensure responsible consumption and production patterns, for example, in order to tackle climate change). Economic growth is, of course, represented and promoted by SDG 8, 'decent work and economic growth', which is fundamentally about creating more jobs, more production and more consumption. If the environmental part of sustainable development looks rather bleak, its social component is at least starting to look rosier.

15

In Chapter 6, Tony Fitzpatrick presents an 'ecosocial' agenda for social reform, with the focus on reform options for a post-productive future. Here Fitzpatrick claims the synergies between social and environmental policies have barely registered to date. We find the familiar oppositions between those who favour remaining close to existing socioeconomic models, that is pro-productivism (based on GDP growth, production and consumption, and so on) and those for whom environmentalism and the ecosocial implies a greater, transformative potential. While the diminishing public sphere is again a major cause for concern here (as we heard in Chapter 4), Fitzpatrick does offer some hope, by encouraging us to think less in terms of oppositions between pro-productivists and post-productivists, and more in terms of commonalities and overlaps. For example, if the policy logic is to create more jobs globally to tackle poverty and inequality (the pro-productive position) then this should be accompanied by reduced working times overall (the post-productivist position). The struggle for sustainability is clearly evident but only by seeking alliances and common ground, as Fitzpatrick suggests, may we begin to take some of the necessary steps to resolve the social and ecological problems and challenges now facing humanity.

Population dynamics have long been inextricably linked to ideas about social sustainability, since the time of Thomas Malthus writing at the turn of the 18th century. Our ability to achieve sustainable development may well depend on the dynamics of the world's population. Certainly, the global human population is rising, and looks set to peak at around 10 billion people, causing an unprecedented 'planetary emergency' according to some accounts (Emmott, 2013). But to what extent are our numbers really our problem? This is the thorny issue taken up by Danny Dorling in Chapter 7. Part of the social sustainability challenge here surely is how to cope with world population dynamics. There may be problems and issues in some of the assumptions underpinning the UN world population projections, fewer babies are being born for example (people are also now leading longer lives, the focus in Chapter 8). Here Dorling considers changing population dynamics for each of the world regions. However, what may ultimately matter most for social sustainability and social wellbeing is how equitable a country is. When a country is equitable, like Finland, people do not have to think of having more children in future to help pay for their own old age. People are treated well enough regardless of how many children they have, or if they have none at all. It may seem impossible to think that this will ever happen to some of the poorest and most inequitable countries but, as Dorling points out, just a century ago Finland was a relatively poor country.

In Chapter 8, Alan Walker critically examines the implications of the major demographic shifts in global population age structures in relation to the thorny question of social sustainably. Here the scope of global ageing is summarised by Walker, and the relationship between ageing and sustainability is considered in the context of global social policy debates, and in the language streams deployed by the international financial institutions, the IMF and World Bank, which reveals the heavy emphasis on the economic dimension, with the exclusion of the environmental and social ones. However, it is with the development of the WHO's policy framework on 'active ageing' in 2002, relabelled 'healthy ageing' in 2015, which brought global ageing policy closer to the UN's sustainable development agenda. Indeed, the WHO now began to integrate its healthy ageing strategy with the SDGs. Walker therefore demonstrates how global discourses on ageing and sustainability have consistently ignored the ageing process and environmental and social sustainability. It is only very recently that attempts have been made to bring these different perspectives together. Nevertheless, existing global social policy frameworks still require more and better alignment if ageing is to become fully integrated with economic, environmental and social sustainability.

The impact of globalization and the movement of people on the making of social policy and global migration complicates the social question, increasing framed as the 'global' social question or 'transnational' social question. Article 13 of the UDHR affirms the right of everyone to 'leave any country' (the right to emigrate), but this is not the same thing as the right to enter a country (the right to immigrate), to work and access benefits. In Chapter 9, Edward Koning considers social conflict on a transnational scale. Policy makers are increasingly being challenged on how to maintain solidarity and cohesion in societies experiencing intergroup tension. Modern welfare states need to decide on the nature of *rights* and how rights may be differentiated, depending on status categories. Policy makers therefore face a difficult decision regarding which of the existing social benefits should be accessible to immigrants, and whether new benefits should be created that exclusively target immigrants to help promote social and economic integration. Residence status remains important here. As Koning notes, few policy makers would prefer not to advocate blatant discrimination between native-born and naturalized citizens, but equally welfare states tend not to grant those without legal status full access to welfare services. But beyond these two extremes, there are tough choices ahead in determining the rights of permanent, temporary and undocumented migrants. Approaches to rights differentiation vary considerably from country to country. Migration does indeed pose a formidable challenge to the future sustainability of the welfare state, even if the challenge turns out to be more political in nature than economic. In the face of growing welfare chauvinism in the electorate, and with the rise of anti-immigrant politicians and anti-immigrant parties (AIPs), the immediate outlook seems bleak for transnational solidarity and the social of social policy, at least in the present climate.

In Chapter 10, Fiona Williams illustrates how an intersectional approach can excavate the 'social' in social policy analysis, not only at national and local/interpersonal scales but at global scales too. Here Williams focuses on the forces at the global scale that have shaped the development of post-financial crisis (austerity) welfare and the global pandemic of COVID-19, which should be understood in terms of the intersections between the crises of global financialised capitalism, of care, of ecology and of racialized transnational mobilities. The four crises are interconnected; they have commonalities in constitution and effect, as well as interlocking dynamics and mechanisms. They are linked by the ways each jeopardizes security, human solidarity and sustainability for future generations. The commonalities include that they challenge the patriarchal, racial and ecosocial dimensions of neoliberal capitalism and its modes of production, reproduction, consumption, accumulation, commodification and growth, of which they are the outcome. An intersectionality approach is able to find synergies and shared understanding across progressive movements for care, decoloniality, environmental and economic justice. Together recent global events and social movements and formations create possibilities for alliances and transformatory alternatives, and they may provide the basis at least for thinking about new welfare states that focus on sustaining the social.

Intersectionality and intersectional analysis are a recurrent theme and approach in this volume, which continues in Chapter 11, where Jane Jenson considers global social policy making and the quasi-concept of social cohesion. It is a quasi-concept, according to Jenson, not least because no shared definition of social cohesion actually exists in the literature. But also, importantly, because of the way it is used empirically by policy makers (often in relation to a set or 'dashboard' of social indicators, for example), while at the same time remaining sufficiently flexible to be deployed by policy makers in policy instruments, at different levels, and within and across different spatial scales; for example, from individuals to communities, and from nation-states to the world regions and increasingly in a global context. Here Jenson examines and compares the work and policy approaches of the international institutions the World Bank, the UN and the WHO, as well as the work of regional actors like the EU. Some of the policy tools, documents and instruments for fostering cohesive social relations appear quite general or broad-brushed, encompassing notions of social, economic and cultural integration, for example, while others are much narrower in scope, operationalizing or interpreting social cohesion according to notions of labour market participation, and other forms of 'work' and job creation initiatives.

In Chapter 12, Gary Craig considers the prospects for global social justice in light of the UN 2030 Agenda seeking to better integrate economic, social and environmental needs for a more just and sustainable world. However, there are major challenges now facing proponents of social justice in an economically globalized world. Where most states are increasingly multicultural, for example, how then should the conception of global social justice be formulated? Can we rely on an almost exclusively Eurocentric or Anglo-American, not to say Judaeo-Christian, understanding of the meaning of social justice? What might a global social justice framework look like in theory and how might it work in practice, and what are some of the likely political consequences if it is accepted by mainstream political and cultural groups? At stake are many thorny issues, but there are some positive developments; international actions and demands for stronger global social justice are growing. However, there will be many challenges ahead on this long and winding road, if the idea of global social justice can be turned into a reality for all.

In Chapter 13, Chris Deeming considers the prospects for improved social governance at the global level, as humanity moves towards more sustainable patterns of consumption and production, and a more socially responsible, equitable, inclusive and just world. In particular, the chapter critically examines the emerging social policies being articulated by the OECD in order to reform global capitalism. This international organization is made up of rich nation states and is in the process of repositioning itself as the international institution responsible for promoting 'global social justice', a highly challenging endeavour. Nevertheless, the OECD is clearly influencing global social governance debates in an effort to build a new consensus against growing social inequality. There are many challenges ahead in securing a new social governance architecture for inclusive economic growth. Yet something of a paradox remains. On one hand, the OECD claims to want to move beyond growth, but on the other it is promoting growth strategies to end poverty and address extreme inequality (forming part of the SDGs). In other words, the 'growth paradigm' is being maintained here, while the opportunities for greater redistribution of resources within and among countries gets crowded out by the dominant discourse sustaining global capitalism, based on the idea that (GDP) growth is always better.

In Chapter 14 (aptly titled 'For better or worse?'), Richard Wilkinson and Kate Pickett point to something of an irony in the age of extreme inequality. In part, represented by the growing worldwide effort to devise new and better measures charting human wellbeing and social progress, a growing academic industry is now devoted to this task. At the same time, however, Wilkinson and Pickett point to the general lack of policy making based on or informed by the knowledge of the *social* determinants of health and wellbeing (indeed, Richard Wilkinson has made a formative contribution to this field). Moreover, even when governments like New Zealand and Scotland have adopted measures of wellbeing in governmental policy, that does not necessarily mean that wellbeing will increase. Nor should substituting or complementing GDP with a dashboard of wellbeing indicators imply that we are necessarily moving beyond GDP or material growth. While higher material standards are clearly needed in low-income countries, where many do not yet have access to necessities, in the rich countries there are sharply diminishing returns to wellbeing associated with endless economic growth. Further improvements in the quality of life for all will therefore depend on major encompassing societal changes. Firstly, there is a pressing need to escape excessive consumerism. Societies need to switch their focus from material throughput and economic output associated with consumerism in order to transition towards social and environmental sustainability. Secondly, and related, the authors maintain that societies really need to address inequality in order to improve population wellbeing overall. If we are serious about the transition to sustainability, then we must reduce the inequality which ramps up status competition and consumerism. Only then might we think about the long-term possibility of substantial social progress.

The concluding chapter, Chapter 15, by Chris Deeming, draws together some of the lessons from the volume as a whole, for thinking through the conceptual 'lynchpin' of the 'social' and the seismic shifts in social policy over time and space. Here we return to the different conceptualizations of the 'social' of social policy discussed in earlier chapters, and reflect on social progress in the first half of the 21st century.

Notes

1   The international financial institutions, the IMF and the World Bank, are considered to be UN agencies, but they have mandates to act independently on economic grounds, in order to maintain global economic stability.

2 The policy approach at the IMF is now claimed to be about 'Forging a Stronger Social Contract'; thus, 'social spending is not just an expense', as Christine Lagarde, Managing Director at the IMF, maintains, 'but rather the wisest of investments in the well-being of our societies': www.imf.org/en/News/Articles/2019/06/14/sp061419-md-social-spending.

3 The Intergovernmental Science-Policy Platform on Biodiversity and Ecosystem Services (IPBES, 2019) reports current negative trends in biodiversity and ecosystems that will undermine Agenda 2030 and progress towards the SDGs, particularly relating to poverty, hunger, health, water, cities, climate, oceans and land (SDGs 1, 2, 3, 6, 11, 13, 14 and 15). Loss of biodiversity is not only an environmental issue, but also a developmental, economic, security, social and moral issue, if we are to preserve human life and the life of other species on earth, according to the IPBES and the Intergovernmental Panel on Climate Change (IPCC, 2019), the intergovernmental body of the UN.

4 For Marxist thinkers like David Harvey (2014) such crises are not altogether surprising, but to be expected, since capitalism is inherently unstable and prone to crises. Crises are essential to the reproduction and reconstitution of capitalism, Harvey maintains, but they also strengthen the case for anti-capitalist politics in the Marxist tradition. For the international institutions (the WTO, the IMF, World Bank and the OECD) and international forums like the G20 the crises appear unexpected: 'the global financial and economic crisis came as a surprise for many international organizations' (one of many such claims appearing in aftermath of the global financial crises, in the UN flagship report, Report on the World Social Situation (RWSS), UN DESA, 2011: 2). Nevertheless, they do point to deficiencies in the capitalist system that need to be overcome in order to preserve or strengthen international capitalism and the world economy; 'inclusive growth' arguably represents the latest paradigmatic response from the international institutions for the remaking of the global capitalist economy (see Chapter 13 in this volume).

5 See Jubilee Debt Campaign, 'Coronavirus: Cancel the Debts of Countries in the Global South', https://jubileedebt.org.uk/actions/stop-coronavirus-debt-disaster; also the statement from over 100 global civil society organizations calling on G20 governments, the IMF and World Bank to immediately cancel debt payments in 2020, https://jubileedebt.org.uk/press-release/call-for-immediate-cancellation-of-developing-country-debt-payments.

6 See Stamp Out Poverty proposals for a 'Climate Damages Tax', www.stampoutpoverty.org/; also the campaign for a 'Robin Hood Tax' on trades by banks and other big speculators, so the finance sector meets the cost of its own crises and makes a fairer contribution to society.

7 See also WEF, 'Coronavirus: A Pandemic in the Age of Inequality, www.weforum.org/agenda/2020/03/coronavirus-pandemic-inequality-among-workers/; and UN plans for tackling the social and economic dimensions of the crisis: 'UN Launches COVID-19 Plan That Could "Defeat the Virus and Build a Better World"', https://news.un.org/en/story/2020/03/1060702.

8 Dr Tedros Adhanom Ghebreyesus, WHO Director-General, opening remarks at 148th session of the Executive Board, 18 January 2021, https://www.who.int/director-general/speeches/detail/who-director-general-s-opening-remarks-at-148th-session-of-the-executive-board.

9 UN Secretary-General António Guterres (2020), for example, is calling for a 'New Social Contract', between Governments, people, civil society and business to integrate employment, sustainable development and social protection. Plus a 'New

Global Deal', based on a fair globalization, to create equal opportunities for all and respect the rights and freedoms of all. The varying responses to the crisis found at national and regional levels, however, means any durable changes are likely to be understood in relation to the specific institutional features and policy legacies of each country, as Daniel Béland observes, https://www.mcgill.ca/maxbellschool/article/how-different-countries-respond-global-crises-social-policy-lessons-past.

10 The challenges associated with creating and sustaining 'social' value in market (value) society were well recognized in the writing on political economy, including Adam Smith, Karl Marx, Karl Polanyi and John Maynard Keynes (see discussions by T. H. Marshall, 1972, David Harvey, 2014, Fred Block and Margaret R. Somers, 2014). In recent work, for example, Bill Jordon (2008, 2021) makes the case for 'social value' based on notions of wellbeing incorporated into policy-making decisions; while Mariana Mazzucato (2018: 229–33, 264–9) discusses the idea of 'public value', urging us to rethink the process of value creation beyond old notions of the public and private sphere. Other initiatives are also attempting to change the way society thinks and accounts for social value: for example, www.socialvalueuk.org/. Some of the problems and challenges associated with defining and conceptualizing 'social value' and operationalizing it in policy terms are discussed by Dowling and Harvie (2014).

11 In the classical tradition, for example, social theorists like Émile Durkheim were concerned with the study of 'social facts', the facts termed 'social' (Durkheim, [1895] 1982: 50), and with the study of 'social solidarity' (Durkheim, [1897] 1952). For Weber, sociology was all about the understanding of 'social action' (Weber, [1922] 1978: 4). Notions and conceptions of the 'social' are not always precisely defined, however, dealing with quite diverse problems, institutions and issues relating to governance. Jean Baudrillard, for example, marked 'the end of the social' with the rise of consumer capitalist society ([1978] 1983: 25, 82), while Gilles Deleuze (1979: ix) considers 'the rise of the social', that is, 'social' workers within the social service state. Nikolas Rose (1996: 327), like Baudrillard, lamented 'the death of the social' with the rise of New Right ideology, but at the same time, he also observes the rise of 'social' policies increasingly being articulated at a supra-national level in the work of international organizations.

12 A 'social question' is usually one that concerns society and/or a social group, increasingly cast as the transnational social question in global times (see Chapters 3 and 15), that demands or provokes political reactions and institutional responses. The so-called social questions were originally conceived in terms of regulating the social. For example, 'social control', 'the pauper question' (poor relief and the workhouse), 'the penal question' (incarceration and the prison) and 'the workers' question' that dominated thinking about the social question, conceived in terms of social welfare planning and the needs of the capitalist economy. As such, the work of social scientists, in the long history of the social sciences, has been directed at state-orientated concerns and the major political issues of the day, the social questions, as Peter Wagner (2001) suggests.

13 As Adam Smith taught us, there are moral limits to markets, to naked self-interest and economic individualism: 'How selfish soever man may be supposed, there are evidently some principles in his nature, which interest him in the fortune of others, and render their happiness necessary to him, though he derives nothing from it except the pleasure of seeing it. Of this kind is pity or compassion, the emotion which we feel for the misery of others, when we either see it, or are made to conceive it' (Smith, [1759] 2009: 13).

14 BLM seeks to bring attention to police violence against African-American people in the USA after the shooting death of African-American teenager Trayvon Martin in February 2012. The Black Lives Matter Global Network is now a global movement in the fight for freedom, liberation and justice, see www.blacklivesmatter.com/. The George Floyd/BLM protests in 550 US cities began in May 2020, in reaction to the murder of George Floyd, quickly spreading worldwide.

15 Article 2 of the UDHR, for example, states: 'Everyone is entitled to all the rights and freedoms set forth in this Declaration, without distinction of any kind, such as race, colour, sex, language, religion, political or other opinion, national or social origin, property, birth or other status. Furthermore, no distinction shall be made on the basis of the political, jurisdictional or international status of the country or territory to which a person belongs, whether it be independent, trust, non-self-governing or under any other limitation of sovereignty; further details are available from the OHCHR': https://www.ohchr.org/EN/UDHR/Pages/UDHRIndex.aspx.

16 The World Youth Report (WYR) found 142 million young people of upper secondary age are out of school, while upper secondary enrolment rates average only 14 per cent in low-income countries. Moreover, almost 30 per cent of the poorest 12–14 year olds have never attended school, some 71 million young people were unemployed, and many millions more are in precarious or informal work.

17 A clear exception here is research looking at the formal institutions of the EU and the social question hanging over the future of a 'Social Europe', with the focus on sustaining social cohesion across diverse EU member states and the challenges associated with social policy development (Mahon, 2002; Jenson, 2010b; Barbier, 2013; Vandenbroucke et al, 2017).

18 The idea of 'Global Social Policy' as a field of study is often conceived, as Deacon et al (1997: 195) observe, in terms of understanding the social policies of international institutions and regional actors, that shape global social redistribution, regulation and provision; and the way in which global actors shape national social policy. In this sense social policy preoccupations are put to the test in the global context.

References

Ayob, N., Teasdale, S. and Fagan, K. (2016) 'How Social Innovation "Came to Be": Tracing the Evolution of a Contested Concept', *Journal of Social Policy*, 45(4): 635–53.

Babb, S. (2013) 'The Washington Consensus as Transnational Policy Paradigm: Its Origins, Trajectory and Likely Successor', *Review of International Political Economy*, 20(2): 268–97.

Banting, K. and Kymlicka, W. (eds) (2006) *Multiculturalism and the Welfare State: Recognition and Redistribution in Contemporary Democracies*, Oxford: Oxford University Press.

Barbier, J.-C. (2013) *The Road to Social Europe: A Contemporary Approach to Political Cultures and Diversity in Europe*, Translated by Susan Gruenheck Taponier, Abingdon: Routledge.

Baudrillard, J. ([1978] 1983) *In the Shadow of the Silent Majorities, Or, the End of the Social*, New York: Semiotext(e).

Bebbington, A., Guggenheim, S., Olson, E. and Woolcock, M. (2004) 'Exploring Social Capital Debates at the World Bank', *Journal of Development Studies*, 40(5): 33–64.

Béland, D. (2007) 'The Social Exclusion Discourse: Ideas and Policy Change', *Policy & Politics*, 35(1): 123–39.

Béland D. and Orenstein, M. A. (2013) 'International Organizations as Policy Actors: An Ideational Approach', *Global Social Policy*, 13(2): 125–43.

Béland, D. and Petersen, K. (2014) 'Introduction: Social Policy Concepts and Language', in D. Béland and K. Petersen (eds) *Analysing Social Policy Concepts and Language: Comparative and Transnational Perspectives*, Bristol: Policy Press, 1–11.

Bell, D. ([1977] 1996) *The Cultural Contradictions of Capitalism*, 20th Anniversary Edition, with a new afterword by the author, New York: Basic Books.

Bellucci, S. and Weiss, H. (2020) '1919 and the Century of the Labour Internationalisation', in S. Bellucci and H. Weiss (eds) *The Internationalisation of the Labour Question: Ideological Antagonism, Workers' Movements and the ILO since 1919*, Cham: Palgrave Macmillan, 1-19.

Block, F. and Somers, M. R. (2014) *The Power of Market Fundamentalism: Karl Polanyi's Critique*, Cambridge, MA: Harvard University Press.

Bøås, M. and McNeill, D. (eds) (2004) *Global Institutions and Development: Framing the World?*, Abingdon: Routledge.

Bogalska-Martin, E. and Matteudi, E. (eds) (2018) *The Social Question in the Global World*, Cambridge: Cambridge Scholars.

Bonoli, G. (2018) 'Active Labour Market Policies for an Inclusive Growth', in C. Deeming and P. Smyth (eds) *Reframing Global Social Policy: Social Investment for Sustainable and Inclusive Growth*, Bristol: Policy Press, 169–87.

Breman, J., Harris, K., Lee, C. K. and Van Der Linden, M. (eds) (2019) *The Social Question in the Twenty-First Century: A Global View*, Oakland, CA: University of California Press.

Clarke, J. (1996) 'Public Nightmares and Communitarian Dreams: The Crisis of the Social in Social Welfare', *The Sociological Review*, 44(1): 66–91.

Clarke, J. (2007) 'Subordinating the Social? Neoliberalism and the Remaking of Welfare Capitalism', *Cultural Studies*, 21(6): 974–87.

Collins, P. H. (2007) 'Pushing the Boundaries or Business as Usual? Race, Class, and Gender Studies and Sociological Inquiry', in C. Calhoun (ed) *Sociology in America: A History*, Chicago, IL: University of Chicago Press, 572–604.

Collins, P. H. and Bilge, S. (2020) *Intersectionality*, Second Edition, Cambridge: Polity.

Corbett, S. and Walker, A. (2017) 'Putting "the Social" Back into Social Policy', in R. Atkinson, L. McKenzie and S. Winlow (eds) *Building Better Societies: Promoting Social Justice in a World Falling Apart*, Bristol: Policy Press, 111–24.

Craig, G. (ed) (2018) *Global Social Justice*, Cheltenham: Edward Elgar.

Craig, D. and Porter, D. (2005) 'The Third Way and the Third World: Poverty Reduction and Social Inclusion Strategies in the Rise of "Inclusive" Liberalism', *Review of International Political Economy*, 12(2): 226–63.

Dalby, S., Horton, S. and Mahon, R. with Thomaz, D. (eds) (2019) *Achieving the Sustainable Development Goals: Global Governance Challenges*, Abingdon and New York: Routledge.

Deacon, B. (2005) 'From "Safety Nets" Back to "Universal Social Provision": Is the Global Tide Turning?', *Global Social Policy*, 5(1): 19–28.

Deacon, B. with Hulse, M. and Stubbs, P. (1997) *Global Social Policy: International Organizations and the Future of Welfare*, London: Sage.

Dean, J. (1996) *Solidarity of Strangers: Feminism After Identity Politics*, Berkeley, CA: University of California Press.

Deeming, C. (2013) 'Addressing the Social Determinants of Subjective Wellbeing: The Latest Challenge for Social Policy', *Journal of Social Policy*, 42(3): 541–65.

Deeming, C. (2016) 'Rethinking Social Policy and Society', *Social Policy and Society*, 15(2): 159–75.

Deeming, C. and Smyth, P. (2018) 'Social Investment, Inclusive Growth That Is Sustainable and the New Global Social Policy', in C. Deeming and P. Smyth (eds) *Reframing Global Social Policy: Social Investment for Sustainable and Inclusive Growth*, Bristol: Policy Press, 11–44.

Deleuze, G. (1979) 'Foreword: The Rise of the Social', in J. Donzelot, *The Policing of Families*, Translated from the French by Robert Hurley, New York: Pantheon, ix–xvii.

Dillard, J., Dujon, V. and King, M. (eds) (2008) *Understanding the Social Dimension of Sustainability*, New York: Routledge.

Dingwerth, K., Witt, A., Lehmann, I., Reichel, E. and Weise, T. (eds) (2019) *International Organizations under Pressure: Legitimating Global Governance in Challenging Times*, Oxford: Oxford University Press.

Dowling, E. and Harvie, D. (2014) 'Harnessing the Social: State, Crisis and (Big) Society', *Sociology*, 48(5): 869–86.

Downes, A. and Lansley, S. (eds) (2018) *It's Basic Income: The Global Debate*, Bristol: Policy Press.

Dujon, V., Dillard, J. and Brennan, E. M. (eds) (2013) *Social Sustainability: A Multilevel Approach to Social Inclusion*, New York: Routledge.

Durkheim, E. ([1895] 1982) *The Rules of Sociological Method*, Edited with an Introduction by Steven Lukes, Translated by W. D. Halls, New York: Free Press.

Durkheim, E. ([1897] 1952) *Suicide: A Study in Sociology*, London: Routledge & Kegan Paul.

EC (European Commission) (2019) *Towards a Sustainable Europe by 2030*, COM(2019)22, Brussels: EC, https://ec.europa.eu/commission/sites/beta-political/files/rp_sustainable_europe_30-01_en_web.pdf.

ECA (United Nations Economic Commission for Africa) (2018) *2018 Africa Sustainable Development Report: Towards a Transformed and Resilient Continent*, Addis Ababa: UN, https://digitallibrary.un.org/record/3801706?ln=en.

ECLAC (United Nations Economic Commission for Latin America and the Caribbean) (2018) *Draft Programme of Work of the ECLAC System, 2020*, LC/SES.37/8, Havana: UN, https://repositorio.cepal.org/handle/11362/43570.

Emmerij, L., Jolly, R. and Weiss, T. G. (2001) *Ahead of the Curve? UN Ideas and Global Challenges*, Bloomington, IN: Indiana University Press.

Emmott, S. (2013) *10 Billion*, London: Penguin.

ESCAP (United Nations Economic and Social Commission for Asia and the Pacific) (2019) *Asia and the Pacific SDG Progress Report 2019*, Bangkok: UN, https://digitallibrary.un.org/record/3813666?ln=en.

Evans, B. and McBride, S. (eds) (2017) *Austerity: The Lived Experience*, Toronto: University of Toronto Press.

Faist, T. (2015) 'The Transnational Social Question: Cross-Border Social Protection and Social Inequalities', in P. Kettunen, S. Michel and K. Petersen (eds) *Race, Ethnicity and Welfare States: An American Dilemma?*, Cheltenham: Edward Elgar, 227–53.

Faist, T. (2019) *The Transnationalized Social Question: Migration and the Question of Social Inequalities in the Twenty-First Century*, Oxford: Oxford University Press.

Fassin, É. and Fassin, D. (2006) *De la question sociale à la question raciale: Représenter la société française*, Paris: La Découverte.

Ferragina, E. and Arrigoni, A. (2017) 'The Rise and Fall of Social Capital: Requiem for a Theory?', *Political Studies Review*, 15(3): 355–67.

Fitzpatrick, T. (2001) 'Making Welfare for Future Generations', *Social Policy & Administration*, 35(5): 506–20.

Fraser, N. and Honneth, A. (2003) *Redistribution or Recognition? A Political-Philosophical Exchange*, Translated by Joel Golb, James Ingram and Christiane Wilke, London and New York: Verso.

Fredman, S. (2016) 'Women and Poverty – A Human Rights Approach', *African Journal of International and Comparative Law*, 24(4): 494–517.

Frey, M., Kunkel, S. and Unger, C. R. (eds) (2014) *International Organizations and Development, 1945–1990*, Basingstoke: Palgrave Macmillan.

Fukuda-Parr, S. and Muchhala, B. (2020) 'The Southern Origins of Sustainable Development Goals: Ideas, Actors, Aspirations', *World Development*, 126: 104706.

Garza, A. (2020) *The Purpose of Power: How to Build Movements for the 21 Century*, London: Doubleday.

Gore, C. (2000) 'The Rise and Fall of the Washington Consensus as a Paradigm for Developing Countries', *World Development*, 28(5): 789–804.

Gore, C. (2015) 'The Post-2015 Moment: Towards Sustainable Development Goals and a New Global Development Paradigm', *Journal of International Development*, 27(6): 717–32.

Gough, I. (2017) *Heat, Greed and Human Needs*, Cheltenham: Edward Elgar.

Guterres, A. (2020) *Tackling the Inequality Pandemic: A New Social Contract for a New Era*, The 18th Nelson Mandela Annual Lecture, 18 July, New York: UN, www.un.org/en/coronavirus/tackling-inequality-new-social-contract-new-era.

Habermas, J. ([1962] 1989) *The Structural Transformation of the Public Sphere: An Inquiry into a Category of Bourgeois Society*, Translated by Thomas Burger, Cambridge, MA: MIT Press.

Harvey, D. (2014) *Seventeen Contradictions and the End of Capitalism*, New York: Oxford University Press.

Hegel, G. W. F. ([1821] 1967) *Philosophy of Right*, Translated with notes by T. M. Knox, Oxford: Oxford University Press.

Hickel, J. (2017) *The Divide: A Brief Guide to Global Inequality and Its Solutions*, London: Heinemann.

Hobson, B. (ed) (2003) *Recognition Struggles and Social Movements: Contested Identities, Agency and Power*, Cambridge: Cambridge University Press.

Honneth, A. (1995a) *The Fragmented World of the Social: Essays in Social and Political Philosophy*, Edited by Charles W. Wright, New York: State University of New York Press.

Honneth, A. ([1992] 1995b) *The Struggle for Recognition: The Moral Grammar of Social Conflicts*, Translated by Joel Anderson, Cambridge: Polity.

ILO (International Labour Organization) (2004) *A Fair Globalization: Creating Opportunities For All, World Commission on the Social Dimension of Globalization*, Geneva: ILO, https://www.ilo.org/fairglobalization/report/lang--en/index.htm.

IMF (International Monetary Fund) (2019) *A Strategy for IMF Engagement on Social Spending*, Policy Paper No 19/016, Washington, DC: IMF, www.imf.org/~/media/Files/Publications/PP/2019/PPEA2019016.ashx.

IMF (2020) *IMF and the Sustainable Development Goals*, 26 February, www.imf.org/en/About/Factsheets/Sheets/2016/08/01/16/46/Sustainable-Development-Goals.

IPBES (Intergovernmental Science-Policy Platform on Biodiversity and Ecosystem Services) (2019) *Summary for Policymakers of the Global Assessment Report on Biodiversity and Ecosystem Services of the Intergovernmental Science-Policy Platform on Biodiversity and Ecosystem Services*, Bonn: IPBES secretariat, https://doi.org/10.5281/zenodo.3553579.

IPCC (Intergovernmental Panel on Climate Change) (2019) *Climate Change and Land: An IPCC Special Report on Climate Change, Desertification, Land Degradation, Sustainable Land Management, Food Security, and Greenhouse Gas Fluxes in Terrestrial Ecosystems: Summary for Policymakers*, IPCC, www.ipcc.ch/site/assets/uploads/sites/4/2020/02/SPM_Updated-Jan20.pdf.

Jenson, J. (2010a) 'Diffusing Ideas for After Neoliberalism: The Social Investment Perspective in Europe and Latin America', *Global Social Policy*, 10(1): 59–84.

Jenson, J. (2010b) *Defining and Measuring Social Cohesion*, London: Commonwealth Secretariat and UNRISD, www.files.ethz.ch/isn/151856/Jenson%20ebook.pdf.

Jenson, J. (2015a) 'The "Social" in Inclusive Growth: The Social Investment Perspective', in R. Hasmath (ed) *Inclusive Growth, Development and Welfare Policy: A Critical Assessment*, New York: Routledge, 108–23.

Jenson, J. (2015b) 'Broadening the Frame: Inclusive Growth and the Social Investment Perspective', in S. McBride, R. Mahon and G. W. Boychuk (eds) *After '08: Social Policy and the Global Financial Crisis*, Vancouver, BC: UBC Press, 40–58.

Jenson, J. (2015c) 'Social Innovation: Redesigning the Welfare Diamond', in A. Nicholls, M. Gabriel, J. Simon and C. Whelan (eds) *New Frontiers in Social Innovation Research*, Basingstoke: Palgrave Macmillan, 89–106.

Jenson, J. (2017) 'Developing and Spreading a Social Investment Perspective: The World Bank and OECD Compared', in A. Hemerijck (ed) *The Uses of Social Investment*, Oxford: Oxford University Press, 207–15.

Jenson, J. (2018) 'Social Politics Puzzling: Governance for Inclusive Growth and Social Investment', in C. Deeming and P. Smyth (eds) *Reframing Social Policy: Social Investment for Sustainable and Inclusive Growth*, Bristol: Policy Press, 273–93.

Jolly, R., Emmerij, L. and Weiss, T. G. (2009) *UN Ideas that Changed the World*, Bloomington, IN: Indiana University Press.

Jordon, B. (2008) *Welfare and Well-being: Social Value in Public Policy*, Bristol: Policy Press.

Jordon, B. (2021) *Social Value in Public Policy*, Cham: Palgrave Macmillan.

Kaasch, A. (2013) 'Contesting Contestation: Global Social Policy Prescriptions on Pensions and Health Systems', *Global Social Policy*, 13(1): 45–65.

Kaasch A. and Deacon, B. (2008) 'The OECD's Social and Health Policy: Neoliberal Stalking Horse or Balancer of Social and Economic Objectives?', in R. Mahon and S. McBride (eds) *The OECD and Global Governance*, Vancouver: UBC Press, 226–41.

Kaufmann, F.-X. (2013) *Thinking about Social Policy: The German Tradition*, Germany Social Policy Volume 1, Translated from the German by Thomas Dunlap, Edited and introduced by Lutz Leisering, Heidelberg: Springer.

Kentikelenis, A., Gabor, D., Ortiz, I., Stubbs, T., McKee, M. and Stuckler, D. (2020) 'Softening the Blow of the Pandemic: Will the International Monetary Fund and World Bank Make Things Worse?', *The Lancet Global Health*, 8(6): e758–9.

Koch, M. and Fritz, M. (2014) 'Building the Eco-social State: Do Welfare Regimes Matter?', *Journal of Social Policy*, 43(4): 679–703.

Koch, M. and Oksana, M. (eds) (2016) *Sustainability and the Political Economy of Welfare*, Abingdon: Routledge.

Laruffa, F. (2018) 'Social Investment: Diffusing Ideas for Redesigning Citizenship after Neo-Liberalism?', *Critical Social Policy*, 38(4): 688–706.

Leisering, L. (ed) (2021) *One Hundred Years of Social Protection: The Changing Social Question in Brazil, India, China, and South Africa*, Cham: Springer.

Lewis, G., Gewirtz, S. and Clarke, J. (eds) (2000) *Rethinking Social Policy*, London: Sage.

Lister, R. (2008) 'Recognition and Voice: The Challenge for Social Justice', in G. Craig, T. Burchardt and D. Gordon (eds) (2008) *Social Justice and Public Policy*, Bristol: Policy Press, 105–23.

Mahon, R. (2002) 'Child Care: Toward What Kind of "Social Europe"?', *Social Politics: International Studies in Gender, State & Society*, 9(3): 343–79.

Mahon, R. (2010) 'After Neo-Liberalism? The OECD, the World Bank and the Child', *Global Social Policy*, 10(2): 172–92.

Mahon, R. (2011) 'The Jobs Strategy: From Neo- to Inclusive Liberalism?', *Review of International Political Economy*, 18(5): 570–91.

Mahon, R. (2013) 'Social Investment According to the OECD/DELSA: A Discourse in the Making', *Global Policy*, 4(2): 150–9.

Mahon, R. (2014) 'The OECD's Search for a New Social Policy Language: From Welfare State to Active Society', in D. Béland and K. Petersen (eds) *Analysing Social Policy Concepts and Language: Comparative and Transnational Perspectives*, Bristol: Policy Press, 81–100.

Mahon, R. (2015) 'Integrating the Social into CEPAL's Neo-structuralist Discourse', *Global Social Policy*, 15(1): 3–22.

Mahon, R. (2019) 'Broadening the Social Investment Agenda: The OECD, the World Bank and Inclusive Growth', *Global Social Policy*, 19(1–2): 121–38.

Marshall, T. H. (1972) 'Social Policy in Context', *Sociology*, 6(2): 326–7.

Mazzucato, M. (2018) *The Value of Everything: Making and Taking in the Global Economy*, London: Allen Lane.

McNeill, D. (2004) 'Social Capital and the World Bank', in M. Bøås and D. McNeill (eds) *Global Institutions and Development: Framing the World?*, Abingdon: Routledge, 108–23.

Narayan, D. and Petesch, P. (ed) (2002) *Voices of the Poor: From Many Lands*, New York: Oxford University Press, http://hdl.handle.net/10986/14053.

Narayan, D., Chambers, R., Shah, M. K. and Petesch, P. (2000b) *Voices of the Poor: Crying Out for Change*, New York: Oxford University Press, http://hdl.handle.net/10986/13848.

Narayan, D., Patel, R., Schafft, K., Rademacher, A. and Koch-Shulte, S. (2000a) *Voices of the Poor: Can Anyone Hear Us?*, New York: Oxford University Press, http://documents.worldbank.org/curated/en/131441468779067441/Voices-of-the-poor-can-anyone-hear-us.

O'Brien, R., Goetz, A., Scholte, J. and Williams, M. (2000) *Contesting Global Governance: Multilateral Economic Institutions and Global Social Movements*, Cambridge: Cambridge University Press.

OECD (Organisation for Economic Co-operation and Development) (2019) *Policy Coherence for Sustainable Development 2019: Empowering People and Ensuring Inclusiveness and Equality*, Paris: OECD Publishing, https://doi.org/10.1787/a90f851f-en.

OECD (2020) *Beyond Containment: Health Systems Responses to COVID-19 in the OECD*, Paris: OECD Publishing, https://read.oecd-ilibrary.org/view/?ref=119_119689-ud5comtf84&title=Beyond_Containment:Health_systems_responses_to_COVID-19_in_the_OECD.

Oldekop, J. A., Horner, R., Hulme, D., Adhikari, R., Agarwal, B., Alford, M., Bakewell, O., Banks, N., Barrientos, S., Bastia, T., Bebbington, A. J., Das, U., Dimova, R., Duncombe, R., Enns, C., Fielding, D., Foster, C., Foster, T., Frederiksen, T., Gao, P., Gillespie, T., Heeks, R., Hickey, S., Hess, M., Jepson, N., Karamchedu, A., Kothari, U., Krishnan, A., Lavers, T., Mamman, A., Mitlin, D., Monazam Tabrizi, N., Müller, T. R., Nadvi, K., Pasquali, G., Pritchard, R., Pruce, K., Rees, C., Renken, J., Savoia, A., Schindler, S., Surmeier, A., Tampubolon, G., Tyce, M., Unnikrishnan, V. and Zhang, Y.-F. (2020) 'COVID-19 and the Case for Global Development', *World Development*, 134: 105044.

Pateman, C. (1998) 'The Patriarchal Welfare State', in A. Gutmann (ed) *Democracy and the Welfare State*, Princeton: Princeton University Press, 231–60.

Pilbeam, P. (2000) *French Socialists before Marx: Workers, Women and the Social Question in France*, Montreal: McGill-Queen's University Press.

Razavi, S. (2016) 'The 2030 Agenda: Challenges of Implementation to Attain Gender Equality and Women's Rights', *Gender & Development*, 24(1): 25–41.

Razavi, S. (2019) 'Indicators as Substitute for Policy Contestation and Accountability? Some Reflections on the 2030 Agenda from the Perspective of Gender Equality and Women's Rights', *Global Policy*, 10(S1): 149–52.

Razavi, S. and Hassim, S. (2006) 'Gender and Social Policy in a Global Context: Uncovering the Gendered Structure of "the Social"', in S. Razavi and S. Hassim (eds) *Gender and Social Policy in a Global Context: Uncovering the Gendered Structure of 'the Social'*, UNRISD, Basingstoke: Palgrave Macmillan, 1–39.

Rodrik, D. (2006) 'Goodbye Washington Consensus, Hello Washington Confusion? A Review of the World Bank's "Economic Growth in the 1990s: Learning from a Decade of Reform"', *Journal of Economic Literature*, 44(4): 973–87.

Rose, N. (1996) 'The Death of the Social? Re-figuring the Territory of Government', *Economy and Society*, 25(3): 327–56.

Sachs, J., Schmidt-Traub, G., Kroll, C., Lafortune, G. and Fuller, G. (2018) *SDG Index and Dashboards Report 2018*, New York: Bertelsmann Stiftung and SDSN.

Sen, A. (2013) 'The Ends and Means of Sustainability', *Journal of Human Development and Capabilities*, 14(1): 6–20.

Smith, A. ([1759] 2009) *The Theory of Moral Sentiments*, Introduction by Amartya Sen, New York: Penguin.

Smith, S. S. and Kulynych, J. (2002) 'It May be Social, But Why Is It Capital? The Social Construction of Social Capital and the Politics of Language', *Politics & Society*, 30(1): 149–86.

Stjernø, S. (2005) *Solidarity in Europe: The History of an Idea*, Cambridge: Cambridge University Press.

Stone, D. (2020) *Making Global Policy*, Cambridge: Cambridge University Press.

Taylor, S. R. and Mahon, R. (2019) 'Gender Equality from the MDGs to the SDGs: The Struggle Continues', in S. Dalby, S. Horton and R. Mahon with D. Thomaz (eds) (2019) *Achieving the Sustainable Development Goals: Global Governance Challenges*, Abingdon and New York: Routledge, 54–70.

Tilly, C., Castañeda, E. and Wood, L. (2019) *Social Movements, 1768–2018*, Fourth Edition, New York: Routledge.

UN (United Nations) (2019a) *Mainstreaming of the Three Dimensions of Sustainable Development Throughout the United Nations System: Report of the Secretary-General*, https://digitallibrary.un.org/record/3800940?ln=en.

UN (2019b) *The Sustainable Development Goals Report 2019*, New York: UN, https://doi.org/10.18356/55eb9109-en.

UN (2020a) *World Economic Situation and Prospects 2020*, New York: UN, https://doi.org/10.18356/ee1a3197-en.

UN (2020b) *Policy Brief: The impact of COVID-19 on women*, New York: UN, www.unwomen.org/-/media/headquarters/attachments/sections/library/publications/2020/policy-brief-the-impact-of-covid-19-on-women-en.pdf?la=en&vs=1406.

UN (2021) *World Economic Situation and Prospects 2021*, New York: UN.

UNCTAD (United Nations Conference on Trade and Development) (2020a) *Trade and Development Report 2020: From Global Pandemic to Prosperity for All: Avoiding Another Lost Decade*, Geneva: UN, https://doi.org/10.18356/aea7b3b9-en.

UNCTAD (2020b) *Transforming Trade and Development in a Fractured, Post-Pandemic World*, Geneva: UN, https://unctad.org/system/files/official-document/osg2020d2_en.pdf.

UNCTAD (2020c) *Impact of the COVID-19 Pandemic on Trade and Development: Transitioning to a New Normal*, New York: UN, https://unctad.org/system/files/official-document/osg2020d1_en.pdf.

UNGA (United Nations General Assembly) (2000) *United Nations Millennium Declaration*, A/RES/55/2, https://digitallibrary.un.org/record/422015?ln=en.

UNGA (2015) *Transforming Our World: The 2030 Agenda for Sustainable Development*, A/RES/70/1, https://sustainabledevelopment.un.org/post2015/transformingourworld/publication.

UNGA (2020) *Declaration on the Commemoration of the Seventy-Fifth Anniversary of the United Nations*, A/75/L.1, https://undocs.org/en/A/75/L.1.

UNIATF (United Nations Inter-agency Task Force on Financing for Development) (2019) *Financing for Sustainable Development Report 2019*, New York: UN, https://doi.org/10.18356/9444edd5-en.

UNIATF (2020) *Financing for Sustainable Development Report 2020*, New York: UN, https://doi.org/10.18356/6fab9229-en.

UN DESA (United Nations Department of Economic and Social Affairs) (2011) *Report on the World Social Situation 2011: The Global Social Crisis*, New York: UN, https://doi.org/10.18356/e40a0e7f-en.

UN DESA (2019a) *Disability and Development Report 2018: Realizing the Sustainable Development Goals by, for and with Persons with Disabilities*, New York: UN, https://doi.org/10.18356/a0b1b1d1-en.

UN DESA (2019b) *State of the World's Indigenous Peoples: Implementing the United Nations Declaration on the Rights of Indigenous Peoples*, 4th Volume, New York: UN, https://doi.org/10.18356/5cb401e7-en.

UN DESA (2019c) *World Youth Report 2020: Youth and the 2030 Agenda for Sustainable Development*, New York: UN, https://doi.org/10.18356/0c6f53e0-en.

UN DESA (2020) *World Social Report 2020: Inequality in a Rapidly Changing World*, New York: UN, https://doi.org/10.18356/7f5d0efc-en.

UN Women (2018) *Turning Promises into Action: Gender Equality in the 2030 Agenda for Sustainable Development*, New York: UN Women, https://doi.org/10.18356/917ed83e-en.

UN Women (2019) *UN Women Annual Report 2018–2019*, New York: UN Women, www.unwomen.org/en/digital-library/annual-report.

UN Women (2020) *Annual Report 2019–2020: The World for Women and Girls*, New York: UN Women, www.unwomen.org/en/digital-library/annual-report.

Vallance, S., Perkins, H. C. and Dixon, J. E. (2011) 'What Is Social Sustainability? A Clarification of Concepts', *Geoforum*, 42(3): 342–48.

Vandenbroucke, F., Barnard, C. and De Baere, G. (eds) (2017) *A European Social Union after the Crisis*, Cambridge: Cambridge University Press.

Vosko, L. (2002) ' "Decent Work": The Shifting Role of the ILO and the Struggle for Global Social Justice', *Global Social Policy*, 2(1): 19–46.

Wacquant, L. (2006) 'From Slavery to Mass Incarceration: Rethinking the "Race Question" in the United States', in D. Macedo and P. Gounari (eds) *The Globalization of Racism*, Abingdon: Routledge, 94–110.

Wacquant, L. (2014) 'Marginality, Ethnicity and Penality in the Neo-Liberal City: An Analytic Cartography', *Ethnic and Racial Studies*, 37(10): 1687–711.

Wagner, P. (2001) *A History and Theory of the Social Sciences: Not All That Is Solid Melts into Air*, London: Sage.

Weber, M. ([1922] 1978) *Economy and Society: An Outline of Interpretive Sociology*, Volume 1, Edited by Guenther Roth and Claus Wittich, Berkeley, CA: University of California Press.

Weiss, T. G., Carayannis, T., Emmerij, L. and Jolly, R. (2005) *UN Voices: The Struggle for Development and Social Justice*, Bloomington, IN: Indiana University Press.

WHO (World Health Organization) (2011) *World Report on Disability 2011*, Geneva: WHO and the World Bank, https://apps.who.int/iris/handle/10665/44575.

WHO (2013) *Global and Regional Estimates of Violence Against Women: Prevalence and Health Effects of Intimate Partner Violence and Non-Partner Sexual Violence*, Geneva: WHO, https://apps.who.int/iris/handle/10665/85239.

WHO (2014) *Global Status Report on Violence Prevention 2014*, Geneva: WHO, UNDP, UNODC, https://www.who.int/violence_injury_prevention/violence/status_report/2014/report/report/en/.

WHO (2017) *Violence Against Women*, Key Facts, 29 November, https://www.who.int/news-room/fact-sheets/detail/violence-against-women.

Wilkinson, R. and Pickett, K. (2009) *The Spirit Level: Why More Equal Societies Almost Always Do Better*, London: Allen Lane.

Wilkinson, R. and Pickett, K. (2018) *The Inner Level: How More Equal Societies Reduce Stress, Restore Sanity and Improve Everyone's Wellbeing*, London: Allen Lane.

Williams, F. (2000) 'Principles of Recognition and Respect in Welfare', in G. Lewis, S. Gewirtz and J. Clarke (eds) *Rethinking Social Policy*, London: Sage, 338–52.

Williams, F. (2021) *Social Policy: A Critical and Intersectional Analysis*, Cambridge: Polity.

Winlow, S. and Hall, S. (2013) *Rethinking Social Exclusion: The End of the Social?*, London: Sage.

WBG (Women's Budget Group) (2020b) *Crises Collide: Women and Covid-19*, https://wbg.org.uk/analysis/reports/crises-collide-women-and-covid-19/.

World Bank (1996) *World Development Report 1996: From Plan to Market*, New York: Oxford University Press, https://doi.org/10.1596/978-0-1952-1107-8.

World Bank (1997) *World Development Report 1997: The State in a Changing World*, Washington, DC: World Bank, https://doi.org/10.1596/978-0-1952-1114-6.

World Bank (2005) *Economic Growth in the 1990s: Learning from a Decade of Reform*, Washington, DC: World Bank, https://doi.org/10.1596/0-8213-6043-4.

World Bank (2006) *World Development Report 2007: Development and the Next Generation*, Washington, DC: World Bank, https://doi.org/10.1596/978-0-8213-6541-0.

World Bank (2007) *World Development Report 2008: Agriculture and Development*, Washington, DC: World Bank, https://doi.org/10.1596/978-0-8213-6807-7.

World Bank (2020a) *The Sustainable Development Agenda and the World Bank Group: Closing the SDGs Financing Gap*, Washington, DC: World Bank, http://pubdocs.worldbank.org/en/259801562965232326/2030Agenda-2019-final-web.pdf.

World Bank (2020b) *Global Economic Prospects, June 2020*, Washington, DC: World Bank, http://hdl.handle.net/10986/33748.

World Bank (2021) *Global Economic Prospects, January 2021*, Washington, DC: World Bank, https://doi.org/10.1596/978-1-4648-1612-3.

Yuval-Davis, N. (2011) 'Beyond the Recognition and Re-distribution Dichotomy: Intersectionality as Stratification', in H. Lutz, M. T. Herrera Vivar and L. Supic (eds) *Framing Intersectionality: Debates on a Multi-Faceted Concept in Gender Studies*, Farnham: Ashgate, 155–70.

2

'No such thing as society'?
Neoliberalism and the social

John Clarke

Introduction

Neoliberalism, in its many variants, has involved a sustained attack on ideas, institutions and formations of the 'social', including those of traditional social welfare systems and more recent movements towards social reform. This disposition is pungently described by Wendy Brown (2018: 16) as 'the neoliberal attack on the social, which includes an attack on equality, social belonging and mutual social obligation, and also an attack on the replacement of traditional morality and traditional hierarchies (including racial hierarchies) by social justice and social reform'.

But does this mean that neoliberalism is simply 'anti-social'? As Brown indicates, there are certainly arguments for treating it as such, not least the impacts on health, wellbeing and longevity that have followed in the train of neoliberalism's inequality-generating policies and practices in many places. The turn to 'austerity' that was the dominant response to the global financial crisis intensified such consequences (see, for example, Stuckler and Basu, 2013). Nevertheless, this chapter will argue that the view of neoliberalism as 'anti-social' risks reifying a particular conception of the social and misses critical ways in which neoliberalism not merely contests but has sought to reconstruct older conceptions and institutions of the social. Instead, we might take a more conjunctural view of the processes of neoliberalization, highlighting three questions in particular:

- What conceptions of 'the social' has neoliberalism promoted (rather than attacked)?
- What has happened to older conceptions of 'the social' (expressed in social welfare and wider notions of public-ness)?

- What are the 'emergent' possibilities through which people lay claim to the idea and sensibility of 'the social'?

The remainder of this chapter is devoted to a discussion of these questions.

In search of the social

Two orientations underpin the discussion. This chapter takes a view of the social that treats it as a shifting and contested field, composed of imaginings, representations and their institutionalizations rather than a fixed formation more or less associated with the 'Golden Age' of welfare states (Huber and Stephens, 2001).

Such conceptions of the social tend to locate it in a long history of struggles (in the Global North) to mitigate, redress and reform the effects of capitalism that began with the workers' movements of the late 19th century and culminated in the social democratic accomplishments of the period following the Second World War. Some (like Esping-Anderson, 1985, 1990) celebrated these social democratic accomplishments; others, such as Jacques Donzelot (1984, 1988), traced the de-politicizing effects of this 'invention of the social'. But both views seem to over-identify the social with those welfarist formations.

In more general terms, the social appears as the conceptual and political poor relation of political economy. In both conventional and critical variants, the domain of the social is secondary, grasped as a phenomenon whose character derives from the big political forces and their dynamics. In contrast, other conceptual and political interventions from the margins (from multiple margins, indeed) have made efforts to make the significance and the recurrent contestation of the social both visible and productive, most notably feminists and feminist scholarship (of many varieties). This more dynamic conception of the social has at least three critical aspects. First, it means treating the social as the site of the (complex) relations and practices of social reproduction. Second, it demands thinking of the social as continually traversed by governmental strategies that seek to embed the devices and desires that will deliver the correct ordering of the population and its capacities (as Foucault knew, government in this sense is always seeking to make better people). Third, the social remains a contingent and contested field, rather than a set of fixed relationships and positions.

The study of welfare states came rather late to the discovery that welfare was contested by politics other than those of class, centring on challenges to the ways in which welfare citizenship was constructed and constrained through categoric distinctions built around gender, 'race' and ethnicity, sexuality and disability (see, inter alia, Fiona Williams writing in Chapter 10; Lewis et al, 2000). In thinking about the social in these terms, we can draw on Catherine Hall's comments in her study of metropole–colony relations across England and Jamaica, where she argues that the social is continuously engaged and reworked by projects and processes seeking to map, reorder and remake the social body:

> Marking differences was a way of classifying, of categorising, of constructing boundaries for the body politic and the body social. Processes of differentiation, positioning men and women, colonisers and colonised, as if these divisions were natural, were constantly in the making, in conflicts of power ... The mapping of difference, I suggest, the constant discursive work of creating, bringing into being, or reworking these hieratic categories, was always a matter of historical contingency. The map constantly shifted, the categories faltered, as different colonial sites came into the metropolitan focus, as conflicts of power produced new configurations in one place or another. (Hall, 2002:17, 20)

Although the temporal and spatial focus of this chapter is different, this view of a contingent and contested social provides a vital foundation for thinking about the shifting relationships between neoliberalism and the social.

The second condition for the discussion that follows centres on the challenge of thinking about neoliberalism *conjuncturally*, rather than as an epochal formation. This implies exploring the accumulating forces, tensions, contradictions and antagonisms that are condensed together into making a specific historical moment. In particular, it requires attention to the political and cultural formations that exist alongside the dominant tendency, the place occupied by neoliberalism for the past 30 years. In approaching this challenge, it is useful to return to Raymond Williams' distinction between 'epochal' and 'authentic historical' analysis:

> In what I have called epochal analysis, a cultural process is seized as a cultural system, with determinate dominant features: feudal culture or bourgeois culture or a transition from one to the other. This emphasis on dominant and definitive lineaments is important and often, in practice, effective. But it then happens that its methodology is

preserved for the very different function of historical analysis, in which a sense of movement within what is ordinarily abstracted as a system is crucially necessary, especially if it is connected with the future as well as the past. In authentic historical analysis it is necessary at every point to recognize the complex interrelationships between movements and tendencies both within and beyond a specific effective dominance. It is necessary to examine how these relate to the whole cultural process rather than only to the selected and abstracted dominant system. (Williams, 1977: 121)

Williams argues that the temptations, and risks, of 'epochal analysis' involve treating the epochal dominant as a 'static type' abstracted from the 'real cultural processes' that are its conditions. Instead, he points to the importance of crafting an 'authentic historical analysis' that is attentive to the internal dynamic relations of specific moments:

We have certainly to speak of the 'dominant' and the 'effective', and in these senses of the hegemonic. But we find that we have also to speak, and indeed with further differentiation of each, of the 'residual' and the 'emergent', which in any real historical process, and at any moment in the process, are significant both in themselves and in what they reveal of the characteristics of the 'dominant'. (Williams, 1977: 121–2)

This chapter will certainly speak of the dominant – neoliberalism – and its shifting shapes and strategies, not least those that have arisen as neoliberalizing processes find new ways of dealing with its residual and emergent others. That will be the focus of the next section of the chapter. The following two sections consider the residual and the emergent more directly in their own terms.

Neoliberalism: from anti-social to remaking the social

Neoliberalism has certainly had an anti-social disposition, visible in several dynamics. There is a core commitment to the *individualization* of society, treating it as a multitude of self-seeking individuals engaging only in market or market-like transactions (embodying the conventional *homo economicus* of neoclassical economic theory). This individualization works through multiple imaginary figures, inviting/inciting subjects to see themselves as producers and consumers, as entrepreneurs and investors, as life planners and budget managers. This individualization is simultaneously an *economization* of the social, refusing to recognize forms of social relationship and interaction beyond the transactional. But these two dynamics are interwoven with a third, *familialization*. Indeed, it could be argued that the critical attention to neoliberalism's individualization has tended to obscure this other dynamic, in which neoliberal processes tend towards what might be called possessive–competitive familialism. For example, in the United Kingdom, the recurring political–cultural incitement of people to be 'hard working' and 'responsible' was aimed less at individuals and more at families (invoking a nation of 'hard working, responsible families'). This emphasis was foreshadowed by Margaret Thatcher's famous observation that 'there is no such thing as society' which concluded that 'there are only individual men and women and their families'. This individual–familial nexus provided a foundation for the anti-social policy logics of neoliberalism, in particular the dismantling or reform of collective or public institutionalizations of the social: public services, collective housing provision, the varieties of welfare state, and so on. It is also argued elsewhere (Clarke, 2007), that it is worth considering different sets of processes that have been in play in neoliberalism's 'subordination of the social'. These have included its subjugation to brutal market logics, its privatization and domestication (locating the social in the realm of the familial household), its spatial and scalar 'narrowing' as a residual setting and its valorization (treating it as the source of potential value, whether through processes of marketization or privatization of public resources or through its role as a setting for the creation and discovery of subjects of value, people who can be monetized in different ways, such as loan systems).

These arguments focus fundamentally on neoliberalism's dominant character but certainly do not exhaust its repertoire of strategies for governing the social. To explore these involves opening up the political–cultural dynamics of neoliberalism to greater scrutiny, not least its interaction with alternative conceptions of the social. Such interactions emerge more visibly when we consider 'actually existing neoliberalisms' rather than treating it as an abstracted general position. At this point we have to consider the ways in which neoliberal policies have found ways of cohabiting with other political and cultural processes and ways of imagining the social. Neoliberalism has proved remarkably adaptable (Peck, 2010) and this includes accommodations with different types of political regimes and forms of political culture. Neoliberalization has been conducted through dictatorships, authoritarian regimes, forms of liberal democracy and, of course, through a variety of international organizations like the World Bank and International Monetary Fund (IMF) seeking to make the world safe, and profitable, for capital during the so-called 'Washington Consensus' era with the 'stabilize, liberalize and privatize' mantra (Williamson, 2008). Similarly, it has been enacted through conservative, neo-conservative, liberal, authoritarian and social democratic political programmes. This tends to confirm the hegemonic status of neoliberalism, but looked at from the other side, that dominance has been accomplished by learning to adapt, co-opt, incorporate and ventriloquize these many others. As Williams argued, the relationship between the dominant and the emergent is a critical issue for conjunctural analysis, and one exemplary focus for this dynamic has been questions of equality: of gender, 'race' and sexuality, especially (see inter alia Duggan, 2003; Lamble, 2013; Ludwig, 2016). Different neoliberalisms have found it possible to accommodate and incorporate social, political and cultural movements generated around equality by rendering them 'individual' matters (of choice, especially) and by folding them into what Harzig, Juteau and Schmitt (2003) call the 'master narrative' of diversity (but see also Cooper, 2004). Meanwhile, other neoliberalisms have been equally comfortable with political regimes of a more conservative, reactionary or restorationist character that have refused such diversity politics as undermining 'the social fabric' and 'social order'.

More generally, the social constitutes a field that governing processes, including neoliberal ones, continually strive to occupy, dominate and direct. Governing processes are always directed towards finding ways of ordering the population (differentiating, hierarchizing, sorting, improving and more) and aim to institutionalize strategies that have the objective of making the people who they should be. Neoliberalism features here as a project or process committed to transforming the social, working through strategies of economization, individualization and familialization that aim to create (or 'release' in the naturalizing imagery of neoliberalism's advocates) the array of responsible, dynamic and entrepreneurial selves; and, in reverse, to discipline and punish those who fail their new obligations. But alongside this, neoliberalization processes find ways of accommodating other versions of the social, especially those that can be folded into an individualizing narrative of choice, empowerment and liberation. It equally finds it possible to accommodate familial, patriarchal, heteronormative and repressive conceptions of the social and how it should best be ordered. Neoliberalism has proved able to cohabit with (and borrow from) a very wide range of social imaginaries, shape-shifting and acquiring new voicings as it borrows and bends from them.

The institutionalization of neoliberal rule in 'actually existing neoliberalisms' has involved extensive political and governmental work: finding partners, building alliances, making compromises (both material and discursive) that seek to co-opt, absorb and incorporate other possibilities. The social is central to this understanding of the pragmatics of neoliberalism, since it is the terrain on which people live their everyday lives, find points of attachment, investment and identification (as well as distinction, detachment and refusal). Without underestimating neoliberalism's destructive, ruthless and authoritarian capacities, it matters to understand how it seeks to enrol and engage people in specific places. As Ludwig argues:

> neoliberalism also needs to be investigated as political project that engages people, deploys their hopes and promises them a good life, more freedom, wealth or personal fulfilment. Sexual politics need to be investigated as technologies of power that help to organize acceptance and consensus within neoliberalism. (Ludwig, 2016: 426)

In the process, new mappings of the social are elaborated through political and governmental projects and processes. The neoliberal remaking of the social has extended well beyond its articulation with the economic, producing new assemblages of people, positions and practices. Such changes have necessitated the remaking of ways of life, the elaboration of sets of distinctions and relationships within a population and between populations (in neoliberal's globalizing effects). It has required the inculcation of habits and practices appropriate to dominant conceptions of a 'modern people' who need to step forward to take their place in a global world.

However, this poses some difficult political and analytical challenges for thinking about neoliberalism and its others. It suggests that we should be wary of thinking of policies, strategies and conceptions of the social as 'essentially' neoliberal, attending instead to the complex political work of borrowing and blending, incorporation and ventriloquism that goes on as neoliberal processes seek to find means of ruling that enrol populations into the desired ways of thinking and being. It may be that the processes of being co-opted or incorporated into neoliberal political and governmental projects strips the alternative or radical possibilities from these alternative conceptions of the social. For example, Andrea Muehlebach's (2012) remarkable exploration of the rise of 'the moral neoliberal' in Italy points to the paradoxical, and apparently contradictory, strands of thought and feeling that underpinned the growth of voluntary care work in Italy, strands that included Catholic and socialist lineages. Muehlebach argues that the apparent opposition between such orientations and seemingly rational, market-centred neoliberalism conceals a larger unity. This larger view, she argues, 'allows us to grasp neoliberalism as a form that contains practices and forces that appear as oppositional yet get folded into a single order' (Muehlebach, 2012: 8). Her exploration of the connections between neoliberal rationality and other-oriented sentiments allows her:

> to grasp neoliberalism as a complex of opposites that can contain what appear as oppositional practices, ethics and emotions … Neoliberalism thus appears not simply as malleable, but a process that may allow for the simultaneity and mutual dependency of forms and practices that scholars think of in oppositional terms. Neoliberalism is a force that can contain its negation – the vision of a decommodified, disinterested life and of a moral community of human relationality and solidarity that stands opposed to alienation. (Muehlebach, 2012: 25)

This is a significant argument about the shape-shifting and multi-vocal dynamic of neoliberalism, but it leaves us with two questions. First, is there an outside or a beyond to neoliberalism: something, somewhere, some orientation that is not neoliberal or has not (yet) been neoliberalized? Second, do those elements that are incorporated in neoliberalism necessarily remain neoliberal? Might they, in some place, at some time, be dis-incorporated or rearticulated to an alternative political project?

Abstractly, this matters: it seems wrong to treat incorporation as a one-way and one-time political process. In contrast, articulation, and the possibilities of dis-articulation and rearticulation seem a more fluid and dynamic way of thinking about such processes of ideological/ discursive or cultural work. With this in mind, we now turn back to questions of what Williams called 'the residual', and its relations to the dominant.

Tracing the residual

When Williams writes about the residual, he is not treating it as simply as a historical left-over. Rather he is pointing to the significance of persistence. Here his understanding of the residual can be used to think about the persistence of ideas of the social, the public and social welfare (and their diverse institutionalizations). Williams argues that:

> The residual, by definition, has been effectively formed in the past, but it is still active in the cultural process, not only and often not at all as an element of the past, but as an effective element of the present. Thus certain experiences, meanings and values which cannot be expressed or substantially verified in terms of the dominant culture, are nevertheless lived and practised on the basis of the residue – cultural as well as social – of some previous social and cultural institution or formation. (Williams, 1977: 122)

In this light, it can be argued that forms of collective social provision remain the focus of deep social and cultural attachments, not least because they speak to experiences, problems and desires that cannot be effectively addressed within the terms of the dominant. So, to what extent have older conceptions of the social persisted in the face of neoliberalism's anti-social and re-socializing tendencies? The persistence of many of the problems and experiences that collective welfare provision was supposed to address – poverty, unemployment, ill-health, education and so on – serve to keep older images of the social alive, even if in subordinate ways. The intensification of those 'social problems' under neoliberal rule has constantly been accompanied by demands for more and better welfare, even as welfare states have been dismantled and restructured.

Indeed, the persistence of those experiences (as structural features of the social organization of capitalism) has sustained the 'residual' imaginary of social welfare and wellbeing. In its turn, this persistence of residual identifications, attachments and desires has supported the persistence of aspects of state welfare, public services and other forms of collective support and provision. As some versions of path-dependency theory argued, such attachments formed a critical feature of the 'resilience' of welfare states. For example, Paul Pierson argued that a variety of factors, but especially those located in popular politics, coalesced to make radical revision, or abolition, of welfare states unlikely:

> There are strong grounds for scepticism about the prospect for any radical revision of the welfare state in most countries. Almost nowhere have politicians been able to assemble and sustain majority coalitions for a far-reaching contraction of

> social policy ... The reasons have already been outlined. The broad scale of public support, the intensity of preferences among programme recipients, the extent to which a variety of actors (including employers) have adapted to the existing contours of the social market economy, and the institutional arrangements which favour defenders of the status quo make a frontal assault on the welfare state politically suicidal in most countries. (Pierson, 2001: 416)

Welfare states (in their different guises) have proven unevenly resistant to unlocking under neoliberal rule. This has been visible both in the persistence of a range of social/public institutions (for example, the NHS in the UK) and the forms of care and support that they provide. There are two important qualifications to the 'resilience' story. The first is that the period following the financial crisis of 2007–08 has had contradictory effects on such social provision. On the one hand, 'austerity' politics and policies have extensively undermined public spending on social provision, even as austerity increased the need for public support of different kinds (see, for example, Cooper and Whyte, 2017; Evans and McBride, 2017; McBride and Evans, 2017). The years of austerity and a retreat of the state have hampered national and global responses to the pandemic according to the UN (UNCTAD, 2020), which warns of a 'lost decade' if national governments choose to adopt austerity as their response to the severe global economic crisis now unfolding. At the same time, however, the multiple effects of 'austerity' appear to have undermined neoliberal rationality, generating (in the UK at least) a growing level of public support for some forms of welfare provision. Secondly, the assemblages that we call welfare states have been extensively modified, reworked and given new responsibilities for ensuring neoliberalized populations. Three particular directions in which the welfare state has been reorganized to make it more compatible with the perceived needs of capital in neoliberal times are the drive towards 'workfare', the contractualization of citizenship, and the subsidizing of capital. But we should also take account of the revitalization of nationalism and nativism in the remaking of welfare policies: for example, in the Orbán government's mix of anti-immigration and familialist policies that attempt to secure Hungary against its Others: to make Hungary a place where 'people benefit from being Hungarians'.[1]

Popular experiences and expectations have been cast in multiple cultural registers, with talk of rights, entitlements, justice, fairness, security, care and more. Such discourses have been subjected to a long process of reworking that has combined both curtailment and renegotiation (in different places). In the UK, for example, the attack on welfare involved combining a demonization of the poor, the 'rebalancing' of rights and responsibilities expressed in the idea of citizenship, and a recrafting of the meaning of 'fairness', a much trumpeted 'British value' that was reworked to mean 'fairness for all who earn it' in the dominant 'moral economy of austerity' (Clarke, 2014). Despite such attempts to actively residualize the residual (treating its imagery as 'old thinking' or 'out of time'), such conceptions of the social persist and indeed, from time to time, are brought to bear explicitly, increasingly coming to bear on the obligations that governments owe their citizens in turbulent times, even allowing for the equally persistent tensions about who might count as 'their' citizens. For example, Sharma, writing about Dalit women in India, argues that they mobilized a complex, heteroglossic variety of conceptions of rights, entitlements and justice in enacting themselves as citizens:

> They positioned themselves as knowledgeable and deserving citizens, who had been short-changed by a corrupt local administration and who deserved government resources as their right; this was a direct challenge to official caricatures of their identities as unaware, irresponsible, and immoral. Furthermore, they used standard bureaucratic mechanisms, On the other hand, however, they used the older idiom of 'mai-baap' and the parental duty it invoked, to hold officials accountable. 'Mai-baap' referenced a different time and moral universe where just rulers, like good parents, were ethically bound to care for their wards. (Sharma, 2011: 974)

However, as Sharma notes, such bases for claims making are open to denial by state officials as being out of time and inappropriate. Residual formations are always vulnerable to such attempts at closure.

Emergent possibilities of the social

In contrast, new imaginings and practices of solidarity, security and collective welfare have continued to emerge as responses to the neoliberal subordination, degradation and impoverishment of the social. These emergent concerns have been articulated in diverse local, national and transnational movements: mobilizations and forms of association that operate in angular and discordant relationships with the dominant tendency.

Williams locates the emergent in a view that 'new meanings and values, new practices, new relationships and kinds of relationship are continually being created' while warning that 'it is exceptionally difficult to distinguish between those which are really elements of some new phase of the dominant culture … and those which are substantially alternative or oppositional to it' (Williams, 1977: 123). Neoliberalism's recurring failures, and the contradictions, dislocations and antagonisms that they generate, have been a fertile terrain for re-imaginings of the social. In particular, the exhaustion of neoliberal strategies around the social and the public realm (for example, contracting out, marketization and so on) has become increasingly visible. In the UK, the collapse of contracting corporations such as Carillion, the failures of semi-privatized public service providers (for example, educational trusts or the probation service) and the mishaps of contracted out services (notably, the practice of disability assessment) have all contributed to this sense of exhaustion. The experience of 'austerity' policy and practice, most particularly the devolution of fiscal stress, has intensified the sense of a degraded public realm, most visible in the 'hollowing out' of cities and towns where municipal authorities increasingly lack the capacity to respond to such tendencies (see, for example, Peck 2012; Phinney, 2018).

Despite this, there has been a significant move towards the 'remunicipalization' of public services, most notably the provision of water (see, for example, Pigeon et al, 2012). At stake in such processes are not only the economic, political and legal processes of shifting ownership and control of resources, but also a mix of older and emergent imaginings of what water is and how it might be controlled and managed. In an article exploring Italy's anti-water privatization struggles, Muehlebach sets up some of the critical questions at stake in conflicts over forms of ownership and control of this resource:

> This paper explores water as a commons (or what Italians call *bene comune*) through the rise and fall of Italy's antiwater privatization movement. I suggest that the power of this movement lay in its insistence that water could only be governed as a commons if it simultaneously also included the recuperation of the democratic process as collective social and practical activity as well. I show that this process of recuperation gave life both to effective forms of mass political action as well as a new round of dispossession on the part of the Italian state. This article thus expands on a point made by a long line of theorists on Marx's concept of

'primitive' or 'original' accumulation by arguing that Italians were not only dispossessed of their right to publicly own water but of their capacity to effective democratic action as such. (Muehlebach, 2018: 343; see also Bakker, 2007)

These debates reflect a growing interest in ideas and practices of commoning. Commoning identifies practices of governing natural resources for collective use and is interwoven with a political imaginary of how social life might, and should, be organized. Linebaugh has made the case for the value of treating 'the commons' as an active process:

> To speak of the commons as if it were a natural resource is misleading at best and dangerous at worst – the commons is an activity and, if anything, it expresses relationships in society that are inseparable from relations to nature. It might be better to keep the word as a verb, an activity, rather than as a noun, a substantive. (Linebaugh, 2007: 279)

Globally the interest in commoning has expanded, bringing together the exploration of existing practices of commoning, the creation of policies and procedures for 'governing the commons' and the elaboration of a politics of commoning as an anti-capitalist and anti-individualist ecological economics. This interest has also been developed through discussions about whether a 'social commons' can be imagined, such that issues of social protection, wellbeing and welfare can be rethought as communal resources and rights (see, inter alia, Barbagallo and Federici, 2012; Mestrum, 2015; Williams, 2015). Francine Mestrum has claimed that:

> When welfare states or social protection are perceived as commons, after a defining and regulating process, they can contribute to collective and individual welfare, as emerging from collective and participatory action. The commons sustain our common being, our being together, our co-existence. They go beyond individual interests. (Mestrum, 2015: 6)

These emergent ways of thinking about – of imagining – the social, point to new possibilities of articulating the economic, the political and the social and give the question of social reproduction a much more central place in such imaginings. They speak to the interwoven crises – of production, of sociality, of the environment and of social reproduction – and precisely identify that interweaving as the fundamental condition of the present.

Finally, there are emergent politics and practices that seek to construct solidarities across national boundaries, many directed at supporting and sustaining migrants in the current world of global flows and intensified boundary work (Yuval-Davis et al, 2019). Versions of 'sanctuary' spaces, 'welcome cultures' and practices of support have recurrently appeared in the Global North as 'national' citizens try to find ways to refuse the demonization, exclusion and repression of migrants and to find ways of living and working in solidarity with them (see, for example, Bhimji, 2016; Cantat, 2016; Hamman and Karakayali, 2016; Rajaram, 2016; Tazzioli and Walters, 2019), Cantat examines forms and practices of solidarity, including that of 'Mediterranean solidarity', which articulates connections within and across the Mediterranean, repositioning 'Europe' in the process. She argues that:

> The emergence of new political subjectivities that bring together refugees from a range of horizons and activists in solidarity with them challenges the geography of borders and separation promoted by the EU. For some of the participants, it is also integral to anti-capitalist struggles in the contemporary era: fighting processes of migrant illegalisation is seen as an indispensable aspect of worker solidarity under condition of global capitalism. This contests the binary conceptualisations of politics underpinning state power. Where migrants are spoken about as exterior to political communities in Europe, these joint struggles and their use of the narrative around Mediterranean identity in sites as far away as Germany insists on the interiority of a migrant presence and claims their possibility of and right to belonging. (Cantat, 2016: 28)

I am not suggesting that these emergent conceptions of the social provide a coherent and integrative political programme (although they do overlap and intersect in some interesting ways). The point is to recognize that the dominant, that continually shapes shifting neoliberalization processes, continues to encounter alternatives that insist on its failings, its contradictions and its disasters, while indicating that other ways of organizing the social, other ways of living together, are possible. Such emergent alternatives are, of course, subject to different political cultural tactics aimed to neutralize, incorporate or merely dismiss them. They are denounced as unrealistic and utopian.

They fail to promise the endless growth without which capitalism makes little sense. They are reduced to fantasies of a 'social' or 'sharing' economy, or the creation of 'social enterprises'. But they persistently recur as other ways of thinking and imagining in the face of the multiplying catastrophes of actually existing neoliberalism.

Conclusion: 'people want the social back'

In the aftermath of the Grenfell Tower fire in June 2017 in London – a disaster that appallingly embodied the neoliberal degradation of the social in many ways – one local Member of Parliament, David Lammy (Labour, Tottenham), said in an interview: ' "I knew that appetite for the end of austerity existed in our cities ... but the [2017] election proved it goes beyond that now. People want the social back. They are clear that you cannot contract everything out" ' (Adams, 2017). This was a fascinating evocation of the social, directly addressing the failures of neoliberal governance. But which social might this be? It is possible that Lammy's evocation of the social draws on a rather complex mixture of residual and emergent elements. In his interview Lammy referred to an older public realm, invoking social provision and a civic culture of support: ' "Even in the 70s and 80s when my mother picked up her pay packet every Friday from Tottenham town hall ... there was a proper civic society, we had a civic glue. A lot of that has gone" ' (Adams, 2017). In Lammy's view, councils like Kensington and Chelsea simply don't know how to do 'civic' anymore.

> 'They believe they are there for the upper middle class folk of Notting Hill, who rely on their bin collections, and want their roads fixed, and don't want high-rise blocks looking like eyesores so they get them cladded. That's about it for them in terms of public services.' (Adams, 2017)

He describes the borough council as the epitome of 'light-touch' regulation, which puts every service out to competitive tender or outsources it, a tendency that has infected all local government since the 1980s. The result of this philosophy, he believes, was that when the crisis happened it was not only that the council failed to act, it was more that the habit of intervention was not in their make-up (Adams, 2017).

But as a black MP representing a North London constituency, Lammy must know that the public services and civic culture of the 1970s and 1980s in Britain were structured around a series of exclusions and subordinations that worked though intersections of 'race', class and gender, their 'universalism' more promised than realized. Therefore, at stake in getting the social 'back' is the challenge of rethinking it one more time, to address both the present failures of the neoliberal 'neo-social' (to borrow Fabian Kassl's phrase, 2006) and the limitations and contradictions of the older social democratic/labourist version. What is at stake in conceptions of the social is too vital to be left to nostalgia, even as we seek to evoke residual conceptions of why the social was once valued, and why it continues to be the focus of emergent imaginaries. The social persists in posing challenges that simply cannot be answered within the terms of the neoliberal dominant.

Note

1   https://thehungaryjournal.com/2019/02/10/orban-announces-major-family-protection-package/.

References

Adams, T. (2017) David Lammy Interview, *The Guardian*, 2 July, www.theguardian.com/politics/2017/jul/02/david-lammy-mp-grenfell-tower-interview-blair-brown-black.

Bakker K. J. (2007) 'The "Commons" Versus the "Commodity": Alter-globalization, Anti-privatization and the Human Right to Water in the Global South', *Antipode*, 39(3): 430–55.

Barbagallo, C. and Federici, S. (2012) 'Introduction: Care Work and the Commons', *The Commoner*, 15: 1–21, www.commoner.org.uk/wp-content/uploads/2012/01/commoner_issue-15.pdf.

Bhimji, F. (2016) 'Contesting the Dublin Regulation: Refugees and Migrant Claims to Personhood and Rights in Germany', *Intersections EEJSP*, 2(4): 51–68.

Brown, W. (2018) 'Where the Fires Are: Wendy Brown talks to Jo Littler', *Soundings: A Journal of Politics and Culture*, 68: 14–25. https://www.lwbooks.co.uk/sites/default/files/s68_02brown_littler.pdf

Cantat, C. (2016) 'Rethinking Mobilities: Solidarity and Migrant Struggles Beyond the Narrative of Crisis', *Intersections EEJSP*, 2(4): 11–32.

Clarke, J. (2007) 'Subordinating the Social? Neoliberalism and the Remaking of Welfare Capitalism', *Cultural Studies*, 21(6): 974–87.

Clarke, J. (2014) 'Imagined Economies: Austerity and the Moral Economy of "Fairness"', *Topia: Canadian Journal of Cultural Studies*, 30–31: 17–30.

Cooper, D. (2004) *Challenging Diversity: Rethinking Equality and the Value of Difference*, Cambridge: Cambridge University Press.

Cooper, V. and Whyte, D. (eds) (2017) *The Violence of Austerity*, London: Pluto Press.

Donzelot, J. (1984) *L'invention du social: Essai sur le déclin des passions politiques*, Paris: Fayard.

Donzelot, J. (1988) 'The Promotion of the Social', *Economy and Society*, 17(3): 395–427 (Translated by G. Burchell).

Duggan, L. (2003) *The Twilight of Equality? Neoliberalism, Cultural Politics, and the Attack on Democracy*, Boston, MA: Beacon Press.

Esping-Anderson, G. (1985) *Politics against Markets: The Social Democratic Road to Power*, Princeton, NJ: Princeton University Press.

Esping-Andersen, G. (1990) *The Three Worlds of Welfare Capitalism*, Princeton, NJ: Princeton University Press.

Evans, B. and McBride, S. (eds) (2017) *Austerity: The Lived Experience*, Toronto: University of Toronto Press.

Hall, C. (2002) *Civilising Subjects: Metropole and Colony in the English Imagination 1830–1867*, Chicago, IL: University of Chicago Press.

Hamman, U. and Karakayali, S. (2016) 'Practicing Wilkommenskultur: Migration and Solidarity in Germany', *Intersections EEJSP*, 2(4): 69–86.

Harzig, C., Juteau, D. with Schmitt, I. (eds) (2003) *The Social Construction of Diversity: Recasting the Master Narrative of Industrial Nations*, New York: Berghahn Books.

Huber, E. and Stephens, J. (2001) *Development and Crisis of the Welfare State: Parties and Policies in Global Markets*, Chicago, IL: University of Chicago Press.

Kassl, F. (2006) ' "Activating Youth Welfare" – An Example for the Neo-social Re-arrangement of German Social Policy', in G. Marston and C. McDonald (eds) *Analysing Social Policy: A Governmental Approach*, Cheltenham: Edward Elgar, 145–63.

Lamble, S. (2013) 'Queer Necropolitics and the Expanding Carceral State: Interrogating Sexual Investments in Punishment', *Law Critique*, 24: 229–53.

Lewis, G., Gewirtz, S. and Clarke, J. (eds) (2000) *Rethinking Social Policy*, London: Sage.

Linebaugh, P. (2007) *Magna Carta Manifesto: Liberties and Commons for All*, Berkeley, CA: University of California Press.

Ludwig, G. (2016) 'Desiring Neoliberalism', *Sexuality Research and Social Policy*, 13: 417–27.

McBride, S. and Evans, B. (eds) (2017) *The Austerity State*, Toronto: University of Toronto Press.

Mestrum, F. (2015) *Social Commons: A New Alternative to Neoliberalism*, 27 August, http://eng.globalaffairs.ru/valday/Social-Commons-a-new-alternative-to-neoliberalism-17656.

Muehlebach, A. (2012) *The Moral Neoliberal: Welfare and Citizenship in Italy*, Chicago, IL: University of Chicago Press.

Muehlebach, A. (2018) 'Commonwealth: On Democracy and Dispossession in Italy', *History and Anthropology*, 29(3): 342–58.

Peck, J. (2010) *Constructions of Neo-Liberal Reason*, Oxford: Oxford University Press.

Peck, J. (2012) 'Austerity Urbanism', *City: Analysis of Urban Trends, Culture, Theory, Policy, Action*, 16(6): 626-55.

Phinney, S. (2018) Detroit's Municipal Bankruptcy: Racialised Geographies of Austerity', *New Political Economy*, 23(5): 609–26.

Pierson, P. (2001) 'Coping with Permanent Austerity: Welfare Restructuring in Affluent democracies', in P. Pierson (ed) *The New Politics of the Welfare State*, Oxford: Oxford University Press, 410–56.

Pigeon, M., McDonald, D. A., Hoedeman, O. and Kishimoto, S. (eds) (2012) *Remunicipalisation: Putting Water Back into Public Hands*, Amsterdam: Transnational Institute.

Rajaram, P. K. (2016) 'Whose Migration Crisis? Editorial Introduction', *Intersections EEJSP*, 2(4): 5–10.

Sharma, A. (2011) 'Specifying Citizenship: Subaltern Politics of Rights and Justice in Contemporary India', *Citizenship Studies*, 15(8): 965–80.

Stuckler, D. and Basu, S. (2013) *The Body Economic: Why Austerity Kills*, New York: Basic Books.

Tazzioli, M. and Walters, W. (2019) 'Migration, Solidarity and the Limits of Europe', *Global Discourse*, 9(1): 175–90.

UNCTAD (United Nations Conference on Trade and Development) (2020) *Transforming Trade and Development in a Fractured, Post-Pandemic World*, Geneva: UN, https://unctad.org/system/files/official-document/osg2020d2_en.pdf.

Williams, F. (2015) 'Towards the Welfare Commons: Contestation, Critique and Criticality in Social Policy', in Z. Irving, M. Fenger and J. Hudson (eds) *Social Policy Review* 27, Bristol: Policy Press, 93–111.

Williams, R. (1977) *Marxism and Literature*, Oxford: Oxford University Press.

Williamson, J. (2008) 'A Short History of the Washington Consensus', in N. Serra and J. E. Stiglitz (eds) *The Washington Consensus Reconsidered: Towards a New Global Governance*, Oxford: Oxford University Press, 14–30.

Yuval-Davis, N., Wemyss, G. and Cassidy, K. (2019) *Bordering*, Cambridge: Polity.

3

The social question: reconciling social and economic imperatives in policy

Bradley W. Bateman

Introduction

In its original form, the 'social question' referred to the welfare of workers in the Second Industrial Revolution. As the scale of production grew in the late 19th century, and as people increasingly left the countryside to perform wage labour in urban areas, fundamental questions of social democracy and equity came to the fore. How would the rights of labour be established against the power being concentrated in the hands of capital? Would working class people have the right to vote? Should workers have bargaining power through unions? All of these questions grew from the underlying question of what share of the total output the workers deserved and whether (or how) they would receive that fair share.

At the same time, another set of nascent social questions arose about the welfare of workers that went beyond the basic question of their right to a fair share of what they helped produce. The second social question arose from the tendency of capitalist economies to cycle through periods of boom and bust. Periods of boom drew workers into the huge new factories, and periods of bust threw them into unemployment. Thus, in addition to the questions about workers' basic rights in the new vertically integrated industrial landscape, there were questions of the fate of those displaced by the cyclical nature of capitalist production.

The third social question, relating to inclusion and sustainability in the 21st century, provides a chance to consider how traditional Keynesian ideas once again bear relevance in the continued attempt to balance our economic and social life, with capitalism again plunged into another crisis from the COVID-19 pandemic. The social questions, then, are the focus of this chapter.

The first social question

The economic theories of the early 19th century offered little hope that workers could earn higher wages. In the models of the classical economists such as David Ricardo and T. Robert Malthus, wages were always driven down to the subsistence level. Hence, the idea of economics as the 'dismal science'. Part of the reason for this dismal result is that their models assumed that people were always living at any time on the output from the previous year; the output set aside for workers was referred to as 'the wage fund' and it was assumed that its size was fixed by how much was left after rent and profits were distributed to the owners of land and capital. This way of conceptualizing economic existence had been developed in the 18th century by economists such as Adam Smith and the Physiocrats and reflected an agricultural mode of production; but even as industrial output became greater, the classical economists continued using the earlier conception of living each year on the total output of the previous year. Yet while they understood that there were temporary aberrations that could cause wages to rise, in the long run they believed that the wage fund dictated subsistence wages, no matter the level of total output.[1]

Only later in the 19th century did economists abandon the idea that society lived each year off a fund of things produced in the previous year. Perhaps driven by the fact that the Second Industrial Revolution was industrializing so much of total output, economists in many countries began to consider instead models of how *current* output is distributed between the different classes of society. As early as the 1860s, younger theorists like W. Stanley Jevons, Carl Menger and John Bates Clark began to develop new marginalist models that looked at how markets distributed output. These models suggested that in competitive markets each productive class (workers, capitalists, landowners) earned a return (wages, profits and rents) equal to the value of what they produced.[2] Thus, like their classical predecessors, they offered little hope that workers would earn a higher wage than the market was already paying them. The models were much more analytically sophisticated and they directly addressed one aspect of the social question, 'What did workers deserve and could they hope to receive fair payment?' The result, however, did not offer much more hope than had Ricardo or Malthus.

But if neither the classical nor the 'neoclassical' economists offered much hope for higher wages, there remained the question of the plight of the workers who were periodically unemployed by the trade cycle.

Could anything be done to increase their welfare or to protect them against the periodic waves of unemployment?

In the 19th century economists on both the right and left talked openly of the problems for workers caused by the 'trade cycle'; they observed the large fluctuations in employment across the trade cycle and began to understand periodic mass unemployment as a feature of capitalist production. Karl Marx (1867) referred to the fluctuating pool of unemployed as the 'industrial reserve army' and Alfred Marshall (1890) referred to it as 'the Residuum'. But economists offered few solutions for the cyclical problem of recurring unemployment. Marx was not always clear, for instance, whether the downturns generated by the cycle were manifestations of capitalism's tendency to self-destruction, or whether they were part of the cyclical nature of capitalism. Because the downturns might be a part of capitalism's demise, he was not focused on theoretical work that might show how to mitigate them.[3] Marshall (1919, 1923) began to develop theoretical explanations for the trade cycle after he published his great synthetic exposition of neoclassical microeconomics, *The Principles of Economics* (1890). However, he never developed sophisticated models of how the economy as a whole operated (macroeconomics); thus, he lacked the apparatus to make clear, effective recommendations for battling the unemployment created by the trade cycle.

The really path-breaking theoretical work that would eventually lead to what we now call macroeconomics began at the turn of the 20th century, led most notably by Knut Wicksell (1898), the great Swedish economist.[4] Much of this early macroeconomic work centred on interest rates, banking and financial markets. To the extent that this work suggested economic policies, it was largely focused on fluctuations in the price level; avoiding inflation and deflation were the primary goals of the early theorists of the trade cycle. Their work, however, lacked a theoretical basis for explaining how the financial markets caused the fluctuations in employment that resulted as output went up and down.[5]

John Maynard Keynes was the first economist to work out an integrated theory that could tie together dysfunction in the financial markets with the mass unemployment that occurred as a result. Keynes' first two books of economic theory, *A Tract on Monetary Reform* (1923) and *A Treatise on Money* (1930), followed very much in the vein of the emerging macroeconomic literature, focusing largely on financial markets and prices. But the second book, which Keynes meant to be a path-breaking work, was a critical failure and threw him back on a small circle of young Cambridge economists (the Circus) with whom he worked to try to figure out why he had failed so badly.[6] Their advice to him was that he had tried to demonstrate the effects of government policies on prices while assuming that the economy remained at full employment. They helped him to see clearly that he needed a theoretical model that could more fully explain the fluctuations of a capitalist economy. In addition to being able to explain why prices went up and down, he needed to be able to show how employment fluctuated over the course of the cycle. Hence the title of his magnum opus: *The General Theory of Employment, Interest, and Money* (1936).

Keynes' theoretical model made it very easy to conceptualize how economic policy could be used to combat the trade cycle. When the economy was in a slump, for instance, the authorities could increase government spending to increase the total demand for goods and services. Likewise, they could increase output by cutting income taxes to stimulate consumer demand. In either case, the stimulus would, in turn, increase the demand for labour and increase total employment. Conversely, if an economy was overheating, government spending could be reduced or income taxes could be raised. Because this kind of counter-cyclical policy could be used to stimulate or dampen aggregate demand, it came to be called demand management.

By the time Keynes published *The General Theory* in the depths of the Great Depression, however, many countries had already started to explore the use of demand management as a way to stimulate their economies. In Sweden, for instance, a rapprochement was established between urban and rural interests. This pragmatic political compromise bridged a historical gap between farmers, who wanted higher food prices and lower prices on manufactured goods, and urban workers, who wanted exactly the opposite. The agreement created new common ground by supporting deficit spending that would benefit both groups. Peter Hall (1989) collected the story of 'proto-Keynesian' economic policies from many countries; each demonstrates an instance of the use of demand management policies in the inter-war years that arose without any reference to Keynes or his theoretical work.[7]

Just as we often find Keynes' name attached to demand management policy, we frequently find it attached to the Bretton Woods institutions and the modern welfare state (Townsend, 2004). But as in the case with demand management, it is not true that the welfare state was born out of his theoretical work. Even before 'proto-Keynesian' demand management had become a policy idea for addressing mass unemployment, the nascent welfare state had already been born as a bulwark against many of the social dislocations created by large-scale industrial capitalism. One plank of the early welfare state, for instance, was unemployment insurance to provide temporary income to those thrown out of work during the downward turns in the trade cycle.

The first modern welfare state is usually said to have been established by Bismarck in Germany in the 1880s in response to the uncertainty created for industrial workers.[8] Bismarck's welfare state was a nascent system of insurance against the cyclical vicissitudes of capitalist production. Like the proto-Keynesian spending policies in the inter-war years, however, Bismarck's welfare state had no theoretical underpinning in economic theory. Like those 'proto-Keynesian' demand management policies of the inter-war years, Bismarck's early system of social security was a pragmatic political response to pressing economic problems.[9]

Only with the creation of the modern British welfare state in 1945 was there a system of social security on offer that was built on the rationale of Keynesian economic theory.[10] Keynesian theory allowed William Beveridge, the architect of Britain's welfare state, to address the argument that a welfare state was only financially feasible if full employment was maintained; full employment was necessary both to generate the tax revenue needed to pay for the welfare state and to keep expenditure on unemployment insurance as low as possible. Beveridge used Keynes' work to provide the policies that would sustain full employment.[11]

Beveridge's (1942) plan for the British welfare state drew attention in many other countries, but was by no means the model for every post-war welfare state. In a sense, it did not need to be; many forces were converging to bring countries to a similar policy position. By this time, for instance, some form of the welfare state had been implemented in almost all industrial nations. And, as explained earlier, most industrialized countries had also developed demand management policies to help deal with the Depression. Finally, there was widespread evidence in many countries that the huge deficits run during the Second World War had created strong domestic demand and high employment. Thus, in the immediate post-war world there were full employment policies, welfare states and combinations of the two, but the changing social policy landscapes internationally were not directly attributable to either Beveridge or Keynes.

Nonetheless, Keynes' work did, *after the fact*, become the basis for virtually all post-war full employment policy and in that capacity also became central to welfare state policy around the world; his work provided the framework in which the intuitions behind full employment policy and the modern welfare state could be easily modelled. His place at the centre of post-war full employment policy came about in no small part through the mid-century econometric revolution that changed the economics profession. On the one hand, national income statistics began to be collected across the industrial democracies; on the other hand, Keynes had built his theoretical model on the variables defined by those emerging statistical categories (for example, aggregate consumption and the levels of government expenditure and private investment). Thus, the emerging revolution in economic measurement and forecasting was built on his model and it was used increasingly after 1945 to formulate full-employment, demand-management policies around the world. In this sense, the financially viable modern welfare state very much came to depend on the recommendations of 'Keynesian' economic policy. Demand management policies may originally have been forged from political coalitions and practical experimentation, but the study of their effectiveness carried out after the war was done using Keynes' model, and this meant that the formulation of future policy was soon being generated using Keynesian econometric models.

In fact, Keynesian economic policies defined the mainstream of economic policy making through the entire 'Trente Glorieuses', or glorious 30 years, following the Second World War (1945–75). Keynesian policy defined the means to fulfil the commitment to full employment in most industrial democracies until the mid-1970s, when the economic shocks created by the two oil embargoes brought the post-war prosperity to a halt.

In this sense, Keynes plays a central role in the answer to the original social question. Keynes, of course, did not provide the answer to the fundamental questions of political rights and representation, such as universal suffrage or the right to union organizing, but he *did* provide the model that would underpin full employment policy with his *General Theory*. His model was used as the basis for both the fiscal and monetary policy making that was used to ameliorate the trade cycle and to make the welfare state financially viable.

The 30 years of economic growth after the Second World War, together with the improved social welfare created by the welfare state, helped foster a new set of social questions. In a world with expanded suffrage and the emergence of class interests advanced by that increased suffrage, more people began to question their traditional lack of rights and representation. For instance, the shape of the welfare state in different countries helped accelerate questions about the role of women in the workplace. What kind of rights did women have to equal treatment in the workplace? Everything from childcare to reproductive rights had a new valence. Likewise, the full inclusion of traditionally marginalized peoples and groups could now be seen in a new and different way.

Of course, the welfare state alone is not responsible for creating the second social question that arose around difference and diversity; but as a part of the policies that helped to solve the original social question it helped to lay the groundwork for the emergence of the second social question.

The second social question

Much as the questions about rights and representation within the first social question were answered through cultural and political struggle, not through the application of economic theory, so, too, the issues at the heart of the second social question required cultural and political struggle. Basic issues such as women's rights and the inclusion of traditionally marginalized groups required existing moral and ethical frameworks to be challenged, reinterpreted and refocused. Just as the classical and neoclassical economists had been unable to suggest remedies for the low pay of late 19th century industrial workers, they offered little that might facilitate better treatment for traditionally marginalized groups.

Mainstream economics was not static, however. While it is correct to say that Keynesian economic theory and Keynesian economic policy were important influences during the '30 glorious years', there was always an anti-Keynesian movement within the profession which sought to overthrow Keynes' hegemony. This took various forms, from the Austrian economists who had migrated to America to escape Hitler, to the emerging school of Chicago economics being cultivated by Milton Friedman and George Stigler. The common thread connecting all the anti-Keynesian efforts was a desire to diminish the role of the state in the economy. In Keynesian theory, the state could improve economic outcomes; his opponents wanted his authority diminished for exactly this reason. They did not trust power in the hands of the state and they did not want to pay the taxes necessary to pay for the welfare state.[12]

There are many ways to track the progress of the various threads of anti-Keynesian activity, but much of their eventual success depended on the economic devastation wrought by the two oil embargoes in the 1970s. The two embargoes had the simultaneous effects of causing a rapid rise in prices (inflation) and a major downturn in economic activity (stagnation). This was an unlikely pairing and the anti-Keynesians used its existence to argue that Keynesian economics had failed.

Traditionally, the trade cycle was defined by either inflation paired with high employment or deflation paired with high unemployment. Keynesian policy could be used easily and effectively against either pair. If the economy was overheating on the upswing and prices were rising, there were many ways to decrease demand: raise taxes, cut government spending or raise interest rates. Likewise, if the economy was in a recession and there was high unemployment and falling prices, it was easy to increase demand: cut taxes, increase government spending or lower interest rates. The new pairing of inflation with high unemployment, however, which was labelled stagflation (stagnation in growth with high inflation), did not lend itself to such easy (Keynesian) policy solutions.[13]

The oil embargoes had not been caused by Keynesian policies, of course, but inflation *had* first started to edge up as early as 1968 as a result of what was then the longest peacetime expansion in American history. The anti-Keynesians initially seized on the rising government expenditures in 1966–67 as the reason for the inflation; President Lyndon Johnson had increased government expenditure as a part of his War of Poverty while simultaneously trying to raise defence expenditure to escalate the Vietnam War. It did not matter that his Keynesian advisors had argued against simultaneously tackling these two problems; what mattered was that a president who was widely known to use Keynesian advisors had tripped the economy into problems with an anti-poverty programme. Nor did it matter that after 1968, when Richard Nixon occupied the White House, the Federal Reserve did Nixon's bidding and executed a loose monetary policy to stimulate the economy and that this had further exacerbated inflation.

In the end, the argument moved beyond the question of who was to blame for the stagflation and came to focus on the fact that Keynesian policies could either fight inflation or fight unemployment; and no matter which one was chosen, it would only make the other problem worse. Finally, there was traction for anti-Keynesian policies.

Initially, the policies and economic theories that filled the void created by this perceived failure of Keynesian economics were a mixture of new and old. One of the new ideas was something called supply-side economics. The crux of this idea was actually quite old: if you taxed people less, it was argued, they would invest more. But if the policy itself was old news, its consequences were articulated in a fresh new way that seemed to address the issue of stagflation: creating new productive capacity through new investment would allow an increase in employment and output without further raising prices. Special interest groups across the industrial democracies seized on this policy and it had some purchase in the policy arena for at least two decades despite having little or no grounding in economic theory and no clear empirical support.

The old theory that first stepped into the breach created by the demise of Keynesian economics in the late 1970s and early 1980s was monetarism, or the idea that the solution to inflation was to carefully limit the growth of the money supply. The idea that 'inflation was always and everywhere a monetary phenomenon' had its earliest Western origins in the influx of gold from the Americas into Europe's feudal economies in the 15th and 16th centuries and the soaring inflation that this influx had caused. Milton Friedman and Anna Schwartz (1963) had established the modern, empirically argued version of this argument in their classic *Monetary History of the United States*. Friedman became monetarism's public face in the 1970s with his argument that monetary authorities could provide the best outcomes by setting a target for the steady, stable growth of the money supply, rather than by trying to influence interest rates.

Monetarism was soon to be more thoroughly discredited than Keynesianism. Its legitimacy rested on the question of whether the stock of money circulated at a steady rate; Schwartz and Friedman's great work had consisted in part in showing that it had circulated at a steady rate over many decades (in the United States). But changes in the financial system and financial regulation that began shortly after their book was published caused the rate of circulation (referred to as its velocity) to begin to change unpredictably in the 1980s. Thus, just as the Federal Reserve Bank began to use the monetarist tool of closely targeting the growth rate of the money supply, they had to regularly abandon those targets to avoid economic catastrophe. If velocity is unstable, monetary targeting of the type Friedman prescribed simply does not work.

The demise of monetarism left one strong anti-Keynesian idea afloat in mainstream economics: new classical macroeconomics. One might actually argue that it left two new anti-Keynesian ideas afloat, as new classical macroeconomics was itself built on another late 20th century innovation: rational expectations theory.

Taken together, the result(s) of rational expectations theory and new classical macroeconomics was to produce a simple theoretical counter to Keynesian economics. New classical economists assume that economic agents know the underlying process that drives the economy: rational expectation theorists assume that economic agents, on average, understand and correctly forecast the outcomes of those underlying processes. In a theoretically elegant way, the assumptions are combined to demonstrate that any action that the government takes to affect the economy will be undone by agents acting so as to move the economy in the opposite direction. The result is that any Keynesian demand management policy meant to stimulate the economy will be ineffective; economic agents will see what is happening and act so as to counteract the new demand management policies. The only recourse of a government is to abide by strict rules (for example, balanced budgets, strict limits on interest rate policy). Anything else causes unemployment, poor growth and/or inflation.

Ultimately, the global financial crises demonstrated that neither new classical assumption was an accurate portrayal of the world. People are not, on average, omniscient as regards the economy; and demand management policy *can* effectively counter a rapidly emerging recession.[14]

One of the sets of economic agents who were frequently argued to portray the assumptions of new classical macroeconomics most accurately were bond traders. They had been collectively dead wrong, however, about the onset of the global financial crisis and about the effect of the policies implemented to address the crisis. Likewise stock traders, who lost trillions of dollars when the market crashed in 2007–08; they were another set of economic agents often argued to demonstrate the rational foresight assumed in the new classical economics, but they also completely failed to foresee what happened.

In the aftermath of the global financial crisis, a new mainstream consensus emerged that Keynesian demand management policy can be effective in combating the short-term effects of a collapse in the economy.[15] During the reign of new classical macroeconomics, Keynesian policy had been largely absent from mainstream economic policy discussion. There had been some renewal of interest among policy makers in the first decade of the 21st century, but this was largely a pragmatic turn and did not reflect a change within the economics profession.[16] Throughout the 1990s and the first decade of the new century the consensus of the profession had been that active policy management was ineffective and that only rule-based policy that fostered the credibility of the authorities was effective. The crux of the argument was that the rules that generated credibility were the rules that defenestrated policy: balancing the budget and keeping interest rates at levels mandated by financial prudence, for instance.

In every way, then, the turn away from Keynesian economics and towards new classical macroeconomics was a part of the neoliberal turn in both economics and economic policy. The underlying argument is that markets work and governments do not. Likewise, it is a central tenet of new classical macroeconomics that individual actions are the lens through which to see the world, and individual autonomy is the frame for policy discussion. The 'social question' for neoliberals is how to limit the role of government and diminish the welfare state. In that sense, the new classical macroeconomics that reigned during the anti-Keynesian decades following the oil embargoes offered a solution to a quite different 'social question'.

However, new classical macroeconomics offered no tools for addressing the 'second social question' as more traditionally understood. In no way does new classical macroeconomics address the questions of difference and diversity. To the extent that neoliberalism is a theory based on libertarian ideas, neoliberals (to include new classical macroeconomists) would almost certainly say that they disavow discrimination of any kind. But to the extent that surmounting the traditional barriers created by gender, ethnicity or disability require cultural and political struggle, neoliberalism is an unlikely resource. On the one hand, libertarians see individuals as autonomous and do not easily engage in discussion of cultural struggle (except to fight against ideas of social solidarity and social democracy), since it hypothetically violates individual autonomy to suggest to someone a change in their attitude toward others. On the other hand, the neoliberals' right-wing funding sources want to maintain the cultural status quo.[17]

The third social question

The highly individualistic focus of the new classical macroeconomics reflects the fact that it is an offshoot of traditional, marginalist (or neoclassical) economic theory. In fact, like the 19th century giant of neoclassical microeconomics Alfred Marshall (mentioned earlier), the new classical economists wanted to graft marginalist thinking onto the intuitions of the early classical economist David Ricardo. Simple models of individual choice paired with laissez-faire conclusions have a strong mutualism across mainstream economics. But working from this common root, modern neoclassical economics does not offer much hope for helping with the emerging concern for social inclusion. To the extent that inclusion continues to cover concerns for full social participation regardless of gender, ethnicity or ability, traditional market tools *can* easily be used to demonstrate (and quantify) the effects of discrimination. Yet while it has been used in this way, such a treatment of discrimination and exclusion are rarely, if ever, a part of how the subject is taught. One is much more likely to find an argument against the minimum wage or rent controls than one is an argument for social inclusion. The drift of mainstream economics is much more towards the neoliberal idea that government is necessarily a bad thing than it is towards the idea that government can help those who are socially excluded.[18]

There are well-known exceptions to this drift in mainstream economics, such as the work of the late Tony Atkinson (2015) or of the Nobel Prize laureate Joseph Stiglitz (2015). Likewise, the recent turn to more empirical economics has produced interesting work like Card and Krueger (1994), on the economic impacts of minimum wages for example, and Mullainathan and Shafir (2013) on managing with less. But the influence of economic theory on social policy is still much more likely to come from the point of view that the state is an impediment than it is from the point of view that the state is an effective means to solve social problems.

Still, the turn to the third social question of inclusion and sustainability provides a chance to see how traditional Keynesian policies once again bear relevance. It may be that the mainstream of the economics profession only conceives of the legitimacy of Keynesian demand management as a short-run tool for addressing economic dislocation, but this is far better than the neoliberal idea implicit in new classical macroeconomics that the state is always and everywhere ineffective unless it is, paradoxically, defenestrated. In fact, Keynesian economic policies are much more powerful than simply being a tool for short-run boosting of the economy; they have important potential to address both aspects of the third social question.

Perhaps this is most intuitive in the case of sustainability. If societies are to successfully address climate change, it will require immense investment. Whatever route we take to cut our dependence on fossil fuels, it will mean building out new infrastructure to generate clean energy: solar, wind or geothermal. New technology needs to be researched, factories need to be financed, and the new infrastructure will need to be built. All of this means stimulating aggregate demand and increasing the number of people in employment.

The increases in expenditure needed to convert to green energy can also help to achieve more social inclusion. This is true from at least two perspectives. As regards inclusion of members of groups that have traditionally been marginalized, training for green jobs can be directed to job training centres and schools in the neighbourhoods where excluded groups live. Just as importantly, the new research and construction can generate jobs that pay above the social minimum, thus helping to address the growing problems of income inequality and socioeconomic exclusion.

Of course, green energy is not the only industry where the fight against climate change can create jobs (ILO, 2019). Creating more forests, planting more trees, reclaiming wetlands, and designing pedestrian-friendly urban areas are all investments that would increase jobs and employment. Nor do investments have to be made to help fight climate change in order to be effective at providing more well-paying jobs. Building more housing and more schools creates jobs and can help mitigate inequality and increase inclusion.

Conclusion

The question naturally arises how Keynes came to see such a different role for the state than is held by so many mainstream economists. After all, he identified throughout his life as a Liberal, and he abhorred government control of personal lives, such as anti-sodomy laws. How does someone who respects and understands the autonomy of the individual become an advocate for the state?

The answer, perhaps, can be found in some of his early popular writing. Keynes first came to prominence as the author of *The Economic Consequences of the Peace*, which argued against the system of reparations imposed on Germany in the peace settlement following the First World War. His argument is underpinned not by an idea about individual rights and freedom, however, but rather by a focus on social stability and the legitimacy of the capitalist system.

He argues that European capitalism is built on a system of great inequality that people are only willing to accept because they believe it provides stability and the promise of a better life for their children and grandchildren. Thus, government action that supports economic stability has a warrant that exceeds the utilitarian calculus of the individual.

Such an approach, of course, offers a very different response to the coronavirus pandemic than one sees from most economists. Rather than starting with questions about the monetary value of a human life, or focusing on how quickly the economy can be 'restarted', a Keynesian approach might ask first how people can best be taken care of. A Keynesian would be more concerned with the effective use of the government to stabilize people's welfare, as we have seen across Western economies, rather than risking the appearance that people are expendable in the service of returning to economic growth.

Keynes would have understood that if society could not seriously address the pandemic, then the ensuing instability might make a return to economic growth through any familiar means an undesirable end. Ensuring things like adequate healthcare and unemployment insurance would take priority, and the necessary fiscal measures would be taken to support the economy. He would recognize the state's vital investment function in the necessary public goods and services that create social value. All of this has to be paid for, but of course Keynes would not advocate for a return to austerity. The return to prosperity for all requires stability and legitimacy, policy makers should now seize the opportunity to 'build back better' rather than adopt austerity according to the UN (UNCTAD, 2020), by creating more sustainable, resilient and inclusive societies.

Notes

[1] The term 'classical' is usually used to refer to economists from Smith to Marx. There is, of course, a wide range of opinion within the work of this group, but it remains fair to say that no one in the group had an optimistic outlook for the possibility of wages rising in the long run. A common feature of their agriculturally influenced mode of theorizing is that they imagined that each year a society produced a surplus above the minimum needed to reproduce itself. In the long run, they understood this surplus as being all distributed to the landowners and capitalists, leaving the wages fund fixed at the level necessary to sustain workers at the minimal level.

[2] To be more precise, they argued that workers received a wage equal to the value of the output attributable to the last worker hired. The theory was used to demonstrate the other two classes were paid on a similar basis, according to the value of the last unit of land or capital employed.

[3] Marx and Engels advocated some ameliorative social policies in *The Communist Manifesto* (1848), but Marx does not offer ameliorative remedies in *Das Kapital* (1867).

[4] Classical political economists of the 18th and early 19th century were much more focused on the economy as a whole than the microeconomic theorists who dominated economics by the end of the 19th century. See Murphy (2009) for a discussion of early 'macroeconomic' thinking. Laidler (1999) offers an excellent survey of macroeconomic thinking before Keynes.

[5] Patinkin (1982) argues that Keynes was the first economic theorist to work out a model that explained fluctuations in output and aggregate employment.

[6] Volumes XIII and XXIX of Keynes' *Collected Writings* (1989) contain much of the extant archival material and correspondence between Keynes and the members of the Circus. See also Moggridge (1992).

[7] Canada is, perhaps, the only country where it happened that the initial experiments with demand management were the direct result of Keynes' influence. Robert Bryce, a young Canadian who sat through the lectures in which Keynes worked out his *General Theory*, returned home from Britain after the book was published and went to work in the civil service, where he introduced Keynes' ideas.

[8] As Gøsta Esping-Andersen (1990) has pointed out, both the definition and the origin of the modern welfare state are subject to disagreement. Recently,

Boyer (2018) has argued that the origins of the modern British welfare lie in the Poor Laws.

[9] Bismarck established the welfare state as a conservative move to increase loyalty to the state and in an effort to dampen the appeal of left-wing labour politics.

[10] Backhouse and Nishizawa (2010) and Backhouse et al (2017) provide excellent explanation of the many threads of British thought that fed into the creation of the welfare state.

[11] Beveridge and Keynes had a sometimes tumultuous relationship. Beveridge's initial response (1942) to *The General Theory* was negative. See Moggridge (1992) and Marcuzzo (2010).

[12] In the United States, the desire to delegitimize Keynes and his work also carried an explicit connection to issues of diversity and difference. The strongest political pressure against Keynesian policy came from the American South, where white supremacy was an important part of the opposition to Keynesian policies. White supremacists wanted to make sure that the welfare state would not grow and be extended to relieve the many problems created by discrimination against black Americans. See Logan (1970) for an explanation of the racist origins of the early opposition to the welfare state in the American South.

[13] One might say (correctly) here that stagflation did not lend itself to easy *Keynesian* policy solutions. But the truth is that it did not lend itself to *any* easy policy solutions. In the range of solutions offered by alternative schools of thought within economics, only supply-side economics appeared to be relatively 'easy' in the sense that its imposition did not portend further economic dislocations as a result. But supply-side economics never has garnered any credible empirical evidence to support it. Of the anti-Keynesian solutions such as monetarism and Austrian economics there would be predictable dislocation, especially wide-scale unemployment, as a result of the effort to combat inflation.

[14] Perhaps the best evidence of a change in attitude about the idea that demand management can be effective in a sudden recession is the writing of Richard Posner (2009a, 2009b). Likewise, Posner accepts Keynes' argument that people are not always omniscient about where the economy is going.

[15] It would not be correct to say that there was a widespread turn to Keynesian policy as a 'regular' tool of economic policy making. But as a short-term policy, it came to be seen as effective in the face of a rapid downturn in demand.

[16] See Bateman, Hirai and Marcuzzo (2010) for transnational comparisons of how Keynesian policies began to return after the start of the new century.

[17] See, for example, Teles (2010).

[18] See Kwak (2017) for an explanation of the way that introductory economic reasoning has been misapplied in recent decades to build a case against any attempt to mitigate inequality.

References

Atkinson, A. B. (2015) *Inequality: What Can Be Done?*, Cambridge, MA: Harvard University Press.

Backhouse, R. and Nishizawa, T. (eds) (2010) *No Wealth but Life: Welfare Economics and the Welfare State in Britain, 1880–1945*, Cambridge: Cambridge University Press.

Backhouse, R. E., Bateman, B. W., Nishizawa, T. and Plehwe, D. (eds) (2017) *Liberalism and the Welfare State: Economists and Arguments for the Welfare State*, Oxford: Oxford University Press.

Bateman, B. W., Hirai, T. and Marcuzzo, C. (eds) (2010) *The Return to Keynes*, Cambridge, MA: Harvard University Press.

Beveridge, W. (1942) *Social Insurance and Allied Services*, Cmd. 6404, London: HMSO.

Boyer, G. R. (2018) *The Winding Road to the Welfare State: Economic Insecurity and Social Welfare Policy in Britain*, Princeton, NJ: Princeton University Press.

Card, D. and Krueger, A. B. (1994) 'Minimum Wages and Employment: Case Study of the Fast-Food Industry in New Jersey and Pennsylvania', *American Economic Review*, 84(4): 772–93.

Esping-Andersen, G. (1990) *The Three Worlds of Welfare Capitalism*, Princeton, NJ: Princeton University Press.

Friedman, M. and Schwartz, A. (1963) *A Monetary History of the United States, 1867–1960*, Princeton, NJ: Princeton University Press.

Hall, P. A. (ed) (1989) *The Political Power of Economic Ideas: Keynesianism Across Nations*, Princeton, NJ: Princeton University Press.

ILO (International Labour Organization) (2019) *Work for a Brighter Future: Global Commission on the Future of Work*, Geneva: ILO, https://digitallibrary.un.org/record/3827525?ln=en.

Keynes, J. M. (1923) *A Tract on Monetary Reform*, London: Macmillan.

Keynes, J. M. (1930) *A Treatise on Money*, London: Macmillan.

Keynes, J. M. (1931) *Essays in Persuasion*, London: Macmillan.

Keynes, J. M. (1936) *The General Theory of Employment, Interest, and Money*, London: Macmillan.

Keynes, J. M. (1989) *Collected Writings*, Volume 30 (Bibliography and Index), London: Macmillan.

Kwak, J. (2017) *Economism: Bad Economics and the Rise of Inequality*, New York: Pantheon Books.

Laidler, D. (1999) *Fabricating the Keynesian Revolution*, Cambridge: Cambridge University Press.

Logan, R. W. (1970) *The Betrayal of the Negro: From Rutherford B. Hayes to Woodrow Wilson*, New York: Collier Books.

Marcuzzo, M. C. (2010) 'Whose Welfare State? Beveridge versus Keynes', in R. Backhouse and T. Nishizawa (eds) *No Wealth but Life: Welfare Economics and the Welfare State in Britain, 1880–1945*, Cambridge: Cambridge University Press, 189–206.

Marshall, A. (1890) *The Principles of Economics*, London: Macmillan.

Marshall, A. (1919) *Industry and Trade*, London: Macmillan.

Marshall, A. (1923) *Money, Credit, and Commerce*, London: Macmillan.

Marx, K. (1867) *Das Kapital: Kritik der politischen Oekonomie* (Capital: A Critical Analysis of Capitalist Production), Hamburg: Verlag von Otto Meissner.

Marx, K. and Engels, F. (1848) *Manifest der Kommunistischen Partei* (The Communist Manifesto), London: Workers' Education Association.

Moggridge, D. (1992) *Maynard Keynes: An Economist's Biography*, London and New York: Routledge.

Mullainathan, S. and Shafir, E. (2013) *Scarcity: The New Science of Having Less and How It Defines Our Lives*, New York: Picador.

Murphy, A. (2009) *The Genesis of Macroeconomics*, Oxford: Oxford University Press.

Patinkin, D. (1982) *Anticipations of the General Theory?*, Chicago, IL: University of Chicago Press.

Posner, R. A. (2009a) 'How I Became a Keynesian', *New Republic*, 23 September: 34.

Posner, R. A. (2009b) *A Failure of Capitalism: The Crisis of '08 and the Descent into Depression*, Cambridge, MA: Harvard University Press.

Stiglitz, J. E. (2015) *The Great Divide: Unequal Societies and What We Can Do About Them*, New York: W. W. Norton.

Teles, S. M. (2010) *The Rise of the Conservative Legal Movement: The Battle for Control of the Law*, Princeton, NJ: Princeton University Press.

Townsend, P. (2004) 'From Universalism to Safety Nets: The Rise and Fall of Keynesian Influence on Social Development', in T. Mkandawire (ed) *Social Policy in a Development Context*, Basingstoke: Palgrave Macmillan, 37–62.

UNCTAD (United Nations Conference on Trade and Development) (2020) *Trade and Development Report 2020: From Global Pandemic to Prosperity for All: Avoiding Another Lost Decade*, Geneva: UN, https://doi.org/10.18356/aea7b3b9-en.

Wicksell, K. (1898) *Geldzins und Güterpreise* (*Interest and Prices*), Jena: Gustav Fischer.

4

Disputing the economization and the de-politicization of 'social' investment in global social policy

Jean-Michel Bonvin and Francesco Laruffa

Introduction

Since the mid-1990s, a new vocabulary of the 'social' has appeared in global social policy discourses, involving concepts such as 'social cohesion', 'social capital', 'social inclusion' (reducing 'social exclusion') and 'social economy' (Graefe, 2006: 197; see for example Levitas, 1996; Fine, 1999; Jayasuriya, 2006). In particular, one of the most interesting developments in thinking about the 'social' in the 21st century is the emergence of the social investment perspective on welfare reform (Esping-Andersen, 2002; Jenson, 2010; Morel et al, 2012; Hemerijck, 2013, 2018; Deeming and Smyth, 2015). In global social policy discourses more generally, 'social investment' (SI) is now actively promoted by international organizations like the Organization for Economic Co-operation and Development (OECD), the International Monetary Fund (IMF) and the World Bank Group (WBG), as well as regional actors like the European Union (EU) and the European Commission (EC) and UN Regional Commissions like the Economic Commission for Latin America and the Caribbean (ECLAC) (Mahon, 2010; Jenson, 2017; Deeming and Smyth, 2018). SI is fast becoming one of the most important frameworks for thinking about the 'social', but this worldwide development remains highly problematic.

The chapter is structured in four main sections. The first two sections summarise the problems with the SI perspective before introducing the capability approach (CA). The third section presents social policy as an essential precondition for an effective democracy. Finally, the fourth section explores the implications of treating welfare reform itself as a political–democratic matter. Throughout the chapter, the aim is to highlight the differences of this conception with the SI perspective on social policy.

The social investment perspective

The SI perspective emphasizes the positive contribution of social policy not only to human wellbeing (for example, through the reduction of poverty and social marginalization) but also to economic progress. Thus, in contrast to theories that see a trade-off between social and economic goals, SI attempts to reconcile them, making social equity go hand in hand with economic efficiency (Taylor-Gooby, 2008; Vandenbroucke et al, 2011: 5; Hemerijck, 2013: 134).

Despite its merits, the SI approach has been criticized for adopting an economic framework, with the risk of replacing debates on social values with the economic rationale (Nolan, 2013). In particular, putting at its very core the concept of 'human capital' (for example, Hemerijck, 2013: 142), SI tends to extend the economic logic to non-economic spheres, such as education and health. The 'social' is thus partly transformed into an investment object and an economic entity. Hence, SI entertains an ambiguous relationship with 'neoliberalism'. While SI surely provides an alternative to austerity and welfare retrenchment, it largely accepts the normative–epistemological dimension of neoliberalism (Laruffa, 2019). This is especially true with respect to the 'economization of the social', which is an essential element of neoliberalizing policy processes (Foucault, 2008), whereby economic criteria are essentially extended to 'non-economic' domains.

Moreover, the economization of the 'social' seems also to entail its de-politicization (Madra and Adaman, 2014). Indeed, the utilitarian calculus of efficiency maximization, which underlies the logics of returns on investment, does not require democratic deliberation and can in principle be delegated to an elite of experts, as long as it proves competent enough. Thus, once the economic discourse becomes the dominant framework for decision making, political choices tend to be removed from public discussion and are transformed into technocratic issues to be solved by experts (Clarke, 2004, and writing in Chapter 2 of this volume). Finally, the theory and policy framing of 'human capital' is equally problematic because seeing individuals largely as commodities rather than as democratic citizens reinforces this de-politicization tendency, making them objects of employability-enhancing social policy interventions rather than their own active selves.

Amartya Sen's CA (for example, Sen, 1999, 2009) provides a theoretical framework, and its linked methodology, able to overcome the double problem of economization and de-politicization of the 'social'. In contrast to economization and its focus on maximizing GDP or the employment rate, the CA requires thinking about policy making in terms of its contribution to the achievement of 'final ends' (Richardson, 2015). On the other hand, the CA conceives welfare reform in political–democratic terms rather than as a matter for technocratic management. As the problems of economization and de-politicization of the 'social' are linked, so too are the solutions. Indeed, while reducing social policy choices to an issue of economic calculation (economization) seems to preclude public debate and can be delegated to experts (de-politicization), framing the 'social' in terms of final ends entails potential disagreement about those ends and thus politicization. Disagreement over the ends of policies demands democratic deliberation and discussion to be settled, and conflict and democratic struggle may arise in the process. The point is that while within the economic framework the goals of public action are already given (for example, maximizing economic growth through the increase of employment and productivity rates), the CA emphasizes open-ended and underspecified goals, thereby leaving to democratic deliberation the definition of the goals of public action.

Yet this capability for democratic participation cannot simply be taken for granted and should be promoted by public action itself. Hence, following Olson (2006), this chapter argues that, from a capability perspective, the connection between social policy and democracy is crucial and deploys itself in a twofold way. On the one hand, social policy is interpreted as an essential factor in enabling 'equal citizenship' or equal ability of 'functioning as a citizen' (Anderson, 1999), establishing the social preconditions of political equality. On the other hand, welfare reform itself is framed as a political–democratic matter. Thus, in this conception, welfare reform proposals cannot be developed entirely by 'experts' and citizens should be included in the formulation, implementation and evaluation of social policies.

The capability approach and the importance of conversion factors

The CA is a normative framework originally formulated by Amartya Sen for the evaluation of human wellbeing in the field of development. It is centred on the notion of 'capability' defined in terms of substantive individual freedoms that people have 'to lead the kind of lives they value – and have reason to value' (Sen, 1999: 18). With this focus, the CA provides an alternative framework for the evaluation of wellbeing, social justice and the progress of societies with respect to mainstream economics, which generally uses either material resources or (individual/social) utility as central evaluative measures. In this context, economization implies the extension of the economic rationale (focused on promoting either material wellbeing or preference satisfaction, or a combination of the two) to the 'social'; the CA offers an alternative to economization, providing an evaluative framework based on different normative and epistemological assumptions.

On the one hand, the CA provides an alternative to utilitarian frameworks that focus only on utility (or preference satisfaction) for assessing wellbeing. Here the argument is that disadvantaged social groups may adapt their preferences to their deprived situation so that a framework based exclusively on individuals' happiness would not register important forms of injustice, which are made invisible by the process of preferences adjustment. Moreover, individuals may have other objectives in life than maximizing their own happiness. For example, in order to pursue their political ideals, people may be ready to sacrifice their own wellbeing. In this context, the CA is concerned not only with people's happiness and life satisfaction but also with their political agency.

On the other hand, the exclusive focus on material resources is rejected because they are envisaged as means rather than ends and policies should focus on what intrinsically matters rather than on what is only instrumentally important since there is no automatic relationship between the two. For example, economic growth may be associated with *worsening* living conditions (for example, greater pollution). Moreover, focusing on resources implies ignoring those inequalities that emerge in the presence of equality of resources. These inequalities originate from the varying capacities of individuals to transform resources into actual freedom to lead a valuable life. From this perspective, 'conversion factors' are an essential concept in the CA, which emphasizes that resources still need to be converted into real freedom.

However, the concept of 'conversion factors' can be used more broadly: rather than only intervening in the relationship between resources and capabilities, they can refer to all those factors that mediate the translation of resources, formal freedoms and rights into real freedoms and real rights (that is, capabilities). In this context, conversion factors may facilitate the conversion process (they are then called 'enabling conversion factors') or undermine and hinder it ('constraining conversion factors'). Moreover, conversion factors can be external or internal to the individual and capabilities are always the result of the interaction between internal and external conversion factors. For example, disability can be considered an internal conversion factor (that is, a personal characteristic) that potentially hinders the process of converting formal freedoms and rights into real ones. However, the negative impact of disability on capabilities can be reduced through specific social interventions and public policies, such as providing accessible public transportation, anti-discrimination laws and so on.

The interaction among the different conversion factors determines the conversion rate at which inputs (resources and formal rights and freedoms) are transformed into outputs (capabilities). Vulnerable groups in society are generally characterized by low conversion rates: they are 'inefficient' in converting inputs into outputs (Chiappero-Martinetti and Salardi, 2008), even if, crucially, the responsibility for this 'inefficiency' may not lie in individuals themselves but involve social and political responsibility (for example, if public transport is not accessible to disabled people their conversion rate is low). In other words, even in the presence of formal equalities in resources, rights and freedoms, vulnerable groups will tend to enjoy low levels of capabilities because of low conversion rates. Hence, from a capability perspective, tackling the social question is not only a matter of equalizing resources or formal rights, but of properly tackling the issue of conversion factors. Redistribution per se is not enough; it needs to be complemented by efforts aiming at shaping 'society' in a more equitable way.

As already noted, conversion factors may have a positive or a negative impact on the process of transforming resources, rights and formal freedoms into capabilities. While disability may constrain the conversion process, good health facilitates it. The same is true for external conversion factors: public policies and social institutions, including social norms, do not always play a positive role in the conversion process (see for example Nambiar, 2013, on the constraining role of institutions when routines and habits limit individual freedom). How should we then distinguish between enabling (or empowering) and constraining (or disabling) social institutions?

For answering this question, it is possible to use two criteria based on Sen's distinction between the process and the opportunity aspects of freedom (for example, Sen, 2009). While process freedom refers to the respect for individual freedom during the process that leads to a certain decision, the opportunity aspect of freedom looks at the consequences of that decision for the quality of life of the people targeted by it (interpreted in terms of available real opportunities for human flourishing). Accordingly, the two criteria used to determine whether any given social institution is empowering or not can be formulated through the two following questions: (a) Does this specific social institution rely upon a participatory process that guarantees equal participation of the people involved or targeted by that institution and equal consideration of their viewpoints or aspirations? (b) Does this institution promote the enhancement of the capabilities of the people involved? The next two sections develop a perspective on social policy whereby the latter is conceived as an enabling conversion factor in this twofold sense, starting with an analysis of the consequences of social policy (opportunity freedom) and then turning to the process of policy making (process freedom).

Social policy as conversion factor of democracy

Assessing social policy as a conversion factor in terms of its consequences implies asking how far it positively, or negatively, affects individuals' capabilities. In the SI perspective, social policy is often assessed in terms of its consequences for various dimensions of wellbeing, such as health, education and income. Also, a central criterion in this perspective is the capacity of social policy to promote employment. Thus, social policy should help individuals participate in the labour market, with a special emphasis put on good jobs (that is stable, well-paid, with social rights attached, and so on). While these dimensions and criteria are important also from a capability perspective, one aspect that is often ignored in the SI approach is the potential contribution of social policy in promoting individuals' political agency. For this reason, this section focuses on the contribution of social policy to enhance people's capability for democratic citizenship.

This capability is of central importance in Sen's approach: democracy is indeed one of the fundamental means of development as well as one of its central goals (Sen, 1999; on the importance of democracy in the CA, see also for example Anderson, 2003; Crocker, 2006). Crucially, rather than a formalistic understanding of democracy based on the mere existence of certain institutions, the CA requires assessing democracy on the extent to which 'different voices from diverse sections of the people can actually be heard' (Sen, 2009: xiii). In other words, what matters is individuals' capacity for effective political participation, that is, their 'capability for voice' (Bonvin, 2012). This illustrates Sen's preference for participatory ways of making the 'social'.

From this perspective, the central question is: to what extent does social policy support citizens' effective political participation? Indeed, while democracy involves political equality, that is, an equal formal right to participate in the government of public affairs, in reality it is possible to observe the existence of 'political poverty', defined as 'the inability of groups of citizens to participate effectively in the democratic process' (Bohman, 1997: 333). In this context, political poverty can be interpreted as the result of difficulties in converting a formal right to participate in public affairs into a real right (capability).

Of course, non-participation could also result from a free choice (for example, the rich may lock themselves away). Yet there are some important reasons for doubting that this is systematically, or even often, the case. As Offe (2014: 11) argues, the opportunity to participate is 'genuine' or 'real', as opposed to merely formal, 'if the behavioural evidence suggests that whether or not participants make use of that opportunity is *randomly* distributed, rather than distributed in its statistical probability by opportunity-constraining social and economic conditions, such as education and economic status' (emphasis in the original). Given that a lot of empirical studies have shown that the distribution of non-participation is not even among social groups and is highly concentrated among vulnerable social groups whereas participation is strongly correlated to indicators of individuals' life chances (education, income, labour market status and so on), then non-participation cannot be considered as the outcome of a free choice (Offe, 2014: 12). Moreover, political poverty is not only problematic in itself: it also produces negative consequences for other dimensions of social disadvantage. Indeed, governments will tend to implement policies that are biased in favour of those social categories that are known to participate and are therefore better able to defend their interests, at the expense of the interests of those that do not participate (Offe, 2014: 2). Political poverty may then be interpreted as a kind of 'corrosive disadvantage' (Wolff and De-Shalit, 2007), which is not only a deprivation of a capability in itself but one that has also negative effects on other capabilities, undermining other dimensions of wellbeing and freedom.

Crucially, political poverty does not emerge from individuals' failures or incapacities alone but, as is the case for any lack of capabilities, it emerges from the interaction between individual and collective conversion factors. Furthermore, also individual conversion factors, such as education and income, may be improved (or worsened) by public action, thereby involving political responsibility.

What, then, is the role of social policy in reducing political poverty, that is, in supporting the effective political participation of marginalized groups? The answer to this question involves the reduction of marginalization itself through redistribution. Indeed, given the evidence that low income, unemployment and social exclusion are associated with lower political participation, a generous social policy, which redistributes income, promotes employment and reduces other forms of social marginalization, positively contributes to citizens' political empowerment. In other words, redistribution is a prerequisite towards a participatory way of making the 'social', insofar as it facilitates vulnerable people's participation in the polity and society. From this perspective, it seems that there is no difference between SI and the CA. Indeed, even if in the social investment approach democracy and the problem of political inequality are not specifically and explicitly addressed, the improvement of socioeconomic outcomes that is targeted by SI should have positive spill-over effects on political empowerment and reduce political inequality. Thus, the democratic question would be addressed indirectly in SI.

However, there is some evidence that SI policies do not necessarily enhance vulnerable people's political participation (Marx and Nguyen, 2018). This may result from two reasons: on the one hand, SI policies may miss their target and benefit mostly the least vulnerable among their beneficiaries (Bonoli et al, 2017), thus failing to empower the most marginalized people; on the other hand, the SI perspective conceives of individuals mainly in terms of human capital, which certainly empowers them as productive workers but may have negative consequences on their political empowerment as democratic citizens.

The latter argument is especially visible in the case of education policy. Van de Werfhorst (2007), for instance, finds that people educated in vocational programmes are less active citizens (in terms of political interest and participation) than people taught in general education. Thus, emphasizing the merits of vocational training in transmitting work-relevant skills, SI may neglect the importance of other competences that are needed for enhancing political empowerment and promoting active democratic citizenship. The kind of education policy emphasized by the CA substantially differs from the one at the core of SI (Bonvin and Laruffa, 2019). Rather than investing only in 'human capital' in order to make individuals fit for the labour market, education in the CA also aims to promote their political agency as democratic citizens. In this context, education should above all undermine the process of adaptive preferences, nourishing individuals' 'capacity to aspire' (Appadurai, 2004). In this perspective, education should promote a diffuse 'sense of entitlement' (Hobson et al, 2011), which increases people's ability to exercise rights but also the 'self-efficacy to make claims' and the 'ability to imagine alternatives' (Hobson et al, 2011: 173, 174). Thus, even though both approaches insist on reducing socioeconomic disadvantage, they have a very different view of the 'social': while SI sees people as human capital to be invested in, thus running the risk of abandoning those who do not appear as a profitable investment, the CA envisages all people as democratic citizens who are to be provided with the necessary capabilities to function as equal citizens (Anderson, 1999).

Social policy as a political–democratic matter

The previous section, taking the perspective of opportunity freedom (that is, centred on consequences), argued that social policy can play an important role as an enabling conversion factor of democracy. In this context, social policies that aim to promote capabilities should conceive the targeted individuals not only as 'receivers' of welfare benefits and services and as 'doers' interested in having valuable opportunities for agency (within and beyond the labour market) but also as 'judges'; that is, democratic citizens that should have a say on the direction of social change (Bonvin and Laruffa, 2018). This requires attaching high priority in social policy theorizing to the goal of reducing 'political poverty'.

However, reducing political inequalities is not only a matter of improving the distribution of economic and educational resources. Indeed, the literature on policy feedback clearly shows that the *modalities* of social policy delivery are central for enhancing or undermining individuals' self-perception as citizens (Dósa, 2018). Establishing the socioeconomic preconditions of political equality then requires articulating redistribution and recognition, whereby the focus is on promoting citizens' equal respect (Anderson, 1999). In other words, not only social policy outcomes but also *processes* are of fundamental importance in order to promote capabilities. Burchardt and Vizard (2011) highlight this point, emphasizing the importance of the treatment dimension (where the focus is on immunity from lack of dignity and respect) and the autonomy dimension (where the focus is on choice and control in relation to critical decisions that affect a person's life) in policy interventions.

This section thus considers the process aspect of freedom, which focuses on the process of social policy formulation rather than on social policy (desired) outcomes. From this perspective, the importance of democracy in the CA influences not only the goals but also the policy-making process itself, which requires treating social policy as a political–democratic object.

This is in line also with Bifulco and Mozzana (2011), who argue that one central criterion for establishing whether, and the extent to which, state intervention is capacitating is the degree of democratic deliberation involved in the process. Thus, state action focused on individuals' capabilities should, in order to define and promote the common good, rely on public deliberation.

In other words, the CA requires conceiving of individuals as citizens not only at the 'end', as a desired outcome of social policy, but also during the whole process of formulating, implementing and evaluating social policy itself. This framework emphasizes the importance of taking effective account of citizens' views and values.

In this context, the difference between the CA and the SI perspective on welfare reform is very significant (Laruffa, 2019). Indeed, SI largely relies on a 'technocratic' approach, whereby scientific evidence is purported to provide the normative basis for formulating welfare reform proposals. The latter are framed as necessary steps, required by the new conditions of a highly competitive and globalized 'knowledge-based economy'. In this perspective, reform is presented as a value-free process of adaption to a changed world, a matter of 'modernization', whereby scientific knowledge about current socioeconomic trends appears to be a sufficient informational basis for formulating welfare reform proposals without the need for any further political discussion.

The problem with this view is that it suffers from a new kind of paternalism, where experts act as the exclusive holders of relevant knowledge, thus neglecting the importance of public deliberation in forming, and possibly changing, individual and collective preferences about what should be pursued. This may in turn undermine citizens' capacity to aspire and imagine more emancipatory futures, promoting instead processes of adaptive preferences and adaptations to the status quo. Indeed, institutions that do not develop individuals' capability for voice risk promoting adaptive preferences (Bonvin and Farvaque, 2005). In contrast, the 'receiver–doer–judge' model inspired by the capability perspective (Bonvin and Laruffa, 2018) emphasizes not only that the three dimensions are equally important and no trade-off is allowed between them (for example, a lack of political agency cannot be compensated with increasing welfare benefits, expanding service provision or making social policy more employment-friendly) but also that these dimensions are deeply interconnected. For example, in the field of employment policies, the enhancement of 'capability for work' involves the freedom to have a job one has reason to value, which requires taking into account people's values and thus their 'voice' (Bonvin, 2012). In other words, what constitutes a 'valuable' job cannot be defined once and for all exclusively by experts but demands taking into account the values and voices of the people involved. In this view, a proper implementation of the 'receiver' and 'doer' dimensions within social policies is conditional upon a due consideration of the 'judge' dimension.

These insights were implemented in the context of the EU-funded research project Re-InVEST, which aimed to rethink the SI paradigm from a capability perspective. In this context, instead of focusing on the economic impact of social policy, as SI all too often does, the project insisted on its potential in promoting individuals' capabilities, rights and wellbeing. Moreover, in order to avoid the technocratic or expertocratic trap, this project included not only academics but also civil society organizations (NGOs and trade unions) and, through a participatory-action-research methodology (Hearne and Murphy, 2019), vulnerable and marginalized social groups. The project thus aimed not only at producing scientific research outputs but also at realizing different 'actions', such as public events or parliamentary hearings, with a view to engaging with the public sphere and possibly influencing the political agenda.

Hence, a methodology was adopted that allowed the professional knowledge of the civil society organizations to be merged with the academic knowledge produced by scientific research and the knowledge of citizens themselves, which they derive from their lived experience. The goal was to establish 'knowledge alliances' (Novy, 2012) with a view to co-constructing knowledge and policies. In this context, social scientists are invited to play less the role of experts than that of facilitators of deliberative democracy, strengthening the voice of marginalized groups in the public debate on welfare reform. The contention is that social policies should also be conceived as 'knowledge alliances' where the lived experience of vulnerable people is considered as an adequate informational basis (among others) for the design, implementation and evaluation of social policies.

Conclusion

In the recent phase, often dominated by austerity and welfare cuts, promoting a 'productivist' vision of the 'social' seems to be a valuable strategy for encouraging the political and economic elites to 'invest' in the 'social'. However, this strategy is not without risks. In particular, emphasizing the economic benefits of social policy entails the economization and de-politicization of the 'social', whereby social policy can be reduced to a technocratic exercise of calculating the costs and benefits of social interventions in order to then implement those that have been assessed as the most efficient.

This chapter has developed an alternative perspective on the 'social' based on Amartya Sen's CA. This framework counters both the economization and the de-politicization of the 'social'. Rather than the economic consequences of social policy, the model considers the 'final ends' of public action, which requires a democratic debate on the 'good society'.

Given the central importance of democratic deliberation in this approach, it has been argued that social policy should be framed as an enabling conversion factor of democracy, and assessed against its capacity to perform this task. This has two dimensions. On the outcome side, social policy should support the conversion of the formal right to political participation, which in a democracy is equally distributed among the population, into an effective (or real) right. The goal here is to reduce 'political poverty' and participatory inequalities. On the process side, social policy itself should be an object of democratic deliberation rather than technocratic management. This demands taking account of citizens' values and aspirations at all stages of the policy process, from the formulation and implementation of policy until its evaluation.

Merging the outcomes-oriented and the process-oriented perspectives, enabling social policies (as external conversion factors) can be said to promote capabilities both during the implementation process and as an outcome of this process. This means that they:

- successfully combine with internal conversion factors, complementing them or compensating possible individual deficits in order to promote capabilities, including the capability for democratic citizenship, and with a special focus on challenging patterns of inequality;
- nourish people's 'capacity to aspire' and 'sense of entitlement', thereby contrasting the phenomenon of adaptive preferences and creating a culture of rights and participation;
- rely on public discussion rather than (solely) on 'experts' for defining the 'common good' and the goals to be pursued by enabling institutions themselves;
- treat individuals with respect and recognition.

In conclusion, framing social policy as an enabling conversion factor of democracy, and as a democratic object itself, has many important implications for tackling inequality and promoting social sustainability. Clearly, all issues involved in this reframing of the 'social' as a political–democratic matter cannot be tackled in this short contribution. However, it is hoped that these reflections will encourage further discussion on the possibility, and on the modalities, of moving beyond an economized and de-politicized view of 'the social' in favour of a more engaged democratic and deliberative approach to welfare reform.

References

Anderson, E. (1999) 'What Is the Point of Equality?', *Ethics* 109(2): 287–337.

Anderson, E. (2003) 'Sen, Ethics, and Democracy', *Feminist Economics*, 9(2–3): 239–61.

Appadurai, A. (2004) 'The Capacity to Aspire: Culture and the Terms of Recognition', in V. Rao and M. Walton (ed) *Culture and Public Action*, Palo Alto, CA: Stanford University Press, 59–84.

Bifulco, L. and Mozzana, C. (2011) 'La dimensione sociale delle capacità: fattori di conversione, istituzioni e azione pubblica' [The social dimension of capabilities: conversion factors, institutions and public action], *Rassegna Italiana di Sociologia*, 3: 399–416.

Bohman, J. (1997) 'Deliberative Democracy and Effective Social Freedoms: Capabilities, Resources, and Opportunities', in J. Bohman and W. Rehg (eds) *Deliberative Democracy: Essays on Reason and Politics*, Cambridge, MA: MIT Press, 321–48.

Bonoli, G., Cantillon, B. and Van Lancker, W. (2017) 'Social Investment and the Matthew Effect: Limits to a Strategy', in A. Hemerijck (ed) *The Uses of Social Investment*, Oxford: Oxford University Press, 66–76.

Bonvin, J.-M. (2012) 'Individual Working Lives and Collective Action: An Introduction to Capability for Work and Capability for Voice', *Transfer: European Review of Labour and Research*, 18(1): 9–18.

Bonvin, J.-M. and Farvaque, N. (2005) 'What Informational Basis for Assessing Job-Seekers? Capabilities vs. Preferences', *Review of Social Economy*, 63(2): 269–89.

Bonvin, J.-M. and Laruffa, F. (2018) 'Human Beings as Receivers, Doers and Judges. The Anthropological Foundations of Sustainable Public Action in the Capability Approach', *Community, Work and Family* 21(5): 502–18.

Bonvin, J.-M. and Laruffa, F. (2019) 'Education as Investment? A Comparison of the Capability and Social Investment Approaches to Education Policy', in M. A. Yerkes, J. Javornik and A. Kurowska (eds) *Social Policy and the Capability Approach: Concepts, Measurement and Application*, Bristol: Policy Press, 19–39.

Burchardt, T. and Vizard, P. (2011) '"Operationalizing"the Capability Approach as a Basis for Equality and Human Rights Monitoring in Twenty-First-Century Britain', *Journal of Human Development and Capabilities*, 12(1): 91–119.

Chiappero-Martinetti, E. C. and Salardi, P. (2008) 'Well-being Process and Conversion Factors: An Estimation', Human Development, Capability and Poverty International Research Centre Working Paper Series, no 3, https://pdfs.semanticscholar.org/e524/a21d0ae 7f06c12bd3de824d53cb4e5edd7ce.pdf?_ga=2.77856407.20553976 09.1582312575-892120130.1575313478.

Clarke, J. (2004) 'Dissolving the Public Realm? The Logics and Limits of Neo-liberalism', *Journal of Social Policy*, 33(1): 27–48.

Crocker, D. (2006) 'Sen and Deliberative Democracy', in A. Kaufman (ed) *Capabilities Equality: Basic Issues and Problems*, New York: Routledge, 155–97.

Deeming, C. and Smyth, P. (2015) 'Social Investment after Neoliberalism: Policy Paradigms and Political Platforms', *Journal of Social Policy*, 44(2): 297–318.

Deeming, C. and Smyth, P. (2018) 'Social Investment, Inclusive Growth That Is Sustainable and the New Global Social Policy', in C. Deeming and P. Smyth (eds) *Reframing Global Social Policy: Social Investment for Sustainable and Inclusive Growth*, Bristol: Policy Press, 11–44.

Dósa, M. (2018) 'Welfare and Citizenship: The Case for a Democratic Approach to the Welfare State', *Intersections*, 4(1): 45–65.

Esping-Andersen, G. (ed) (2002) *Why We Need a New Welfare State*, Oxford: Oxford University Press.

Foucault, M. (2008) *The Birth of Biopolitics: Lectures at the Collège de France, 1978–79*, Basingstoke and New York: Palgrave Macmillan.

Graefe, P. (2006) 'The Social Economy and the American Model Relating New Social Policy Directions to the Old', *Global Social Policy*, 6(2): 197–219.

Hearne, R. and Murphy, M. (2019) *Participatory Action Research: A Human Rights and Capability Approach*, Maynooth: Maynooth University Press.

Hemerijck, A. (2013) *Changing Welfare States*, Oxford: Oxford University Press.

Hemerijck, A. (2018) 'Social Investment as a Policy Paradigm', *Journal of European Public Policy*, 25(6): 810–27.

Hobson, B., Fahlen, S. and Takacs, J. (2011) 'Agency and Capabilities to Achieve a Work–Life Balance: A Comparison of Sweden and Hungary', *Social Politics: International Studies in Gender, State & Society*, 18(2): 168–98.

Jayasuriya, K. (2006) *Statecraft, Welfare, and the Politics of Inclusion*, Basingstoke and New York: Palgrave Macmillan.

Jenson, J. (2010) 'Diffusing Ideas for After Neoliberalism: The Social Investment Perspective in Europe and Latin America', *Global Social Policy*, 10(1): 59–84.

Jenson, J. (2017) 'Developing and Spreading a Social Investment Perspective: The World Bank and OECD compared', in A. Hemerijck (ed) *The Uses of Social Investment*, Oxford: Oxford University Press, 207–15.

Laruffa, F. (2019) 'Social Welfare Discourses and Scholars' Ethical-Political Dilemmas in the Crisis of Neoliberalism', *Ethics and Social Welfare*, 13(4): 323–39.

Levitas, R. (1996) 'The Concept of Social Exclusion and the New Durkheimian Hegemony', *Critical Social Policy*, 16(46): 5–20.

Madra, Y. and Adaman, F. (2014) 'Neoliberal Reason and Its Forms: De-Politicisation Through Economisation', *Antipode*, 46(3): 691–716.

Mahon, R. (2010) 'After Neo-Liberalism? The OECD, the World Bank and the Child', *Global Social Policy*, 10(2): 172–92.

Marx, P. and Nguyen, C. G. (2018) 'Political Participation in European Welfare States: Does Social Investment Matter?', *Journal of European Public Policy*, 25(6): 912–43.

Morel, N., Palier, B. and Palme, J. (eds) (2012) *Towards a Social Investment Welfare State? Ideas, Policies and Challenges*, Bristol: Policy Press.

Nambiar, S. (2013) 'Capabilities, Conversion Factors and Institutions', *Progress in Development Studies*, 13(3): 221–30.

Nolan, B. (2013) 'What Use Is "Social Investment"?', *Journal of European Social Policy*, 23(5): 459–68.

Novy, A. (2012) '"Unequal Diversity" as a Knowledge Alliance: An Encounter of Paulo Freire's Dialogical Approach and Transdisciplinarity', *Multicultural Education & Technology Journal*, 6(3): 137–48.

Offe, C. (2014) 'Participatory Inequality in the Austerity State: A Supply Side Approach', Working Paper der DFG-KollegforscherInnengruppe Postwachstumsgesellschaften, No 1/2014, Jena, www.kolleg-postwachstum.de/sozwgmedia/dokumente/WorkingPaper/wp1_2014.pdf.

Olson, K. (2006) *Reflexive Democracy: Political Equality and the Welfare State*, Cambridge, MA: MIT Press.

Richardson, H. (2015) 'Using Final Ends for the Sake of Better Policy-Making', *Journal of Human Development and Capabilities*, 16(2): 161–72.

Sen, A. (1999) *Development as Freedom*, New York: Knopf.

Sen, A. (2009) *The Idea of Justice*, Cambridge, MA: Belknap Press.

Taylor-Gooby, P. (2008) 'The New Welfare State Settlement in Europe', *European Societies*, 10(1): 3–24.

Vandenbroucke, F., Hemerijck, A. and Palier, B. (2011) 'The EU Needs a Social Investment Pact', OSE Paper Series, Opinion Paper 5, www.ose.be/files/OpinionPaper5_Vandenbroucke-Hemerijk-Palier_2011.pdf.

Van de Werfhorst, H. G. (2007) *Vocational Education and Active Citizenship Behavior in Cross-National Perspective*, AIAS Working Paper 62, Amsterdam: University of Amsterdam.

Wolff, J. and De-Shalit, A. (2007) *Disadvantage*, Oxford: Oxford University Press.

5

The social dimension of sustainable development at the UN: from Brundtland to the SDGs

Iris Borowy

Introduction

Sustainable development (SD) is widely accepted as a form of development we, as humankind, should but do not have at the moment. Discussing SD, therefore, is not discussing reality but plans for desired changes based on perceived reality. Depending on who does the planning, perceptions of reality as well as desires for change may differ. This chapter discusses some of those plans with regard to the 'social' dimension of SD.

The social forms one of the cornerstones of the standard tripartite system of SD, consisting of environmental, economic and social dimensions (Elkington, 1997), often, in Wikipedia and elsewhere, illustrated as a triangular graph, with the three dimensions occupying three corners or overlapping bubbles. Recently, it has been complemented by the cultural dimension (Magee et al, 2012). This concept goes back to the Brundtland Commission (officially World Commission on Environment and Development) and its landmark report *Our Common Future*, published in 1987. It famously defined sustainable development as 'development that meets the needs of the present without compromising the ability of future generations to meet their own needs' (WCED, 1987: 43). This often-cited reference to intergenerational justice has shaped the popular understanding of SD, while inter-regional (social) justice has received a lot less attention. As just one case in point, there is no section entitled 'social' in a 2014 exhaustive, four-volume publication on *Sustainable Development*, and topics that could be interpreted as social are conspicuously under-represented (Blewitt, 2014).

This relative neglect is in contrast to the intent of the Brundtland Commission, whose members left little doubt that they considered the social a central component of SD, inextricably linked to economic and environmental concerns. Thus, in a passage cited much less frequently, the report went on to state that this definition entails 'the concept of "needs", in particular the essential needs of the world's poor, to which overriding priority should be given', as well as the concept of environmental limitations (WCED, 1987: 43). In addition, the report insisted that the times in which human activities and effects could be 'neatly compartmentalized within nations, within sectors (energy, agriculture, trade), and within broad areas of concern (environment, economics, social)' were over (WCED, 1987: 4). The Commission clearly meant the social dimension to be as important as the others, and human needs to be the manifestation of this social dimension.

The report never explicitly defined what those future 'needs' would be. This vagueness was a strength of the report, since it focused on the universally true principle, leaving it up to different stakeholders to define what this would mean for their time, place and circumstances, and arguably 'consensus on a vague concept was better than disagreement over a sharply defined one' (Daly, 1996: 2). However, vagueness was also its weakness, since it facilitated an appropriation of the idea by various interests (Redclift, 2005), leading Jim MacNeill, Secretary-General and moving force of the Brundtland Commission, to quip that ' "infinity" was the ever-expanding number of self-serving interpretations of sustainable development' (MacNeill, 2013). Few attempts have been made, so far, to establish a more precise, broadly acceptable definition. One suggestion, published in a volume specifically dedicated to the social and economic dimensions of SD, remains modest, explaining that a 'socially sustainable system must achieve fairness in distribution and opportunity, adequate provision of social services, including health and education, gender equity, and political accountability and participation' (Harris and Goodwin, 2001: xxix). But who gets to decide whether this is an adequate list? Other people and groups have certainly made different choices.

While opinions may differ on what exactly should be included in the social component of SD, the connection itself is not difficult to draw. Poverty and social exclusion act both as drivers and as the ostensible justification for further economic growth. However, endless economic growth is clearly incompatible with an environmentally sustainable world. In reverse logic, this means that an environmentally sustainable world, with resource extractions, waste production and pollution on a level that leaves the life-support systems intact for many generations of humans, requires an end to ongoing material growth, which, in turn, requires a situation in which communities around the world have access to sufficient goods and services for their wellbeing. In short: no environmental sustainability without socioeconomic sustainability. In a world in which the material provisions of parts of the world population are not yet met but the global system already depletes existing resources beyond regeneration capacity, the obvious answer would be increased economic redistribution, not a popular idea among those people who would have to give up part of their material wealth (Borowy, 2017, 2019).

This dilemma tied into the principal question of what was even the suitable frame of reference to discuss the social (or economic) dimension of SD: local, regional or global? While many social issues are experienced locally, they are often the outcome of much larger dynamics, which, in turn, are open to different interpretations. The most important difference in this context doubtless involved two contradictory worldviews. Simplifying what was admittedly a more nuanced situation, policy makers, negotiators and regular people in different parts of the world had distinct approaches to developmental shortcomings: those from high-income countries tended to view industrial development as a global process which had reached different places to different degrees and which, though largely beneficial, needed to be modified in order to address increasingly serious manifestations of environmental destruction. The issues showed up locally or globally, but underlying processes such as industrialization, bringing jobs and improving living standards while causing air and water pollution, was global and needed global responses. Those from low-income countries tended to view recent economic development as a function of imperialism and ongoing power asymmetries, which had enabled some countries to amass wealth at the expense of others and whose discriminating structures were still in place in the form of unequal trade, finance and political systems. In this view, the appropriate framework was not one global society, caught in various local forms of a single challenge, but two antagonistic societies, of which one had to defend itself against the encroachments of the other (Rivarola and Appelqvist, 2011). Depending on the view chosen, SD might require important transformations in one, global society, or in the interaction between two separate, potentially antagonistic societies. Or, put more bluntly, the question was: who was responsible for environmental, economic and social problems, and who, consequently, would have to change?

If SD was necessary to save the humankind from self-destruction, and a functioning social component was necessary to make SD work, saving the planet would require an agreement on the following questions:

- What does the social component of SD consist of?
- Is a one-world or fragmented-world approach more just, acceptable and useful or, in other words, who is perceived as needing to change?

This chapter explores how these questions were addressed at critical junctures of the SD debates between the 1970s and today.

The social dimension of SD before Brundtland

While some elements of sustainability thinking arguably date back centuries debates leading to the modern SD concept began with doubts regarding the benefits of unlimited industrialization and economic growth for the environment and human lives in the 1960s (Mebratu, 1998). Several widely read publications focused on the difficulty of reconciling economic development with environmental conservation, but some such as *The Affluent Society* by John Kenneth Galbraith, *Toward a Steady-State Economy* by Herman Daly or *Small Is Beautiful* by Ernst Friedrich Schumacher specifically considered the ramifications of different economic pathways for normal people's lives. Though they differed substantially in recommendations, they shared an outlook that the continuation of a system based on constant increases in production and consumption would weaken rather than strengthen most people's wellbeing in terms of health and life satisfaction and that future development should be based on different economic structures as well as different values and principles. These books were mostly written by academics of the Anglo-Saxon world, and they were read and discussed predominantly in North America and Europe, that is, in regions that were sufficiently wealthy to debate consumption as a problem instead of merely a way to satisfy urgent material needs. Thus, the idea that there might be a point at which economies produced enough so that further growth should be used to create more public goods such as education and healthcare (Galbraith), or at some point more economic growth created more problems of pollution and inequality than benefits, thereby becoming uneconomic (Daly) and that when people had what they needed they would be happier focusing on spiritual rather than material needs (Schumacher) resonated with industrialized societies.

Meanwhile, decolonization and the entry of many newly independent countries in the UN brought the topic of global inequality to the forefront of international discussions. Here, the perspective was not one of superfluous material provision, but of continued poverty in the Global South because of perceived continued Northern control over global trade and financial regulations.

The mainstream response to this was the organization of development assistance, treating the societies in Africa and Asia like a part of the world that supposedly needed help to overcome its development deficiencies through bilateral or multilateral development assistance. One initiative to review this process was the Pearson Commission, established by the World Bank in 1968 to discuss the past record and future strategies of international development. While generally positive about the record of development efforts, it did see the continued socioeconomic disparity between different parts of the world as a problem and called on high-income countries to provide 0.7 per cent of their Gross National Product (GNP) as development aid, a figure that was soon after adopted by the UN General Assembly (Commission, 1969; UNGA, 1970). The idea entailed only a minimal element of redistribution, and it was perfectly compatible with the mainstream industrialization development model. There was no binding agreement, and 50 years later industrialized countries had provided less than half of what would have been needed to meet the target of 0.7 per cent GNP (Shah, 2014). But the declaration and the ensuing practice did establish enough of a precedent to establish the principle that rich countries had a moral responsibility to provide financial support for the poor. There was a one-world aspect to it, in that, in theory, such assistance should be forthcoming simply because different societies coexisted in the same world, unrelated to other interests. But the stronger attitude was one of a fragmented world in which 'under-developed' countries needed to change in order to become what 'developed' countries already were. Pope Paul VI exemplified this attitude in an encyclical letter of 1967, arguing:

> Given the increasing needs of the under-developed countries, it should be considered quite normal for an advanced country to devote a part of its production to meet their needs, and to train teachers, engineers, technicians and scholars prepared to put their knowledge and their skill at the disposal of less fortunate peoples. (Pope Paul IV, 1967)

His reference to education formed a standard element of a social approach to development.

In early 1972, preparations for the UN Conference on the Human Environment (UNCHE) in Stockholm that summer demonstrated the difficulty of reconciling concerns about environmental limits, spurred by the environmental movement in the North, with demands for changes in income distribution, supported in Southern countries, and economic growth, coveted by all participants. Above all, negotiations revealed the profound distrust of Southern governments, who suspected that this new-found interest in the environmental repercussions of industrialization might be a thinly disguised neo-colonialist strategy to prevent Southern countries from gaining the material affluence already enjoyed in the North. These fears were reinforced when news about the *Limits to Growth* study suggested that Northern experts were about to change the rules of global economics, postulating limits to industrial activities, which would obstruct the development of Southern countries more than that of the already industrialized North (Borowy, 2014). Thus, the conference report, while acknowledging the burdens of economic growth, explicitly rejected the idea of a non-growing economy. However, the Action Plan for the Human Environment included recommendations regarding a better distribution of environmentally relevant scientific knowledge and technology (UN, 1973: 45, 5 and passim). This redistributory approach was substantially reinforced during negotiations for a New International Economic Order (NIEO), which followed at the United Nations soon after (UNGA, 1974). Proposals repeated the demand for easier technology transfer but also included improving the terms of trade, gaining better access to international transportation and to markets of industrialized countries, establishing a code of conduct for transnational corporations, increasing development assistance and reducing the debt burden of low-income countries (UNGA, 1974). After several years of fruitless negotiations under UN auspices between demanding Southern and stonewalling Northern delegates, the initiative faded. But their demands and the underlying concept of Northern policies perceived as tied to Southern poverty remained and would repeatedly re-emerge in future negotiations.

Thus, it clearly served as model for the last chapter of the World Conservation Strategy (WCS), published in 1980 by the International Union for Conservation of Nature (IUCN) and the United Nations Environment Programme (UNEP). In addition to key demands of the NIEO, including the increase of development aid to the 0.7 per cent of GNP, a reformation of the international monetary system and an acceleration of disarmament, it also contained references to social lives. Crucially, it included the demand that redistribution should entail the reduction of consumption in industrialized countries in that 'the affluent constrain their demands on resources, and preferably reduce them, shifting some of their wealth to assisting the deprived.' As social goals the text also called for:

> 'people-centred' development, that achieves a wider distribution of benefits to whole populations (better nutrition, health, education, family welfare, fuller employment, greater income security, protection from environmental degradation); that makes fuller use of people's labour, capabilities, motivations and creativity; and is more sensitive to cultural heritage. (IUCN, 1980: 20)

The chapter was entitled 'Towards Sustainable Development', the first time this expression appeared in print in the report by an international organization. Clearly, social topics were considered an integral component of this ideal together with robust stipulations regarding North–South redistribution.

However, it was only after the Brundtland Commission issued its report that SD grew from an obscure idea known to a handful of people within the development community to an everyday expression routinely used in academia, advertising and politics and, arguably, widely accepted as an aspirational goal for individual, national and global behaviour.

Framing the social dimension by the Brundtland Commission

The central task of the Brundtland Commission was 'to propose long-term environmental strategies for achieving sustainable development by the year 2000 and beyond' and to suggest ways in which environmental concern could be 'translated into greater co-operation among developing countries and between countries at different stages of economic and social development' (WCED, 1987: ix). It was a tall order, not only because of the mounting environmental challenges but also because Commission members represented different worldviews. The commissioners came from 22 different countries:[1] seven people came from the rich OECD countries, four from communist countries, and 11 from countries that could be grouped under 'developing countries'. Over a period of almost three years commissioners met eight times to discuss relevant issues, based on reports and draft chapters that experts in the field had written.

Controversies appeared throughout about the degree to which solutions would follow a one-world rather than a North–South approach and the degree to which recommendation should address redistributive aspects. These differences showed when, at one of the earliest meetings, several delegates from the Global South suggested that Northern countries should provide financial compensation for the exploitative policies to which Southern countries had been subjected in the past. The demand appeared bizarre and patently counterproductive to Northern commissioners and was dropped as being unhelpful for the Commission agenda (Borowy, 2014: 60).

This lengthy process of commissioning draft reports, discussing controversial topics within the Commission, with experts and in public meetings, and revising the texts through further discussions, eventually produced an eminently rich report which touched on a long list of political, economic and social issues. Among them was the whole repertoire of standard social policy questions, with whole chapters dedicated to population, food security, energy, urban lives and peaceful coexistence, and in addition there were sub-chapters on health, the commons and on managing distribution and mobility. There were not many social topics that were not at least mentioned in passing. Further highlighting the importance of social policies, the report pointed out that economic and social development could and 'should be mutually reinforcing' in that money used for education and health could increase human productivity, while the resulting income could 'accelerate social development by providing opportunities for underprivileged groups or by spreading education more rapidly' (WCED, 1987: 54). As crucial social desirables, the text cited the improvement of the position of women in society, the protection of vulnerable groups and the promotion of local participation in decision-making processes (WCED, 1987: 38). The final report recommended the classical series of social interventions including public health programmes (notably regarding malaria and nutrition), population control programmes that raise the status of women, expanding education and empowering vulnerable groups (WCED, 1987: 103–16). None of these were particularly controversial, and all mainly referred to required changes in the Global South.

By contrast, the question of social justice was far more sensitive. As a measure against inequality the text called for economic growth combined with 'vigorous redistributive policies' (WCED, 1987: 50). Actually, the specific recommendation was only mildly vigorous, limited to future income increases, which should disproportionately go to low-income people, and merely within a country. It was understood that more radical recommendations would not be acceptable in industrialized countries (Borowy, 2014: 127), so nothing was mentioned about a possible redistribution of existing income, or of wealth, or about financial transfers from high- to low-income countries. Still, having a blueprint for some form of redistribution at all potentially opened the door for more far-reaching ideas. One avenue for North–South redistribution was through automatic fund raising, arguably the most innovative feature, though it was first presented at the UN Conference on Human Settlements (HABITAT) in 1976. It meant taxing the exploitation of international commons, like the oceans or Antarctica, or international financial transactions, such as IMF drawing rights. Also, implicitly but clearly, the text spelled out the need for high-income countries to adapt their lifestyles to a level of consumption to which all people in the world could aspire, though it did not go beyond mild exhortation (WCED, 1987: 57).

Seeing that some topics would be unacceptable and some dilemmas unsolvable, commissioners focused on those aspects on which they could agree: on environmental pressures resulting from poverty, requiring poverty reduction, and on the need for more modern, more environmentally friendly technology. By contrast, they downplayed the environmental pressures which resulted from wealth and from high-consumption lifestyles. This strategy led to a certain pro-growth bias, which observers criticized afterwards (Sachs, 1993). A few controversial issues that had come up during discussions were downplayed or omitted, notable with regard to high consumption levels in rich societies, risk of advanced technology, such as its tendency to increase labour productivity and, thereby, increase unemployment in low-income countries (Borowy, 2014: 145–7). At the same time, the production process produced a compromise worldview which endorsed, on the one hand, a Northern one-world view while at the same time highlighting a Southern emphasis on poverty and consumption inequality. Thus, the report emphasized in its first words of the first chapter:

> The Earth is one but the world is not. We all depend on one biosphere for sustaining our lives. Yet, each community, each country, strives for survival and prosperity with little regard for its impact on others. Some consume the Earth's resources at a rate that would leave little for future generations. Others, many more in number, consume far too little and live with the prospect of hunger, squalor, disease, and early death. (WCED, 1987: 27)

Basically, the Brundtland Commission argued that unlimited consumption by one part of the world population was responsible for suffering, disease and early death in another part, and that reframing the world as a unified political entity was the way to stop this from happening. At its core, this argument was not about poverty, it was about wealth, (in-)equality and global *social* policy.

The reception and reinterpretation of SD in recent years

Not surprisingly, these sensitive elements received short shrift in the otherwise remarkable response which the report had in virtually all UN organizations and numerous other organizations, national governments and NGOs. Out of a broad range of issues and recommendations, stakeholders tended to focus on those more compatible with their interests, often the supposed compatibility of poverty reduction, economic growth and environmental protection (Borowy, 2014: 178–96).

Obviously, these issues would not disappear but would emerge again at the 1992 UN Conference on Environment and Development (UNCED) at Rio de Janeiro, reflecting both the 20-year anniversary of the Stockholm Conference and recommendations of the Brundtland Commission.

The context could not be more different from that of the Brundtland Commission: rather than a small group of dedicated individuals, sincerely dedicated to coming to an agreement in the interest of the general good, UNCED was a large-scale conference, bringing together representatives from 175 nations, including 110 heads of states, 1,500 officially accredited NGOs and 7,000 journalists (Johnson, 1993: 5). Arguably the most important, though not the only, outcome was Agenda 21, a detailed blueprint of proposed policy changes and their estimated price tags.

The tension between industrialized and low-income countries has often been described (Palmer, 1992; Johnson, 1993). The vision of UNCED was that of 'global bargain' whereby a real commitment by G77 countries to shift their development onto an environmentally responsible path (including rainforest preservation) would correspond to a real commitment by industrialized countries to help finance such a shift (Johnson, 1993: 5). It was a good plan but bound to fail as soon as one side was unwilling to agree to concessions. Disagreements centred on various issues, above all the question of finances. Low-income countries expected financial assistance for SD beyond the regular development assistance, as well as a fulfilment of the two-decades-old promise of Northern countries to provide 0.7 per cent of their gross domestic product (GDP) as development aid. Industrialized countries, above all the US under President George Bush, were unwilling to make far-reaching commitments, especially without any anti-corruption measures or any control over how these funds would be spent. And, of course, these debates masked more deep-seated disagreements regarding who was to blame for existing environmental and socioeconomic problems.

Regarding the social dimension, the most noteworthy aspect may be the degree to which Agenda 21 took a collective approach. In addition to several chapters dedicated to already well-rehearsed topics of social concern, health, 'demographic dynamics' (meaning population growth), 'human settlements' (urbanization), poverty and consumption, another section addressed the roles of major social groups, notably women, children, youth, indigenous groups, workers, NGOs, farmers and business as well as the scientific communities. These chapters were remarkably uncontroversial, suggesting that this was either an overlooked avenue through which social progress within an SD context might have been made or, more probably, that the framing of these chapters was too general to appear threatening to anybody. Other aspects of social change proved controversial enough. The Vatican had tried, successfully, to limit all references to contraception but could not prevent some clear language as to the connection between family planning and SD (Johnson, 1993: 157–65). But the most bitter disagreement was about the role of consumption. Representatives of OECD countries, above all the US, flatly refused to consider changes in their high-consumption lifestyles or even to acknowledge they were part of the problem. Nevertheless, the language in Agenda 21 was remarkably clear:

> Poverty and environmental degradation are closely interrelated. While poverty results in certain kinds of environmental stress, the major cause of the continued deterioration of the global environment is the unsustainable pattern of consumption and production, particularly in industrialized countries, which is a matter of grave concern, aggravating poverty and imbalances. (Johnson, 1993, §4.3: 152)

Consequently, Agenda 21 explicitly included 'achieving sustainable consumption patterns' in its list of recommended actions (Johnson, 1993, §4.8: 153). However, if Northern countries were unwilling to curtail their economic activities, Southern countries were similarly unwilling to accept limits to their economic development, including the unlimited use of resources on their land. In Article 33.3, Agenda 21 firmly embraced wealth as the priority development goal, citing 'economic growth, social development and poverty eradication' as 'the first and overriding priorities in developing countries' and 'essential to meeting national and global sustainability objectives' (Johnson, 1993: 451). Some potentially transformative proposals of the Brundtland Report were lost. For instance, the idea of automatic financing had shrunk to a vague reference to 'innovative approaches' to funding mechanisms in a single paragraph (Johnson, 1993, §33.1: 450).

Nevertheless, even the very subdued references to limited consumption and the need for changes in the global economic distribution were sufficient to alarm right-wing groups, mostly in the US, who began attacking sustainable development and Agenda 21 as a global ploy to rob middle class people in industrialized countries of their property and freedom. For example, the Post-Sustainability Institute, headed by Rosa Koire, warned that Agenda 21 aimed at defunding communities and reducing the independence of Americans (Post-Sustainability, undated), while Heidenreich, on 'tv.disclose', pointed out that it was the UN's little-publicized plan to depopulate 95 per cent of the world by 2030 (Heidenreich, 2017). Revelations of this sort have been picked up by other conspiracy theorists whose YouTube submissions can appear involuntarily comical to the unconvinced (see for example American TruthFl, 2020). They have not grown into a large, mainstream movement, but they have managed to activate sufficient conspiracy concern to get several US state legislatures to outlaw Agenda 21 (SPLC, 2014).

UNCED was just one of a series of 11 UN conferences that, between 1990 and 1992, addressed topics of social concern, including human settlements, the lives of women and children, human rights or, in 1995, 'social development'. Most of these meetings came with calls for financial assistance from industrialized countries. It was not a good time for such calls: the end of European communism had shifted attention of donors towards the collapsed Eastern European economies, and ministries of development were losing ground in industrialized countries. By 1995, the perceived avalanche of conferences with mounting financial demands provoked an initiative by the Development Assistance Committee of the OECD to translate these various demands into a manageable format. The result was a list of seven developmental goals, which formed the nucleus of the Millennium Development Goals (MDGs) of a global initiative jump-started at the UN Millennium

Summit in 2000. The OECD goals were largely accepted as the programme, complemented merely by one additional goal from UN negotiations, to the detriment of much more far-reaching plans included in the Millennium Declaration presented by Kofi Annan (Borowy, 2015).

This process narrowed the comprehensive approach of SD to a few, specific questions of health and poverty reduction, goals everybody could agree on. In some ways, this change strengthened the position of social topics such as health, education or the empowerment of women. But it also reinterpreted development from a global concern to a component of a challenge related to Southern deficiencies. By 2005, this process had produced eight goals, measured by targets and indicators (Borowy, 2015). Of these goals, the first referred to poverty reduction, the second to education, the third to gender equality, and goals four through six to health issues. None of these were categorized as SD. Instead, goal seven referred to ensuring 'environmental sustainability', reflecting a restricted view of sustainability as a purely environmental concept. The choice of respective targets, again, reveals a focus on health issues (sanitation and drinking water) and a crucial but unquantifiable integration of 'principles of sustainable development into country policies and programmes', while some indicators (land covered by forest, per capita CO_2 emissions and species extinction) were clear markers of environmental limits. The question of distribution was, to some extent, addressed in goal eight, to 'develop a global partnership for development'. Its targets and indicators took up old NIEO demands of an 'open, rule-based, predictable, non-discriminatory trading and financial system' measured by the access low-income countries had to markets and in tariff reduction, in overall ODA and in ODA dedicated to social services. It also included debt management and universal access to essential drugs. They were the only part of the goals which involved high-income countries. More sensitive issues like consumption or automatic financing were excluded from the agenda (UN, undated a). For all practical purposes, the MDGs reflected an approach where high-income countries would assist low-income countries to change so as to outgrow their deficiencies.

Conceptually, this reductionist approach had something of a retrograde character. But it did put into motion a process in which global development was promoted, monitored and publicized to an unprecedented degree. While none of the goals were particularly new or radical, the precise manner in which they were defined in quantifiable terms and the rise of the internet as a globally accessible medium allowed the United Nations Development Programme

(UNDP), which became the central caretaker institution, to draw attention to successes and shortcomings like never before. For the first time in history, anybody with access to the internet could seemingly 'see' whether global development was going well or not. It was a massive transformation of the understanding of social life in the world, both for the high profile that social topics like health and female literacy achieved and for the way in which such knowledge distribution, in itself, became a social process.

In many ways, the outcome of the MDGs was impressive. Its final report, published in 2015, celebrated that several goals had been achieved and that for the rest there had been substantial improvements: the ratio of people living in extreme poverty, child mortality, material mortality, deaths from malaria and tuberculosis had all declined substantially. More than 2 billion people had gained access to improved sanitation, and the proportion of external debt service to export revenue in developing countries fell from 12 per cent in 2000 to 3 per cent in 2013. However, meanwhile, global CO_2 emissions had increased by over 50 per cent (UN, 2015). Even more disconcerting were the issues on which the report remained silent: 5 out of the 60 indicators originally agreed on (UN, undated a) were not mentioned. Virtually all addressed economic inequality: 1.2 (poverty ratio gap), 1.3 (share of poorest quintile in national consumption) and 1.4 (growth rate of GDP per person employed). Whether these issues were ignored because the numbers were considered too scarce, too unreliable or too controversial, or for another reason, remains unclear, but the silence indicates the sensitivity of the topic.

Adding a goal entitled 'sustainable' to the list of goals testifies to the degree to which this label had become a required entity in development activities. But this could not gloss over the fact that its restricted approach was a far cry from the one-world view that characterized SD. However, the format of non-binding but globally endorsed goals to which many governments as well as international organizations gave financial and political support was so convincing that in 2012, three years before the end of the MDGs and on the 20-year anniversary of UNCED, the governments of two Southern countries (Colombia and Guatemala) initiated a process for a new round of goals, this time with a decidedly larger horizon and a clearer one-world basis. This time, they were called Sustainable Development Goals (SDGs) (UN, undated b). While they copied the form of the MDGs, consisting of goals supported by targets to be measured by indicators, the breadth, focus and overall approach has been very different.

Rather than addressing development as something to be achieved by Southern countries, supposedly with the help of the industrialized world, they approach development as a global endeavour, in which all countries have a stake and a responsibility. So, while some goals predominantly address developmental requirements of countries in the South, such as hunger, education or sanitation, others are predominantly about requirements of high-income countries in the North, notably with regard to climate change, consumption patterns and global partnership.

A comparison of the social topics addressed over the course of four decades (Table 5.1) shows some continuities as well as some distinct differences. Health, education, poverty and women's rights are constant issues, whose importance for SD all initiatives recognize. Beyond that, interestingly, the profiles of the Brundtland report and of the SDGs are most similar, while Agenda 21 puts more emphasis on group-based activities and the MDGs pursue a relatively narrow approach. Thus, the SDGs can be regarded as an adoption of the Brundtland goals with the tools of the MDGs.

Table 5.1: Social goals

	Brundtland Report	Agenda 21	MDGs	SDGs
Children		✓	✓	
Consumption	✓	✓		✓
Demographic dynamics/population growth	✓			✓
Energy	✓			✓
Education	✓	✓	✓	✓
Farming/farmers	✓	✓		
Health	✓	✓	✓	✓
Hunger/food security	✓		✓	✓
Inequality	✓	✓		✓
Minorities		✓		
Peace	✓			✓
Poverty	✓	✓	✓	✓
Sanitation	✓		✓	✓
Urban lives/cities	✓			✓
Women	✓	✓	✓	✓
Workers		✓		

Finally, while the environmental part of SD looks rather bleak, its social component appears rosier; though progress in these fields has been uneven. Between the 1970s and today, core social indicators such as poverty levels, life expectancy or urban living conditions have almost universally improved, though the record is less clear in terms of inequality. While the spectacular rise of the middle class in China and, to a lesser extent, in other emerging economies like India and Brazil, has lowered the global Gini-coefficient, effectively making the world a more equal place, the difference between the very poor and the very rich has widened, as an obscenely disproportionate percentage of economic gains have gone to the top of global incomes (Milanovic, 2016). At the same time, with all other social indicators so closely linked to relative and absolute poverty levels, inequality remains the defining feature of development (UN, 2019: 3).

Conclusion

During the last 40 years SD has grown from an expression familiar only to a small group of development experts to one that produces half a billion hits when searched on Google. During the same period, its discourse has consistently included an important social component, albeit with changes in composition and degree. Several classic topics of social welfare, such as health, poverty or education, were already discussed in the 1970s, so that the Brundtland Commission could adopt, complement and systematize them. True to its understanding of the tripartite nature of SD in which the social entailed a key position, the Brundtland Commission discussed a long list of social topics, whose range was not reached again until the establishment of the SDGs 30 years later.

The defining topics of the SD negotiations have been poverty and inequality. While they seem tightly connected – a society with lots of very poor people is likely to also be very unequal since it is rare that everybody in society is very poor – the approach is actually quite different. Conceptually, poverty can be addressed in a fragmented world in which alleviation focuses specifically on the poor without changing the lives of other parts of society. Reducing inequality requires taking society as a whole into account, including and especially the circumstances of the wealthy. Consequently, the MDGs, which had originated largely in discussions within the OECD, focused on poverty and followed a fragmented world approach, which did not question the lives and policies in the Global North. However, a fragmented-world approach could also be attractive to low-income countries to buttress demands for development assistance and other compensatory payments.

In this sense, a one-world approach is politically, and psychologically, more demanding since all decisions have repercussions everywhere. The thrust of negotiating efforts is not so much a bargain in which different parts of the world supply different contributions, as was tried at Rio in 1992, as a recognition that in a shared one world there are no issues that concern only one part of the world. The sensitivity of this approach has been obvious with regard to consumption, whereby observers and activists have long argued that high consumption rates in the Global North was related to poverty and environmental degradation in the South, while delegates from industrialized countries have long downplayed or denied this connection. While the one-world approach was comparatively weak in the MDGs, it has returned strongly with the SDGs. If its global reach has not been enough to satisfy its supporters, it has been sufficient to trigger its enemies, as those who feel threatened by Agenda 21 have seamlessly shifted their attention to the SDGs (DeWeese, 2015). Nevertheless, the reason for the rise of the one-world paradigm seems more grounded in facts than in ideology: in a world in which formerly poor countries of the Global South have become wealthy, or at least modestly comfortable, and in which challenges of mass consumption, hazardous waste or energy are felt in similar ways in many places in many countries, it makes increasingly less sense to divide the world into two opposing camps. Thus, the strong demonstration of social connectedness of the SDGs stands in stark contrast to the growing nationalism evident around the world. One is tempted to see this as a competition between two strands that will shape the following decades: one of increasing political separation and another of increasing social connection. If that is true, SD, by contradicting nationalism, populism and parochialism, is an eminently political and social concept.

Note

[1] Norway, Italy, Saudi Arabia, Zimbabwe, Ivory Coast, Mexico, Germany, Sudan, Hungary, PR China, Canada, Colombia, Brazil, Japan, Guyana, USA, Algeria, Indonesia, Nigeria, India, the USSR and Yugoslavia.

References

American TruthFl (2020) *Agenda 21? The Plan to Depopulate 95% of the World by 2030*, www.youtube.com/watch?v=MKWgYOQnPBM.

Blewitt, J. (ed) (2014) *Sustainable Development*, Volumes I–IV, Abingdon: Routledge.

Borowy, I. (2014) *Defining Sustainable Development for Our Common Future: A History of the World Commission on Environment and Development (Brundtland Commission)*, Abingdon: Routledge.

Borowy, I. (2015) 'Negotiating International Development: The Making of the Millennium Development Goals', *Regions & Cohesion/ Regiones y Cohesión/Régions et Cohésion*, 5(3): 18–43.

Borowy, I. (2017) 'Sustainable Development in Brundtland and Beyond: How (Not) to Reconcile Material Wealth, Environmental Limits and Just Distribution', in E. Vaz, A. Melo and C. J. de Melo (eds) *Environmental History in the Making*, Volume I, New York: Springer, 91–108.

Borowy, J. (2019) 'Sustainability and Redistribution', in J. Meadowcroft, D. Banister, E. Holden, O. Langhelle, K. Linnerud and G. Gilpin (eds) *What's Next for Sustainable Development? Our Common Future at Thirty*, Cheltenham: Edward Elgar, 120–37.

Commission on International Development (1969) *Partners in Development*, London: Pall Mall Press.

Daly, H. (1996) *Beyond Growth*, Boston, MA: Beacon Press.

DeWeese, T. (2015) A New Agenda 21 Threatens our Way of Life, https://newswithviews.com/DeWeese/tom267.htm.

Elkington, J. (1997) *Cannibals with Forks: The Triple Bottom Line of 21st Century Business*, Oxford: Capstone.

Harris, J. and Goodwin, N. (2001) 'Volume Introduction', in J. Harris, T. Wise, K. Gallagher and N. Goodwin (eds) *A Survey of Sustainable Development: Social and Economic Dimensions*, Washington, DC: Island Press.

Heidenreich, K. (2017) Agenda 21? The Plan to Depopulate 95% of the World by 2030, www.disclose.tv/agenda-21-the-plan-to-depopulate-95-of-the-world-by-2030-313560.

IUCN (International Union for Conservation of Nature) (1980) *World Conservation Strategy – Living Resource Conservation for Sustainable Development*, Gland: IUCN-UNEP-WWP.

Johnson, S. (1993) (Introduction and commentary), *The Earth Summit: The United Nations Conference on Environment and Development (UNCED)*, London, Dordrecht and Boston: Graham & Trotman and Martinus Nijhoff.

MacNeill, J. (2013) 'Brundtland Revisited', CIC, 4 February 2013, OpenCanada.org, 12 May 2013.

Magee, L., Scerri, A. and James, P. (2012) 'Measuring Social Sustainability: A Community-Centred Approach', *Applied Research in the Quality of Life*, 7(3): 239–61.

Mebratu, D. (1998) 'Sustainability and Sustainable Development: Historical and Conceptual Review', *Environmental Impact Assessment Review,* 18(6): 493–520.

Milanovic, B. (2016) *Global Inequality: A New Approach for the Age of Globalization*, Cambridge, MA: Harvard University Press.

Palmer, G. (1992) 'The Earth Summit: What Went Wrong at Rio?' *Washington University Law Review,* 70(4): 1005–28.

Pope Paul VI. (1967) *On the Development of People: Populorum Progressio*, On the Development of Peoples, www.papalencyclicals.net/paul06/p6develo.htm.

Post-Sustainability Institute website (undated) Nexus between Redevelopment and United Nations Agenda 21, www.postsustainabilityinstitute.org/redevelopment-and-un-agenda-21.html.

Redclift, M. (2005) 'Sustainable Development (1987–2005): An Oxymoron Comes of Age', *Sustainable Development,* 13(4): 212–27.

Rivarola Puntigliano, A. and Appelqvist, Ö. (2011) 'Prebisch and Myrdal: Development Economics in the Core and on the Periphery', *Journal of Global History,* 6(1): 29–52.

Sachs, W. (1993) 'Global Ecology and the Shadow of "Development"', in W. Sachs (ed) *Global Ecology: A New Arena of Political Conflict*, London: Zed Books, 3–21.

Shah, A. (2014) 'Foreign Aid for Development Assistance', *Global Issues,* 24 September 2014, www.globalissues.org/article/35/foreign-aid-development-assistance.

SPLC (Southern Poverty Law Center) (2014) *Agenda 21: The UN, Sustainability and Right-Wing Conspiracy Theory*, www.splcenter.org/20140331/agenda-21-un-sustainability-and-right-wing-conspiracy-theory.

UN (United Nations) (undated a) *Millennium Development Goals and Indicators*, http://mdgs.un.org/unsd/mdg/Host.aspx?Content=Indicators/OfficialList.htm.

UN (undated b) *The Sustainable Development Agenda*, www.un.org/sustainabledevelopment/development-agenda/.

UN (1973) *Report of the United Nations Conference on the Human Environment*, New York: UN, www.un.org/ga/search/view_doc.asp?symbol=A/CONF.48/14/REV.1.

UN (2015) *The Millennium Development Goals Report 2015*, New York: UN, https://doi.org/10.18356/6cd11401-en.

UN (2019) *The Sustainable Development Goals Report 2019*, New York: UN, https://doi.org/10.18356/55eb9109-en.

UNGA (United Nations General Assembly) (1970) *International Development Strategy for the Second United Nations Development Decade*, A/RES/2626(XXV), https://digitallibrary.un.org/record/201726?ln=en .

UNGA (1974) *Declaration on the Establishment of a New International Economic Order*, A/RES/S-6/3201, https://digitallibrary.un.org/record/218450?ln=en .

WCED (World Commission on Environment and Development) (1987) *Our Common Future*, Reprinted 2005, Oxford: Oxford University Press, https://sustainabledevelopment.un.org/content/documents/5987our-common-future.pdf.

6

Paradigm lost? Blocking the path to ecosocial welfare and post-productivism

Tony Fitzpatrick

Introduction

Having been bricked deeply into the masonry of modern societies, no discussion of how to redesign the architecture of economy, society and natural environment can sensibly proceed without extensive reference to social policies. Inevitably, there will be disagreements about what this entails. Yet can we at least agree on some broad categories to focus debate?

This chapter begins by defining an ecosocial agenda and presents post-productivism as one instance of this. Though the former is deliberately broad-spectrum, what it denotes – the development of synergies across social and environmental policies – has barely registered to date (Fitzpatrick, 2017). Being comprehensive, it also contains some familiar divisions: between those who favour remaining close to existing socioeconomic models and those for whom environmentalism and the ecosocial implies a greater, transformative potential. 'Post-productivism' belongs to the latter tendency.

Two key challenges, or blockades, are outlined. The first deals with process. Several scenarios for the future of the labour market are outlined, one of which involves 'employment-centred welfare' and one is termed the 'part-time labour market'. The second challenge concerns the contemporary context. What should we do about a capitalism that has wreaked havoc on democracy?

The ecosocial and post-productivism

'Ecosocial policy' possesses at least three features (Fitzpatrick, 2014, 2017: 232–40; see also Koch and Fritz, 2014).

Firstly, a recognition that social and environmental policies must converge across three domains: (1) research and scholarship, (2) government legislation, policy making and institutional reorganization, at local, national and international levels, (3) the practices and ethos of relevant agents (professionals, practitioners, service users, activists and so on).

Secondly, such convergence involves a search for creative synergies which enable multiple strategies to be pursued and multiple goals to be realized. For instance, energy-efficient buildings emit less CO_2, especially when powered through renewable sources, and reduced consumption benefits poorer households especially since their energy costs are proportionately high (Fitzpatrick, 2014: ch 6). Such synergies also imply reconsideration of some big questions regarding the proper functions of and relationship between (a) public and private sectors, (b) states, markets and civic spaces.

Finally, the above would depend upon and make a vital contribution to a new social politics of the 21st century. This needs to be *more equal*, so that the benefits and burdens of sustainability can be shared out fairly. It needs to be *more participative and democratic*. If environmental and ecosocial policies are to be effective they must garner popular support, and so active citizens must see themselves as agents of ecological and social change. This implies the decentralization of political power. It therefore needs to be *more local*, so that less strain is placed upon ecosystems and the links connecting governors and governed are shorter and so more effective, regarding the accountability of the former. It needs to be *more socially responsible and cooperative*, based upon an understanding of interdependencies (not only between people now living, but between present and future and between humans and non-humans).

The ecosocial therefore signifies a new framework for politics, economics and public policy which would place less strain on people and communities, on social institutions and on ecosystems, by improving their resilience, flexibility, resources and capabilities. It aims at greater social and ecological wellbeing and sustainability.

There are two subgenera within the ecosocial: post-productivism and pro-productivism. This chapter will invoke the latter but not examine their respective merits in any depth. Pro-productivism is therefore not illustrated in Figure 6.1 (Goodin, 2001; Fitzpatrick, 2004a; Van der Veen and Groot, 2006). Post-productivism represents a form of the ecosocial which does not sacrifice diversity but nevertheless pushes more towards a particular reform agenda (the subdivisions in Figure 6.1).

Figure 6.1: Ecosocial policy: three levels of classification

Post-productivism is a composite of elements that appear immiscible. It implies using productivity gains for ends that are non-productive and utilizing greater efficiencies so that we can indulge in inefficient and even uneconomical activities. It involves a revaluation of the values and practices upon which so much of contemporary society is based: acquisitive materialism, status competition and wage dependency.

Post-productivism says, then, that (1) environmental preservation and sustainability should prevail even at (2) a cost to economic growth, productivity and efficiency. If (1) assists or at least does not threaten (2), then fine. But (2) should not be the arbiter of (1).

There are two more specific claims that can be associated with post-productivism (Fitzpatrick, 2004b, 2004c). Firstly, that we must pay more attention to time in three senses:

- As a currency or form of social and economic exchange (Gregory, 2015). Directly or indirectly, local currency schemes imply 'timebanking', where people contribute their time to a central pool of distribution and then use their deposits to purchase time from others. The aim is to encourage types of cooperation and recognize types of communal transaction that fall below the radar of the formal, commercial, wage-earning economy.
- As a return for increased prosperity (Coote and Franklin, 2013). The expectations of previous generations (machines will displace labour and create more leisure time, leading to drastic social changes) have not been fulfilled. Prosperity has flowed into heightened patterns of consumption rather than into reduced employment hours (Graeber, 2018). Post-productivism supports a systematic and justice-enhancing re-emphasis upon the latter.

- As a personal, as much as a social, resource; that is, as disposable time (Goodin et al, 2008). Rather than surrendering a third of our working-age lives in exchange for a wage and a pension, employment time would need to be organized more flexibly according to the needs and demands of individuals. Reductions in employment hours are important, but less so if unaccompanied by greater autonomy regarding the employment hours which remain.

All of this implies a radical restructuring of principles, priorities and institutional relations. The economic sphere must serve the imperatives of (a) the social, such that more time is released from the necessities of wage-earning, and (b) the ecological, so that energy flows are decarbonized and based upon renewable resources (Pullinger, 2014).

The point about time being a personal resource leads to a second claim which suggests we ought to value being rather than having. Fitzpatrick (2018) articulates this via the lens of Epicureanism, such that we ought to seek a combination of wisdom and happiness by prioritizing needs which are both natural and necessary. This means developing a disposition conducive to *ataraxia*: peace of mind, freedom from anxiety and irrational fears. Here it is proposed (Fitzpatrick, 2018: ch 7) that, in a modern context, an Epicurean ethics requires significant social reform, including:

- A reduction in the systemic economic, political, cultural and ecological insecurities which contemporary capitalism facilitates, depends upon and encourages.
- Revitalized public spaces and the use of urban land. This includes increasing the frequency of green spaces, revitalizing public space and reorganizing infrastructures so that they emit less pollution and CO_2.

A post-productivist society, then, is not about a medieval return to nature. It is happy to utilize the productivity gains of modern automation and technology, but also wants to rescue the human and the natural from the algorithmic governance of contemporary capitalism. It means possessing the rights, the opportunities and the resources needed to switch technology off and unplug ourselves from the circuitry of the perma-streamed hyper-connectedness of the 24/7 economy, set within a new economic architecture which empowers people in employment and consumer entitlements but which also confines labouring–consuming to just one locale of an ecosocial terrain.

As such, post-productivism corresponds to the ecosocial principles listed earlier (equality, participation and democracy, localism, social responsibility and cooperation) but does so by emphasizing the centrality of time and of social conditions which facilitate *ataraxia*. It can potentially act as a locus for cross-boundary consensus between the subdivisions in Figure 6.1 while pointing towards a more specific agenda for reform.

The rest of the chapter is devoted to exploring two key challenges that post-productivism encounters.

The futures of the labour market

Much has been written about the implications of future technologies, particularly automation, artificial intelligence and algorithms, for jobs, wages and, therefore, for employment security and social cohesion (for example, McKinsey Global Institute, 2017). How many jobs will be displaced? What kind of jobs will be displaced? Will technologies create new jobs to replace those lost?

Estimates of job losses by the 2030s have ranged from the modest (Nedelkoska and Quintini, 2018, estimated that 14 per cent of jobs may disappear, necessitating retraining) to the prominent estimate by Frey and Osborne (2013) that approximately 47 per cent of jobs will disappear. And this may affect middle-income jobs as much as, and perhaps more than, low-skilled ones (Rajadhyaksha and Chatterjee, 2018). Many professional occupations will be streamlined as sophisticated computer programs become more and more capable of rendering diagnoses, marking essays, researching legal documents, calculating insurance premiums and even interacting verbally with clients and customers. Reassurances that this will represent just another of capitalism's waves of creative destruction (PwC, 2018: 36–49), such that new jobs will appear to replace old ones, and that the future may even be one of high employment, could be confounded by the possibility that new jobs and industries will be automated from their inception (Ford, 2015).

As sophisticated as many of these analyses are, they have obvious uncertainties built into them. What happens in the future is clearly affected by what we anticipate will happen and how we act accordingly. One solution to uncertainty lies less in prediction and more in normative debate about what we want to happen. Instead of predicting the future and using this to sequester the normative, we might build outward from the normative: what *ought to happen* frames what *can happen* rather than vice versa. This is where post-productivism enters the picture.

Imagine the following three scenarios.

Scenario 1: Visionless turbulence

For four decades the free market orthodoxy has been that deliberate attempts to mould the future will be counterproductive and harmful. Since unrestrained markets find their own equilibrium, and since the information age is even more opaque to rationalistic models than the former era (energy harnessed by mass industry), state blueprints threaten to be even more damaging than the Keynesian management, high public spending, mixed economies and powerful trades unions of old. Governments may keep a hand resting lightly on the wheel, guiding some R&D over here, directing some incentives over, but nothing more intrusive. So, while the future will be volatile, governments should not hamper the innovators, re-engineer the winners and losers, or inhibit the profit motive (Heath, 2017; Worstall, 2017).

Scenario 2: Employment-centred welfare

Since free markets typically harm low-income households, averting such turbulent blindness could involve a government-run redirection of social resources. We might prefer a future where the labour displaced by new technologies is reabsorbed into the economy elsewhere. There are three basic strategies.

(i) A fiscal, arms-length approach would restructure the gates, switches and relays of the economy via taxation, spending and borrowing priorities. For instance, some have called for a 'robot tax' so that dislodged workers can be compensated and retrained (Delvaux, 2016; Delaney, 2017).

(ii) There is a more regulatory, managerial version of (i) involving state control and statutory interventions (Datta, 2017; Knight, 2018). For instance, we might create new synergies between the education and economic sectors to match labour demand to supply more effectively (West, 2018: ch 6). Or we might even prohibit the spread of new technologies into some sectors, on the grounds that the social cost of not doing so could be too high.

(iii) If (i) and (ii) are found to be insufficient as means to this employment-centred future, we might favour a make-work or job-guarantee approach where we simply create jobs to soak up displaced labour (Paul et al, 2018; Summers, 2018). Would such jobs pay for themselves on the basis that supply creates its own demand? Or, even if they are not cost-effective, would spending money on job creation nonetheless be less expensive overall than dealing with the social problems of high unemployment: inequalities, poverty, intergenerational immobilities, poor mental and physical health, and social unrest?

The problem with the latter possibility is that if workers in such jobs understand that rationale then they may estimate their own social value and status in the eyes of others as being minimal. They would be required to labour for x hours a week for what remains a second-class citizenship. Option (iii) might therefore lead to high social spending without an adequate amelioration of social problems.

The attraction of employment-centred welfare is that it corresponds most closely to long-established habits, values, relationships and practices. So, if the labour market is going to face massive and long-term disruption, it seems logical to persist with familiar cultural expectations in which social wellbeing is delivered largely via labour market participation. We cope with uncertainty by clinging to the familiar.

The disadvantage is that it potentially neglects the opportunity to remould society–economy relations in ways that recognize the downsides of a life dedicated to spending, say, approximately 35–40 hours per week in waged work for (due to increased longevity and an escalating pensions bill) approximately 50–55 years. Even many of those lucky enough to enjoy occupations which involve mental stimulation, social respect and professional autonomy can eventually be burnt out by the prospect of such Sisyphean labours.[1]

Scenario 3: Part-time labour markets

An alternative would be to retain some aspects of those employment-centred habits, values, relationships and practices, but in the context of an economy in which greater space is made for informal, non-waged, non-contracted activities. This is the post-productive option. It implies a two-way movement: more people moving into the labour market but less aggregate time being spent in wage-earning due to systemic reductions in working hours (De Spiegelaere and Piasna, 2017).

The justification for a part-time option, then, is to avoid the harms created by 'underwork' on one side – as has long been understood, unemployment engenders insecurity, alienation, loss of purpose and self-esteem – and overwork on the other. Excessive hours at wage-earning creates its own problems and challenges for family life and emotional wellbeing (Golden and Wiens-Tuers, 2008), with evidence suggesting that 'presenteeism', for example going to work even while ill, is a growing problem (Garrow, 2016).

Reductions in labour hours is not, in itself, a novel suggestion. From the late 1990s, the European Union's Working Time Directive guaranteed workers a 48-hour limit on their working week.[2] The main problem with such a directive is that a 48-hour maximum is far less progressive than it would have seemed generations ago.

More radical objectives are needed, whether this is framed as a longer weekend[3] or the eventual goal of a 21-hour working week. Yet it is clear that such objectives encounter massive obstacles, especially since developing a part-time economy would require effective synergies of social and ecological priorities. This is undoubtedly why no enduringly successful scheme to reduce average working hours below the 35–40 per week norm can be found. The challenges are simply enormous.

Blockade 1: Loaded dice

Think of the collective action problem (CAP). Individuals act rationally in terms of their own personal needs and desires, yet create a situation which is detrimental to all. It makes sense for Farmer Joe to graze more and more cows on a shared field since each additional cow yields more profit. However, beyond a certain point overgrazing means that the restorative capacities of the field are fatally undermined. The grass cannot recover, the cows cannot feed and everyone suffers. Yet despite a common interest in preserving the field, translating that interest into common action is difficult. Not when each cow generates a benefit which accrues solely to Joe, while the burdens of each additional animal are borne by everyone. The personal trumps the communal.

So why would an organization reduce the working hours of its staff? A pro-productivist argument succeeds. If reductions result in an improved productivity which outstrips the hours lost, then greater growth and higher profits may result. If planned well, a business could gain a competitive advantage. As such examples spread, others might follow suit and so, gradually, a communal interest is served by individual firms pursuing a more rational form of self-interest.

But a *post*-productivist approach does not have the same recourse. If the aim is to reduce hours regardless of the impact on productivity, profits and so on, why would an organization do so? Some organizations might possess a hippy-ish ethos and selfless concern for staff but, across the entire economy, they are likely to be in a minority. Other organizations might be willing to hire more workers to compensate for the reduced hours, yet this brings costs in terms of reorganization, hiring, training and so forth that reduces the appeal of doing so.

Thus, while our system might be less rational and desirable than an alternative in which we make room, and time, for other activities, we are constrained like Farmer Joe to foreground parochial, short-term self-interest. The latter might create a CAP, an employment-based society undermining social wellbeing by creating a lot of 'precariat' jobs that are repetitive and menial, without the remuneration or security that people need, but those burdens are borne largely by those on low incomes whose situation can safely be blamed on their personal inadequacies (or on 'job-stealing immigrants').

A pro-productivist approach might succeed in breaking us partially away from this, but only by keeping us tethered to existing sources of economic value, in which social–moral worth is measured by economic status and contribution. Any working-time reductions engineered by pro-productivism might inevitably be modest as a result. In short, a social and economic system based upon perpetual competition, profit-maximisation and cost–benefit calculi will typically load the dice against those who want more free time.

At this point we might invoke the state. If the farmers will not act in their common interest then a powerful agency must intervene to coordinate activity through legislation, taxation and so on. But here the CAP reappears on a global stage. If a national state sees that reduced hours gives its economy a competitive advantage, then good. But if this is not the case and, indeed, if the economy is likely to take a hit then why would the state take the risk? The disincentives faced by individual organizations are here scaled up to individual states.

Perhaps, therefore, rather than being characterized as a contribution to social reform and political economy, post-productivism has to be thought of as nothing more than a lifestyle choice. The 'slow movement' is a loose assemblage of writers and practitioners who advocate a slower pace in order to properly emphasize the quality of life (Honoré, 2005). If enough people go down this road then, surely, policy makers will eventually have to incorporate such preferences into their decision making.

This is an idealized expectation. The CAP is inescapable. You might educate pupils in the virtues of slowness but, once the lesson is over, they will re-enter a world of positional goods where the costs of being 'left behind' are enormous. The affluent can choose to downsize. For everyone else the risk of stepping to one side comes from inflation and reliance on casualized jobs.

Post-productivism finds itself in a dilemma, therefore. It has to imagine a re-engineering of society and economy but, regarding the CAP, does not have the relative feasibility of pro-productivist arguments.

Diminishments of the public sphere

Now imagine that we can wish the above challenge away and not have to worry about it. Would this imply that we should prioritize post-productivism? The 'public sphere' implies at least the following.

Firstly, *geosocial places* which are open to all free of charge and without restriction: urban zones, town squares, parks and playgrounds, community centres, unowned parts of the countryside. Sometimes, such spaces can be occupied, often temporarily, by specific functions: marketplaces, fairs, carnivals, rallies, marches.[4]

Secondly, a *virtual commons* such as online spaces for interaction that are open to all. In the 1990s and early 2000s the internet offered intercommunicative websites, dedicated chatrooms and various email networks. From the mid-2000s, social networks and social media came to dominate and reconfigure such exchanges, particularly Facebook, Twitter and Instagram.

Finally, a more abstract *civic agora* necessary to the wellbeing of society, the interactive flourishing of social participants and the healthy deliberations essential to political liberties and democracy. Here, what are otherwise private, enclosed spaces (family, domestic domains, workplaces, devotional places) 'open out' in a wider atmosphere of civil society. This civic space is also tied, via what we typically call the public sector, to the creation of non-excludable public goods where, ideally, distinctions of class, gender, sexuality, dis/ability, ethnicity and so forth are irrelevant. The civic agora and public sector are therefore spaces in which people assume, and can confidently anticipate they will have access to, their roles as citizens.

In short, the public sphere implies the absence or at least the minimization of boundaries, restrictions and excludability. Sadly, each of these layers has been deteriorating in recent decades, particularly (though not only) in those countries which have stripped themselves down for the delectation of market forces. It is not that the public sphere has vanished, more that is has been desiccated and shrivelled. We can identify three key phases in this process over the last half century.

Firstly, following a prevailing sense of social crises and ungovernability in the 1970s, the medication prescribed by the free market Right[5] softened up those institutions vital for the civic culture upon which democracy depends. The initial rationale for this masked itself as pro-democratic, that is, in opposition to the presumed 'elective dictatorship' of the socialist state, such that economic liberties were presented as the condition for a resurgence in political liberties. Yet it soon became clear that the assumption here was that whenever economic liberalism and political democracy are in conflict, democracy must give way.

For democracy enables people to get together and place restrictions (via consumers' rights, workers' rights, state redistribution, socialized production and ecological regulation) on the spontaneous interplay of market relations. Thatcherism therefore involved an assault on those 'intermediate institutions' (lying between state and civil society) which were seen as inhibiting both profit-making and a business-friendly government: the BBC, trades unions, local government, universities, the ethos of public service, public sector professionals (Marquand, 2004: 63–115). Those institutions which counterbalanced the reach of powerful market actors began to contract in scope, reach, frequency and influence.

The implications for geosocial places became apparent early on. Physical, especially urban, spaces were subject to privatization and colonized by commercialized enclosures (like shopping malls), with cities being remade as retail outlets. The ideology of 'private good, public bad' demanded that public buildings and land be sold to developers, including school sports and playing fields, which would contribute to rates of obesity. Under assault, local authorities would remodel themselves accordingly, either as the willing clones of Thatcherite domination or as those struggling with a lack of funds and desperate to defend key services. Geosocial places would be commodified and sold back to us via entry fees or conditional access.

Yet, secondly, for a long time none of this seemed to matter very much to very many people. In the 1990s history was assumed to have ended, in that the great ideological battles of old were over: liberal democratic capitalism had won. The Soviet Union was dismantling itself, and China had long settled into its market reforms; the globalization of finance and trade rang the death knell of protectionism; new information and communication technologies were making national boundaries less relevant. If anything, surely this signalled a kaleidoscopic enlargement of internationalized public spaces, swirling around us 24/7. The buzz-talk for a new millennium was of a global civil society, global citizenship and post-national, cosmopolitan identities and associations (Keane, 2003).

Finally, the first two decades of the new century punctured many of those complacencies. The events of 9/11, and its subsequent aftermath, tested the principles and self-images of the civilized West, often finding them wanting. The crash of 2007–08 confirmed that there was indeed a pernicious gap between reality and self-representation, highlighting the extent to which the priorities of the previous three decades – how to cut income tax and public spending, how to deregulate, how to re-motivate the poor – were misguided. The social exclusion to be concerned about, symbolized by a massive growth in inequalities, had occurred at the social top, not at the social bottom. Yet the sea-gods of politics and economics were not to be thwarted. The old totems prevailed after 2008, not because they worked but because gods depend upon a blind worship of their idols, incantations and icons. No new, unifying model of economic organization emerged. In its absence, many people imbibed the defensive isolationism of Trump, Brexit and a nationalist populism that hovered towards neo-fascism.

The weeds of this pathology germinated everywhere. As became belatedly clear, expectations that social networks would herald some McLuhanite Global Village Hall, or a fractal, 'rhizomatic' re-empowerment of social relations, were wishful at best and delusional at worst.[6] Reactionary movements would be funded by billionaires, such as climate change deniers the Koch brothers (Oreskes and Conway, 2011). Autocratic states would establish troll farms and wage online war via bots. Those who practised 'fake news' blamed it on others. A 'white working class' was suddenly a handy weapon in the distracting culture wars that the privileged fight whenever they want disadvantaged and struggling households to focus upon identity grievances (Schäfer, 2017). This helps protect their privileges against socioeconomic wars over public goods and the distribution of material resources.

Hierarchies had learned to masquerade as anti-hierarchical grassroots; insiders masked themselves as insurgent outsiders ready to wage a social war on behalf of the very groups they otherwise needed to oppress. The vertical learned to represent itself as the horizontal. And this reimagining of the powerful as the real victims, for example of self-appointed experts who think that facts and research should trump your feelings and opinions, was devastatingly effective because it identified and exploited social malignancies which had been growing for decades. Democracy could not have been under such threat by the 2010s unless it had been systematically undermined over the previous four decades.

Hence, the new tribalisms looked disturbingly like some of the political and religious tribalisms of old. By the second half of the 2010s, public spaces would be awash with neo-fascist tropes and repertoires, aided and abetted by American Republicans and British Brextremists mesmerized by their electoral successes, high on their own supply and as careless of the damage they caused as any reckless adolescent. The ideals at the centre of the 250-year experiment with democracy, of a common good, of bipartisan consensus, of open deliberation, of trust, rationality, verifiability and evidence-based policy making, were being eroded. In the 1930s the centre had held because its locale, at an equidistance from extreme Right and Left, remained clear. As we approached the 2020s, such compass points no longer seemed so assured. The public spaces open to the *flâneur*, in which we wander for the sheer joy of the stroll, sharing vocabularies and norms, encountering strangers without fearing the unknown, were becoming deserted, increasingly populated by subsurface monsters tempted above ground by the encroaching shadows. Disorder and disorientation became prevalent. Society came to resemble the politics of a playground in which adults are silenced by the tantrums of the toddlers.

All of these factors, then, have led to the feeling that geosocial, virtual and agoric spaces are frayed and fractured.

Blockade 2: Lengthening queues

The implications of that fracturing are this. We not only face massive social and environmental problems due to the diminishments of the public sphere; we are also now less resilient at coping with them and possess less capacity to address them effectively. Consider that which is both source and symptom of such problems: inequality.

The pernicious effects of widening inequalities have been well documented (by Wilkinson and Pickett, Chapter 14 in this volume). For instance:

- higher death rates and a deceleration in life expectancy increases;
- larger divisions between asset holders and the wage dependent (creating downward pressure on salaries and upward pressure on rents);
- greater mental health problems;
- lower levels of civic engagement;
- more traffic accidents;
- more household debt;
- reduced opportunities for children from low-income backgrounds;
- widening gaps in educational attainment (helping to consolidate middle and upper class privileges);
- declining influence of organized labour, producing a bonanza for CEOs, shareholders and middle management;
- the resulting dominance of money in politics, undermining the egalitarianism upon which genuine democracy depends.

All of this puts more pressure on the welfare state and public services. Schools and hospitals in many areas become patchwork services reliant upon the dedication of overworked, underpaid and often unappreciated staff. And as the public sector struggles to carry the extra weight of social problems, this merely fuels the prejudices of those who loaded it with that extra bulk in the first place.

Hence, the very ideology which first heralded and then generated massive inequalities also reduced the capacity of the state to cope with, let alone solve them. The long-established prejudice which says that the private sector is, by definition, less bureaucratic, more efficient, more user-friendly, more innovative and more accountable than the public sector shows no signs of abating (Mazzucato, 2018). Large parts of state activity have been outsourced, marketized and either fully or semi-privatized, funnelling public money into private hands but with the state still expected to underwrite liabilities and rescue things once risks become too high and/or profits too low for the private sector. This has often been called the privatization of profit and the socialization of risk. None of which matters ideologically, since even these failures can be woven into an unfalsifiable narrative whereby it is always the state which erred, supplying further 'proof' that additional pro-market reform is needed.

Similar stories can be told about climate change. Inequalities fuel global warming via overconsumption, status competition and intergroup rivalry, heightening the vulnerabilities of already vulnerable groups (Fitzpatrick, 2014). Perceived unfairness in the distribution of social burdens, in addition to a suspicion of political elites, makes it less likely that electorates will support government action or that social communities will pull together. There is a correlation between inequality and adverse impacts on environmental quality (Nazrul Islam, 2015). Despite some welcome improvements in adapting towards mitigating climate change (Fitzpatrick, 2017), the overall story has been one of inaction and buck-passing. And the longer states have remained paralysed near the foot of the mountain, the steeper and higher the mountain becomes.

All of which suggests that as the queue of problems we face gets longer, our capacity to reduce the queue's size through collective solutions is undermined. Thus, the queue gets longer still and so on in a vicious circle.

If so, then the post-productivist agenda hardly seems like a priority. As with Blockade 1, we can certainly make *pro*-productivist arguments for increased free time. For instance, so long as household incomes are decent, we can propose that less wage dependency plus allowing people greater control over their time is a way to address some of the maladies of inequality, for example by improving mental health and child wellbeing (more time for play, reading and so on).

Whatever the cogency of such claims, they are more likely to receive a hearing than the suggestion that reducing working time is a good in and of itself. It may be, but even sympathetic commentators might be tempted to say: how important is it given the inventory of harms, risks and challenges we currently face and which were documented earlier? Post-productivism surely comes towards the end of a very long queue of priorities.

Paradigm regained?

Is that it, then? Can we make a case for an ecosocial approach and a new politics of time, but only within a pro-productivist framework?

If we treat pro- and post-productivism as ideal types, this might suggest two possible strategies. The first is to contrive a third ideal type, borrowing elements from both. In this rapprochement we might, for instance, combine pro- and post-productivism along an evolutionary timeline. We firstly make an economic case for ecosocial reform, such that green social policies are most likely to be adopted and supported if they are consistent with prevailing views regarding the good of prosperity, employment dependency and growth. Then, as the moral case for environmentalism inserts itself more fully into our social background assumptions, so other 'ways of living' can be promoted, including the principle of extensive reductions in the working week.

The ecosocial therefore allows post-productivism to get its foot in the door. Then, if this drives a culture shift and popular support towards the idea of further working-time reductions, the latter reconfigures the former. We start off by appealing to the imperatives of wealth, employment and growth and thereby facilitate an ethos of post-material wealth, part-time employment and post-growth economics. Hence, post-productivism first piggybacks on pro-productivism, then hops off and takes up the running.

The second strategy is a more Machiavellian version of the first. We seek a rapprochement not in order to disseminate a principle, but only as a Trojan horse strategy in which we agitate for a part-time approach by highlighting the moral and social deficiencies of dedicating so much of our lives and social energies to wage-earning. In short, the only appeal to the first ideal type is as camouflage for ambushes by the second.

The obvious problem with the second strategy is that, by potentially making it appear superficial, it undermines the genuineness of any consensus and so either leads to breakdown in the rapprochement or, more likely, a situation where none forms in the first place. The obvious problem with the first strategy is that (as indicated earlier) the vested interests and established practices of existing economic and cultural orthodoxies constitute a permanent roadblock to anything more than some relatively modest reductions in average working hours.

In short, if we treat pro- and post-productivism as paradigms, or ideal types, then the latter might well be a non-starter. The alternative is therefore one of a genuine multi-perspectivism where we do not make up our minds prematurely (see Fitzpatrick, 2020). It is not simply that pro-productivists have to be willing to acknowledge the merits of post-productivism and vice versa; it is that each group has to be willing to advocate and campaign for the other across, and according to the demands of, diverse social contexts, institutional domains and political circumstances. We must be multi-locatory, that is, willing to uproot and unsettle ourselves by inhabiting plural roles and identities, and willing to recognize that the strongest consensus accommodates a continuing, dynamic and fluid pluralism. It means eschewing single frameworks and solves-all-problems solutions. The roadblocks have to be invaded and stormed along multiple fronts.

Hence, a multi-perspectivism is one of genuine rapprochement; rather than one of timelines and piggybacking, however, consensus reappears in a new kinetic, agitative and mutable guise.

Conclusion

Hence, no, a multi-perspectivism does not have to lose touch with the everyday precisely because it wants the everyday to aspire to a world beyond itself. Does this address the two blockades? Perhaps.

Firstly, the loaded dice of the CAP are still loaded but we can appeal to pro-productivist versions of the ecosocial without imagining that the former exhausts the latter. Secondly, the queue of priorities continues to lengthen, but if working-time reductions can be promoted as a means to restore tired social energies and revitalize communities then divisions between pro- and post-productivists appear less schismatic. Instead of jockeying for position, we can encourage fellow sufferers to blame those who lengthened the queue in the first place.

Rather than regard the pro- and post-productivist frameworks as inherently conflictual we ought to stress where, why and how they overlap and how both might help to resolve social and ecological problems. In the wake of the COVID-19 crisis such debates about society and economy have become more heated, yet the basic options outlined earlier persisted and, almost certainly, are unlikely to vanish in the foreseeable future.

Notes

[1]   And it commits resources and effort that could otherwise be earmarked for ecological adaptation and mitigation.
[2]   http://ec.europa.eu/social/main.jsp?catId=706&langId=en&intPageId=205. See also the Department for Business Innovation and Skills (BIS, 2014).
[3]   In 2017 the UK's Green Party called for a three-day weekend, see www.bbc.co.uk/news/uk-politics-39471102.
[4]   Some public spaces may be semi-public and semi-privatized, such as shopping malls.
[5]   Those supporting (1) domination by private capital, (2) the free flow of investment and trade, (3) privatization, deregulation and flexibility, (4) a power imbalance favouring employers and corporations rather than workers and organized labour, (5) a smaller but more powerful state apparatus, (6) bias against public sector provision and non-commercial forms of exchange, (7) an ethos of competitiveness, acquisitiveness and restless consumerism.
[6]   Note the famous quote by Bill Gates, 'The Internet is becoming the town square for the global village of tomorrow', addressing a session of the World Economic Forum (WEF) in Davos, see https://www.weforum.org/agenda/2014/11/what-will-the-future-of-the-internet-look-like/.

References

BIS (Department for Business Innovation and Skills) (2014) *The Impact of the Working Time Regulations on the UK Labour Market: A Review of Evidence*, BIS Analysis Paper Number 5, London: BIS.

Coote, A. and Franklin, J. (eds) (2013) *Time on Our Side: Why We All Need a Shorter Working Week*, London: NEF.

Datta, B. (2017) 'Can Government Keep Up with Artificial Intelligence?', *NOVA Next*, 10 August, www.pbs.org/wgbh/nova/next/tech/ai-government-policy/.

De Spiegelaere, S. and Piasna, A. (2017) *The Why and How of Working Time Reduction*, Brussels: European Trade Union Institute.

Delaney, K. (2017) 'The Robot That Takes Your Job Should Pay Taxes, Says Bill Gates', *Quartz*, 17 February, https://qz.com/911968/bill-gates-the-robot-that-takes-your-job-should-pay-taxes/.

Delvaux, M. (2016) *Draft Report, with Recommendations to the Commission on Civil Law Rules on Robotics (2015/2103(INL))*, Committee on Legal Affairs, European Parliament.

Fitzpatrick, T. (2004a) 'A Post-Productivist Future for Social Democracy?', *Social Policy & Society*, 3(3): 213–22.

Fitzpatrick, T. (2004b) 'Time, Social Justice and UK Social Policies', *Economy and Society*, 33(3): 335–58.

Fitzpatrick, T. (2004c) 'Time and Social Policy', *Time & Society*, 13(2/3): 197–219.

Fitzpatrick, T. (2014) *Climate Change & Poverty: A New Agenda for Developed Nations*, Bristol: Policy Press.

Fitzpatrick, T. (2017) *A Green History of the Welfare State*, Abingdon: Routledge.

Fitzpatrick, T. (2018) *How to Live Well: Epicurus as a Guide to Contemporary Social Reform*, Cheltenham: Edward Elgar.

Fitzpatrick, T. (2020) 'Specters of Democracy: Detouring the Limitations of Rawls and the Capabilities Approach', in J. Mandle and S. Roberts-Cady (eds) *John Rawls: Debating the Major Questions*, Oxford: Oxford University Press, 183–99.

Ford, M. (2015) *The Rise of the Robots*, New York: Basic Books.

Frey, C. B. and Osborne, M. (2013) *The Future of Employment: How Susceptible Are Jobs to Computerisation?*, Oxford: Oxford Martin School, University of Oxford.

Garrow, V. (2016) *Presenteeism: A Review of Current Thinking*, Brighton: Institute for Employment Studies.

Golden, L. and Wiens-Tuers, B. (2008) 'Overtime Work and Worker Well-Being at Home', *Review of Social Economy*, 66(1): 24–49.

Goodin, R. (2001) 'Work and Welfare: Towards a Post-productivist Welfare Regime', *British Journal of Political Science*, 31(1): 13–39.

Goodin, R., Rice, J., Parpo, A. and Eriksson, L. (2008) *Discretionary Time: A New Measure of Freedom*, Cambridge: Cambridge University Press.

Graeber, D. (2018) *Bullshit Jobs: A Theory*, London: Allen Lane.

Gregory, L. (2015) *Trading Time: Can Exchange Lead to Social Change?*, Bristol: Policy Press.

Heath, A. (2017) 'Trust in Free Markets: Robots Are Set to Revolutionise Work for the Better', *The Telegraph*, 23 March.

Honoré, C. (2005) *In Praise of Slow: How a Worldwide Movement Is Challenging the Cult of Speed*, London: Orion.

Keane, J. (2003) *Global Civil Society?*, Cambridge: Cambridge University Press.

Knight, W. (2018) 'Here's How the US Needs to Prepare for the Age of Artificial Intelligence', *MIT Technology Review*, 6 April, www.technologyreview.com/s/610379/heres-how-the-us-needs-to-prepare-for-the-age-of-artificial-intelligence/.

Koch, M. and Fritz, M. (2014) 'Building the Eco-social State: Do Welfare Regimes Matter?', *Journal of Social Policy*, 43(4): 679–703.

Marquand, D. (2004) *Decline of the Public: The Hollowing Out of Citizenship*, Cambridge: Polity.

Mazzucato, M. (2018) *The Entrepreneurial State Debunking Public vs. Private Sector Myths*, New Edition, Middlesex: Penguin.

McKinsey Global Institute (2017) *Jobs Lost, Jobs Gained: Workforce Transitions in a Time of Automation*, Washington, DC: McKinsey Global Institute.

Nazrul Islam, S. (2015) *Inequality and Environmental Sustainability*, DESA Working Paper No 145 ST/ESA/2015/DWP/145, New York: UN DESA, www.un.org/esa/desa/papers/2015/wp145_2015.pdf.

Nedelkoska, L. and Quintini, G. (2018) *Automation, Skills Use and Training*, OECD Social, Employment and Migration Working Papers, No 202, Paris: OECD Publishing.

Oreskes, N. and Conway, E. (2011) *Merchants of Doubt*, London: Bloomsbury.

Paul, M., Darity, W., Hamilton, D. and Zaw, K. (2018) 'A Path to Ending Poverty by Way of Ending Unemployment: A Federal Job Guarantee', *Russell Sage Foundation Journal of the Social Sciences*, 4(3): 44–63.

Pullinger, M. (2014) 'Working Time Reduction Policy in a Sustainable Economy: Criteria and Options for Its Design', *Ecological Economics*, 103: 11–19.

PwC (PricewaterhouseCoopers) (2018) *UK Economic Outlook*, https://www.pwc.co.uk/economic-services/ukeo/ukeo-nov18-final.pdf .

Rajadhyaksha, A. and Chatterjee, A. (2018) *Robots at the Gate: Humans and Technology at Work*, Impact Series 03, London: Barclays.

Schäfer, A. (2017) 'Return with a Vengeance: Working Class Anger and the Rise of Populism', *Items*, 8 August, https://items.ssrc.org/return-with-a-vengeance-working-class-anger-and-the-rise-of-populism/.

Summers, L. (2018) 'A Jobs Guarantee – Progressives' Latest Big Idea', *Financial Times*, 2 July.

Van der Veen, R. and Groot, L. (2006) 'Post-Productivism and Welfare States: A Comparative Analysis', *British Journal of Political Science*, 36(4): 593–618.

West, D. (2018) *The Future of Work: Robots, AI, and Automation*, Washington, DC: Brookings Institution.

Worstall, T. (2017) 'Getting Capitalism Wrong – AI Will Reduce Economic Inequality, Not Increase It', *Forbes*, 25 June, www.forbes.com/sites/timworstall/2017/06/25/getting-capitalism-wrong-ai-will-reduce-economic-inequality-not-increase-it/#2426a990675b.

7

World population prospects at the UN: our numbers are not our problem?

Danny Dorling

Introduction

Human population growth is slowing dramatically, and it is slowing because people are having fewer and fewer babies as compared to their parents, everywhere, without exception. More importantly, they are having fewer than we thought they would have a few years ago when the fertility rates were *already* reducing dramatically and unprecedentedly. Our species has never, ever had so few children. The reason why the total human population of the planet will keep on growing for 50 or 60 or 70 years, but almost certainly not for 80 years, is because people are living longer. It is now no longer because we are having more children.[1]

'The smaller generation to come – worldwide'[2]

On Monday 17 June 2019 the United Nations (UN) revealed momentous news. The world did not notice, but soon it will. The headline of the UN report (prepared by the Population Division, Box 7.1) read '9.7 billion on Earth by 2050, but growth rate slowing'.[3]

Box 7.1: The United Nations Population Division

The Division was established in the early years of the United Nations to serve as the Secretariat of the then Population Commission, created in 1946. Over the years, it has played an active role in the intergovernmental dialogue on population and development, producing constantly updated demographic estimates and projections for all countries, including data essential for the monitoring of progress in achieving the MDGs and now the SDGs, developing and disseminating new methodologies, leading the substantive preparations for the major United Nations conferences on population and development as well as the annual sessions of the Commission on Population and Development. It studies population dynamics and monitors demographic trends and policies worldwide. Population estimates and projections prepared by the Division for all countries on fertility, mortality, international migration, urbanization and population size and structure are widely used by all international bodies. The 2019 Revision of World Population Prospects is the twenty-sixth round of official United Nations population estimates and projections that have been prepared by the Population Division of the Department of Economic and Social Affairs at the United Nations (UN DESA Population Division, 2019).

Source: UN Population Division, www.un.org/en/development/desa/population/about/index.asp (Reproduced with the permission of the United Nations.)

A day earlier the UN projection for the year 2050 had been nearer 9.8 billion, and the projection for 2100 had been 11.2 billion people. Something very significant had occurred.

The United Nations report concentrated on where there will still be the most growth. To quote:

> India is expected to show the highest population increase between now and 2050, overtaking China as the world's most populous country, by around 2027. India, along with eight other countries, will make up over half of the estimated population growth between now and 2050. The nine countries expected to show the biggest increase are India, Nigeria and Pakistan, followed by the Democratic Republic of the Congo, Ethiopia, Tanzania, Indonesia, Egypt and the United States of America.

But the report continued:

> The population size of more and more countries is actually falling. Since 2010, 27 countries or areas have seen a drop of at least one per cent, because of persistently low fertility rates. Between now and 2050, that is expected to expand to 55 countries which will see a population decrease of one per cent or more, and almost half of these will experience a drop of at least 10 per cent.

The UN did not mention the new 2100 prediction in this particular press release. Figure 7.1 shows the number of people the UN estimates

Figure 7.1: Number of people aged 18 in the world, actual to 2020 and UN central predictions thereafter

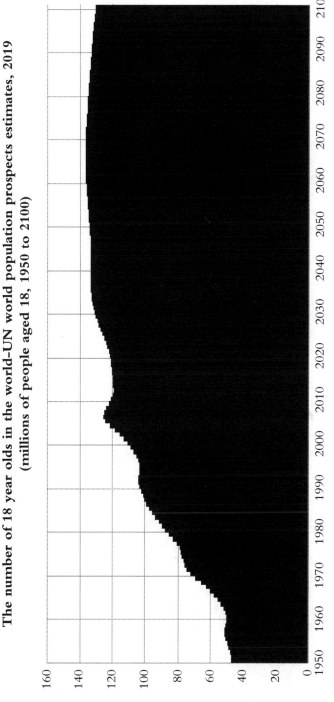

The number of 18 year olds in the world–UN world population prospects estimates, 2019 (millions of people aged 18, 1950 to 2100)

have been, and will be, aged 18 each year from 1950 until 2100. The future they predict is remarkably smooth.

However, some reporters noticed that something was very new: 'The world's population is slowing down and could stop growing – or even begin decreasing – by 2100', one noticed, before adding that '[UN population] division director John Wilmoth said this outcome "is not certain and in the end the peak could come earlier or later, at a lower or higher level of total population"' (Rodriguez, 2019). However, John's central projection for the year 2100 is now 10.9 billion people, 300 million fewer than the UN had said it expected, the day before. It is very unlikely that the future number of 18 year olds on the planet will change as smoothly as suggested in Figure 7.1, as it did not in the past. It is likely to fall long before the 2060s date suggested by the graph.

Human population growth is slowing dramatically, and it is slowing because people are having fewer and fewer babies as compared to their parents, everywhere, without exception. More importantly, they are having fewer than we thought they would have a few years ago when the fertility rates were already reducing dramatically and unprecedentedly. Our species has never had so few children per parent.

If people in a particular place live on average for 80 years rather than 40, they double the number of people found in that place at any one time without a single additional baby needing to be born. The human species is ageing rapidly. More rapidly than we thought prior to Monday 17 June 2019! And this is wonderful news because it is caused by fewer people dying when young and healthcare for the elderly improving. The next update of the United Nations projections will not be published until sometime in June 2021. For now, the numbers in this chapter are the best we have access to.

Figure 7.2 shows the annual change in the number of 18 year olds now predicted to occur each year and the number that did occur each year in the last 68 years. The peaks in the graph occurred in 1955, 1970, 1985, 2005, with the next predicted to be in 2025. The length of time between these peaks in years is 15, 15, 20 and 20.

It is the trend in the corrections to the UN revisions that matters most. In their estimates published in 2011 the UN demographers suggested than 10 billion was most likely by 2100. The subsequent 2013, 2015 and 2017 revisions updated that estimate to just over 11 billion. But now the 2019 revision is reducing that estimate again (UN DESA Population Division, 2019).

Seven years ago, on 11 June 2013, a book by the present author titled *Population 10 Billion* made a guess that the UN was getting it wrong (Dorling, 2013). It was just a guess, but it turned out to be right. The

Figure 7.2: Annual change in the number of people aged 18 in the world, actual to 2020 then predicted

The number of 18 year olds in the world–UN world population prospects estimates, 2019 (annual change in millions of people aged 18, 1950 to 2100)

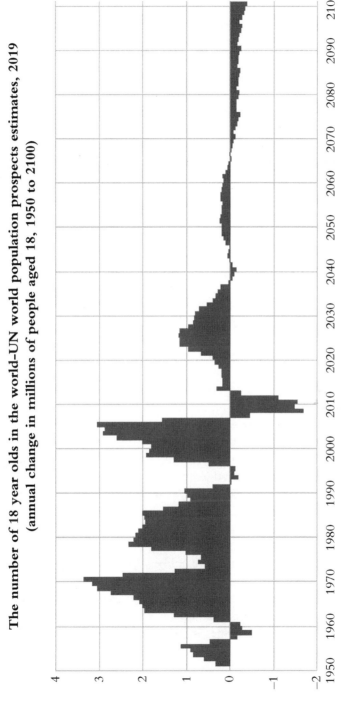

reason the UN was making this mistake, the book said, is that it had failed to notice an echo of a baby boom. It was using current fertility estimates to project forwards, unaware that fertility at the start of this current century was slightly and unusually elevated, due to many people turning 18 around the year 2005. This was an actual increase, as shown by the peak in Figure 7.2.

The slowdown in the growth of this single year age group, and then the fall to come in young adults worldwide, raises all kinds of issues. In general, smaller generations have been more powerful generations in the past. Their bargaining position is better. Each child becomes more precious. But in strange times (like those we currently live in) people begin to try to imagine all kinds of new scenarios. However, 'artificial intelligent' robots are not going to replace the young. The reason why is simple. We are animals, evolved to be acutely aware of just how much attention we are or are not getting from others of our species. That is how we have survived for millennia.

Rutger Bregman's (2020) new book *Humankind* explains it most simply. We were cared for by the old and cared for our young. Most of us are acutely aware of even the smallest slight we receive, the mildest of ignoring. Most of us warm with happiness when we are praised by those we love. Emulating humans to fool other humans with machines is a fool's game because it is to compete with what drove our evolution. Instead, robots are best used to undertake repetitive tasks that our inquisitive natures hate.

What is likely to happen next? Look again at Figure 7.2 showing the future change in the number of 18-year-olds that has now been predicted to carry through to the year 2100. Note how the UN prophesies a rapid move towards stability. To achieve that, every 18 year old has to have slightly more than two children each (because a few babies will still die even in the most utopian of futures). But then look at what has happened most recently. Look at the falls between 2007 and 2013 in the graph and note how that plummeting below the line almost exactly fits the gap that can be seen in the time series between 1991 and 1996, around 17 years earlier.

Young adults in the future are unlikely to conform to what the UN demographers currently predict. If we manage to avoid world war, famine, a very deadly pandemic and severe prolonged global economic crisis, then young people will continue to have fewer and fewer children each, for some time to come. What is more, they will almost certainly have even fewer than the UN experts currently predict. And this has been what a majority of women wanted in the past: fewer children than their (almost always) male partner wanted. And more and more women now get what they want (Dorling and Gietel-Basten, 2017). The views of women on the ideal family size, or whether to have children at all, are far more important than men's views.

If you find it hard to believe that the finest demographic minds the world can muster might still be making a mistake, even though they are at least now finally moving their predictions down towards what reality is telling them, look at Figure 7.3. This graph shows the 'change in change' each year in 18 year olds. This is simply one annual change figure subtracted from the next. To give an example: in 2006, 2007 and 2008 the number of 18 year olds thought to be alive worldwide on 1 July each year was 125.850, 125.386 and 123.692 million, respectively. The change between those three numbers was −0.46 and −1.69 million; the population was falling, and the change in change between those two numbers, the rate of deceleration or acceleration, was −1.23 million, a rapid deceleration (or acceleration in the rate of fall, if you want to see it that way).

Figure 7.3 shows all of those 'change in change' figures derived from the very latest UN population estimates for the world. Each great deceleration, the troughs in 1955, 1972 and 2007, has been greater in magnitude than the last. Now look at what the UN thinks will happen in future, and then start planning for even fewer 18 year olds than that, because this clear downwards trend is still being ignored. The period after 2020 will be a continuation of the trends seen before 2020 in Figure 7.3, not what is revealed here.

But let us take the projections the UN made in 2019 at face value; even if they are not an overestimate they still reveal a dramatic slowdown to come, as Figure 7.4 makes clear. In this graph the vertical axis shows the number of people estimated to have been, or predicted in future to be, living in the world at each date. The horizontal axis shows the annual absolute rate of population change at that time. Acceleration slowed after the 1960s and stopped around 1990. For 2010 onwards we have an obvious slowdown in population growth.

The stabilizing global population to come, worldwide

For children and young adults, everyone aged under 21, Figure 7.5 shows that the deceleration began earlier and the peak is expected to be reached around 2060. Please think what this means. In less than 40 years from now the number of children alive in the world is set to fall. And then the fall accelerates. Note how the line is sloping downwards after 2090. This, as has been repeatedly pointed out here, is a conservative estimate.

Figure 7.3: Annual change-in-change in the number of people aged 18 in the world

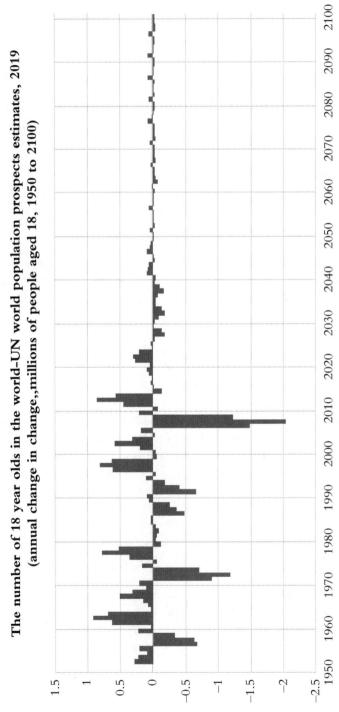

The number of 18 year olds in the world–UN world population prospects estimates, 2019
(annual change in change,,millions of people aged 18, 1950 to 2100)

Figure 7.4: Total world population and annual change in world population, year 1 to 2100

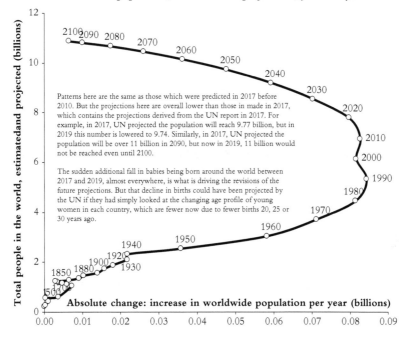

World total human population, with UN 2019 projections, year 1 to year 2100

Patterns here are the same as those which were predicted in 2017 before 2010. But the projections here are overall lower than those in made in 2017, which contains the projections derived from the UN report in 2017. For example, in 2017, UN projected the population will reach 9.77 billion, but in 2019 this number is lowered to 9.74. Similarly, in 2017, UN projected the population will be over 11 billion in 2090, but now in 2019, 11 billion would not be reached even until 2100.

The sudden additional fall in babies being born around the world between 2017 and 2019, almost everywhere, is what is driving the revisions of the future projections. But that decline in births could have been projected by the UN if they had simply looked at the changing age profile of young women in each country, which are fewer now due to fewer births 20, 25 or 30 years ago.

For those aged 21 to 40, Figure 7.6 shows that the deceleration began abruptly in 1980, as they were being born in fewer numbers in the early 1960s, and the peak is expected to be reached around 2080. You might argue that even if such a scenario begins to come true, the rich world will continue to impoverish the poorer countries of the world and the current trends cannot continue. You might suggest that there will be absolute immiseration as the billionaires continue to increase their wealth. But how will the billionaires continue to grow their wealth in a world in which the markets they target are no longer growing, in which there are fewer and fewer young people for them to exploit?

The falling population of Europe

For those aged 81 and over deceleration comes much later; but there are only so many graphs one chapter can include! So consider instead Figure 7.7, which compares Germany, France, Italy and Spain. By 2100 Germany has fallen below 75 million people, France to just 65 million, Italy has now dropped below 40 million and Spain to just 33 million. None of these falls need happen. Each of these countries

Figure 7.5: Total world population aged under 21 and annual change in that population, year 1950 to 2100

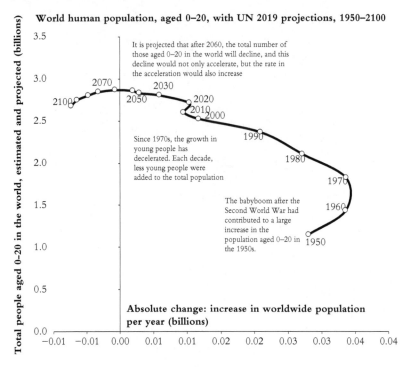

and the European Union that they lie in could open up its borders a little more obviously than each already does, and each need not suffer such falls. However, were they to do so then the populations of the countries that people migrate from will fall even faster than they are already predicted to fall in future, or would rise by less than they are predicted to rise.

The slowing of the rise in the population of Africa

In the 2019 UN report, the population in Egypt in 2050 is projected to be 160 million. It was previously projected to increase to 153 million in the 2017 UN report. The population growth rate accelerated fastest in the 1950s but is now expected to continue to rise until the 2040s. The 2019 UN population report revised the total population in Egypt in 2100 upward from its 2017 projection of 199 million to 225 million, 26 million more. Again this illustrates that the projections are highly variable. There is no great certainty for any particular country, but an overall sense should now be realized that the projections tend to be revised downwards more than they are revised upwards. If more

Figure 7.6: Total world population aged 21–40 and annual change in that population, year 1950 to 2100

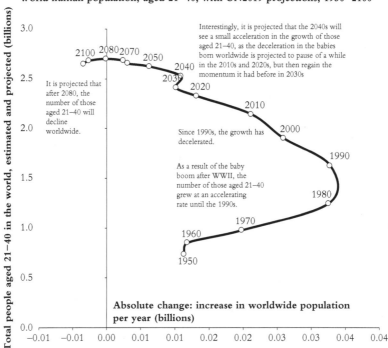

World human population, aged 21–40, with UN2019 projections, 1950–2100

Interestingly, it is projected that the 2040s will see a small acceleration in the growth of those aged 21–40, as the deceleration in the babies born worldwide is projected to pause of a while in the 2010s and 2020s, but then regain the momentum it had before in 2030s

It is projected that after 2080, the number of those aged 21–40 will decline worldwide.

Since 1990s, the growth has decelerated.

As a result of the baby boom after WWII, the number of those aged 21–40 grew at an accelerating rate until the 1990s.

Absolute change: increase in worldwide population per year (billions)

people move from Egypt to Europe then the population of Egypt will not grow as quickly as projected by the UN and the population of the entire world will also grow more slowly as those who move will have fewer children than if they did not move.

Figure 7.8 shows the project trend for Egypt and three other countries in Africa. In 2019, the UN revised its 2017 projections for the population in Nigeria downward. It is now projected that the acceleration between 2020 and 2050 in Nigeria's population will be less rapid. Hence, its population will reach 401 million in 2050, instead of the 411 million which was projected before (in 2017). Comparing the projections made in 2019 with those made in 2017 also reveals a much quicker slowdown in population growth now projected after 2050. The quicker slowdown now makes the projection of the population that will be reached in 2100 fall to 733 million, which is much smaller than the previous projection of 794 million, made just two years earlier: a drop of 61 million.

The most pronounced downward revision the UN made in its 2019 report is in the projections it now presents for the future population

Figure 7.7: Population past and predictions for Germany, France, Italy and Spain, year 1 to 2100

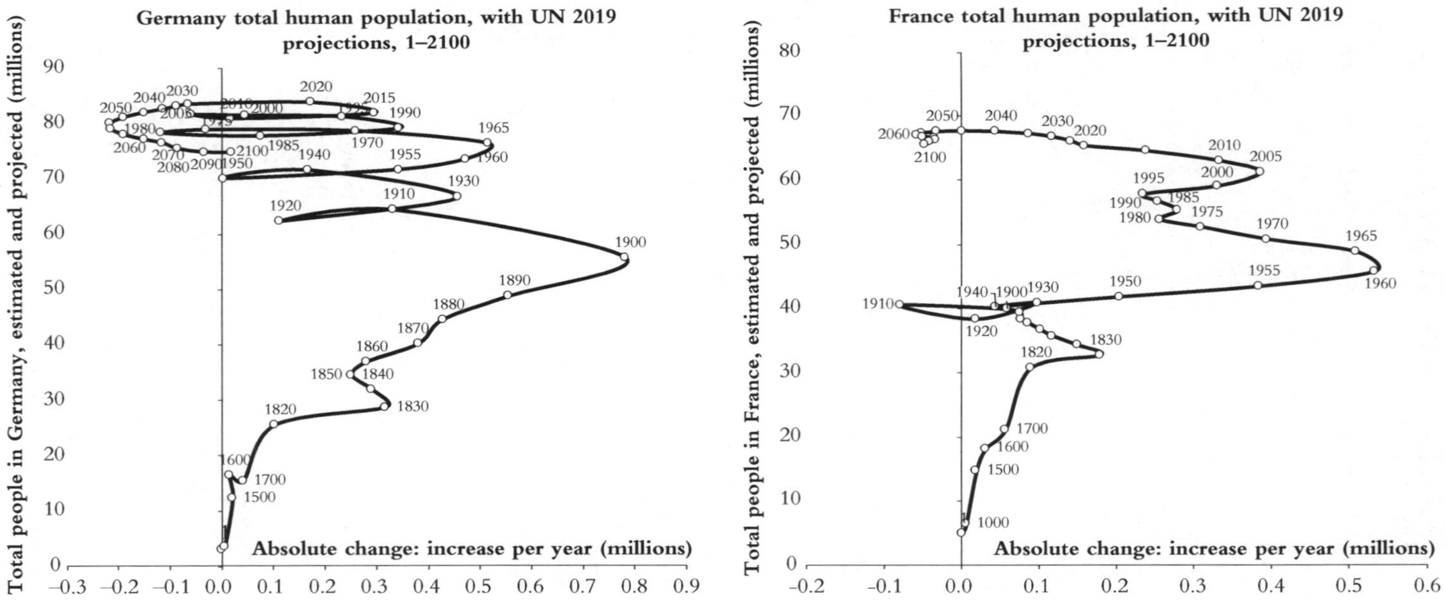

France total human population, with UN 2019 projections, 1–2100

(continued...)

Germany total human population, with UN 2019 projections, 1–2100

Figure 7.7: Population past and predictions for Germany, France, Italy and Spain, year 1 to 2100 (continued)

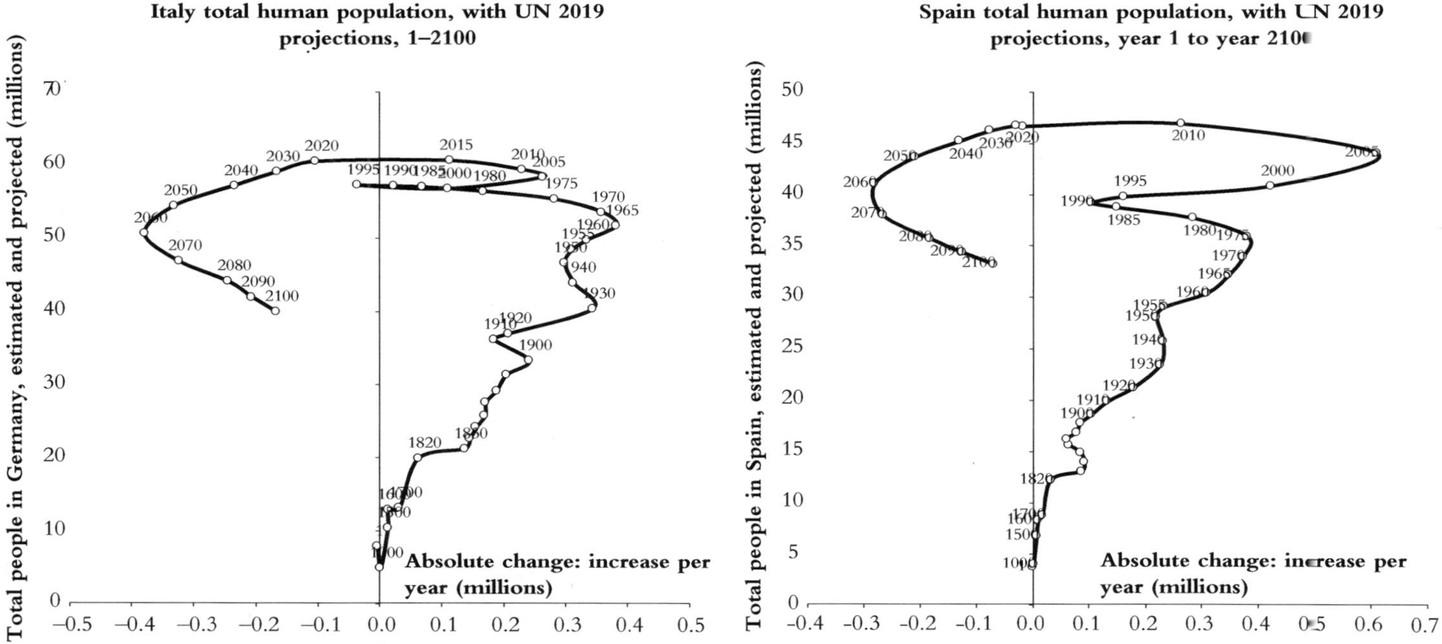

Spain total human population, with UN 2019 projections, year 1 to year 2100

Italy total human population, with UN 2019 projections, 1–2100

Figure 7.8: Population past and predictions for Egypt, Ethiopia, Nigeria and Uganda, year 1 to 2100

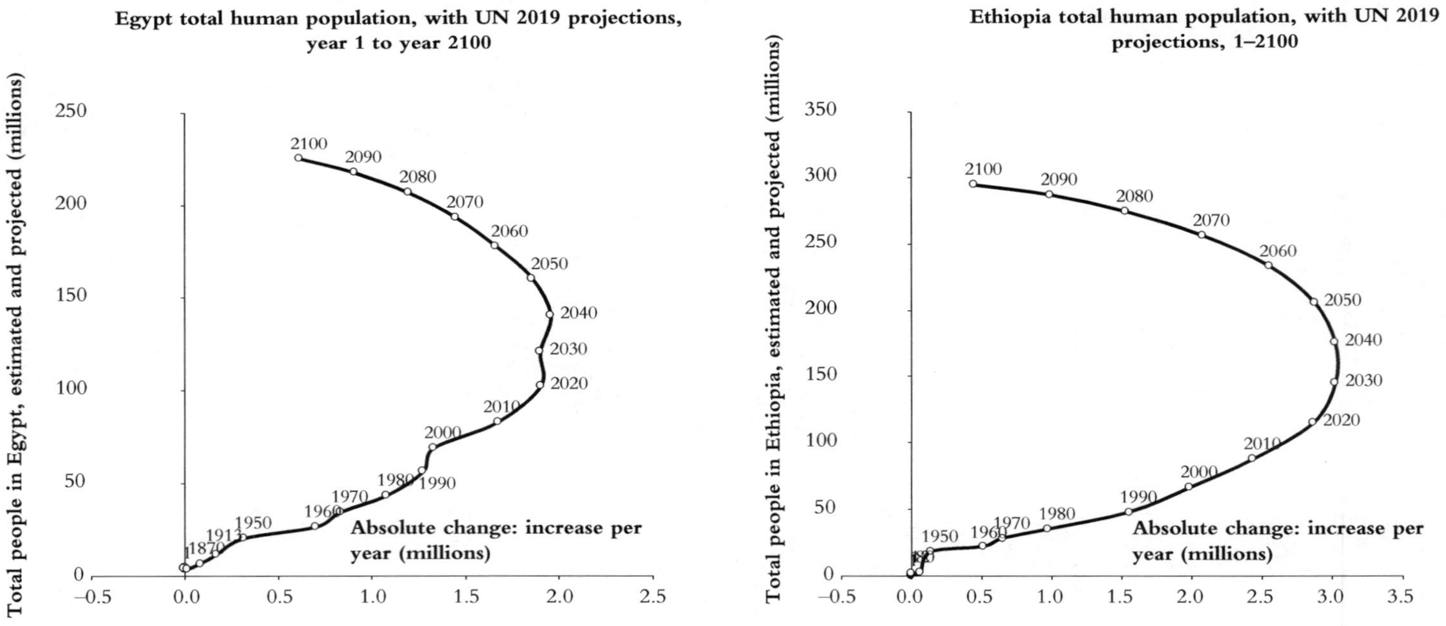

Egypt total human population, with UN 2019 projections, year 1 to year 2100

Ethiopia total human population, with UN 2019 projections, 1–2100

(continued...)

Figure 7.8: Population past and predictions for Egypt, Ethiopia, Nigeria and Uganda, year 1 to 2100 (continued)

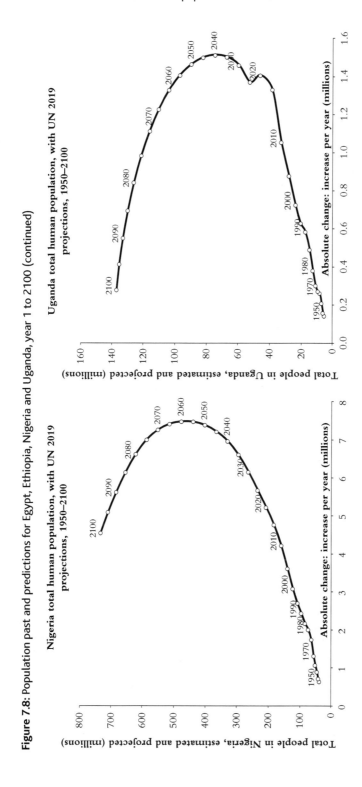

Figure 7.9: Population predictions for Iran, Russia, Bangladesh and Singapore, to the year 2100

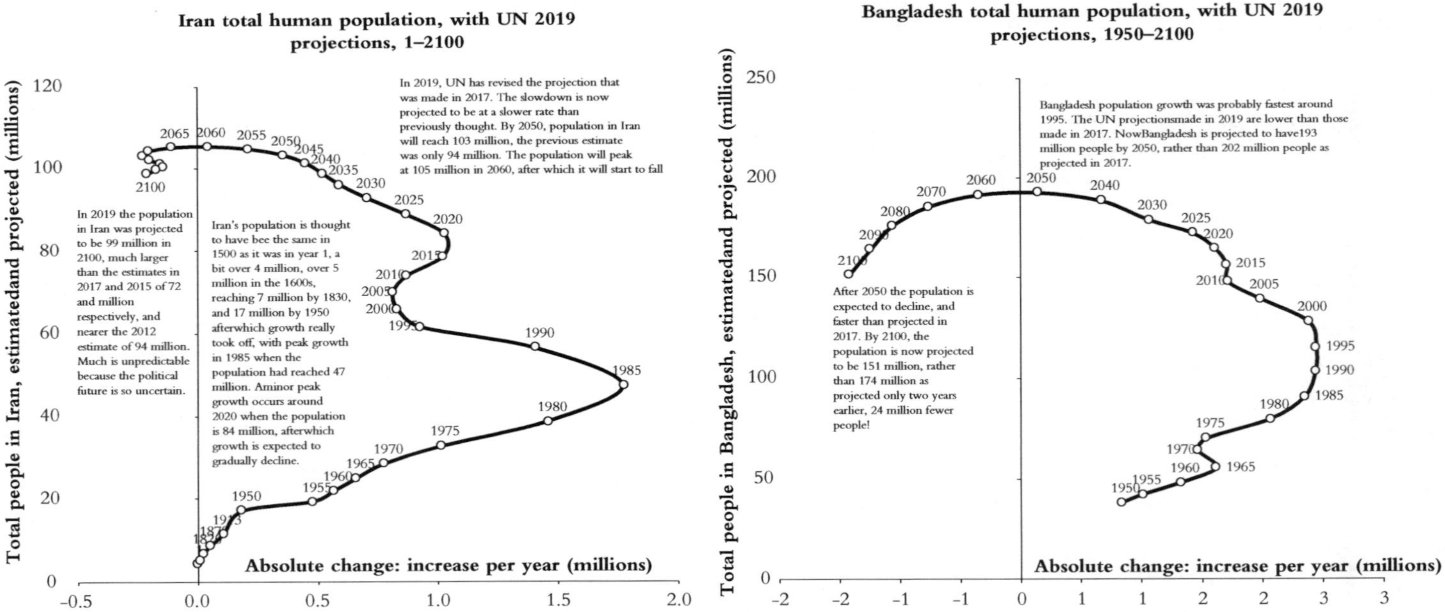

Iran total human population, with UN 2019 projections, 1–2100

Bangladesh total human population, with UN 2019 projections, 1950–2100

In 2019, UN has revised the projection that was made in 2017. The slowdown is now projected to be at a slower rate than previously thought. By 2050, population in Iran will reach 103 million, the previous estimate was only 94 million. The population will peak at 105 million in 2060, after which it will start to fall

In 2019 the population in Iran was projected to be 99 million in 2100, much larger than the estimates in 2017 and 2015 of 72 and million respectively, and nearer the 2012 estimate of 94 million. Much is unpredictable because the political future is so uncertain.

Iran's population is thought to have bee the same in 1500 as it was in year 1, a bit over 4 million, over 5 million in the 1600s, reaching 7 million by 1830, and 17 million by 1950 afterwhich growth really took off, with peak growth in 1985 when the population had reached 47 million. A minor peak growth occurs around 2020 when the population is 84 million, afterwhich growth is expected to gradually decline.

Total people in Iran, estimated and projected (millions)

Absolute change: increase per year (millions)

Bangladesh population growth was probably fastest around 1995. The UN projectionsmade in 2019 are lower than those made in 2017. NowBangladesh is projected to have193 million people by 2050, rather than 202 million people as projected in 2017.

After 2050 the population is expected to decline, and faster than projected in 2017. By 2100, the population is now projected to be 151 million, rather than 174 million as projected only two years earlier, 24 million fewer people!

Total people in Bangladesh, estimated and projected (millions)

Absolute change: increase per year (millions)

(continued...)

Figure 7.9: Population predictions for Iran, Russia, Bangladesh and Singapore, to the year 2100 (continued)

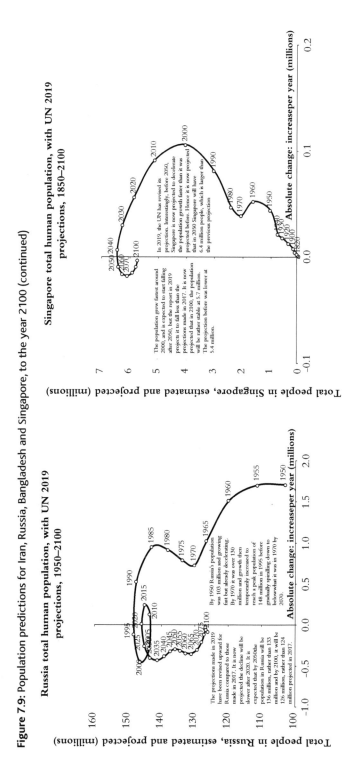

Singapore total human population, with UN 2019 projections, 1850–2100

In 2019, the UN has revised its projection. Interestingly, before 2050, Singapore is now projected to decelerate the population growth faster than it was projected before. Hence it is now projected that in 2050 Singapore will have 6.4 million people, which is larger than the previous projection

The population grew fastest around 2000, and is expected to start falling after 2050, but the report in 2019 projects it to fall less than the projections made in 2017. It is now projected that in 2100, the population will be rather stable at 5.7 million. The projection before was lower at 5.4 million.

Russia total human population, with UN 2019 projections, 1950–2100

The projections made in 2019 have been revised upward for Russia compared to those made in 2017. It is now projected the decline will be slower after 2020. It is expected that by 2050the population in Russia will be 136 million, rather than 133 million and by 2100, it will be 126 million, rather than 124 million projected in 2017.

By 1950 Russia's population was 103 million and growing fast but already decelerating. By 1970 it was over 130 million and growth then temporarily increased to reach a peak population of 148 million in 1995 before gradually spiralling down to belowvehat it was in 1970 by 2070.

Figure 7.10: Population predictions for Myanmar, Indonesia, Fiji and Mexico, to the year 2100

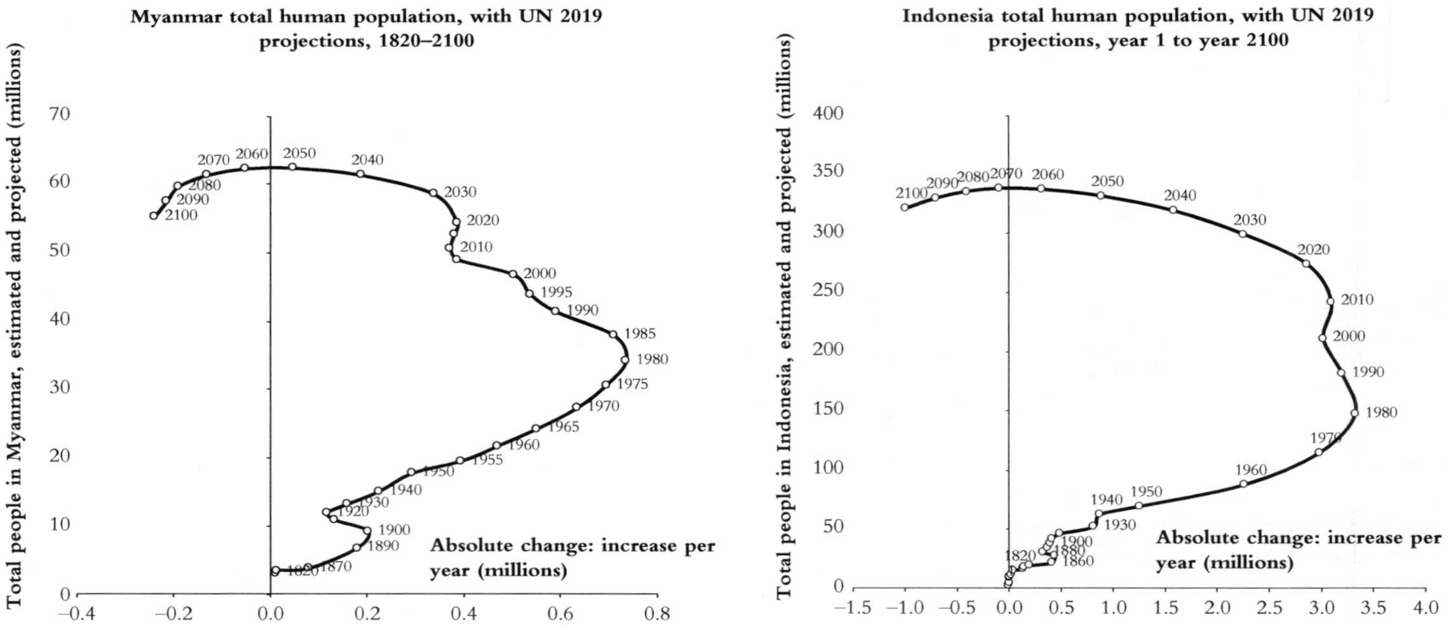

(continued...)

Figure 7.10: Population predictions for Myanmar, Indonesia, Fiji and Mexico, to the year 2100 (continued)

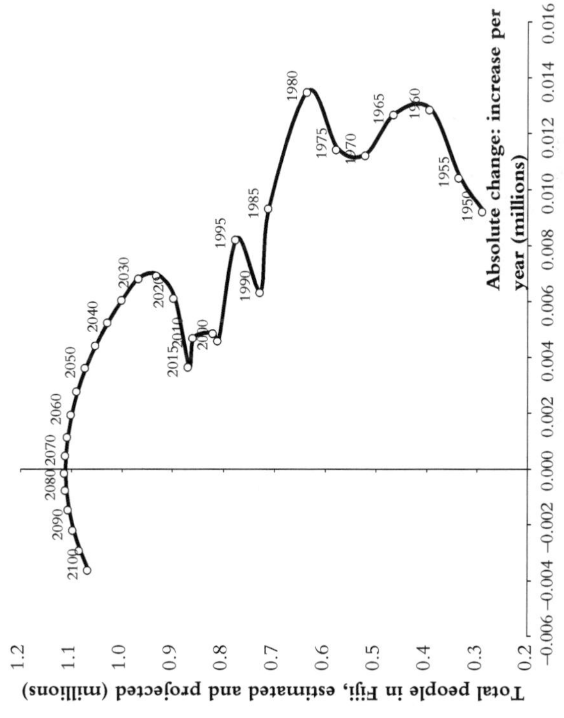

Mexico total human population, with UN 2019 projections, year 1 to year 2100

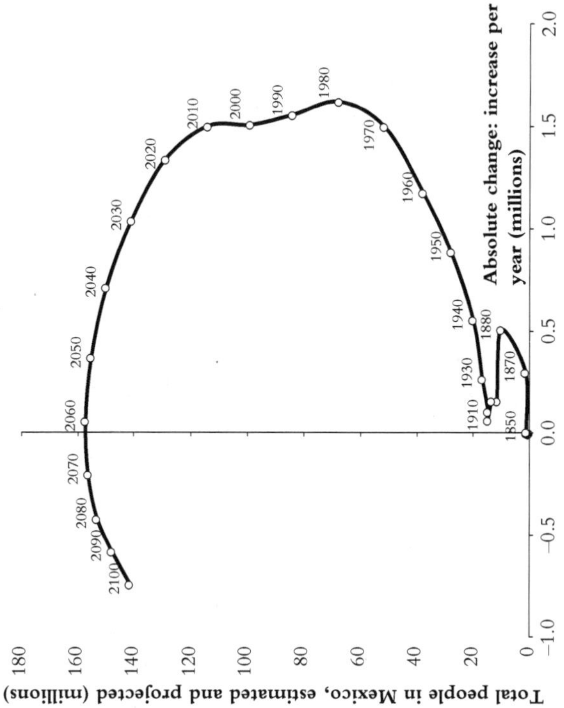

Fiji total human population, with UN 2019 projections, 1950–2100

of Uganda. In 2019, the UN projected that the population in Uganda could be expected to reach 89 million in 2050, and then 137 million in 2100. But in its previous 2017 report, these numbers were 106 and 214 million respectively. The 2019 UN projections reduced the 2017 projection of total world population in 2100 by 309 million. The revision for Uganda alone was down by 77 million.

The population growth rate of Ethiopia accelerated fastest in the 1980s, during the time of famine. The growth rate of the population of Ethiopia is expected to peak about 2030. In 2019, the UN revised the total projection that was made in 2017 upwards. It is now projected that in 2050, the population in Ethiopia will reach 205 million; the previous estimate was 191 million. In 2019, population in Ethiopia was projected to rise to 294 million in 2100, which is higher than the previous estimation of 250 million. Thus the UN projections can rise as well as fall.

The falling populations of Asia

But now head west to Iran, north to Russia, south to Bangladesh and east to Singapore. Fly into the near future and towards the rising sun. Just look at Figure 7.9 and imagine what happens when we slow down. What will happen in all these countries as the population falls?

Keep flying round the world, into the sunrise and the future. Fly over Myanmar, Indonesia, Fiji and Mexico, all shown in Figure 7.10. Contrast the huge growth and acceleration of the population in almost all these places in the 1950s and 1960s with the declaration that has already begun in each place and the huge population falls to soon come. These examples have not been cherry-picked. They are simply a sample drawn with the help of Qiujie Shi, a postgraduate student the author worked with on this and which has been put up on a website which shows graphs for many other countries.[4] This is simply what is expected to happen if current trends continue, and there are many reason to believe that all these UN central population projections are overestimates and that populations will fall earlier and faster than this.[5]

Population falling from the Indian Ocean to across the Pacific

The great irony of our times is that we worry about population numbers (Wallace-Wells, 2019; Thunberg, 2019) even though they are now so surely predicted to fall. The UN estimates of the distant future settling at two children per potential couple do this despite there being no evidence that when fertility falls below two children per couple it will rise again.

The slowdown in the poorest countries of the world

Take the case of Cuba. Its population is already falling. It is now set to almost halve within the next 80 years because the number of children born is already so low on that island and because there is very little migration to Cuba (Figure 7.11). Cuba is one of the most sustainable places on earth. In a recent academic study it was ranked as the most sustainable of all, just above Costa Rica and Sri Lanka (Hickel, 2020). Its people are best placed to weather the future fall in population. However, Cuba need only fall this fast if there is not, say, increased immigration from some African countries. Furthermore, as Cuba has one of the best records of training doctors worldwide, and countries in Africa have the fewest doctors per head, it would make sense to avert the population fall in Cuba based on that growing need for medical staff training and expertise.

Population growth is related to economic inequality. Cuba's population has stabilized so early largely because it is such an equitable country. Nearby, in the USA, population continues to rise, and total fertility rates are only now, finally, falling below two children per couple and only then most surely for the middle class (Ducharme, 2019). Of all the rich nations of the world it is the USA which is most unequal economically; and the USA which has the highest population growth. Inequitable, affluent countries like the USA also suck in migrants because they have so many jobs at the bottom of their economies; so many so very badly paid jobs.

Migration to more equitable affluent countries like Japan and the Nordic countries is much lower as there are far fewer low-paid opportunities. Nevertheless, when people migrate to the USA they have, on average, fewer children than they would have had if they had stayed living in a poorer country. Thus even economic inequality can contribute to a smaller global population. However, it is economic equality that is most closely associated with low population growth: affluence, stability and social wellbeing.

The projections that the UN make are not always as stable as those for Cuba. For example, for nearby Venezuela, which has experienced turmoil in recent years, including its population almost falling in 2015, the pattern is far less smooth. Often there is turmoil, more often than we tend to acknowledge (Scott, 2017). This turmoil is shown

Figure 7.11: Cuba's total population and annual change in its population, year 1820 to 2100

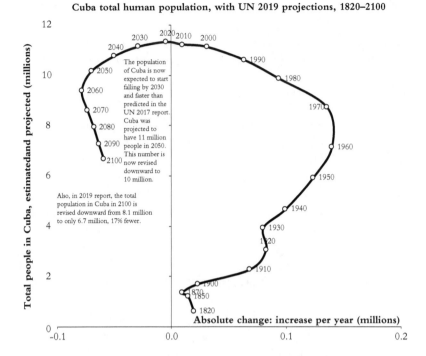

Cuba total human population, with UN 2019 projections, 1820–2100

The population of Cuba is now expected to start falling by 2030 and faster than predicted in the UN 2017 report. Cuba was projected to have 11 million people in 2050. This number is now revised downward to 10 million.

Also, in 2019 report, the total population in Cuba in 2100 is revised downward from 8.1 million to only 6.7 million, 17% fewer.

Figure 7.12: Venezuela's total population and annual change in its population, year 1820 to 2100

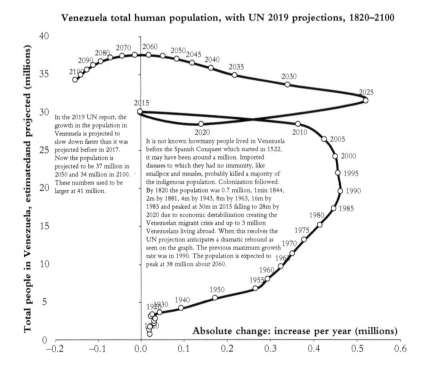

Venezuela total human population, with UN 2019 projections, 1820–2100

In the 2019 UN report, the growth in the population in Venezuela is projected to slow down faster than it was projected before in 2017. Now the population is projected to be 37 million in 2050 and 34 million in 2100. These numbers used to be larger at 41 million.

It is not known how many people lived in Venezuela before the Spanish Conquest which started in 1522, it may have been around a million. Imported diseases to which they had no immunity, like smallpox and measles, probably killed a majority of the indigenous population. Colonization followed. By 1820 the population was 0.7 million, 1min 1844, 2m by 1881, 4m by 1943, 8m by 1963, 16m by 1983 and peaked at 30m in 2015 falling to 28m by 2020 due to economic destabilization creating the Venezuelan migrant crisis and up to 3 million Venezuelans living abroad. When this resolves the UN projection anticipates a dramatic rebound as seen on the graph. The previous maximum growth rate was in 1990. The population is expected to peak at 38 million about 2060.

Figure 7.13: Finland's total population and annual change in its population, year 1 to 2100

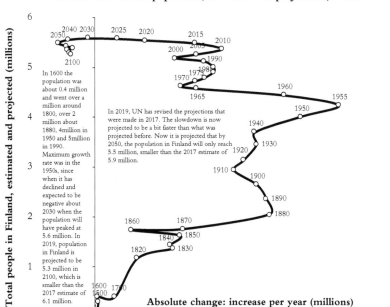

Finland total human population, with UN 2019 projections, 1–2100

in Figure 7.12. And yet even for Venezuela future stability and then a fall are forecast.

Finally consider Finland, the most successful country worldwide in terms of the happiness of its people, very low homelessness, extremely high-quality education, amazing infant health and a host of other factors to be proud of. Finland is also the most equitable country in the world. Surely, you might think, people would be flocking to Finland? Well, some are, in greater and greater numbers; but even given the recent growth in migration to Finland, its population is set to fall shortly after 2025 because its fertility rate is now so very low. Women in Finland cannot be persuaded to have more children, no matter how generous both maternity and paternity pay and conditions are made.

When a country is equitable, like Finland, people do not have to think of having more children in future to help pay for their old age (see Wilkinson and Pickett, Chapter 14 in this volume). They have decent pensions. They don't have to have children to provide cheap labour in their corner-shops, or to help tend the farm, or in case just one might be lucky; people are treated well enough regardless of how many children they have, or whether they have none at all. It may seem

Figure 7.14: Fertility rates in the poorest countries on earth, 1960 to 2017

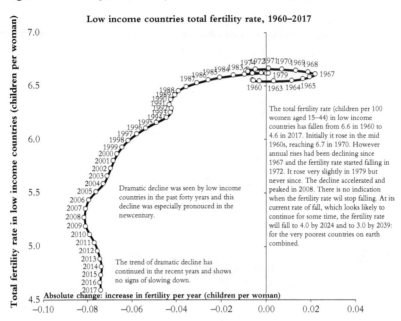

Low income countries total fertility rate, 1960–2017

The total fertility rate (children per 100 women aged 15–44) in low income countries has fallen from 6.6 in 1960 to 4.6 in 2017. Initially it rose in the mid 1960s, reaching 6.7 in 1970. However annual rises had been declining since 1967 and the fertility rate started falling in 1972. It rose very slightly in 1979 but never since. The decline accelerated and peaked in 2008. There is no indication when the fertility rate wil stop falling. At its current rate of fall, which looks likely to continue for some time, the fertility rate will fall to 4.0 by 2024 and to 3.0 by 2039: for the very poorest countries on earth combined.

Dramatic decline was seen by low income countries in the past forty years and this decline was especially pronouced in the newcentury.

The trend of dramatic decline has continued in the recent years and shows no signs of slowing down.

impossible that that will ever happen to some of the poorest and most inequitable countries in the world, but not long ago Finland was also one of the poorest and more inequitable of countries in the world; just a century ago in fact.

Figure 7.14 ends this chapter and the time series of graphs with a different graph, this time of fertility rates themselves for the lowest income countries in the world, and the ones which currently have the highest fertility rates. There are now only 34 such countries: Afghanistan, Benin, Burkina Faso, Burundi, the Central African Republic, Chad, the Comoros islands, the Democratic People's Republic of Korea, the Democratic Republic of the Congo, Eritrea, Ethiopia, Gambia, Guinea, Guinea-Bissau, Haiti, Liberia, Madagascar, Malawi, Mali, Mozambique, Nepal, Niger, Rwanda, Senegal, Sierra Leone, Somalia, South Sudan, the Syrian Arab Republic, Tajikistan, Togo, Uganda, the United Republic of Tanzania, Yemen and Zimbabwe. On average, across all of these, by the time this book is published the average number of children a woman gives birth to in her lifetime will be the same as the current queen of England gave birth to in her lifetime (four). And it is still falling.

What is less certain is the effect the pandemic will have on population numbers. Globally the deaths are (sadly) within the margin of error, at least at present, given that other communicable diseases kill so many more people in poorer countries in the world and that noncommunicable diseases together accounted for more than 7 out of 10 deaths globally in 2019, as the World Health Organization (WHO) reports.[6] What is less certain is what will happen to fertility rates, growing economic insecurity may well put people off having children even more – accelerating slowdown – but it is simply too early to tell long-term implications for world population.

Notes

[1] For a good summary see Darrell Bricker and John Ibbitson (2019).

[2] See also the blog post written for the Intergenerational Foundation and published on 8 July 2019: www.if.org.uk/2019/07/08/the-smaller-generation-to-come-worldwide/ and in Italian on 8 October 2019: https://open.luiss.it/2019/10/08/sempre-meno-giovani-nel-mondo-il-pensiero-di-danny-dorling/.

[3] '9.7 Billion on Earth by 2050, but Growth Rate Slowing, Says New UN Population Report', UN News, 17 June 2019, https://news.un.org/en/story/2019/06/1040621.

[4] See www.dannydorling.org/books/SLOWDOWN/.

[5] For more details, see the book these graphs were produced to illustrate; they could not be included in that book as it contains so many graphs already (Dorling, 2020).

[6] See https://www.who.int/news-room/fact-sheets/detail/the-top-10-causes-of-death.

References

Bregman, R. (2020) *Humankind: A Hopeful History*, London: Bloomsbury.

Bricker, D. and Ibbitson, J. (2019) *Empty Planet: The Shock of Global Population Decline*, London: Robinson.

Dorling, D. (2013) *Population 10 Billion: The Coming Demographic Crisis and How to Survive It*, London: Constable.

Dorling, D. (2020) *Slowdown: The End of the Great Acceleration—and Why It's Good for the Planet, the Economy, and Our Lives*, New Haven, CT: Yale University Press.

Dorling, D. and Gietel-Basten, S. (2017) *Why Demography Matters*, Cambridge: Polity.

Ducharme, J. (2019) It May Not Be a Bad Thing Fewer U.S. Babies Were Born in 2018 than in Any Year since 1986, Time, 15 May, http://time.com/5588610/us-birth-rates-record-low/.

Hickel, J. (2020) 'The Sustainable Development Index: Measuring the Ecological Efficiency of Human Development in the Anthropocene', *Ecological Economics*, 167: 1–10.

Rodriguez, A. (2019) 'The World's Population Could Stop Growing by 2100, UN Report Finds', *USA Today*, 17 December, https://eu.usatoday.com/story/news/nation/2019/06/18/world-population-could-peak-2100-united-nations-report-finds/1490136001/.

Scott, J. C. (2017) *Against the Grain: A Deep History of the Earliest States*, New Haven, CT: Yale University Press.

Thunberg, G. (2019) *No One Is Too Small to Make a Difference*, London: Penguin.

UN DESA Population Division (2019) *World Population Prospects 2019: Highlights*, New York: UN, ST/ESA/SER.A/423, https://population.un.org/wpp/Publications/Files/WPP2019_Highlights.pdf.

Wallace-Wells, D. (2019) *The Uninhabitable Earth: A Story of the Future*, London: Allen Lane.

8

Ageing sustainably

Alan Walker

Introduction

Global ageing is a 21st century phenomenon and has far-reaching consequences for societies, communities, families and individuals, although it is only the economic ones that have dominated both national and global social policy discourses. In the more developed world, the debate about the impact of population ageing began in earnest in the 1980s. As the demographic transformation has reached the less developed world the debate has become global, although the pace of this change in the latter is much more rapid than in the former, which adds urgency to the policy discussions.

This chapter examines the implications of the major demographic shift in population age structures, Global North and South, and suggests how it might be managed sustainably. There are three stages to this analysis. First, the scope of global ageing is summarized, as well as its causes and the closely related transformations in family structure and epidemiology. Second, the relationship between ageing and sustainability discourses is examined, which reveals the heavy emphasis on the economic dimension, with the exclusion of the environmental and social ones. Third, a strategy is advanced to manage ageing sustainably at macro, meso and micro levels. But this would require concerted collective action of a kind that, until the COVID-19 pandemic, had fallen out of favour politically in many parts of the world.

Global ageing

Population ageing is the process by which older people, usually designated as those over the age of 60 or 65, become a larger proportion of the total population. This demographic transition was one of the defining features of the last century and will continue to exert far-reaching influence in the early stages of the present one. Underlying global population ageing are two major demographic changes. On the one hand, fertility rates have declined while, on the other, life expectancy has increased. (This leaves international migration as the only other demographic variable that might influence age distributions but, so far on this score, its overall role has been small.)

Fertility decline has been the primary determinant of population ageing. Between 1950 and 2000 the total fertility almost halved, from 5.0 children per woman of childbearing age to 2.7. It is projected to continue to fall over the next 50 years to below the replacement rate of 2.1 children (see Chapter 7). This threshold had been breached in the majority of more developed countries in the latter part of the last century. As fertility rates decline, falling mortality, especially at older ages, takes over as the main driver of population ageing. This is particularly the case in the more developed countries, where low fertility rates have existed for several decades, and where increasing longevity (caused by falling mortality at older ages) is now the primary engine of population ageing.

Over the second half of the 20th century life expectancy (LE) at birth increased globally by nearly 20 years, from 46.5 years in 1950–55 to 66.0 years in 2000–05 (UN DESA Population Division, 2002: 6). The average gain in life expectancy at birth was 23.1 years in the less developed regions and 9.4 years in the more developed ones. These averages mask huge inequalities and, in multiple respects, ageing is unequal (Cann and Dean, 2009; Walker, 2018). Thus, a person born in one of the more developed regions of the world can expect to outlive, by around 12 years, a person born in one of the less developed regions. If the person is born in one of the *least* developed countries, this difference doubles to more than 24 years (UN DESA Population Division, 2002: 6). Within those regions and within the countries they embrace, there are also big differences in life expectancy and healthy life expectancy (HLE) (Marmot et al, 2020).

The notion that there is a natural biological limit to human life or that there is a gene that programmes us for a specific lifespan are not evidence-based. In contrast, empirical data demonstrate that in the most developed countries for well over 150 years life expectancy has been increasing steadily at an average rate of two years in every ten (Oeppen and Vaupel, 2002). Despite expert projections that this rate of increase would plateau or tail off, the rise has been remarkably linear. Forward projections are discussed in detail in Chapter 7; here it is necessary only to note, first, that the growth in the population aged 61–80 begins to decelerate after the 2020s and, second, that the oldest of the old (81–100) continue to be the fastest growing segment of the global population, at least until the 2040s when it is expected to slow down, but then accelerate after 2080.

As a result of these demographic changes, by 2050 one in six people in the world will be over the age of 65 (16 per cent), up from one in 11 in 2019 (9 per cent). Regions where the population aged 65 years or over is projected to double between 2019 and 2050 include North Africa and Western Asia, Central and Southern Asia, Eastern and South-Eastern Asia, and Latin America and the Caribbean. By 2050, one in four people living in Europe and North America is expected to be 65 or over. The number of people aged 80 years or over is projected by the UN to triple, from 143 million in 2019 to 426 million in 2050 (although note the slightly lower estimates in Chapter 7) (UN DESA Population Division, 2019).

Two other important transitions are related to the demographic one and are caused partly by the same processes. Both have particular resonance in less developed countries because of the speed of demographic change they are experiencing. First, there is the shrinkage in family size resulting from falling fertility and the shift from extended to nuclear families. Second, there is the epidemiological transition from the predominance of acute (mostly infectious) diseases to the prevalence of chronic non-communicable diseases which are associated chiefly with increased longevity. While there are potentially positive aspects to these two transitions, because they are associated with demographic ageing they also have negative consequences. On the one hand, smaller families mean that less childcare responsibilities fall (largely) on women, but they also mean fewer family members are available to care for frail older people. On the other hand, the transformation in the killer disease list has not been matched anywhere by a parallel shift in the orientation of healthcare services, which still focus overwhelmingly on acute medicine, a point this chapter returns to later.

As mentioned, the pace of population ageing in many less developed countries is much faster than in the past. For example, while France had nearly 150 years to adapt to its demographic transition from 10 to 20 per cent of the population being aged 60 and over, countries such as Brazil, China and India will have just over 20 years to make the same adaptation (WHO, 2015a: 43). Moreover, these latter countries are still developing economically while they experience rapid ageing, whereas the former developed before they aged.

Ageing and sustainability

On the face of it, the triumph of public health measures over killer infectious diseases and health-damaging living and working conditions, which enabled longer human life, should be a cause for celebration in the more developed countries, as well as an inspiring goal for the less developed ones. Paradoxically, however, population ageing has invariably been treated by policy makers and the media as if it were a disaster. While age discrimination, or ageism, is not a new problem, the negative policy discourses on ageing took off globally with the first wave of neoliberalism in the 1980s. Sustainability was central to these discourses, but economic not environmental or social sustainability.

The charge was led by the finance-oriented international institutions, notably the World Bank and International Monetary Fund (IMF), and their main focus was the Pay-As-You-Go (PAYG) pension systems of the developed countries. The World Bank in particular stoked global fears concerning population ageing and the future of public pensions:

> Today, as the World's population ages, old age security systems are in trouble worldwide ... formal programs are beset by escalating costs that require high tax rates and deter private sector growth – while failing to protect the old. At the same time, many developing countries are on the verge of adopting the same programs that have spun out of control in the middle – and high – income countries. (World Bank, 1994: 1)

At the time questions were constantly being raised about the sustainability of pension and social protection systems, often in the context of a negative commentary on the 'burden' of population ageing and the risk of intergenerational conflict (Walker, 1990). Partly because of its imposition of loan conditions on less developed countries, the World Bank's multi-pillar prescription for pension systems became widely accepted. As a result, many public PAYG schemes were residualized alongside an expansion in compulsory fully funded and individualized market pensions, with the Chilean defined contribution scheme being used as a model (World Bank, 1994). Take-up of this prescription was patchier in the developed world, with its adoption in the UK and parts of Eastern Europe being attributable to the strong influence of neoliberalism.

The Organisation for Economic Co-operation and Development (OECD) and European Commission (EC) echoed these concerns about financial imbalances in public pension systems, emphasizing the need for retirement reforms. However, their prescriptions also focused on the role of extending working lives as well as the need for parametric pension reforms (EC, 2006; OECD, 2006). The European Union (EU) adopted the 'active ageing' concept (that we will return to later) but interpreted it narrowly as a basis for working longer and retiring later (EC, 1999). Thus, the EU's Lisbon Agenda gave prominence to the goal of raising average retirement ages across EU member states. Once pension and associated retirement age reforms were in train the EU and the OECD switched their attention to rising health and long-term care expenditures, driven partly by increased longevity. So, the policy discourse on pension system sustainability morphed into one on health/long-term care sustainability:

> Health and long-term care expenditure is projected to increase significantly as a proportion of GDP over the next decades in both OECD and BRIICS (Brazil, Russia, India, Indonesia, China and South Africa) countries leading to a doubling of their share of GDP (to around 14 per cent) in 2060. (OECD, 2006)

The EU is closely aligned with the OECD on this issue and, not surprisingly, the HORIZON 2020 programme, which succeeded the Lisbon one, prioritized the goal of raising average healthy life expectancy, partly in an effort to reduce health and long-term care costs.

In summary, sustainability and ageing policy discourses in the latter part of the last century were concerned almost exclusively with economics and, specifically, a neoliberal interpretation of sustainability that took as its starting point minimum state and maximum individual responsibility (Walker and Deacon, 2003). In other words, the path to economic sustainability was via reducing the size of the welfare state and, since older people are the largest beneficiaries, they were the first targets. Not surprisingly, the countries most susceptible to this ideology, proselytized by the international financial institutions, were the most liberal polities, especially the US and UK. Policy attention focused first on pensions, then on health and long-term care, with, in the case of the former, widespread revisions to public pension schemes, ranging from the scrapping of the State Earnings-Related Pension in the UK to the closure of pre-retirement schemes in all EU countries that had them. Looking back it is striking, first, that over several decades of policy debate and action, contextualized by the media's remorseless focus on the public 'burden', it was not ageing at all that was the target, but simply *old age*. It was the costs to exchequers of rising numbers of older people that agitated some politicians and sections of the policy community and media, and not the ageing process itself, that is, the issues of how people become old and what kind of old age they experience (which we return to later). Second, in all of the global and national policy debates about population ageing the topic of environmental sustainability never surfaced. In fact, it was not until the turn of the century and the introduction of the Millennium Development Goals (MDGs) (UNGA, 2000) that the issues of ageing and sustainability began to be considered together, a process that was given added impetus by the Sustainable Development Goals (SDGs) (UNGA, 2015). This new context means that the discussion of ageing at a global level is now closely tied to the development agenda.

The internationally agreed approach to ageing, focused on adjusting to an ageing society and then constructing a society for all ages, was formulated during the build-up to the 1999 International Year of Older Persons (IYOP). The conceptual framework for action comprised four dimensions: the situation of older people's development through the life course; multigenerational relationships; and population ageing and development (UNGA, 1995). This approach was elaborated in the Madrid International Plan of Action on Ageing (MIPAA) (which was co-written by the current author) and adopted during the Second World Assembly on Ageing in Madrid (UN, 2002). MIPAA expanded the IYOP four-dimensional framework into 239 recommendations for policy action, organized into three priority directions: older persons and development; advancing health and wellbeing into old age; and ensuring enabling and supportive environments (UN, 2002). MIPAA specified that success in the progression towards a society for all ages should be measured in terms of social development, the improvement in quality of life of older people, and sustainability throughout the life course of both formal (mainly public) and informal (mainly family) support systems (Sidorenko and Walker, 2004). In contrast to the Vienna International Plan of Action on Ageing (UN, 1982), MIPAA sought to mainstream ageing in the global development agenda, and specifically, to enable older people to contribute fully to and benefit equally from societal development. The idea of older people as both agents and beneficiaries of development was at the core of MIPAA, aiming to 'ensure that people everywhere are able to age with security and dignity to continue to participate in their societies as citizens with full rights'. MIPAA advocated actions focused on realizing human rights and eliminating all forms of discrimination against older people; achieving secure ageing, including the eradication of poverty;

empowering older people; providing opportunities for individual development, self-fulfilment and wellbeing throughout life; ensuring gender equality; recognizing the crucial importance of family, providing healthcare, support and social protection for older people; facilitating partnership between all major stakeholders in the implementation process; harnessing scientific research and expertise; and addressing the situation of ageing indigenous people (see also State of the World's Indigenous Peoples (SOWIP), UN DESA, 2016).

Two types of policy measures were promoted by MIPAA: 'ageing mainstreaming' and 'ageing specific'. Mainstreaming measures are defined as concerted efforts to move towards a wide and equitable approach to policy integration by linking ageing to other frameworks for social and economic development and human rights. More specifically, MIPAA aimed for the integration of the responses to population ageing and the concerns of older people into national development frameworks and poverty eradication strategies. The ageing-specific measures encompass sectoral policy measures designed to address the human needs of older people (income security, health and social care and so on) and simultaneously provide opportunities for continuing integration (inclusion) of people at later stages of their lives into various spheres of societal life, including economic life. Ageing mainstreaming and specific policies should be applied simultaneously and coherently. For example, social security measures to benefit older people have to be synchronized with mainstream spheres of national policy, including development planning and policies aimed at reducing poverty, and incorporated into national budgets. Lastly, while MIPAA had a global reach, because of the wide variations in demographic, social, economic and other dimensions of ageing between world regions, its implementation was via the UN's five world regions (Sidorenko and Walker, 2017).

Despite the wide scope and adoption of MIPAA's recommendations, particularly within the less developed countries it was primarily aimed at, and the bringing together of ageing and development agendas, it is again striking that environmental sustainability was not yet part of those regional and global policy discourses. Similarly with the parallel production of the World Health Organization's (WHO) policy on active ageing (which was contributed to by the current author), which was initially formulated as a major contribution to the Second World Assembly on Ageing in Madrid (WHO, 2002). The refreshing of this policy in 2015, labelled as 'healthy ageing', brought global ageing policy closer to the UN's sustainable development agenda and, specifically, to alignment with its 17 SDGs with their 169 targets (WHO, 2015b,

2020). Indeed, the WHO integrated its healthy ageing strategy with the SDGs, as illustrated by the following examples of specific policies:

SDG 1: No poverty

The rights and wellbeing of older people can be protected by supporting their employment choices as well as providing a safety net for them and their families. Policy examples:

- flexible retirement policies;
- tax-funded minimum pensions;
- changing employers' attitudes towards older workers.

SDG 3: Good health and wellbeing

Optimizing opportunities for good health at all stages of life will ensure that older people can maintain independence and increase their social and economic participation in society, while reducing healthcare costs. Policy examples:

- continued and equitable access to disease prevention, promotion, treatment and rehabilitation through all stages of life;
- robust, integrated systems of health and long-term care oriented around maximizing function in older age.

SDG 11: Sustainable cities and communities

Working to create cities and communities that are sustainable and accessible to all requires a process across the life course that progressively improves the fit between people's needs and the environments in which they live. Policy examples:

- recognize the wide range of capacities and resources among older people;
- protect those who are most vulnerable;
- promote older people's inclusion in and contribution to all areas of community life (WHO, 2002).

The alignment between the WHO's healthy ageing initiative and the SDGs is taken further by the Decade of Healthy Ageing 2020–2030, adopted in 2016 (WHO, 2016). This builds on MIPAA and its regional implementation approach and reflects the central aim of the WHO's active ageing, now healthy ageing, strategies. In fact, it is explicitly linked to MIPAA's three priorities (outlined earlier) and the vision of the SDGs to leave no one behind. However, surprisingly, the Decade departs from the full life-course focus of the active ageing concept and narrows its emphasis to the second half of people's lives. The rationale that 'unique issues' arise in old age and the 'limited attention' later life has received compared to other age cohorts rings hollow when, first, we appreciate the earlier life-course origins of many limitations associated with old age and, second, we take into account the widespread neglect of both early and, especially, midlife in healthy ageing policies (see later). Also, if any age cohort can claim to be neglected in these discussions it is surely those in very late life, the old old, who are the least likely to receive secondary prevention services and are rarely included in active or healthy ageing measures. The Decade initiative comprises three action areas: age-friendly communities, person-centred integrated care, and community-based social care and support. It has an accountability framework, to understand and measure success, which is aligned to the key SDGs.

Is ageing sustainable?

As demonstrated earlier, sustainability has been a central feature of global policy discourses on ageing for four decades; however the overriding, not to say sole, concern has been with economic sustainability and, more often than not, with the long-term costs of PAYG pension systems. Following widespread reforms, the vast majority of public pensions are deemed to be sustainable economically, although scant attention has been paid to their role in social sustainability: the extent to which they enable older people to lead lives of decent social quality (Walker, 2011). This does not prevent those opposed ideologically to public pensions from raising this issue regularly. While ideological conviction is impervious to research evidence it is important to confirm that the policies aimed at extending working lives in line with increases in LE, which most developed countries have enacted or are in the process of doing so, will ensure the economic viability of even the most generous EU pensions (Valkonen and Barslund, 2019). However, the neglect of social sustainability in pension system reforms is demonstrated, for example, by the widespread blunt application of increases in pension ages. Clearly this is a policy that can be accommodated more easily by some workers than others and, therefore, in the absence of other measures, it increases inequalities in income and health. Economic sustainability is achieved at the expense of the low-skilled and most disadvantaged. Those market-liberal regimes that either cut their public pensions to the bone in the first wave of neoliberalism, or maintained only safety-net provision, have no genuine questions of economic sustainability to face, but the question of social sustainability is ever present.

As noted previously, when the designated pension reforms were carried out, attention shifted to the costs of health and long-term care. This new narrative spotlights the projected Exchequer costs of the longevity revolution. Again, this is primarily an economic narrative, not environmental or social. Given the continuing rise in LE in the leading more developed countries, at an average rate of two years in every ten years, and the association between advanced age and multimorbidity, is ageing sustainable even in narrow economist terms? Moreover, what are its environmental consequences? As Danny Dorling shows in Chapter 7, scaremongering about global population size is a red herring. However, while there is a projected deceleration of growth in the 61–80 age group, the picture for the oldest old (81–100) fluctuates. With regard to health status and the need for long-term care, though, we should be *less* concerned about the scale of population ageing and focus much *more* on the circumstances in which people age. This emphasizes the significance of the link made by the WHO between active/healthy ageing and sustainable development. So, let's look at the evidence supporting this connection.

Recent advances in scientific knowledge about the ageing process, based on the combination of biological and social scientific knowledge, and characterized as the 'new science of ageing' (Walker, 2014) pinpoint the importance of recognizing ageing as a lifelong process. The bio-social consensus on human ageing is that it is the result of cumulative wear and tear on the body. Summarizing drastically, two sets of factors are involved and interact with each other – intrinsic (genetic) and extrinsic (social and commercial) – although the exact damage-causing processes are not yet fully understood (Gems and Partridge, 2013; López-Otin et al, 2013). For this present purpose, however, what matters most is that there is no dispute about the fact that the extrinsic factors far outweigh the genetic ones in this biological ageing process, probably by as much as four or five to one. For example, in studies of monozygous twins, only 20 per cent of the variance in longevity has been attributed to inherited genes (Steves et al, 2012). The consensus furthermore rejects the idea of an 'ageing gene', that human beings are programmed to live for a fixed period of time or to age in a certain way (Kirkwood, 2008). The key extrinsic adult risk factors are two-fold. On the one hand, there are factors that are commonly labelled 'behavioural' but which may have social or commercial causes, such as poor diet, tobacco use, lack of physical activity, and alcohol consumption. On the other hand, there are structural risk factors such as deprivation and low socioeconomic status, food poverty, air pollution, excess sugar in food and work-related stress (Kirkwood and Austad, 2000). These risk factors inflict damage on the human body and mind, for example by raising blood pressure, and often result in the non-communicable diseases, or chronic conditions, that are associated with loss of function in later life, or biological ageing. These chronic conditions, sometimes referred to as the 'geriatric giants', include coronary heart disease (CHD), stroke and diabetes, which either truncate lives prematurely or result in disabilities requiring treatment and/or care. For example, high blood pressure is a main risk factor for cardiovascular diseases, especially stroke and CHD (Darnton-Hill et al, 2004).

The life course has been pinpointed as central to an understanding of the causes and human consequences of ageing because none of the biological and environmental interactions occur exclusively in old age (Figure 8.1). In fact, they are all longer term, some lifelong, and have major effects before the onset of conventionally defined old age (that is pension ages). This is chiefly why a social policy aimed at preventing later life disability, such as active ageing, must adopt a life-course orientation (see later). Essential scientific evidence about the associations between social and environmental factors in early and midlife and loss of functional capacity in later life has been produced by national and international analyses of longitudinal datasets. For example, an association between childhood deprivation and high

Figure 8.1: Cumulative risk factors for the development of non-communicable diseases across the life course[1]

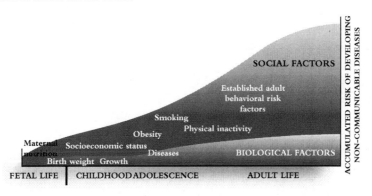

Source: Adapted with permission by Carmen Giefing-Kroell from Aboderin et al (2002: 2).

systolic blood pressure in early old age was highlighted by an analysis of the 1937/39 Boyd Orr cohort (Blane et al, 2004).

One of the most thorough investigations of the relationship between early life conditions and later life outcomes was undertaken by Kuh and colleagues (2012) as part of the UK New Dynamics of Ageing (NDA) ten-year programme (Kuh et al, 2018). A total of nine UK life-course cohorts were used to study the determinants of healthy ageing. Systematic reviews and meta-analysis found, on the one hand, no consistent evidence of associations between later life capability and a range of common genetic markers: the telomere maintenance gene TERT, a genotype related to athletic status ACTN3, genetic variants on the growth hormone and genetic markers of bone and joint health. On the other hand, clear associations were revealed between low socioeconomic status and area deprivation in childhood and lowered levels of functioning in old age. For example, birth weight is positively related to grip strength in old age (and in adult life). Similar associations were found between living in deprived areas in midlife and lower later-life functional capacity. Those living in deprived areas in midlife had lower levels of physical capacity in later life. Associations were also found between childhood education and cognition in old age (Kuh et al, 2012, 2014a): 'There is robust evidence that those in better socio-economic circumstances in childhood as well as adulthood have better [physical] capability at older ages' (Kuh et al, 2012: 1). In scientific terms, this research suggests that socioeconomic factors leave biological imprints on later-life physical development. One of the key policy findings from this research is that action to reduce deprivation in early and midlife is likely to improve health and functional capacity in old age (a fact that makes more puzzling the focus of the WHO's Decade only on later life). Furthermore, policies aimed at improving both living standards and early years' education are likely to increase later-life cognition. In a nutshell, social policy is far more important than genetics in determining the nature of old age and the extent of inequalities in its experience. It is the dominant influence among the non-genetic factors driving ageing and, therefore, it holds the promise of an alternative scenario in which the ageing process is modified to the great benefit of individuals and society.

The basis for a global programme to ensure that ageing is sustainable lies in research evidence, for example from UK NDA Programme, showing that it is possible to modify the ageing process at earlier stages of the life course so that the outcomes in old age are less restricting both physically and mentally. In other words, while ageing is inevitable it is also malleable. In policy terms, measures aimed at modifying the impact of various risk factors and thereby reducing the prevalence and severity of chronic conditions have a high likelihood of extending healthy life expectancy. What sort of measures are required? In the short term, various initiatives might be taken to attempt to mitigate the growth of later-life disability and enable more healthy lifestyles. For example, higher taxes could be levied on tobacco and alcohol and new taxes introduced on saturated fat in foods and sugar in soft drinks and confectionary. Even the relatively modest levy on the sugar content of soft drinks proposed by the UK government in April 2018 could reduce obesity among adults and children by 144,000 per year and prevent 19,000 cases of obesity (Briggs et al, 2016). Smoking-related disabilities in the UK are estimated to drive £760 million per annum in social care costs alone (All Party Parliamentary Group on Smoking and Health, 2017) and there should be a levy on tobacco manufacturers to fund measures to reduce smoking prevalence. Such measures are badly needed in less developed countries too.

National programmes of physical exercise are also urgently required and would be expected to have a significant impact providing they are tailored to specific populations (see later). For example, the active have a 33–50 per cent lower risk of developing Type 2 diabetes than the inactive; and the moderately active have a 20 per cent lower risk of stroke incidence than the inactive (Chief Medical Officer, 2011; Kuh et al, 2014b). The physically active are generally healthier and live longer than the sedentary. Prolonged periods of inactivity are associated with heightened risk of cardiovascular disease, cancer and diabetes (Pate et al, 1995). There is also evidence that physical exercise has a beneficial effect on cognition, as well as other protective effects on health (Lees and Hopkins, 2013). Put crudely, major physical and mental health risks and substantial health and social care costs are, to some extent, the products of inactivity. Despite the fact that an increasing number of countries have national physical activity plans there is no sign of a global improvement in activity levels but, rather, a global 'pandemic of inactivity' (Andersen et al, 2016). Critically, regular activity can diminish the increased mortality risks associated with prolonged sitting.

Another example is the evidence on the beneficial effects of long-term calorie restriction, with adequate intake of nutrients, which decreases the risk of developing most age-associated chronic conditions, including Type-2 diabetes, hypertension, cardiovascular diseases and cancer (Fontana and Partridge, 2015). Indeed, significant health benefits flow from even a 5 per cent weight loss by obese people, resulting in lowered risks for diabetes and heart disease (Magkos et al, 2016). A further example is the need for health professionals to understand the effects of ageing on the body's immune system, especially the reduction in the number of antibody-producing cells in the bone marrow (Pritz et al, 2015). This means that protection from infectious diseases, which cause an estimated one third of mortality above the age of 65, is less than at younger ages and, as a consequence, older people require more frequent vaccination. A final example is the operation of mental stimulation to not only improve brain function but also provide protection from cognitive decline, in a similar way to physical exercise helping to prevent loss of bone and muscle mass (Bertozzi et al, 2017).

Practical questions abound, of course, about any such programmes aimed at physical activity, weight loss and cognitive stimulation. To be effective, such initiatives must be well-funded, tailored to local economic and cultural circumstances and sponsored nationally. As with the longer-term comprehensive strategy set out below, there is a risk of stigma being associated with non-participation. This can be minimized by setting the inclusion bar low and not applying any formal sanctions. Regular television and social media exposure would also assist in gaining wide acceptance. In the longer term it is vital to match the scale of the ageing challenge with an ambitious and comprehensive response. The leading global contender for this role is the idea of 'active ageing' (WHO, 2002). Although the concept of active ageing is contested and often expanded to 'active and healthy ageing' by international institutions (EC, 2020; WHO, 2015a), it remains the most widely accepted strategy on ageing (Walker and Maltby, 2012) and was integral to the 2002 Madrid International Plan of Action on Ageing (UN, 2002). According to the WHO (2002: 3), 'Active ageing is the process of optimising opportunities for health, participation and security in order to enhance quality of life as people age'. This pivotal definition may be mildly criticized for placing too great an emphasis on health and not being sufficiently policy oriented. To counter these objections, while retaining the key life-course focus, an alternative policy-oriented definition has been proffered: 'Active ageing should be a comprehensive strategy to maximise participation and well-being as people age. It should operate simultaneously at the individual (lifestyle), organisational (management) and societal (policy) levels and at all stages of life course' (Walker, 2009: 90).

The life-course focus at the core of the active ageing concept is often overlooked in practice, with old age only being spotlighted. It is one of the seven fundamental principles supporting the implementation of this internationally policy-oriented definition of active ageing. First 'active' should embrace all activities that contribute to both physical and mental wellbeing. This is necessary to counteract the common stereotypes of hyperactive pensioners as the epitome of active ageing. At the same time, the preventative power of physical exercise must not be forgotten (WHO, 2010). Equally important are activities intended to maintain or regain mental capacity, such as the 'five ways to wellbeing' (NEF, 2008). Second, the life-course perspective is essential to recognize that chronic conditions and capabilities in later life are invariably the outcomes of earlier-life social and economic status and exposure to risk factors. To reiterate, the evidence from cohort meta-analyses is that childhood circumstances greatly influence the prospects for active ageing in later life (Kuh et al, 2014b). Third, a preventative approach is crucial. Thus, the explicit goal of a social policy on ageing for sustainability should be to prevent as many as possible of the chronic conditions that can blight or curtail later life. In this regard, it is vital to address not only the low priority allocated to prevention in health and social care but also the neglect of secondary interventions among those already suffering from ill-health or disability (Pope and Tarlov, 1991). Fourth, a comprehensive strategy on active ageing must employ all possible policy levers, upstream primary prevention and downstream secondary prevention and rehabilitation as well as spanning all central and local government departments. Fifth, active ageing should not exclude any age group, as the common stereotype does with the very old and frail. In fact, there is evidence that even minor exercises can improve both physical functioning and mental wellbeing (Grönstedt et al, 2013). Sixth, in public health terms, top-down exhortations or abstract codes of behaviour are unlikely to work for the many. Instead, what is required is an empowerment approach, which seeks to engage different groups of citizens in a dialogue about ageing and the avoidable risk factors, as a counterpart to preventative or remedial actions. This is not easy or straightforward, especially in view of the vested interests involved, and is a non-starter without the political will to get it underway and support it. Finally, it is essential to account for inequality and cultural diversity. For example, gender differences in the application of active ageing are substantial (Foster and Walker, 2013). Furthermore, some forms of activity may be less acceptable or prohibited in certain cultures and so flexibility in implementation is essential.

The underlying objective of this strategy can be demonstrated with reference to a typical life course (Figure 8.2). Physical activity peaks in early adult life and then declines during middle and later life, at vastly different rates due mainly to variable exposure to risk factors; thus the variations in capacity within cohorts are larger than those between cohorts (Kirkwood, 2008). The cumulative impact of physical or mental injuries and/or chronic conditions is that a person's functional

Figure 8.2: Functional capacity and age[2]

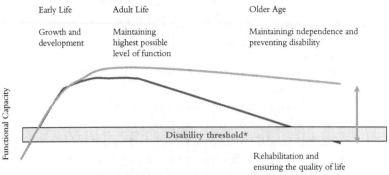

Note: upper line: desired path lower line: path of normal functional capacity.
Source: Adapted with permission from Kalache and Kickbush (1997: 2).

capacity declines until it crosses the disability threshold. The idea of the active ageing strategy is to attempt to slow or prevent the decline in functional capacity and thereby enable people to enjoy disability-free extended lives for as long as possible. Figure 8.2 shows the path of physical capacity but some aspects of cognitive ability also follow a similar one.

Such a transformation from segmented age-group specialisms to an overall life-course approach would, of course, not be easy. Simply contemplating the seismic shift in health services, from acute sickness to prevention and rehabilitation, is sufficient to convey the scale and depth of the necessary changes (not to mention other substantial barriers; Walker, 2018b). The alternative, however, is to proceed as now and tacitly accept the present extent of preventable life-restricting conditions and their human injuries and social and economic costs.

What about the environmental impact of population ageing? An authoritative EU report concluded that it is not likely to lead to significant environmental changes or pressures (EC, 2008). Older generations are generally less mobile and consume, on average, the same or less resources than younger age groups. An important exception is the consumption of heat, gas and other fuels where, in more developed countries, consumption per person is higher on average than for the rest of the population. Also, the trend for healthy and wealthy older people to undertake international travel might increase their carbon footprint (a conclusion that must await the impact of COVID-19).

In contrast, there is substantial evidence of older people's vulnerability to environmental change. For example, fatalities in environmental disasters, such as heatwaves, floods, cold snaps and air pollution tend to occur most among frail older people, particularly but not exclusively in less developed countries (Hatton, 2008). The 2003 heatwave in Europe resulted in an estimated 14,800 deaths in France of which 70 per cent were among those aged 75 and over. One reason for this bias in death rates is the prevalence among older people of the chronic conditions and lowered immunity highlighted earlier, therefore the preventative strategy proposed would assist in reducing older people's vulnerability to environmental disasters caused by heating (while not inhibiting global action against the climate emergency). (This is also the case for the extreme age bias in COVID-19 deaths.) A crucial further step in reducing their vulnerability and promoting social sustainability is the provision of universal public pensions in all less developed countries.

Conclusion

This chapter has demonstrated that global discourses on ageing and sustainability have consistently ignored the ageing process and environmental and social sustainability. It is only very recently that attempts have been made to bring these together. Economic issues continue to dominate global discussions of sustainability. Yet, in existing global policy frameworks, such as active ageing and the SDGs, there is a sound basis for a more progressive approach which would see ageing aligned with economic, environmental and social sustainability. The best starting point would be to embed the life-course approach into national policy thinking and action. Then develop variations of active ageing which reflect specific local customs, culture and levels of economic development. It should focus on all generations, not only older people. Therein lies the potential both to improve the quality of people's lives as they age and to make ageing sustainable now and in the future.

Notes

[1] Reproduced from *Life Course Perspective on Coronary Heart Disease, Stroke and Diabetes: Key Issues and Implications for Policy & Research*, I. Aboderin, A. Kalache, Y. Ben-Shlomo, J. W. Lynch, C. S. Yajnik, D. Kuh and D. Yach, p. 2, WHO/NMH/NPH/02.1, Geneva: WHO, 2002.

[2] Reproduced from *World Health*, 50(4), A. Kalache and I. Kickbush, 'A Global Strategy for Health', pp. 4–5, 1997.

References

Aboderin I., Kalache. A., Ben-Shlomo. Y., Lynch, J. W., Yajnik, C. S., Kuh, D. and Yach, D. (2002) *Life Course Perspectives on Coronary Heart Disease, Stroke and Diabetes: Key Issues and Implications for Policy and Research*, WHO/NMH/NPH/02.1, Geneva: WHO.

All-Party Parliamentary Group on Smoking and Health (2017) *Burning Injustice: Reducing Tobacco-driven Harm and Inequality*, London: UK Parliament.

Andersen, L. B., Mota, J. and Di Pietro, L. (2016) 'Update on the Global Pandemic of Physical Inactivity', *The Lancet*, 388(10051): 1255–6.

Bertozzi, B., Tosti, V. and Fontana, L. (2017) 'Beyond Calories: An Integrated Approach to Promote Health, Longevity and Well-being', *Gerontology*, 63(1): 13–19.

Blane, D., Higgs, P., Hyde, M. and Wiggins, R. (2004) 'Life Course Influences on Quality of Life in Early Old Age', *Social Science and Medicine*, 58(11): 2171–9.

Briggs, A., Mytton, O., Kehlbacher, A., Tiffin, R., Elhussein, A., Rayner, M., Jebb, S. A., Blakely, T. and Scarborough, P. (2016) 'Health Impact Assessment of the UK Soft Drinks Levy', *The Lancet Public Health*, 2(1): e15–e22.

Cann, P. and Dean, M. (2009) (eds) *Unequal Ageing*, Bristol: Policy Press.

Chief Medical Officer (2011) *Annual Report on the State of the Public's Health*, London: Department of Health.

Darnton-Hill, I., Nishida, C. and James, W. (2004) 'A Life Course Approach to Diet, Nutrition and the Prevention of Chronic Diseases', *Public Health Nutrition*, 7(1A): 101–21.

EC (European Commission) (1999) *Towards a Europe of All Ages – Promoting Prosperity and Intergenerational Solidarity*, COM(1999)221 final, Brussels: EC.

EC (2006) *The Demographic Future of Europe – From Challenge to Opportunity*, COM(2006)571 final, Brussels: EC.

EC (2008) *Environment and Ageing*, Brussels: EC Directorate-General Environment.

EC (2020) *European Week of Active & Healthy Ageing*, Brussels: EC, https://ec.europa.eu/eip/ageing/events/european-week-active-and-healthy-ageing-ewaha.

Fontana, L. and Partridge, L. (2015) 'Promoting Health and Longevity Through Diet – From Model Organisations to Humans', *Cell*, 161: 106–18.

Foster, L. and Walker, A. (2013) 'Gender and Active Ageing in Europe', *European Journal of Ageing*, 10(1): 3–10.

Gems, D. and Partridge, L. (2013) 'Genetics of Longevity in Model Organisms: Debate and Paradigm Shifts', *Annual Review of Physiology*, 75: 621–44.

Grönstedt, H., Grönstedt, H., Frändin, K., Bergland, A., Helbostad, J. L., Granbo, R., Puggaard, L., Andresen, M. and Hellström, K. (2013) 'Effects of Individually Tailored Physical and Daily Activities in Nursing Home Residents on Activities of Daily Living, Physical Romance and Physical Activity Level: A Randomised Control Trial', *Gerontology*, 59(3): 220–29.

Hatton, D. (2008) *Older People in Emergencies*, Geneva: WHO.

Kalache, A. and Kickbush, I. (1997) 'A Global Strategy for Health', *World Health*, 50(4): 4–5.

Kirkwood, T. (2008) 'A Systematic Look at an Old Problem', *Nature*, 451: 944–7.

Kirkwood, T. and Austad, S. (2000) 'Why Do We Age?', *Nature*, 408: 233–38.

Kuh, D., Cooper, R., Richards, M., Gale, C., von Zglinicki, T. and Guralnik, J. (2012) 'A Life Course Approach to Healthy Ageing: The HALCyon Programme', *Public Health*, 126(3): 193–5.

Kuh, D., Cooper, R., Hardy, R., Richards, M. and Ben-Shlomo, Y. (eds) (2014a) *A Life Course Approach to Healthy Ageing*, Oxford: Oxford University Press.

Kuh, D., Karunananthan, S., Bergma, H. and Cooper, R. (2014b) 'A Life-course Approach to Healthy Ageing: Maintaining Physical Capability', *Proceedings of the Nutrition Society*, 73: 237–48.

Kuh, D., Hardy, R., Gale, C., Elliot, J., Ben-Shlomo, Y., Cooper, R. and the HALCyon team (2018) 'Healthy Ageing across the Life Course', in A. Walker (ed) *The New Dynamics of Ageing*, Volume 1, Bristol: Policy Press, 59–80.

Lees, C. and Hopkins, J. (2013) 'Effect of Aerobic Exercise on Cognition, Academic Achievement, and Psychosocial Function in Children: A Systematic Review of Randomised Control Trials', *Prevention of Chronic Diseases*, 10: E174.

López-Otin, C., Blasco, M., Partridge, L., Serrano, M. and Kroemer, G. (2013) 'The Hallmarks of Aging', *Cell*, 153: 1194–217.

Magkos, F., Fraterrigo, G., Yoshino, J., Luecking, C., Kirbach, K., Kelly, S. C., de Las Fuentes, L., He, S., Okunade, A. L., Patterson, B. W. and Klein, S. (2016) 'Effects of Moderate and Subsequent Weight Loss on Metabolic Function and Adipose Biology in Humans with Obesity', *Cell Metabolism*, 23(4): 591–601.

Marmot, M., Allen, J., Boyce, T., Goldblatt, P. and Morrison, J. (2020) *Health Equity in England: The Marmot Review 10 Years On*, London: IHE.

NEF (New Economics Foundation) (2008) *Five Ways to Wellbeing*, London: NEF.

OECD (Organisation for Economic Co-operation and Development) (2006) *Health and Long-Term Care – What Are the Main Drivers?*, Paris: OECD Publishing.

Oeppen, J. and Vaupel, J. (2002) 'Broken Limits to Life Expectancy', *Science*, 296: 1029–31.

Pate, R., Pratt, M., Blair, S., Haskell, W., Macera, C., Bouchard, C., Buchner, D., Ettinger, W., Heath, G., King, A., Kriska, A., Leon, A., Marcus, B., Morris, J., Paffenbarger, R., Patrick, K., Pollock, M., Rippe, J., Sallis, J. and Wilmore, J. (1995) 'Physical Activity and Public Health', *Journal of the American Medical Association*, 273: 402–7.

Pope, A. and Tarlov, A. (1991) *Disability in America: Towards a National Agenda for Prevention*, Washington, DC: National Academy Press.

Pritz, T., Lair, J., Ban, M., Keller, M., Weinberger, B., Krismer, M. and Grubeck-Loebenstein, B. (2015) 'Plasma Cell Numbers Decrease in Bone Marrow of Old Patients', *European Journal of Immunology*, 45(3): 738–46.

Sidorenko, A. and Walker, A. (2004) 'The Madrid International Plan of Action on Ageing: From Conception to Implementation', *Ageing & Society*, 24(2): 147–65.

Sidorenko, A. and Walker, A. (2017) 'Policy Options for Responding to Population Ageing', in J.-P. Michel, B. Beattie, F. Martin and J. Walston (eds) *Oxford Textbook of Geriatric Medicine*, Third Edition, Oxford: Oxford University Press, 91–100.

Steves, C., Spector, T. and Jackson, S. (2012) 'Ageing, Genes, Environment and Epigenetics: What Twin Studies Tell Us Now, and in the Future', *Age and Ageing*, 41(5): 581–86.

UN (United Nations) (1982) *Vienna International Plan of Action on Ageing*, https://digitallibrary.un.org/record/170749?ln=en.

UN (2002) *Madrid International Plan of Action on Ageing*, Second World Assembly on Ageing, Madrid, 8–12 April, New York: UN, www.un.org/esa/socdev/documents/ageing/MIPAA/political-declaration-en.pdf.

UN DESA (2016) *State of the World's Indigenous Peoples: Indigenous Peoples' Access to Health Services*, New York: UN, https://doi.org/10.18356/7914b045-en.

UN DESA Population Division (2002) *World Population Ageing 1950–2050*, ST/ESA/SER.A/207, New York, NY, UN.

UN DESA Population Division (2019) *World Population Prospects, The 2019 Revision – Volume I: Comprehensive Tables*, New York: UN, https://doi.org/10.18356/15994a82-en.

UNGA (United Nations General Assembly) (1995) *Conceptual Framework of a Programme for the Preparation and Observance of the International Year of Older Persons in 1999*, Report of the Secretary-General, A/50/114, https://digitallibrary.un.org/record/177179?ln=en.

UNGA (2000) *United Nations Millennium Declaration*, A/RES/55/2, https://digitallibrary.un.org/record/422015?ln=en.

UNGA (2015) *Transforming Our World: The 2030 Agenda for Sustainable Development*, Resolution 70/1, https://digitallibrary.un.org/record/808134?ln=en.

Valkonen, T. J. and Barsland, M. C. (2019) 'Achieving Economic Sustainability in Ageing Societies', in A. Walker (ed) *The Future of Ageing in Europe*, Singapore: Palgrave Macmillan, 53–77.

Walker, A. (1990) 'The Economic "Burden" of Ageing and the Prospect of Intergenerational Conflict', *Ageing & Society*, 10(4): 377–96.

Walker, A. (2009) 'The Emergence and Application of Active Ageing in Europe', *Journal of Ageing and Social Policy*, 21(1): 75–93.

Walker, A. (2011) 'Social Quality and Welfare System Sustainability', *International Journal of Social Quality*, 1(1): 5–19.

Walker, A. (ed) (2014) *The New Science of Ageing*, Bristol: Policy Press.

Walker, A. (2018) 'Ageing and Social Justice', in G. Craig (ed) *Handbook on Global Social Justice*, Cheltenham, Edward Elgar, 213–27.

Walker, A. and Deacon, B. (2003) 'Economic Globalisation and Policies on Aging', *Journal of Societal and Social Policy*, 2(2): 1–18.

Walker, A. and Maltby, T. (2012) 'Active Ageing: A Strategic Policy Solution to Demographic Ageing in the EU', *International Journal of Social Welfare*, 21(S1): 5117–30.

World Bank (1994) *Averting the Old Age Crisis: Policies to Protect the Old and Promote Growth*, New York: World Bank, https://doi.org/10.1596/0-8213-2970-7.

WHO (World Health Organization) (2002) *Active Ageing: A Policy Framework*, Geneva: WHO, www.who.int/ageing/publications/active_ageing/en/.

WHO (2010) *Global Recommendations on Physical Activity for Health*, Geneva: WHO.

WHO (2015a) *World Report on Ageing and Health*, Geneva: WHO, https://apps.who.int/iris/bitstream/handle/10665/186463/9789240694811_eng.pdf;jsessionid=872AF59DEA452A8DB439B68F56E757C8?sequence=1.

WHO (2015b) *Global Strategy and Action Plan on Ageing and Health*, http://www.who.int/ageing/en/.

WHO (2016) *Decade of Healthy Ageing 2020–2050*, www.who.int/ageing/global-strategy/.

WHO (2020) *Healthy Ageing and the Sustainable Development Goals*, www.who.int/ageing/sdgs/en.

9

The political challenges to governing global migration and social welfare

Edward A. Koning

Introduction

The political spotlight on immigrants' use of social programmes seems to be growing brighter and brighter. A key argument for Brexiteers has been that leaving the European Union (EU) would eliminate the entitlements of EU citizens to British social programmes, Donald Trump has done his best to reignite anger about 'illegals on welfare', and government leaders across Western Europe objected to the admission of asylum seekers in the wake of the Mediterranean refugee crisis out of fear that it would place too much pressure on their welfare systems. Indeed, immigration increasingly complicates the social question, inviting dilemmas about the social protection different classes of residents deserve, and about the maintenance of solidarity in societies rife with intergroup tension. Considering the steep rise in global migration patterns projected by the United Nations (for example UN DESA, 2016) and the increasing success of anti-immigrant politicians, this development does not seem likely to abate any time soon.

This chapter reviews how immigration affects the politics of redistribution in Western democracies. The main argument is that the challenges of reconciling migration and welfare are aggravated by the political process. Migration raises complicated questions about the portability of social security arrangements and differentiation in social rights extension. The political sensitivity of issues of immigration and multiculturalism, however, makes it difficult to engage with such questions in a detached manner. The image of the burdensome immigrant has become common in media coverage, the sentiment that welfare should be reserved to native-born citizens is increasingly consequential, and politicians who favour extreme solutions are having a greater influence on policy decisions. For these reasons, it seems unreasonably optimistic to expect that the pressing questions immigration raises about the future of the welfare state will be tackled effectively.

The next section looks at the policy challenge that migration poses to the welfare system. It is then demonstrated that news media frequently depict immigrants as a drain on the system, and do so more now than they did three decades ago. The third section turns the attention to public opinion and shows that while the number of people who believe that immigrants are a leech on the system seems to be in decline, the sentiment is nevertheless having a larger impact on election outcomes. The chapter then turns to party politics, and argues that the increasing success of parties that run on a platform favouring extreme solutions and displaying hostility towards immigrants has produced a climate that discourages constructive and disinterested policy proposals. The final section summarizes these findings and spells out their implications.

Challenges in reconciling migration and welfare

Migration is perhaps the most obvious reason that today's social question has a transnational character. Systems of social rights extension were originally developed to protect members of the nation state (Marshall, 1950), with little anticipation of the massive increase in cross-border mobility that occurred afterwards. And while many observers have exaggerated the extent to which migration and redistribution are at odds, a tension is undeniable. Some of the first scholarly analyses of the relationship between immigration and welfare investigated the worst-case scenario that immigration would make systems of redistribution unsustainable, hypothesizing not only that immigrants would place too heavy a burden on social expenditure, but also that an influx of immigrants would make native-born citizens less willing to support social programmes. Overall, existing research has found little support for these hypotheses (Koning, 2019). This does not mean, however, that reconciling migration and welfare is easy.

For one thing, designing a welfare state in an era of migration raises normative questions that are likely to divide both the electorate and the political elite. Some will argue that immigrants are less deserving of social protection than native-born citizens, either because they believe newcomers have not contributed enough, or because they consider foreign-born individuals as outsiders who do not belong in their country of residence in the first place. Others will insist that human rights considerations require the state to treat all individuals on its territory equally regardless of their place of birth. Besides disagreement on these principled questions, controversy is equally likely to arise regarding the empirical effects of migration on the welfare state. On the one hand, many have theorized that generous welfare states function as a 'magnet' for people who seek social protection, encourage newcomers to take advantage of the system, and will therefore face both an increase in social expenditure and a decrease in social solidarity and cohesion as a result (see also Jane Jenson, Chapter 11 in this volume). Others, on the other hand, have hypothesized that generous approaches will lead to more equality between immigrants and native-born citizens, and that this in turn would reduce existing tensions and alleviate the negative external effects of leaving a class of residents in the margins of society (Sabates-Wheeler and Feldman, 2011). While these competing expectations are theoretically testable, there is currently little agreement in the literature regarding their relative veracity. Moreover, it seems safe to assume that an academic consensus that some of these expectations are incorrect would not prevent them from continuing to influence public and political debate.

Based on these normative and empirical disagreements, two policy issues seem particularly intractable. First, contemporary welfare states need to decide on the nature of *rights differentiation* between native-born citizens and immigrants. Policy makers face a difficult decision regarding which of the existing social benefits should be accessible to immigrants, and whether new benefits should be created that exclusively target immigrants in an attempt to assist their social and economic integration. The residence status of immigrants is of particular relevance here. Few policy makers would advocate blatant discrimination between native-born and naturalized citizens, and similarly rare would be calls to grant people without legal status full access to the complete welfare state apparatus. But beyond these two extremes, it will be difficult to find the right balance in determining the rights of permanent, temporary and undocumented migrants.

For that reason, it is unsurprising that we see wildly different approaches to rights differentiation from one country to another. Some countries have gone very far in disentitling immigrants by placing lengthy residence requirements for access to benefits, demanding immigrants to satisfy eligibility requirements that do not apply to native-born citizens, categorically excluding temporary migrants from a range of services and programmes, or by mandating recent newcomers to rely on family members in times of hardship. Other countries, on the other hand, have implemented very few such restrictions. Instead, they grant most immigrants fundamentally the same social rights as native-born citizens, and even offer social programmes specifically targeted at immigrants, such as state-funded language training, internship programmes or tax credits for employers who hire immigrants.

The second issue regards *portability arrangements* which allow the enjoyment of benefits outside of the country of benefit extension. Even if a state is able to conclude which social rights immigrants should enjoy, a different question is whether these rights should be guaranteed by the country of residence or by the country of origin. This question has become all the more pressing in light of the large increases in temporary and circular migration (Banting and Koning, 2017). Again, there are several considerations that likely inform an answer to this question. For one thing, portability seems more reasonable in the case of contributory benefits that are funded by premiums than non-contributory benefits that are funded by general taxation. If an individual moves out of the country after having built up entitlements to a contributory pension programme, there would likely be fewer objections to them enjoying those pension benefits abroad than if the person would be claiming access to a universal tax-paid pension benefit. Equally important to consider is the origin of migrants. A welfare state could reasonably expect recent newcomers to be protected by their country of origin if they are migrating from Sweden, but not if they are arriving from Somalia.

Again, we see large cross-national differences in the availability and scope of these type of arrangements. By far the most far-reaching system of portability arrangements can be found in the EU. A staple of EU law is the so-called *lex loci laboris*, which mandates that EU citizens should be covered by the social security system of the last member state in which they were gainfully employed, regardless of their country of residence. A more controversial arrangement is that member states are obliged to determine eligibility for contributory programmes based on an applicant's work history in any EU country. (In other words, a person who has worked for four years in Poland and one year in Germany should have the same unemployment insurance as a person who has worked five years in Germany.) Similar, although less extensive, arrangements exist between other countries with long histories of mutual migration, such as the Nordic countries or the Antipodes. But not all migrants can benefit from these kinds of provisions. Rachel Sabates-Wheeler and colleagues (2011) estimate that only about one in four of all migrants in the world benefit from portability arrangements that ensure they are fully protected by either their country of origin or country of residence.

All in all, migration raises many questions regarding the level, structure, coordination and eligibility requirements of social benefits, and the answers are not always obvious. If people are residing in a country without being eligible for legal residence, how does one protect their minimum rights without increasing their chances of staying? If people arrive in a country at an old age from a country that offers little old age protection, how does one avoid poverty during retirement without incurring significant additional expenses? If unemployed immigrants are less protected than unemployed native-born citizens, how can one guarantee equality without necessitating a fundamental overhaul of contributory insurance programs? And if people are in a country for only a few years of their life, which country has the primary responsibility of taking care of them when the need arises? As this small selection of questions demonstrates, migration poses challenges to the configuration of the welfare state that would be difficult to address in any political context. As hard as it might be to formulate ideal responses to these dilemmas, however, it is relatively easy to point out bad ones. For example, several countries blatantly discriminate against temporary migrants in making them pay premiums for unemployment insurance benefits they are never able to draw from because their status mandates them to leave the country if they become unemployed. In other cases, restrictive policy changes have no demonstrable effect other than politicization because they are incompatible with existing national or international legal frameworks. And yet other approaches are downright counterproductive, such as the Dutch approach of making access to transfer benefits conditional on taking language classes, yet demanding people who are in such a socioeconomic position that they might be incentivized by this rule to pay for those lessons themselves. Unfortunately, the context in most Western democracies seems to favour these types of responses over those that are based on detached and even-handed analysis.

The 'burdensome immigrant' in Western media

One important component of this context is the portrayal of immigrants in media outlets. As the rich literature on this subject has amply documented, the depiction of immigrants as a burden on the welfare system is common across Western media, especially when the coverage focuses on refugees and asylum seekers in particular (Philo et al, 2013; Berg-Nordlie, 2018).

This section makes a modest contribution to this large literature by investigating whether images of a burden have become more common over the last four decades or so in the coverage of immigration in major newspapers in four English-speaking Western democracies. More specifically, this analysis measures the frequency of such an image in coverage on immigration from 1981 to 2018 in the *Sydney Morning Herald* and *The Age* in Australia, the *Globe and Mail*, *Toronto Star* and *National Post* in Canada, *The Times*, *The Guardian* and *The Daily Mail* in the UK, and the *New York Times*, *USA Today* and *Wall Street Journal* in the USA. These newspapers were selected because they all have a national scope and a high readership, while also ensuring the inclusion of publications with a different political orientation in each country.[1]

For each of these 11 newspapers, and for each year from 1981 to 2018 for which data were available in database Factiva,[2] the number of articles discussing immigration were counted, and for all of those articles it was established how many included discussion of welfare and social benefits, and, in turn, how many of those used words such as 'burden' in describing the relationship between migration and social benefits.[3] As such, the analysis provides a longitudinal picture of the extent to which major newspapers in these four countries invoke the image of immigrants as a burden on the welfare system.

Overall, in these 11 newspapers about 1 in 7 articles on immigration discusses welfare benefits, and about 1 in 20 articles on immigration discusses welfare benefits in terms of a burden. These numbers are remarkably similar from one country to another, ranging from 12.7 per cent in Canada to 15.8 per cent in the UK on the former indicator, and from 4.6 per cent in Canada to 6.1 per cent in the United States on the latter.

More important for our purposes is that the percentages are increasing over time. As Figure 9.1 shows, in the early 1980s only about 12 per cent of articles on immigration discussed social benefits, whereas that had gone up to about 16 per cent by 2018. Figure 9.2 shows the percentage of articles on immigration that discuss social benefits in terms of a burden, and the increase is even steeper, from about 4 per cent in the early 1980s to almost 6 per cent in 2018. While these increases might not seem very large in absolute terms, they are sizeable in relative terms. They imply that today's consumer of newspapers in these countries is about 30 per cent more likely to read about social benefits in articles about immigration, and about 50 per cent more likely to read about immigration in terms of it burdening the welfare system than its counterpart three decades ago. In other words, these findings suggest that people who read about immigration in newspapers are now more encouraged to think about the costs for the welfare state, and to consider immigration as part and parcel of social policy issues.

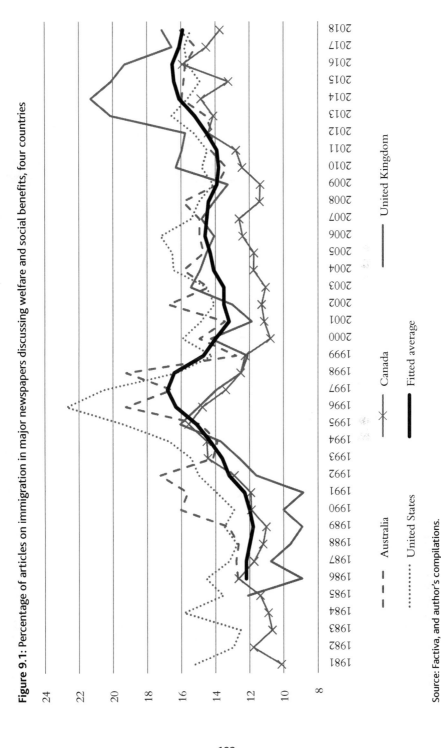

Figure 9.1: Percentage of articles on immigration in major newspapers discussing welfare and social benefits, four countries

Source: Factiva, and author's compilations.

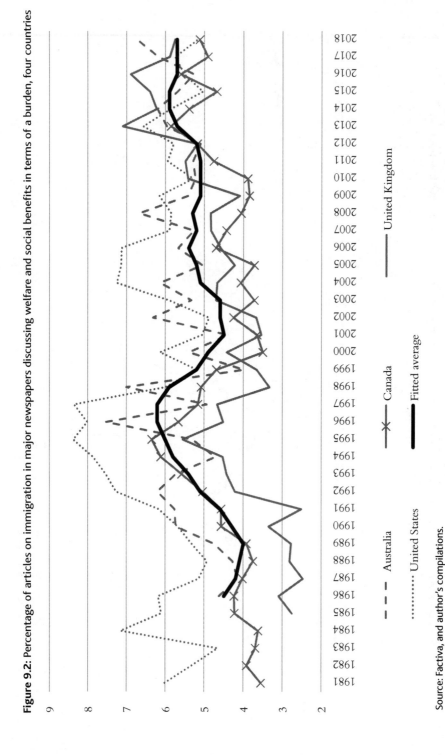

Figure 9.2: Percentage of articles on immigration in major newspapers discussing welfare and social benefits in terms of a burden, four countries

Source: Factiva, and author's compilations.

Electoral relevance of welfare chauvinism

The increasing media attention to the costs of immigration for the welfare system is important primarily because it is likely to inform the views of the electorate. Research on political communication has long emphasized that media have a powerful influence not only on the issues that citizens think about, but also on the considerations they are most likely to associate with those issues. Immigration is no exception. A large body of literature demonstrates that the frequency and tone of media coverage have important consequences for public opinion on immigration. Several experimental and observational studies find that exposure to news about immigration can increase opposition, especially if it depicts immigrants in unflattering terms (Brader et al, 2008; Boomgaarden and Vliegenthart, 2009).

Of particular interest to the current investigation are public attitudes about immigrants' place in the welfare system. There is a rapidly growing literature on public perceptions regarding how much immigrants are making use of the welfare system, and public opinion on the kinds of benefits to which immigrants should be entitled. This literature invariably finds that large portions of the electorate in Western democracies are in favour of limiting immigrants' access to benefits and believe immigrants are taking advantage of the welfare system, and that those sentiments influence voting behaviour (De Koster et al, 2012; Koning, 2017). It is worth noting that these sentiments are not exclusive to those who object to redistribution in general. Quite the contrary, opposition to immigrants' entitlements often goes hand in hand with support for a welfare system in general. In this way, immigration has fragmented coalitions that support egalitarian policies, and made debates about social issues centre more on the types of people who are deserving of support than on the merit of intervening in the market and combating inequality and poverty more generally.

The following will investigate whether views on immigrants' use of welfare benefits have become more politically consequential over time. Existing literature only allows us to infer an answer to such a question indirectly, considering that available studies are case study investigations, survey experiments or cross-national investigations at a single moment in time. However, if it is true that there is now more media attention to immigrants' place in the welfare system and the coverage is now more likely to describe immigration as a burden, we should expect that these issues have become more central to citizens' political considerations.

This investigation is necessarily limited by data availability. Indeed, one of the reasons why scholars have so far paid little attention to longitudinal developments in views about immigrants' welfare use is that there are few available cross-national surveys that have probed respondents' attitudes on this issue the same way at multiple points in time. The most useful data in this regard come from the European Social Survey (ESS), which asked two relevant questions. First, it asked respondents on three occasions (2002, 2008 and 2014) the following question: "Most people who come to live here work and pay taxes. They also use health and welfare services. On balance, do you think people who come here take out more than they put in or put in more than they take out?" Second, it asked respondents twice (2008 and 2016) whether immigrants should gain access to the same social rights as native-born citizens on arrival, after a year, after having worked and paid taxes for a year, after having acquired citizenship, or never.

Figure 9.3 shows the average percentage of respondents expressing reservations about immigrants' place in the welfare system in each available wave across 14 Western European countries.[4] All in all, there is no evidence of an increase in these sentiments over time. If anything, they seem to be on the decline. In 8 of the 14 countries under study, the proportion of respondents who strongly agreed that immigrants take out much more than they contribute was statistically significantly lower in 2014 than in 2002, and only two countries (Austria and

Figure 9.3: Attitudes on immigrants' utilization of and access to welfare in Western Europe

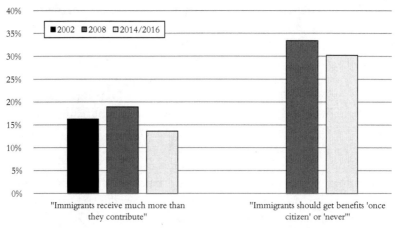

Note: Entries show the average percentage of respondents across 14 countries indicating agreement with the respective statement.
Source: ESS, 2002–16 (www.europeansocialsurvey.org).

Figure 9.4: Effect of attitudes regarding immigrants' utilization of and access to welfare on vote choice

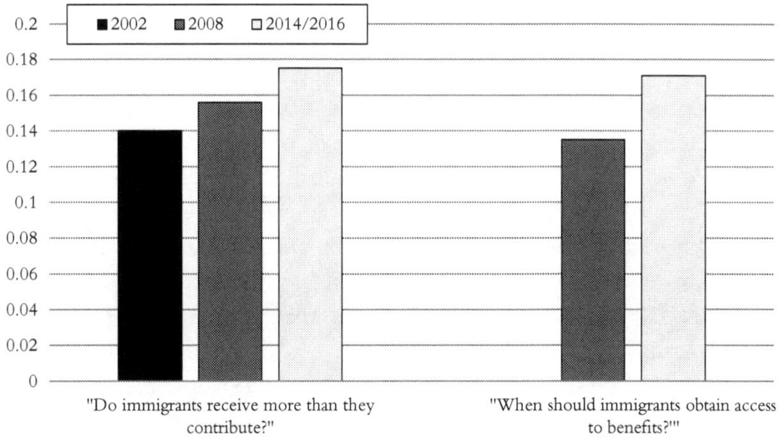

Note: entries show the average Cramer's V measuring the strength of association across 14 countries between the respective variable and party of choice.
Source: ESS, 2002–16.

Portugal) witnessed a significant increase. Similarly, in 7 of the 13 countries for which data are available the proportion of respondents who want to limit immigrants' access to benefits was significantly lower in 2016 than in 2008, and in only three countries (Netherlands, Portugal and Switzerland) did that proportion increase by a statistically significant margin.

While the number of citizens who are worried about immigrants' place in the welfare system is thus not increasing, the political relevance of these sentiments is. Figure 9.4 shows the average association between responses on these questions and respondents' vote choice for each wave of the survey. These data clearly suggest that people's attitudes on immigrants' welfare use are now a better predictor of someone's vote choice than they used to be. On the first indicator, there were significant increases over time for 12 of the 14 countries (in Spain and Ireland, on the other hand, the coefficients remained essentially stable), and significant increases for 11 of the 13 countries on the second indicator (the coefficients did not change over time in Germany and Norway). All in all, these findings imply that West European citizens might not be more welfare chauvinist than they were in the past, but that they are more likely to act on such sentiment in the voting booth. The observation that a person's position on immigrants' welfare entitlements has become a better predictor of their vote choice again underlies the increasing relevance of immigration to social issues, and has important implications for policy making in the area of immigration and welfare.

Political pressures on governing immigration and welfare

Undoubtedly, the most dramatic manifestation of welfare chauvinism's increased electoral relevance is the spread of anti-immigrant parties (AIPs) across Western democracies. Many countries now feature a prominent political party that combines a populist style of campaigning with a nativist insistence that immigrants and immigrant cultures do not belong (Mudde, 2010). These parties tend to blame immigrants explicitly for any economic difficulties that the country might be experiencing, to make the pressure immigration places on the welfare system one of the spearheads of their political campaign, and to favour extreme solutions based on principled rather than evidence-based motivations (De Koster et al, 2012; Koning, 2019). And in sharp contrast to the extreme right of past decades, most of these parties occupy a centrist or even centre-left position on socioeconomic issues. Indeed, these parties often position themselves as the defenders of the welfare state against the pressures of migration, and attract many voters who used to cast their ballots for socialist or social-democratic parties (Bale et al, 2010). The emergence of a party family that is simultaneously pro-welfare and anti-immigrant has transformed the politics of redistribution profoundly. As Figure 9.5 illustrates, these parties have become much more successful over time. Focusing on 15 Western democracies in which these parties have had success,[5] we see that they only garnered about 1 per cent of the vote in the late 1970s, but by now attract almost 14 per cent on average.

As a result of this dramatic growth, AIPs have become more successful in exerting influence over policy making. For one thing, and perhaps most obviously, in some cases these parties have joined coalition governments and therefore became part of the executive. In other instances, mainstream parties were reluctant to formally include AIPs in a coalition, but nevertheless agreed to make policy concessions in exchange for the promise of political support in parliament. Table 9.1 summarizes all formal and informal coalitions that national parties in Western democracies have struck with AIPs. All in all, a total of 21 governments in eight different countries have engaged in these kinds of arrangements.

Even when AIPs do not have such a direct opportunity to shape public policy, they can still exert influence more indirectly. Many researchers have found evidence that some mainstream parties have

Figure 9.5: Average percentage of the electoral vote of AIPs in national legislative elections, 15 Western democracies, 1977–2018

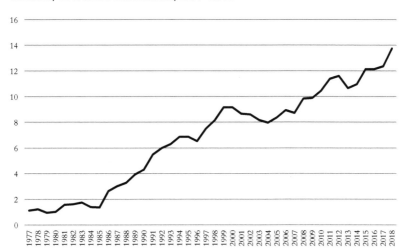

adopted a more restrictive position on immigration in response to the success of AIPs (Bale et al, 2010; Van Spanje, 2010). This could be because mainstream parties have become convinced of some of the ideas that anti-immigrant parties have brought forward, or, more cynically, because they calculated that a more restrictive position would make them regain some of the votes they had lost to AIPs in the past.

More generally, many Western democracies are now characterized by a political climate in which politicians believe it is electorally risky to be seen as 'naïve' or 'politically correct' on issues of immigration. For one thing, this means that politicians likely feel compelled to affirm concerns about immigration-related challenges, including their use of welfare, during electoral campaigns. In a previous study analysing manifestoes of 77 parties in 15 European countries, there were only five manifestoes that did not mention anything about the implications of immigration for the welfare system (Koning, 2017). This politicization of immigrants' welfare use makes normative positions regarding immigrants' place in the welfare system more central to policy making than empirical expectations regarding the effects of alternative policy solutions. In other words, in this political climate the question 'what do immigrants deserve?' is a more important driver of policy positions than the question 'which arrangements produce the most favourable outcomes for the integration of immigrants and the economic health of the welfare system?'

In a context of widespread concern about immigration and its impact on the welfare system, then, it is more important that a policy

Table 9.1: Informal and formal coalitions with AIPs in Western democracies

Country	Years	Arrangement	Parties
Austria	2002–03	Coalition	ÖVP, **FPÖ**
	2003–07	Coalition	ÖVP, **FPÖ**, **BZÖ**
	2017–19	Coalition	ÖVP, **FPÖ**
Denmark	2001–05	Guaranteed support	V, K (+**DF**)
	2005–07	Guaranteed support	V, K (+**DF**)
	2007–11	Guaranteed support	V, K (+**DF**)
	2015–19	Guaranteed support	V, I, K (+**DF**)
Finland	2015–19	Coalition	KESK, **PS**, KOK
Italy	1994–95	Coalition	FI, **LN**, **AN**, CCD, UDC
	2001–06	Coalition	FI, AN, **LN**, UDC, NPSI, PRI
	2011–13	Coalition	PdL, **LN**, MpA
	2018–19	Coalition	**LN**, M5S
Netherlands	2002–03	Coalition	VVD, CDA, **LPF**
	2010–12	Guaranteed support	VVD, CDA (+**PVV**)
New Zealand	1996–98	Coalition	NZNP, **NZF**
	2005–08	Guaranteed support	NZLP, JAPP (+**NZF**)
	2017–current	Coalition	NZLP, **NZF**
Norway	2001–05	Guaranteed support	KRF, H, V (+**FRP**)
	2013–17	Coalition	H, **FRP**
	2017–current	Coalition	H, **FRP**
Switzerland	2003–current	Coalition	All major parties in Federal Council

Note: Initialisms of anti-immigrant parties have been highlighted in bold.

proposal seems 'tough' than that it 'works'. Indeed, in a comparative case study of the Netherlands, Sweden and Canada, I found that economic and fact-based reasoning is rare in contemporary politics of immigration and welfare: politicians more frequently justify welfare restrictions for immigrants by principled than economic arguments, criticisms often target practices that involve few costs or of which the costs are entirely unknown, and solutions rarely fit the ills they are supposed to address (Koning, 2019). All of this means that even when policy changes are supposedly about addressing some of the difficult tensions this chapter started outlining, they are unlikely to be based on the expectation that they are the most likely solutions to address these tensions successfully.

Conclusion

The social question in the age of sustainability has become more vexing now that more and more people live and work in more than one country during their lifetime. No longer can we consider questions of redistribution and social protection exclusively within the terms of a nation state. Instead, states need to coordinate their social security arrangements with each other, recognize the large variability in life history among residents on their territory, and foster solidarity among an increasingly diverse populace. To be sure, this is not easy. Not only does it require significant changes to existing policy arrangements; it raises difficult questions about the responsibility to protect residents with varying levels of ties to the state and about the nature of equality in a welfare regime characterized by rights differentiation.

The main argument of this chapter is that the political process makes this policy challenge even more difficult to address. Three aspects are of particular relevance. First, media increasingly encourage citizens to think of immigrants as a burden on the welfare system. Second, the sentiment that the welfare state should first and foremost take care of native-born citizens now has a larger influence on election results. And finally, the rise of populist parties that insist the welfare state can only survive in the absence of migration has created a political climate that encourages 'tough' approaches to immigration-related challenges, regardless of whether those approaches actually work. Figure 9.6 summarizes this argument.

To be clear, it is not the intention here to suggest definitive statements on the causal linkages between the three compounding factors. The preceding discussion might create the impression of a simple linear sequence of media coverage leading to welfare chauvinism in

Figure 9.6: Challenges to addressing the social question in an era of migration

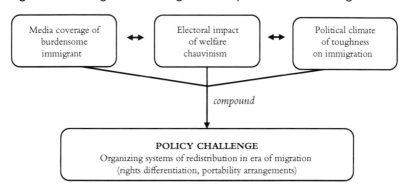

turn affecting the political climate, but reality is likely much more endogenous. After all, the political climate is likely to affect both media coverage (because if politicians are more likely to make comments about immigrants' welfare use, media are more likely to cover those comments) and the electoral relevance of welfare chauvinism (because the emergence of welfare chauvinist politicians gives voters with such sentiments a clearer choice in the voting booth). All this chapter aims to argue, instead, is that these three factors taken together create a massive challenge to tackling the social question in an era of migration.

It would be an exaggeration to describe this challenge as insurmountable. Governments that explicitly position themselves as pro-immigrant (such as the Trudeau government in Canada or the Sánchez government in Spain) or countries in which policy making on immigration-related issues is still largely depoliticized are relatively well placed to formulate effective and inclusionary responses. Nevertheless, if recent developments are any indication, constructive solutions will be increasingly exceptional. As politicians in many countries seem more likely to worry about the electoral consequences of coming across as naïve on immigration than about the rights and life prospects of future newcomers, a more probable scenario is an increase in efforts to push immigrants to the margins of the welfare system, thereby aggravating their socioeconomic difficulties and further accentuating tensions with native-born citizens.

All in all, migration indeed poses a formidable challenge to the future of the welfare state. This is not because, as early scholarly contributions would have it, immigrants will overburden the system and make social expenditure unmanageable. Instead, it is because in many Western democracies immigration has become such a combustible issue that a detached and efficient reconfiguration of the welfare state to cater to its more mobile population seems utopian. Especially in countries where anti-immigrant politics have become mainstream, a more likely scenario is a weakening of systems of social protection for a growing number of residents.

Notes

[1] Certainly, it would be interesting to cast a wider net and include major newspapers from all immigrant-receiving Western welfare states. There are a number of methodological challenges to such an investigation, however. For one thing, Factiva does not include information on many publications from other countries, let alone for all years from 1981 to 2018. Second, cross-national comparisons would be more complicated because of language differences. Indeed, I conducted a similar analysis using the best possible translations of my search terms for the *Süddeutsche Zeitung* in Germany, the *Corriere della Sera* in Italy, *El País* in Spain and *Le Figaro*

in France, and found very different results. These results are not shown but can be made available upon request.

2   Factiva is a subscription database, for further information see https://professional. dowjones.com/factiva/.

3   To count the number of articles on immigration, the search term [migratio★ OR immigratio★ OR migran★ OR immigran★ OR foreigne★ OR asylum OR refug★] was used. Among those articles, it was then measured how many discussed welfare and social benefits by using the search term [welfare OR benefi★ OR 'social assistance' OR payou★]. Finally, it was investigated how many of those articles talked about immigration as a burden by using the search term [burden OR cost OR costs OR drain OR burdensome OR costly OR expensive].

4   All Western European countries for which data were available were included: Austria, Belgium, Denmark, Finland, France, Germany, Ireland, Netherlands, Norway, Portugal, Spain, Sweden, Switzerland and the United Kingdom. The bars on the left-hand side of Figure 9.3 show the percentage of respondents who picked an answer of 8 or higher on a 0–10 scale, where 0 indicates that immigrants contribute much more than they take out, and 10 indicates that immigrants take out much more than they contribute. Unfortunately, the question on when immigrants should gain access to benefits was not asked in Austria.

5   Figure 9.5 shows the average percentage of the vote in parliamentary elections (lower house of parliament only) in Australia, Austria, Belgium, Denmark, Finland, France, Germany, Italy, the Netherlands, New Zealand, Portugal, Sweden, Switzerland and the United Kingdom. Data for France are based on the vote in the first round of its two-round system; data for Germany reflect the regional vote (*Zweitstimme*) of its mixed-member proportional electoral system.

References

Bale, T., Green-Pedersen, C., Krouwel, A., Luther, K. R. and Sitter, N. (2010) 'If You Can't Beat Them, Join Them? Explaining Social Democratic Responses to the Challenge from the Populist Radical Right in Western Europe', *Political Studies*, 58(3): 410–26.

Banting, K. G. and Koning, E. A. (2017) 'Just Visiting? The Weakening of Social Protection in a Mobile World', in A. Triandafyllidou (ed) *Multicultural Governance in a Mobile World*, Edinburgh: Edinburgh University Press, 108–35.

Berg-Nordlie, M. (2018) 'New in Town: Small-Town Media Discourses on Immigrants and Immigration', *Journal of Rural Studies*, 64: 210–19.

Boomgaarden, H. G. and Vliegenthart, R. (2009) 'How News Content Influences Anti-Immigrant Attitudes: Germany, 1993–2005', *European Journal of Political Research*, 48(4): 516–42.

Brader, T., Valentino, N. A. and Suhay, E. (2008) 'What Triggers Public Opposition to Immigration? Anxiety, Group Cues, and Immigration Threat', *American Journal of Political Science*, 52(4): 959–78.

De Koster, W., Achterberg, P. and Van der Waal, J. (2012) 'The New Right and the Welfare State: The Electoral Relevance of Welfare Chauvinism and Welfare Populism in the Netherlands', *International Political Science Review*, 34(1): 3–20.

Koning, E. A. (2017) 'Selecting, Disentitling, or Investing? Exploring Party and Voter Responses to Immigrant Welfare Dependence in Fifteen West European Welfare States', *Comparative European Politics*, 15(4): 628–60.

Koning, E. A. (2019) *Immigration and the Politics of Welfare Exclusion: Selective Solidarity in Western Democracies*, Toronto: University of Toronto Press.

Marshall, T. H. (1950) *Citizenship and Social Class, and Other Essays*, Cambridge: Cambridge University Press.

Mudde, C. (2010) 'The Populist Radical Right: A Pathological Normalcy', *West European Politics*, 33(6): 1167–86.

Philo, G., Briant, E. and Donald, P. (2013) 'The Role of the Press in the War on Asylum', *Race & Class*, 55(2): 28–41.

Sabates-Wheeler, R. and Feldman, R. (2011) *Migration and Social Protection: Claiming Social Rights Beyond Borders*, Basingstoke: Palgrave Macmillan.

Sabates-Wheeler, R., Koettl, J. and Avato, J. (2011) 'Social Security for Migrants: A Global Overview of Portability Arrangements', in R. Sabates-Wheeler and R. Feldman (eds) *Migration and Social Protection: Claiming Social Rights Beyond Borders*, Basingstoke: Palgrave Macmillan, 91–116.

UN DESA (United Nations Department of Economic and Social Affairs) (2016) *International Migration Report 2015: Highlights*, ST/ESA/SER.A/375, New York: UN, www.un.org/en/development/desa/population/migration/publications/migrationreport/docs/MigrationReport2015_Highlights.pdf.

Van Spanje, J. (2010) 'Contagious Parties: Anti-Immigration Parties and Their Impact on Other Parties' Immigration Stances in Contemporary Western Europe', *Party Politics*, 16(5): 563–86.

10

Bringing in 'the social': an intersectional analysis of global crises and welfare

Fiona Williams

Introduction

This chapter illustrates how an intersectional approach can excavate 'the social' in social policy analysis, not only at national and local/ interpersonal scales but at global scales too.[1] It focuses on the forces at the global scale that have shaped the development of post-financial crisis (austerity) welfare and it explains how this should be understood in terms of the intersections between the crises of global financialized capitalism, of care, of ecology and of racialized transnational mobilities. In elaborating this framework, the chapter aims to extend the application of intersectionality to social policy, and, in line with this, to bring 'the social' into a political economy analysis of neoliberal welfare.

Intersectionality provides an understanding of social inequalities and power as complex, interlinked, shifting and multifaceted, constituting both penalties and privileges. It is an approach in which analysis and practice are closely linked (Box 10.1). It has enjoyed an important comeback in the social sciences and humanities since the 2000s from its origins in black feminist theory and politics of the 1980s. Yet the application to social policy of its contemporary tenets around theory, method and praxis has been both relatively limited and relatively recent. While it has been used to inform research and analysis of the multiple dimensions of social exclusion, discrimination and hierarchy at local and national scales in austerity welfare societies (for example, Bassel and Emejulu, 2018; Women's Budget Group, 2017), less consideration has been given to developing an intersectional approach at a global scale, in spite of important feminist, post-colonial and ecological resistance to, and scholarship on, global capitalism.

Box 10.1: What is intersectionality?

Intersectionality is a way of understanding and analysing complexity in the world, in people and in human experiences. The events and conditions of social and political life and the self can seldom be understood as shaped by one factor. They are generally shaped by many factors in diverse and mutually influencing ways. When it comes to social inequality, people's lives and the organization of power in a given society are better understood as being shaped not by a single axis of social division, be it 'race' or gender or class, but by many axes that work together and influence each other. Intersectionality as an analytic tool gives people better access to the complexity of the world and of themselves.

Source: Collins and Bilge (2020: 2).

At the same time, most social policy scholarship on post-crisis welfare notes the different ways in which states have cut back their social expenditure and the effect this has had in reproducing inequalities. In so doing they locate these as the outcome of the political economy of neoliberalism and the particular economic contradictions of global capitalism which led to the global financial crisis (Seymour, 2014; Farnsworth and Irving, 2015). This chapter argues that, while locating austerity measures in welfare in this way is crucial, it only tells part of the story. An intersectional approach helps to 'socialize' a political economy analysis of the crises of global capitalism that emerges out of imperial, colonial, post-colonial, patriarchal and planetary forms of exploitation, expropriation and expulsion. And these are particularly salient to understanding the landscapes of austerity welfare and to the possibilities for transforming it.

The chapter begins with a contextualizing summary of the importance of intersectionality in the context of a continuing marginalization in many areas of mainstream social policy of social critiques based upon gender, 'race', disability, sexuality, age and environmentalism. It then elaborates the intersections of global crises of finance, care, ecology and racialized transnational mobility. The conclusion indicates what the analysis offers for thinking about transformatory alternatives to neoliberal welfare and neoliberalizing policy processes.

Intersectionality and retrieving 'the social'

In the context of neoliberalism, austerity politics, crises driving migration, heightened awareness of sexual and racial harassment and assault, and ecological disasters, recent decades have seen activism from anti-capitalist, environmentalist, disability and grassroots organizations, as well as the resurgence of feminism and anti-racism, transnational movements for indigenous people's and migrants' rights, and for LGBTQI+ rights. This has energized the development of critical thinking as well as possibilities for consolidating that energy. One element of this has been the development of theoretical, methodological and political interpretations of intersectionality. This development, with its potential to unearth – through lived experiences and struggles – the multiple complexities of social power and inequalities as well as participatory and transformative possibilities for social justice, is particularly suited to addressing the social of social policy.

This development is especially important at a time of concerns about the limited acknowledgements in mainstream social sciences of the insights from critiques of both the earlier social movements from the 1970s and 1980s as well as the contemporary activist critiques such as decolonizing the curriculum, or analysis of climate change (see Williams, 2016; Gough, 2017; Bhambra et al, 2018; The Rhodes Must Fall Movement, 2018). For example, in July 2019 the UK Social Policy Association published a commissioned report: *The Missing Dimension: Where Is 'Race' in Social Policy Teaching and Learning?* (Craig et al, 2019). The report examined curricula of social policy courses, journal and conference content over the previous five years, and BAME (black, Asian and minority ethnic) representation amongst student and staff. It found the lack of focus on 'race' and racism to be 'dismal'. This is in spite of the fact that policies around immigration, securitization and austerity since that time have all had detrimental effects on the citizenship rights of minority ethnic and migrant groups (Chattoo et al, 2019: 2–3). In a review of the social policy scholarship, Ann Orloff concluded that although the debates between feminists and mainstream scholars in comparative social policy had been productive, 'the mainstream *still resists the deeper implications* of feminist work, and has difficulties assimilating concepts of care, gendered power, dependency and interdependency' (Orloff, 2009: 317, emphasis added). More recently, Mary Daly and Emanuele Ferragina (2018) note the lack of integration of comparative family policies research into comparative studies of the welfare state and of austerity.

Intersectionality has a long history associated with black feminist struggle and critical analysis. It originally spoke to an experience in which the 'race' and gender of women of colour decentred them within both feminist and anti-racist/black movements of the 1970s and 1980s (Cohambahee River Collective, [1977] 1995; Moraga and Anzaldúa,

1983; Lewis and Parma, 1983). It emerged as an analytic concept in the 1980s to encapsulate this political and institutional problem of invisibility, elaborated by socio-legal black feminist scholar Kimberlé Crenshaw (1989).

Intersectionality has developed as theory, method and praxis. It concentrates on excavating the lived experience. It operates not as a grand and totalizing theory but as an 'orientation' (May, 2015: 3). In recent years it has begun to be applied to social movements and practice, to politics, and to social and public policy intervention (Williams, 2018a; Hankivsky and Jordan-Zachary, 2019; Irvine et al, 2019; Collins and Bilge, 2020). Key aspects in these applications of intersectionality include attention to the complexity of social inequalities and power, a focus on change and fluidity, and challenging fixed and essentialist approaches in which social positions or economic systems are seen as given, natural or over-determining. Relationality, the contingencies of time and place, the contested, contradictory and unsettled nature of phenomena (including welfare states, their policies and practices) also characterize intersectional policy analysis, as do ideas that emerge from the margins and inform resistance. As Hankivsky and Jordan-Zachary note, it enables an understanding of:

> the differential impacts of policy on diverse populations … it draws attention to aspects of policy that are largely uninvestigated or ignored altogether: the complex ways in which multiple and interlocking inequities are organized and resisted in the process, content and outcomes of policy. In so doing, the exclusionary nature of traditional methods of policy, including the ways in which problems and populations are constituted, given shape and meaning, is revealed. (Hankivsky and Jordan-Zachary, 2019: 2)

Politically it marks the importance of alliances across difference as a way to transformative change. This has clear relevance to social policy's concerns with understanding social inequalities and social justice, how to research and make visible those that are hidden, and how to avoid 'universalistic politics (that overemphasizes commonalities to the neglect of differences) … and particularistic politics (that overemphasize differences to the neglect of commonalities)' (Irvine et al, 2019: 12). In other words, how to develop support for combining universalist policies with difference.

So intersectionality offers social policy a more rigorous framing of how the social relations of power and inequality are experienced and operate within and across social groups. The concept is used to inform an understanding of social policy, and the intersections of its forces, institutions, contradictions and contestations both within and across different scales: macro, meso and micro, or global, supra/national and local/interpersonal.[2] Elsewhere the intersections of social relations and social forces within and across each scale are analysed (Williams, 2018b, 2021), but this chapter concentrates on the intersections of those crises at the global scale which mutually shape social policies at national, local and interpersonal scales.

Intersecting global crises

Crisis carries several meanings. Here it is used to denote the outcome of systemic tensions or contradictions, derived from the writings of Marx (Marx and Engels, 1886). In addition, the Gramscian idea of crisis being an interregnum when 'the old is dying and the new cannot be born [in which] a great variety of morbid symptoms appear' (Gramsci, 1971: 276) is relevant.[3] As important is the need to ensure that the claim to a *global* crisis needs to clarify for whom there is a crisis and whether all regions of the world experience the crisis similarly. These meanings and questions cover all four crises discussed here – of financial capitalism, of care and social reproduction, of environment and of racialized transnational mobilities – in different ways. What they share is that they have emerged from an enduring tension inherent in their relationship with capitalism as an economic system of production and consumption and into the specifics of a racial, extractavist and patriarchal neoliberalism. This has reached a critical point where, singly and in aggregate, they endanger current and future ecosocial, human and non-human wellbeing and sustainability, not to mention the capacity to deal with global pandemics. These crises have also generated significant international mobilization and struggle which potentially challenges the hegemony of neoliberalism. For now, the main point is that it is in this conjuncture of intersecting crises that we should understand the shaping of national and supranational social policies.

The global financial crisis

Capitalism of the 21st century has, especially in the US and UK, been dominated by finance capital in which, in the context of depreciated wages, products are only available for many through borrowing via credit or mortgages. Behind the crisis was the accumulation of mass inability to repay debts leading to many banks going bust. The global financial crisis was uneven in its impact, starting in the US and UK as a 'North Atlantic Financial Crisis', before affecting Western Europe, but having less effect elsewhere such as Australia. In the UK, after a bank bailout, the crisis became the justification for an austerity welfare programme from 2009 by the Coalition and subsequent Conservative governments with devastatingly unequal and precarious outcome (Taylor-Gooby, 2013; Hills, 2015). It was not the only country to introduce some form of austerity welfare although these differed across the varieties of neoliberal welfare regimes (Jessop, 2015; Olafsson et al, 2019). In the case of Spain, Portugal, Italy and Greece, austerity was imposed from above by the EU, European Central Bank and International Monetary Fund (IMF) with deleterious consequences to poverty and inequality in those countries (Béland and Mahon, 2016: 88–9). In explaining this shift many social policy analysts of the UK have noted its use as an economic tool, rebalancing capital's power from wages to profits (Seymour, 2014) and as an ideological tool, seeking to transform not only the relationship between the economy, the state and the individual, but the very social relations of everyday life (Tyler, 2013). By 2019, in the UK 14 million were in poverty and 1.5 million destitute (UNHRC, 2019). This has created multiple intersections of social exclusion, discrimination and hierarchy, marked by class, gender, 'race', ethnicity, religion, migrant status, nationality, place and generation. It is women, especially lone parents and women of colour, people with disabilities, and migrant women and men, who have been particularly affected by welfare reforms and public services cuts (Shutes, 2016; Women's Budget Group, 2017; Bassel and Emejulu, 2018; Dwyer, 2019; Ryan, 2019). It is this complexity that requires an analysis that can deal with the 'social' at global scale.

To begin with, Nancy Fraser's feminist critique of the North Atlantic Financial Crisis is used as a template. Its premise is that most analyses of the crisis are gender blind, and the obverse, that feminist theory lacks a framework that links social changes affecting gender relations to this crisis (Fraser, 2013). She argues that current global crises are multidimensional and that we need an integrated approach to understand how these dimensions relate to each other. She provides this through a critical reinterpretation of Karl Polanyi's *The Great Transformation* (Polanyi, [1944] 1957), a tripartite analysis of the history of capitalist crisis over the 19th and first half of the 20th century. In brief, Polanyi's argument is that capitalism's self-destructive impulse lies in its turning land, labour and money into 'fictitious commodities'. The marketization of each of these domains led to despoiling the land, demoralizing the labourer and destroying the value of money through speculation. In Fraser's view, it is the integrated nature of this analysis that is important, along with Polanyi's recognition of the significance of political mobilization, in this case through the conflict between capital and labour, as the key to effect social and economic change. Fraser updates this mobilization to include the significance of feminist, anti-racist and environmentalist struggles. Thus, she rewrites Polanyi's three crisis-prone constituents of land, labour and money as the interlinked systemic crises of ecology, social reproduction and finance, respectively. She argues that the same impulse of 'fictitious commodification' is seen today in each of these global crises with a similar result of destroying the value of the planet's resources, of care and of money, respectively. Thus, in relation to the last of these, money, Fraser argues that it was speculation that fuelled the global financial crisis in which investment was destabilized and devalued. This led not only to austerity policies with disproportionate and detrimental policies for low-income groups, but also to undermining the capacity of money to store value for the future. The endangering of future societies is at the heart of Fraser's analysis. Before explaining what this means for the crises of social reproduction and ecology, it is suggested that there is a dimension missing in her analysis.

While Fraser mentions the three most significant areas of struggle today as feminist, anti-racist and environmentalist, she only identifies crises attached to the first and last of these – social reproduction and ecology. Issues of racism, immigration and post-colonialism tend to be folded into her explication of these two rather than also providing an understanding of the specificity of the relationship between the logics of capitalism and imperialism over time. Since the 1990s, there has been a dramatic dovetailing of immigration and domestic racializing policies (de Genova, 2018). First, contradictions between the demands of global capitalism for mobile labour and state tightening of border controls (supported by ethno-nationalist populist politics) as well as the acceleration and diversification of transnational migration and asylum-seeking has created growing injustices and inequalities (Faist, 2019). Second, global widening of social, economic and geopolitical inequalities has disproportionately affected minority ethnic groups and indigenous people, as the UN State of the World's Indigenous Peoples (SOWIP) series clearly shows (UN DESA, 2011, 2017, 2019). Michael Dawson, in a critique of Fraser, says: 'it is "apparent" when we observe the rise of racial strife in the United States and ethno-religious conflict in Europe that racial and ethnic logics are generating crises as deep and perhaps even more dangerous than those of capital, reproduction, the ecology, or politics' (Dawson, 2016: 145). Thus, the logics of white supremacy and capitalism have given rise over time to both exploitation and expropriation.

We return to how to define this omitted crisis later. What is important here is that it points to an understanding of capitalist development from the 18th century as not determining but inextricably tied into the politics of slavery abolition, imperialism, colonialism, eugenics, post-colonial racism, globalization and post-racial racism (Wallerstein, 2004; Bhattacharyya, 2018). It is not just, as Fraser critiques, that Polanyi's theory of the history of capitalism's tendency to self-destruction ignores the difficulties that women have had to sell their labour power, but also that it omits recognition of the significance of racialized labour because it is based on a conception of a worker who sells their labour power only for it to become commodified (Bhambra and Holmwood, 2018). But this is a worker who is free to do so in the first place. An enslaved worker's labour power is embodied in their enslavement and carries no such freedom to be sold into commodification. To be fair to Fraser, in a later response to Dawson's critique mentioned above she begins to delineate this distinction between exploitation (the commodifiable worker) and expropriation (the unfree worker) and how they intersect over time and space in regimes of 'racialized accumulation' (Fraser, 2016a).

The crisis of social reproduction and care

Social reproduction refers to activities of care, intimacy, affection and domestic labour that contribute to human flourishing, repair and sustenance: raising children, looking after older frail people, organizing and managing the feeding and cleaning of households, holding social networks together, which is generally unpaid and taken for granted. Across the world women are predominantly responsible for unpaid care and domestic work (ILO, 2016). The basic and enduring contradiction between capitalism and social reproductive work is that while part of it, keeping the current and future workforce socialized, healthy and replenished, is essential for economic production, at the same time this work is constituted as separate, part of the natural work carried out both unpaid and paid by women, and devalued. Care is constituted through heteronormative and patriarchal power relations in which classed, racialized, sexualized, generational and disabled inequalities are clearly writ. Of course, it is also about love. However, it is in the imperative for profits extracted from people's labour that capitalism exerts intense pressure on, and endangers, the capacity of people to care for their close others. And, it is in those struggles, by women, disabled and older people, for the state to make visible, remunerate and support this work that this tension is revealed most clearly.

The present era of globalized financialized capitalism (Fraser, 2016b) has heightened this contradiction to the point of crisis. The necessity of female employment as part of the principle of 'hard-working families' coexists with social expenditure cutbacks in support for caring responsibilities and poor pay and working conditions in which women experience intense strains between the demands of work and care as well as limitations on their earning power. At a social level, this crisis is precipitated by declining fertility rates (as Danny Dorling argues in Chapter 7) and ageing populations with increased proportions of older people (discussed by Alan Walker in Chapter 8).

This crisis of social reproduction has been central to much recent feminist analysis and is variously called the 'crisis of care' (Williams, 2012, 2018b; Floro, 2012) or 'depletion through social reproduction' (Rai et al, 2014). (For the distinction between 'care' and 'social reproduction', see Bhattacharya, 2017; Williams, 2018b; Mezzadri, 2019). However, there are differences of 'race', class, disability and geopolitics in the ways women experience these tensions or the shifts in regimes. For example, there has been a global increase in women's involvement in the labour market as well as greater reliance on women's wages in both the Global North *and* South (ILO, 2009; OECD, 2015). In poorer regions care crises result from unemployment, wars, ethnic conflict, climate change disaster and chronic illnesses. These place enormous responsibilities on women to maintain sick, young and old family members with little infrastructural support for basic amenities, and often precipitate women into seeking work through migration, often into care and domestic work in developed countries where social expenditure cuts and neoliberal policies have led to the marketization of low-paid care work. At the same time, professional households in developed countries ease their work–care imbalance by employing migrant or minority ethnic women to do their households' cleaning and caring. In many countries, this is facilitated by state fiscal benefits to those households (Carbonnier and Morel, 2015). In effect, the employment of working class women, women of colour, migrant status or lower caste women in this way merely obscures those hidden reproductive processes and displaces the effects of the care crisis on to the care workers, their families and the countries from which they migrate (Williams, 2012). While this takes on a new form of worldwide relationship between poorer and richer countries, it also perpetuates a historical racial division of the reproductive labour of care work and domestic service provided by women of colour (Glenn, 1992). What the existence of this crisis challenges are the priorities of macroeconomic policies of productivism, market competition and consumerism, which require the invisibility and subservience of the very processes of human interdependence that enable human flourishing.

The ecology crisis

The third global crisis is that of climate change and the environment, known as the Anthropocene (Lewis and Maslin, 2015): that the extent of human activity upon the planet's resources, especially through fossil fuel burning, has accumulated carbon in the atmosphere and oceans to the point that without significant intervention in the immediate term human life is endangered through global warming. The world is already experiencing the consequences of accelerating floods, bushfires, drought, heatwaves and storms, while in the future the sustainability of the planet and the whole ecosystem is at risk (WMO, 2019). Resource exploitation, of cotton, tea, coffee, was part of imperialism and colonial expansion through to global capitalism today, leading some to suggest that, given capitalism's exploitative relationship with nature, a more accurate term is 'Capitalocene' (Gill, 2019: 5) or 'racial Capitalocene' (Manchanda, 2019: 2) in terms of who effects and is affected by that exploitation.

The environment and climate change raise profound ecosocial questions of equity, equality and justice across populations and regions, and over generations (see Tony Fitzpatrick, Chapter 6). A degraded environment affects health and wellbeing in unequal measures: while the wealthy may benefit from forms of environmentally harmful consumption, it is disproportionately poor people, nationally, regionally, globally, whose lives are affected (Snell and Haq, 2014). The UN's Migration Agency, the International Organization for Migration (IOM), notes that in 2018 alone 17.2 million new displacements from disasters in 148 countries and territories were recorded (Ionesco, 2019). Within these populations women suffer significantly: they constitute the majority farmers and carers and are more dependent upon land and resources such as water and fuel which are threatened by climate change (Action Aid, 2019). This is mirrored in the developed world. 'Environmental racism' has been used to describe the ways in which marginalized and minority groups are disproportionally subjected to environmental hazards such as living in proximity to toxic waste, or having limited access to clean air, water and other natural resources (Pulido, 2016; Anthony, 2017).

In 2019–20, the global COVID-19 pandemic represented the deadliest of a series of epidemics and is another form of environmental risk to sustainability. It constituted a micro-biological aspect of the macro-exploitation of planetary resources carrying similar challenging features, outcomes and lessons. It is associated with urban incursion into natural habitats flourishing in high-density urban areas in which 68 per cent of the world population now lives (WEF, 2020). Some epidemics, such as Zika, travelled on the climate-changing winds of El Niño. COVID-19 respects neither class nor borders, yet is more deadly for the old and physically vulnerable, relatively worse for men, and more devastating for socio-economically deprived groups causing disproportionately greater sickness and death among racial minorities (Qureshi et al, 2020). In the UK, it exposed forms of institutionalised racism that give rise to poorer health outcomes for BAME groups (IHE, 2020; Qureshi et al, 2020) as well as, in more general terms, the policies of austerity. This included the inadequacies of a National Health Service that had suffered underfunding and understaffing, the latter caused by deliberately holding down wages and instituting migration restrictions; the lack of social protection to those in the deregulated economy; the inflexibility and inadequacy of income maintenance; and the major shortcomings of national sovereignty. As with the financial crisis, the markets, always focused on the short-term, were unable to stop themselves from falling. Like the effects of climate change, it presents random, unpredictable risks. This challenges the basis of welfare states that are built on a range of relatively predictable risks. They both require robust multi-scalar global, national and local governance for interdependent political and expert cooperation to develop social and physical protection. And, with climate change it challenges the assumption that the welfare state is only afforded and legitimated through the continuation of consumerism, globalization, economic growth and exploitation of the earth's resources, and therefore forces a rethinking of capitalism's commitment to economic growth and development, and the possibilities for future ecosocial policy, as Tony Fitzpatrick argues in Chapter 6 (see also Gough, 2017).

The racialized crisis of transnational mobilities

Identifying the contemporary conditions of transnational mobilities as a *crisis* can be problematic. To call the flight of populations from wars, fragile states, ethnic conflicts, collapsing economies, environmental disasters, crime, violence and the poverty of geopolitical inequalities, a 'migrant *crisis*' or a 'refugee *crisis*', as termed by politicians and media, is to risk misrecognition of the dynamics that have contributed to the problems experienced by migrants and refugees, and to contribute to a growing ethno-nationalist populism (Sager, 2018; Gray and Franck, 2019). Such representation detracts from the experiences and suffering of those who are migrants, refugees or asylum seekers, which have involved death at sea or suffocation in the back of a packed lorry. By 2016, over 3,000 refugees attempting to enter Europe by sea drowned; worldwide it was over 4,000 (IOM, 2016). The crisis-panic of today correlates migrants with danger, illegality, conflict, violence and terrorism. In doing so, it has legitimated the ratcheting up of coercive border controls, detention and deportation policies, which now characterize immigration controls across the world: the precaritization of work and citizenship together (Geiger and Pécoud, 2010). It is these restrictive legal and social policies of immigration that lead to the desperate conditions in refugee camps, such as Sangatte on the French coast, and that *create* the illegalization of immigrants and the so-called crisis (Sager, 2018).

Yet there *is* a crisis in both the experiences of refugees and migrants and the abdication of responsibility by global, supranational and national governance to address this dehumanization and the wave of xenophobia that reproduces it. Global social governance is about the 'management' of migration, but remains some distance from the demands of migrants' rights' movements: it is presumed that it can be managed in a technocratic, 'top-down' manner (Rother, 2018). In relation to Europe, Nicholas de Genova calls this, 'an unresolved *racial crisis* that derives fundamentally from the postcolonial condition of "Europe" as a whole' (de Genova, 2018: 1765, his emphasis). This is called here the 'racialized crisis of transnational mobility' in order to capture the conjuncture between three processes at work: the dehumanization of migrants and refugees at national, supranational and global scales; its contagion with heightened racist policies and practices within national politics; and the rise of ethno-nationalist populist politics. Although migrants seeking asylum are not usually the same migrants who end up in, say, care and domestic work, hospitality and agriculture (although they may be), many in both groups are, one way or another, survival migrants. In other words, the distinction between economic migrants and refugees/asylum seekers holds only to a certain degree. They are linked through, first, the political debates that set state sovereignty against human rights and humanitarianism, often in an appeal to a (mythically) homogeneous and/or imperial history and, second, in an everyday struggle to survive in which support has been minimized; a form of necropolitics which Lucy Mayblin and colleagues call 'social policy as slow violence' (Mayblin et al, 2019).

At the same time, from the 1990s, it is the growing assumption of a 'post-racial Europe' that intensifies this amnesia and dilution of policies and practices within Europe to combat racial/migrant/refugee injustices (Sian et al, 2013). It has created a political discourse in destination countries in which an economic cost/benefit analysis of migration, with migrants as units of labour, predominates over the ethics of international solidarity, interdependence, hospitality or human rights. In common with the other three crises, all these developments point to the ways in which the discourses of welfare, sustainability, social protection, solidarity and human rights are being further jeopardized.

Conclusion: the crises intersect

This chapter has aimed to expand, refine and connect the social dimensions of global crises, which shape and are shaped by welfare states. The four crises are interconnected: they have commonalities in constitution and effect, as well as interlocking dynamics and mechanisms. They are linked by the ways each jeopardizes security, human solidarity and sustainability for future generations. The commonalities include that they challenge the patriarchal, racial and ecosocial dimensions of neoliberal capitalism and its modes of production, reproduction, consumption, accumulation, commodification and growth of which they are the outcome: '[I]n a time of ecological crisis, populations already depleted by exploitation or expropriation or both become increasingly vulnerable to expulsion' (Bhattacharyya, 2018: 37).

Some of the intersections have already been noted: neoliberalism and the financial crisis have given rise to greater precarity of labour and to austerity cuts in social expenditure. These hit women hardest by removing support for caring responsibilities, by its impact on those who work in care services, as well as those who have care needs. Most developed countries have come to depend upon migrant workers to keep down their labour costs of health and social care services enforced by social expenditure cuts and, at the same time, those rights of migrant workers have been curtailed (Williams, 2012). While this dependence drains care capacities from migrants' countries of origin, the migration restrictions have depleted the healthcare capacities of countries, revealed especially in the COVID-19 crisis. Declining citizenship rights and the backlash against multiculturalism reduce migrant workers to units of labour or 'surplus populations' (Bhattacharyya, 2018). In the UK, policies introduced to restrict the rights of asylum-seekers or migrants to housing or income support have subsequently been extended to other groups of benefit claimants as part of austerity policies. This interweaving of people both exploited *and* expropriated that extends beyond (but mostly includes) racialized groups is part of the 'new logic of political subjectivation' of financialized capitalism (Fraser, 2016b: 176). In particular, debt, the very motor of the global financial crisis, not only leads to housing dispossession in the developed world but also creates the means by which agricultural workers in developing countries lose their land to corporations finding new forms of profitable energy, and face expulsion, the third consequence of this logic.

Flood disasters in low-income countries hit women hardest in terms of exacerbating and endangering both their caring and earning responsibilities. Furthermore, climate change is currently leading to greater displacement of people and enforced mobility into a world in which mobilities are increasingly restricted. At the same time, the COVID-19 pandemic required a stasis which is potentially threatening to those without local resources. However, the intersection of these crises needs to be conceptualized carefully (Sager, 2021). Dangers that climate change brings are often intensified by the apocalyptic threat of the clamour of displaced refugees and conflicts as resources become scarce. Yet these feed into the very ethno-nationalist and populist excluding discourses that have degraded the lives of migrants and refugees and limited the collective capacity to fight pandemics.

Within the present neoliberal policy paradigm, the market is seen as the dynamic and flexible solution to solve the financial, environmental, mobility and care crises, through green technologies or access to care markets. However, not only do these tend to deal with the short term rather than the long term, and therefore to postpone the basic tensions they precipitate, but they do not attend to the existing inequalities and distributional imbalances of which they are part. The more that climate change and its policies fall on degraded welfare states and depleted care systems, the more the poorest groups will suffer. Globally, this creates a 'tragic contradiction between growth, climactic instability and egregious inequality. All strategies to eliminate global poverty are untenable unless the shares of the poor are raised: in other words unless a more equitable model of the global economy is introduced' (Gough, 2017: 83). This is true, but it is also the case, as has been argued, that poor people are created by a post-colonial geopolitics which is regionalized, gendered and racialized, and whose capabilities for sustainability are being depleted.

The framework this chapter offers is important in a number of respects. First, it centres the social: it makes social reproduction and care, ecology and the environment, and transnational mobility as central to an analysis of post-crisis welfare states as the financial aspects of the global economy. None of these crises or their intersections is manifested in national welfare states in the same way, but depends on legacies, social formations and path dependencies.[4] Second, making conceptual alliances across different arenas enables us to think about social justice and how to struggle for it. This is in keeping with intersectionality's orientation, to link theory and method to praxis. Singly and together, the implications of these crises profoundly challenge the principles and practices of neoliberal patriarchal and racial global financialized capitalism. Importantly, they are also contested by global, national and local social justice activists and movements. These raise questions not only about growing inequalities and precariousness but also about the ethical, cultural and material dimensions of sustainability and human flourishing. An ethic of care is central: how to ensure that people will be cared for, and how to care for the depleting resources of the world. It provides a view of people who are connected to their environment and by what they have in common. In this way, conceiving of care as a collective social good needs to be central to global justice.

More importantly, this understanding finds synergies across progressive movements for care, decoloniality, environmental and economic justice and together these create possibilities for alliances and transformatory alternatives. They share concerns about global sustainability and crises whose geopolitical effects are unequally spread; they understand citizenship as based on participatory democracy and presume interdependence and decolonized solidarity as a way of being. They invoke care for the other and care for the world. Each envisions a society reorganized to create the conditions of time, security and space to support care of the individual and collective, and to instate value in human labour. It is in the invocation of the 'Commons' or the 'Eco-Commons' as a way of reclaiming the world's resources of land, water, space, time, creativity, public services, health and care from their increasing commodification and depletion that the basis for a new thinking of welfare states may take root.

Notes

[1] See Fiona Williams (2021) for more extensive discussions of the issues raised here.
[2] It should be noted that intersectionality as a theoretical orientation has different versions and applications, and is not without its criticisms. These are discussed in Williams (2021). My own approach in social policy incorporates feminist, anti-racist

and post-colonial intersectional approaches with salient social relations of class, disability, age, sexuality and so on, with a political economy approach to welfare states (Williams, 2021).

[3] Much relevant political literature refers to the contemporary crisis of democracy, especially seen in the distrust of political elites, the rejection of social democracy and the rise of ethno-nationalist populist leaders (Streeck, 2014; Brown, 2015). This is important, but it is of a different order to, and more consequential of, the economic, social and planetary crises discussed here.

[4] Elsewhere a framework is applied that translates this global scale of crises into the intersections, the institutional, discourses, contestations and social relations of family, nation, work and nature at the national scale (Williams, 2021).

References

Action Aid (2019) Climate Change and Gender, www.actionaid. org.uk/about-us/what-we-do/womens-economic-empowerment/ food-hunger-and-sustainable-livelihoods/climate-change/ climate-change-and-gender.

Anthony, C. (2017) *The Earth, the City, and the Hidden Narrative of Race*, New York: New Village Press.

Bassel, L. and Emejulu, A. (2018) *Minority Women and Austerity Survival and Resistance in France and Britain*, Bristol: Policy Press.

Béland, D. and Mahon, R. (2016) *Advanced Introduction to Social Policy*, Cheltenham: Edward Elgar.

Bhambra, G. K. and Holmwood, J. (2018) 'Colonialism, Postcolonialism and the Liberal Welfare State', *New Political Economy*, 23(5): 574–87.

Bhambra, G. K., Gebrial, D. and Nisancioglu, K. (2018) *Decolonising the University*, London: Pluto Press.

Bhattacharya, T. (ed) (2017) *Social Reproduction Theory: Remapping Class, Recentering Oppression*, London: Pluto Press.

Bhattacharyya, G. (2018) *Rethinking Racial Capitalism*, London: Rowman & Littlefield.

Brown, W. (2015) *Undoing the Demos: Neoliberalism's Stealth Revolution*, New York: Zone Books.

Carbonnier, C. and Morel, N. (2015) *The Political Economy of Household Services in Europe*, Basingstoke: Palgrave Macmillan.

Chattoo, S., Craig, G., Atkin, K. and Flynn, R. (eds) (2019) *Understanding 'Race' and Ethnicity: Theory, History, Policy, Practice*, Bristol: Policy Press.

Cohambahee River Collective ([1977] 1995) The CRC Statement, http://circuitous.org/scraps/combahee.html.

Collins, P. H. and Bilge, S. (2020) *Intersectionality*, Second Edition, Cambridge: Polity.

Craig, G., Cole, B. and Ali, N. (2019) *The Missing Dimension: Where Is Race in Social Policy Teaching and Learning?*, Report for the Social Policy Association, www.social-policy.org.uk/uncategorized/.

Crenshaw, K. (1989) 'Demarginalising the Intersection of Race and Sex: A Black Feminist Critique of Anti-discrimination Doctrine, Feminist Theory and Antiracist Politics', *University of Chicago Legal Forum*, 139: 139–67.

Daly, M. and Ferragina, E. (2018) 'Family Policy in High-Income Countries: Five Decades of Development', *Journal of European Social Policy*, 28(3): 255–70.

Dawson, M. (2016) 'Hidden in Plain Sight: A Note on Legitimation Crises and the Racial Order', *Critical Historical Studies*, 3(1): 143–61.

De Genova, N. (2018) 'The "Migrant Crisis" as Racial Crisis: Do *Black Lives Matter* in Europe?', *Ethnic and Racial Studies*, 41(10): 1765–82.

Dwyer, P. (ed) (2019) *Dealing with Welfare Conditionality: Implementation and Effects*, Bristol: Policy Press.

Faist, T. (2019) *The Transnationalized Social Question: Migration and the Question of Social Inequalities in the Twenty-First Century*, Oxford: Oxford University Press.

Farnsworth, K. and Irving, Z. (eds) (2015) *Social Policy in Times of Austerity: Global Economic Crisis and the New Politics of Welfare*, Bristol: Policy Press.

Floro, M. S. (2012) 'The Crises of Environment and Social Reproduction: Understanding their Linkages', *Journal of Gender Studies*, 15(32): 13–32.

Fraser, N. (2013) 'A Triple Movement? Parsing the Politics of Crisis after Polanyi', *New Left Review*, 81: 119–32.

Fraser, N. (2016a) 'Expropriation and Exploitation in Racialized Capitalism: A Reply to Michael Dawson', *Critical Historical Studies*, 3(1): 163–78.

Fraser, N. (2016b) 'Contradictions of Capital and Care', *New Left Review*, 100: 99–117.

Geiger, M. and Pécoud, A. (eds) (2010) *The Politics of International Migration Management*, Basingstoke: Palgrave Macmillan.

Gill, S. (2019) 'Towards Planetary Governance?', *Global Affairs*, 5(2): 131–7.

Glenn, E. N. (1992) 'From Servitude to service Work: Historical Continuities in the Racial Division of Women's Paid Reproductive Labour', *Signs*, 18(1): 1–44.

Gough, I. (2017) *Heat, Greed and Human Needs*, Cheltenham: Edward Elgar.

Gramsci, A. (1971) *Selections form the Prison Notebooks*, London: Lawrence & Wishart.

Gray, H. and Franck, A. K. (2019) 'Refugees as/at Risk: The Gendered and Racialized Underpinnings of Securitization in British Media Narratives', *Security Dialogue*, 50(3): 275–91.

Hankivsky, O. and Jordan-Zachary, J. (eds) (2019) *The Palgrave Handbook of Intersectionality in Public Policy*, Cham: Palgrave Macmillan.

Hills, J. (2015) *Good Times, Bad Times: The Welfare Myth of Them and Us*, Bristol: Policy Press.

IHE (Institute for Health Equity) (2020) *Health Equity in England: The Marmot Review 10 Years On*, London: IHE.

IOM (International Organization for Migration) (2016) 'Migrant, Refugee Deaths at Sea Pass 3,000 as Arrivals near 250,000', *IOM Website*, 26 July, https://www.iom.int/news/migrant-refugee-deaths-sea-pass-3000-arrivals-near-250000.

Ionesco, D. (2019) 'Let's Talk About Climate Migrants, Not Climate Refugees', www.un.org/sustainabledevelopment/blog/2019/06/lets-talk-about-climate-migrants-not-climate-refugees/.

ILO (International Labour Organization) (2009) *Global Employment Trends for Women*, Geneva: ILO.

ILO (2016) *Women at Work: Trends*, Geneva: ILO.

Irvine, J., Lang, S. and Montoya, C. (2019) *Gendered Mobilizations and Intersectional Challenges*, London: Rowman & Littlefield.

Jessop, B. (2015) 'Neoliberalism, Finance-Dominated Capitalism and Enduring Austerity: A Cultural Political Economy Perspective', in K. Farnsworth and Z. Irving (eds) *Social Policy in Times of Austerity: Global Economic Crisis and the New Politics of Welfare*, Bristol: Policy Press, 87–112.

Lewis, G. and Parma, P. (1983) 'Review Essay of American Black Feminist Literature', *Race & Class*, XXV: 86–91.

Lewis, S. L. and Maslin, M. A. (2015) 'Defining the Anthropocene', *Nature*, 519: 171–80.

Manchanda, N. (2019) 'Whither Race in Planetary Governance? A Response to Stephen Gill', *Global Affairs*, 5(2): 145–8.

Marx, K. and Engels, F. (1886) *The Manifesto of the Communist Party*, London: International Publishing Company.

May, V. M. (2015) *Pursuing Intersectionality, Unsettling Dominant Imaginaries*, New York: Routledge.

Mayblin, L., Wake, M. and Kazemi, M. (2019) 'Necropolitics and the Slow Violence of the Everyday: Asylum Seeker Welfare in the Postcolonial Present', *Sociology*, 54(1): 107–23.

Mezzadri, A. (2019) 'On the Value of Social Reproduction: Informal Labour, the Majority World and the Need for Inclusive Theories and Politics', *Radical Philosophy*, 2(04): www.radicalphilosophy.com/article/on-the-value-of-social-reproduction.

Moraga, C. and Anzaldúa, G. (eds) (1983) *This Bridge Called My Back: Writings by Radical Women of Color*, Watertown, MA: Persephone Press.

OECD (2015) *Labor Force Survey 2015*, Paris: OECD, https://stats.oecd.org/Index.aspx?DataSetCode=LFS_SEXAGE_I_R.

Olafsson, S., Daly, M., Kangas, O. and Palme, J. (eds) (2019) *Welfare and the Great Recession: A Comparative Study*, Oxford: Oxford University Press.

Orloff, A. S. (2009) 'Gendering the Comparative Analysis of Welfare States: An Unfinished Agenda', *Sociological Theory*, 27(3): 317–43.

Polanyi, K. ([1944] 1957) *The Great Transformation: The Political and Economic Origins of Our Time*, Boston: Beacon Press.

Pulido, L. (2016) 'Flint, Environmental Racism, and Racial Capitalism', *Capitalism Nature Socialism*, 27(3): 1–16.

Qureshi, K., Kasstan, B., Meer, N. and Hill, S. (2020a) *Submission of Evidence on the Disproportionate Impact of Covid-19, and the UK Government Response, on Ethnic Minorities in the UK*, https://ghpu.sps.ed.ac.uk/wp-content/uploads/2020/04/Qureshi-Kasstan-Meer-Hill_working-paper_COVID19-ethnic-minorities_240420.pdf.

Rai, S., Hoskyns, C. and Thomas, D. (2014) 'Depletion: The Social Cost of Reproduction', *International Feminist Journal of Politics*, 16(1): 86–105.

Rother, S. (2018) 'Angry Birds of Passage – Migrant Rights Networks and Counter-hegemonic Resistance to Global Migration Discourses', *Globalizations*, 15(6): 854–69.

Ryan, F. (2019) *Crippled: Austerity and the Demonization of Disabled People*, London: Verso.

Sager, A. (2018) *The Migrant Eye's View Toward a Normative Theory of Mobility*, Cham: Palgrave Macmillan.

Sager, A. (2021) 'The Uses and Abuses of "Migrant Crisis"', in T. Fouskas (ed) *Immigrants, Asylum Seekers and Refugees in Times of Crisis: International perspectives*, Athens: European Public Law Organization, 15–34.

Shutes, I. (2016) 'Work-related Conditionality and the Access to Social Benefits of National Citizens, EU and Non-EU Citizens', *Journal of Social Policy*, 45(4): 691–707.

Sian, K. P., Law, I. and Sayyid, S. (2013) *Racism, Governance, and Public Policy: Beyond Human Rights*, New York: Routledge.

Seymour, R. (2014) *Against Austerity: How We Can Fix the Crisis They Made*, London: Pluto Press.

Snell, C. and Haq, G. (2014) *A Short Guide to Environmental Policy*, Bristol: Policy Press.

Streeck, W. (2014) 'How Will Capitalism End?', *New Left Review*, 87: 35–64.

Taylor-Gooby, P. (2013) *The Double Crisis of the Welfare State and What We Can Do About It*, Basingstoke: Palgrave Macmillan.

The Rhodes Must Fall Movement (2018) *The Struggle to Decolonise the Racist Heart of Empire*, London: Zed Books.

Tyler I. (2013) *Revolting Subjects: Social Abjection and Resistance in Neoliberal Britain*, London: Zed Books.

UN DESA (United Nations Department of Economic and Social Affairs) (2011) *State of the World's Indigenous Peoples*, New York: UN, https://doi.org/10.18356/e92ca6a3-en.

UN DESA (2017) *State of the World's Indigenous Peoples*, Education, 3rd Volume, New York: UN, https://doi.org/10.18356/66ce8e42-en.

UN DESA (2019) *State of the World's Indigenous Peoples: Implementing the United Nations Declaration on the Rights of Indigenous Peoples*, 4th Volume, New York: UN, https://doi.org/10.18356/5cb401e7-en.

UNHRC (2019) *Visit to the United Kingdom of Great Britain and Northern Ireland: Report of the Special Rapporteur on Extreme Poverty and Human Rights*, Human Rights Council, Forty-first session, A/HRC/41/39/Add.1, https://digitallibrary.un.org/record/3806308?ln=en.

WEF (World Economic Forum) (2020) 'Coronavirus Isn't an Outlier, It's Part of Our Interconnected Viral Age', www.weforum.org/agenda/2020/03/coronavirus-global-epidemics-health-pandemic-covid-19/.

Williams, F. (2012) 'Converging Variations in Migrant Care Work in Europe', *Journal of European Social Policy*, 22(4): 363–76.

Williams, F. (2016) 'Critical Thinking in Social Policy: The Challenges of Past, Present and Future', *Social Policy & Administration*, 50(6): 628–47.

Williams, F. (2018a) 'Intersectionality, Gender and Social Policy', in S. Shaver (ed) *Handbook on Gender and Social Policy*, Cheltenham: Edward Elgar, 37–54.

Williams, F. (2018b) 'Care: Intersections of Scales, Inequalities, and Crises', *Current Sociology*, 66(4): 547–61.

Williams, F. (2021) *Social Policy: A Critical and Intersectional Analysis*, Cambridge: Polity.

Women's Budget Group and Runnymede Trust (2017) 'Intersecting Inequalities: The Impact of Austerity on Black and Minority Ethnic Women in the UK', http://wbg.org.uk/wp-content/uploads/2018/08/Intersecting-Inequalities-October-2017-Full-Report.pdf.

WMO (World Meteorological Organization) (2019) 'United in Science', Report by the Science Advisory Group for the UN Climate Action Summit, https://public.wmo.int/en/resources/united_in_science.

11

Global social policy and the quasi-concept of social cohesion

Jane Jenson

Introduction

This conceptualization of 'the social' has a much longer history than some of the others that this collection considers. We most often trace the concept of social cohesion back to Émile Durkheim's 1893 work, *The Division of Labor in Society*. Writing at the end of a century of immense social change in Europe and mounting political uncertainties in both national states and transnational empires, Durkheim worried about the consequences of economic and social transformations for the capacity of societies to cohere as well as the social mechanisms permitting that to happen. Recently, however, academic and policy analysts have located the concept in the work of an even earlier theorist. As explicit preoccupation with social cohesion in post-colonial and post-conflict settings has mounted, the tendency has been to retrieve the position of Ibn Khaldun.[1] He developed the concept of *asabiyyah* (solidarity or cohesion) in his 14th century masterwork of historical sociology, *Muqaddimah* (Khaldun, 1958 [1377]). Albeit separated by half a millennium, both these social theorists sought the social processes and mechanisms that allowed societies to cohere even as social, economic and political conflicts or instability reshaped them. As this chapter describes and assesses, this concern for cohesive social relations during crisis and change continues to motivate both actions and analysis of institutions and actors now intervening at several scales, including global social policy.

'Social cohesion': a quasi-concept

Social cohesion is a concept that has always operated at the intersection of intervention and analysis. Indeed, it respects the definition of a quasi-concept: a hybrid, making use of empirical analysis and thereby benefiting from the legitimizing aura of the scientific method, but simultaneously characterized by an indeterminate quality that makes it adaptable to a variety of situations and flexible enough to follow the twists and turns of policy that everyday politics sometimes make necessary (Bernard, 1999: 48).[2] Varied policy communities working at numerous scales invoke the quasi-concept. Social cohesion is analysed in local communities and across regions. Supranational and international organizations as well as national institutions adopt a lens they label social cohesion. The disciplinary variety is also immense, ranging from sociology and economics to psychology and epidemiology. When observers are fearful of 'crisis' they tend to invoke the conditions of social cohesion, with the result that its (dreaded) absence receives more consideration than the characteristics of its presence.

In recent decades, the literature on social cohesion has flourished at all scales, albeit in waves and at different times in various parts of the globe. Always associated with moments of social instability, it is not surprising that in this era of globalizing economic relations, multiple and massive migration streams due to political and environmental instabilities, and on-going political violence, attention has turned to issues of social order, stability and cohesion. This mushrooming of political and academic attention has occurred in both the Global South and North (for recent overviews see Schiefer and van der Noll, 2017; Delhey et al, 2018; Fonseca et al, 2019). Concern with increasing ethnic and other forms of social diversity initially underlay interest in the Global North (Jenson, 1998; Dragolov et al, 2013; Spoonley and Tolley, 2013). In the last decades, the literature has flourished for other places, recounting innovative interventions to assess and increase social cohesion in conflict-affected and fragile contexts, during peace-building and following economic crisis across the globe (Green et al, 2009; King and Samii, 2014; OECD, 2011). Given such wide-ranging applications, it is hardly surprising that one key characteristic of the quasi-concept is the lack of any shared definition or location in causal processes.

Definitional uncertainty: why it matters

Like John Milton's *Paradise Lost*, social cohesion is most often lamented for its absence, for an earlier or aspirational condition of social harmony (Schiefer and van de Noll, 2017: 579–80). Although social cohesion is identified either as a key ingredient in assuring positive outcomes such as health, peace or growth or as a positive thing in itself, the actual analysis tends to focus on the absence of social cohesion. Anxiety arises with the fear that it is 'missing' or in decline. One of the waves of policy concern about social cohesion swelled in the mid-1990s, particularly in the European region and in the so-called 'white dominions', which were all experiencing immigration flows coming from new source countries of the Global South. The Council of Europe (CoE) was a leader in European conceptual development and interventions (Farrell and Thirion, 2013).[3] Outside Europe, national policy communities in Canada, Aotearoa/New Zealand and Australia promised to identify practices to foster or protect social cohesion (Beauvais and Jenson, 2002; Peace et al, 2005; Markus and Kirpitchenko, 2007). Attention also extended to social cohesion as a support for successful pluralism or post-conflict peace-building in several regions and at different scales of policy action (for example, Marc et al, 2013; Cox and Sisk, 2017; Jenson, 2019).

Despite interest waxing and waning over the years, there is one constant about this quasi-concept: no shared definition of social cohesion exists. Thus, for example, we can read in 1998:

> Despite lively conversation about social cohesion in policy circles, there is surprisingly little effort to say what it is. Any survey of the literature immediately reveals that there is no consensus about either the definition of social cohesion or its links to a whole family of concepts often used when discussing it. (Jenson, 1998: 4)

In 2017, the situation was similar: 'Scholars of social cohesion argue, however, that – beyond the emphasis on social cohesion as a desirable characteristic of a community, and the common narrative of social cohesion being in decline – there is little agreement on what social cohesion precisely entails' (Schiefer and van der Noll, 2017: 580; also, for example, Burns et al, 2018). Definitions often vary by disciplinary positioning, with psychology and often economics turning to individual factors that seem to compose social cohesion while sociology, politics or social policy tend to emphasize institutional and distributional dimensions in their definitions.

While policy makers may consider definitional floundering and disputes as arcane or irrelevant academic posturing, the issue is crucial for social policy communities: from the definition follows the intervention. Varying a definition and its associated mechanisms will relocate policy intervention from individuals to communities or vice versa for instance, or from individual and group encounters to socioeconomic distributional patterns for example (Beauvais and Jenson, 2002: 6; Peace and Spoonley, 2019: 108).

One long-standing stream of policy analysis rests on the treatment of social cohesion as a synonym for social capital, most often measured by indicators of trust among individuals and trust in institutions (Jenson, 2010). The notion of social capital has been particularly influential in the fields of health and economics and for some interventions by international organizations and non-governmental international organizations. An early use of this definition was in epidemiology, where data collection measured individuals' level of social capital (participation and trust in their neighbours or distrust of 'others') and correlated it with individual health outcomes. The argument was that higher rates of social capital were a buffering mechanism between income inequality and a variety of negative health outcomes (for example, Kawachi et al, 1997; Uphoff et al, 2013, for an overview). This approach launched a lively debate among health experts about whether the social determinants of health depended primarily on community characteristics or on class-based distributional patterns (for example, Muntaner and Lynch, 1999; Wilkinson, 1999; Kushner and Sterk, 2005).

When global social policy communities plump for a definition of social cohesion as social capital there are consequences for programme design. For example, a major publication by the World Bank asserts that social cohesion exists when social ties are many and structured (Marc et al, 2013: 3). Social cohesion is defined as ' "convergence across groups" [that] means that individuals and groups are connected in such a way that they feel it is better to collaborate than compete, and they trust in the fundamentals of the overall social norms and networks that govern their behavior' (Marc et al, 2013: 40). For practice, this emphasis has structured interventions designed to bring people together to encourage them to uncover and identify their understandings and priorities. Thus, in post-conflict or refugee settings this might mean organizing various kinds of mediation. The United Nations-led 2015–16 *Regional Refugee and Resilience Plan* (3RP) for Lebanon and Jordan brought together 200 or more partners from the regional and international levels and proposed, among other things:

> planned social cohesion interventions [that] aim to develop local conflict mitigation mechanisms, involving relevant municipal and community stakeholders. Stakeholders will be helped to conduct participatory conflict analysis, to

identify the main sources of tensions, and will be trained on conflict resolution skills such as negotiation, problem solving and mediation. ... Such initiatives aim to enhance positive interaction in all affected communities, building on existing community and municipal structures.[4]

Donors, whether from non-governmental or international organizations, now organize a range of community-driven development (CDD) interventions to foster trust, taken as the indicator of social cohesion's shared values (Marc et al, 2013: ch 7; for a critical discussion, King and Samii, 2014).

An alternative understanding of the underpinnings of social cohesion identifies social practices that structure distribution of economic, social and political resources. For example, assessing the possibilities for growth, the Development Centre of the Organisation for Economic Co-operation and Development (OECD) defined a cohesive society as one 'that works towards the well-being of all its members, fights exclusion and marginalisation, creates a sense of belonging, promotes trust, and offers its members the opportunity of upward social mobility' (OECD, 2011: 51). The practices following from this definition were job creation as well as access to social rights and services. Proponents of this approach rejected targeted social assistance, calling instead for 'broader social cohesion objectives' to reduce income inequalities as well as to improve access to basic services and opportunities for decent jobs and upward social mobility. The model was one of 'inclusive growth', encompassing more effective redistribution policies and comprehensive social protection programmes to foster social cohesion, as well as sustainable development. In this understanding of social cohesion, inclusion, both social and economic, and social mobility were the objective.

In preparation for the 2013 World Development Report (WDR) that also focused on 'jobs', policy analysts Andrew Norton and Arjan de Haan (2012: 3, 9–10) provided a useful overview of social policy approaches to social cohesion, which they understood as an essentially 'normative' concept (what we term here a quasi-concept) linked to social citizenship. As did the OECD, they pointed out that this understanding of social cohesion implied a goodly emphasis on universalism in social policy, as well as a clear role for the state as the guarantor of such citizenship rights. For them, social cohesion implied three things: a set of rules around social membership and/or national citizenship, norms around fairness and equity, and security of access to livelihoods and basic services.

Nevertheless, while identifying social cohesion as one of three intermediary pillars of development (alongside living standards and productivity), the 2013 WDR continued to perpetuate the concept's ambiguities. It thus chose simply to list a few common threads identifying social cohesion as generally a positive concept that involves a process with varied outcomes (World Bank, 2012: 128). For the authors of this WDR, the relevance of social cohesion as a social glue was its intermediary status between jobs and development.[5] In a chain of argumentation, analysis could focus on either its causes or its consequences, or on both.

Social cohesion: cause or effect?

In the late 1300s, Ibn Khaldun proposed his concept of *asabiyyah*, treating the waxing and waning strength of such patterned solidarities as a *cause* of the cyclical rise and fall of the power and influence of one group over another (Alatas, 2006: 401). For Durkheim, the positioning was different. Cohesion was the *outcome* of social organization, and the institutions that worked to sustain it, such as the law, organization of labour, or religion. He saw this cohesive solidarity and its sustaining institutions as under stress from the heavy tendencies of industrialization, urbanization and massive population movements across the European continent (Durkheim, [1893] 2014).

In the last decade of the past century, similar concerns came to the fore, as governments, international actors and ordinary citizens began to worry about the state of social cohesion, and differences as to causal positioning persisted. Some policy communities sought the contributions of social cohesion to societal wellbeing, being primarily interested in social cohesion as a driver of wellbeing and identifying its consequences. Others pursued the conditions fostering social cohesion, seeking the conditions and practices that drove it. Such positions on social cohesion do not always neatly distinguish one institutional actor from another, however. The same organization may sometimes use the quasi-concept both ways, depending on the reason or goals for which they deploy the notion.

Social cohesion as a driver of positive outcomes preoccupies a large group of global social policy interventions, as it did Ibn Khaldun. In the health sector, the social determinants of health approach sometimes includes calls for fostering social cohesion in order to help equalize health outcomes or to improve public health. The World Health Organization (WHO), for example, built on a long tradition in academic research of assessing the impact of social cohesion, or more notably its absence, for health outcomes. The approach provoked some intense debate because of its emphasis on social relations, via 'the attribution of the effects of income inequality on population health to the breakdown of social cohesion (for example, cooperation, reciprocity, trust, civic participation)' (Muntaner and Lynch, 1999: 60; Wilkinson, 1999). In other words, where social relations among individuals had deteriorated, the claim was that it was possible to see a correlation with poorer health outcomes. Such outcomes ranged from negative effects on mental health to reduced resilience to catastrophic weather events (for example, Fone et al, 2007). The Commission on the Social Determinants of Health (CSDH) of the WHO, in its path-breaking report *Closing the Gap*, positioned social cohesion similarly, identifying it as one of the factors that is causally aligned with good health outcomes, alongside material circumstances, psychosocial factors, (individual) behaviours and biological factors (CSDH, 2008: 43).

A number of other interventions in the domain of global social policy also follow from the proposition that social cohesion drives peace and reduces violence. This position is prevalent in organizations, whether intergovernmental or non-governmental, working in post-conflict situations and among those focused on social development, whether in 'fragile states' or not. It is also often found in settings with concentrated numbers of refugees. For example, civil war has displaced thousands of refugees to Jordan, where massive population movement presents numerous challenges for the receiving country. In the 2019 *Response Plan for the Syrian Crisis*, the Jordanian government, along with donors and UN agencies, made a strong commitment to 'enhance social cohesion' among Jordanian and Syrian schoolchildren and among adults, by interventions particularly at the municipal level. The goal was to overcome vulnerabilities, both individual and collective, and thereby promote more peaceful and resilient communities (Government of Jordan, 2019).[6] Work by the World Bank also treats social cohesion as a driver for overcoming fragility in post-conflict settings. As summarized by Elizabeth King, the expectation is that 'by improving public goods provision or enhancing cohesion, CDR [community driven reconstruction] may reduce the risk of renewed conflict by lessening local grievances or facilitating economic development, which may in turn reduce the incentives to participate in violence' (King, 2013: 15).

This perspective, and the projects following from it, share the notion that was also present in health studies that social cohesion is primarily about connections among individuals. Other designs for action that treat social cohesion as a driver of wellbeing, however, place less emphasis on individuals and more on social cohesion as a social phenomenon. Work by both the World Bank and the OECD exemplify this approach, although the shift in perspective is sometimes only partial. For example, the Bank's 2013 WDR identified social cohesion as one of the pillars of development, building on the notion that there were interactions along pathways between social cohesion and jobs and vice versa (World Bank, 2012: 138–9). For this analysis, the Bank proposed indicators of social cohesion at both individual and country level (World Bank, 2012: 127). The second group of indicators emphasized institutions.[7] Indeed, institutions have been a long-standing focus of Bank work on social cohesion. In an early presentation, for example, Jo Ritzen (at the time a vice-president of the World Bank) summarized the claim this way:

> It is my contention that a country's social cohesion – contributing to the inclusiveness of its communities *and* responsive political institutions – has a vitally important role in managing the effectiveness of that country's policy response to the vagaries of the global economy. (Ritzen and Woolcock, 2000: 9)

Work at the OECD has paid more attention to social relations. In 2012, the OECD Development Centre provided its definition of a cohesive society (quoted earlier), thereby creating a wide-ranging (and often cited) list of qualities of cohesion according to what it accomplishes. Yet, as did the WDR 2013, the OECD's approach also recognized interactions on the pathways to and from social cohesion. In addition, it said: 'Social cohesion is both a means to development and an end in itself, and is shaped by a society's preferences, history and culture' (OECD, 2011: 51). Attention went not only to the consequences of a cohesive society but also the factors that work to foster cohesion. In taking this stance, the OECD joined the company of those, including Émile Durkheim, who also focused on social cohesion as an outcome.

Seeking to identify *the drivers of social cohesion*, global social policy communities list causal factors that foster it, ranging from values to policy choices about how to manage diversity or to promote social development. But again, there is more emphasis on what hinders social cohesion than on what actually brings it into existence.

In analyses that claim values drive social cohesion there are several different positions, but in essence they come down to the idea that cohesion results from acceptance of common values and principles that promote shared feelings of citizenship or of a shared destiny. The scale of intervention that follows is primarily local or national.

Proponents of this position identify policy domains such as education as particularly useful for teaching the values, principles and practices of living together. If in many contemporary situations the goal is to teach the normality and advantages of valuing societal diversity, historically it was more common to insist that citizenship education depended on teaching a set of shared values that would provide the foundation for social cohesion.

An emphasis on shared values has deep roots in European societies divided by religious belief and language and has shaped theories of social cohesion for well over a century.[8] At the broad European scale, attention to values characterized the treatment of social cohesion by the CoE for many years.[9] One, albeit only one, way of assuring a trajectory towards social cohesion involved following a set of 'European' (sometimes termed 'universal') values leading to rights, including social rights.[10] The pathway ranged from practices to recognize and provide reasonable accommodation of cultural diversity to promotion of respect for diversity via the education system and values promoted in curricula. The CoE encouraged a range of other organizations to invest in education to ensure inclusive values, both cultural and social.[11] The other side of the coin, of course, is that educational institutions can also reinforce inter-communal distancing, creating bonds of shared values and worldviews within communities but not across them, as has historically been the case, for example, in Lebanon (Aoun and Zahar, 2017).

At the international level the work sponsored by the World Bank and cited earlier also stressed values and principles as drivers of social cohesion (Marc et al, 2013: 47–8):

> Convergence across groups that is based on shared intersubjective meanings facilitates social cohesion. Intersubjective meanings encompass beliefs of individuals, communities, and societies about themselves, how the world works, and their own agency in confronting change and making decisions that affect their own lives ... These understandings are motivated by reasons that go beyond interests, incentives, and values. ... a convergence based on shared intersubjective meanings implies that everyone in the society should share the same understanding of what the points of convergence are and how it is to be achieved. It does not mean that all people need to believe the same things and behave in the same way, but that at least a minimum of overlap should exist between various

meaning systems, and that people's understandings of the world and the behavior that comes with it must have some elements of compatibility.

This caveat about not requiring, or imposing, homogeneity of values is common, but the difficult question about 'how much' agreement and 'whose values' continues to plague approaches that consider social cohesion as driven, or fostered, by shared values.

There is another model that identifies public policies intended to manage diversity as the driver of social cohesion, however (Banting, 2008: 2). In the last decades of the 20th century, multiculturalism emerged as a favoured policy tool in several countries, before losing favour. Will Kymlicka summarizes multiculturalism policies (abbreviated as MCP) this way:

> This term covers a wide range of policies, but what they have in common is that they go beyond the protection of the basic civil and political rights guaranteed to all individuals in a liberal-democratic state to also extend some level of public recognition and support for minorities to express their distinct identities and practices. The rise of MCPs therefore goes beyond the broader politics of civil rights and nondiscrimination. (Kymlicka, 2013: 101)

Many people identify such policies as having helped countries avoid the conflictual and often violent clashes associated with mobilized differences. Thus, Prime Minister Justin Trudeau expressed this belief in the role of public policy when he said in November 2015:[12] 'Canada has learned how to be strong not in spite of our differences, but because of them, and going forward, that capacity will be at the heart of both our success, and of what we offer the world.' Of course, not everyone shares this belief that multicultural policies foster social cohesion. For example, also in autumn 2015 Chancellor Angela Merkel of Germany labelled multiculturalism 'a sham', a claim that repeated her 2010 pronouncement that it had 'utterly failed'.[13] What she meant by multiculturalism were policy practices that allowed immigrants to live their lives in parallel to other Germans.[14] This is not what is usually meant by multiculturalism policies for proponents such as Kymlicka. However, so discredited now is multiculturalism as a policy perspective in much of Europe that the CoE has abandoned the term and selected 'interculturalism' instead. In a 2008 White Paper, the CoE called for policies promoting intercultural dialogue, with the policy advocated as 'a powerful instrument of mediation and reconciliation: through critical and constructive engagement across cultural fault-lines, it addresses real concerns about social fragmentation and insecurity while fostering integration and social cohesion' (CoE, 2008: 17). By 2015 the Committee of Ministers to Member States on Intercultural Integration recommended that cities follow the 'urban model of intercultural integration', with social policies 'to prevent conflict and foster equal opportunities and social cohesion'.[15] This recommendation was the follow-up to an initiative on *Intercultural Cities* co-sponsored by the CoE and European Union (EU) several years earlier. In other words, for these two large regional policy communities, the policy interventions for intercultural practice should take place at the local level, their claim being that even in the most cosmopolitan and seemingly least-rooted settings that are contemporary urban areas, the right policies can foster social cohesion.

Global social policy communities have increasingly expanded their policy toolbox since the economic crisis of 2008 and the various refugee 'crises' around the globe. The 'right policies' for a cohesive society have become those in which socioeconomic equality and inclusive growth are objectives because, as the claim goes, social cohesion follows from less poverty and more social mobility. In this cluster are found approaches to social development that now identify social cohesion as one positive outcome of work, employment and jobs.

The supranational EU was ahead of many deploying such policy tools, in part because it has a quite particular approach to 'cohesion'. Its broad social policy agenda is part of this approach, in the sense that cohesion is sought via the eradication of poverty and social exclusion as well as modernization of social protection, all of which require social investment, activation of the labour force and a higher employment rate to generate social inclusion.[16] Social cohesion was among the objectives in the Europe 2020 strategic project, and socioeconomic as well as cultural integration was the identified route.[17]

Increasingly, additional organizations in the global social policy community are identifying economic and social inequalities as hindering social cohesion and calling for direct interventions. The OECD, which relaunched itself onto the terrain of social cohesion in 2011, did so via a model stressing social inclusion and social mobility as well social capital as drivers of social cohesion (OECD, 2011: 59). The UNDP took up the theme again with its 2015 Human Development Report (HDR), *Rethinking Work for Human Development*. In this perspective, a key driver of social cohesion is work: paid and unpaid, formal and informal and so on. While social cohesion is not the only objective of policy, it is one of the positive outcomes: 'Work provides livelihoods, income, a means for participation and connectedness, social cohesion, and human dignity.'[18] The 2030 Development Agenda is linked to the issue of work and there is an explicit linkage of social development to social cohesion for peace: 'In conflict and post-conflict situations it is important to focus on productive jobs that empower people, build agency, provide access to voice, offer social status and increase respect, cohesion, trust and people's willingness to participate in civil society' (UNDP, 2015: 22).

But attention to social development as a driver of social cohesion goes well beyond policy interventions around work. Policy communities have both advocated and expressed scepticism about reliance on social protection policy interventions in situations of ethnic diversity in fragile settings. Concerns are similar to those expressed about ethnic diversity in long-standing welfare states (for this debate see, among others Kymlicka, 2015). For proponents, extending social protection, in the form of food aid, cash transfers and so on, has the potential to foster social cohesion but others claim it is similarly likely that that extension of social protection could generate feelings of hostility and greater tension. Elsa Valli and colleagues (2018) have provided an overview of this dispute as well as contributing to the discussion. They conducted an experimental study for UNICEF (United Nations Children's Fund) in Latin America to test whether social protection interventions had the ability to foster social cohesion, particularly between refugees and host communities. The former were Colombians and the host country was Ecuador. The policy treatment came from a six-month intervention of the World Food Programme (WFP). The results were mixed, with measures of social cohesion rising among the incoming Colombians but with little change in the host population.

Overall, then, as this section indicates, the lack of agreement about this quasi-concept goes beyond definitional ambiguity. The global social policy community demonstrates no greater belief in or scepticism about the notion than do those working exclusively at a local or national scale. Disagreements persist about where to position social cohesion in a causal chain: as cause, as effect, or as intermediary factor or variable. Does this mean there is no consensus whatsoever?

Conclusion: points of agreement

The literature using the quasi-concept of social cohesion is now extensive, covering most portions of the globe. No region escapes the pressures following from refugee flows due to environmental, political or economic pressures, or the choices about how to ensure wellbeing for citizens in the face of globalizing and unstable economic and political relations. While this chapter has stressed the uncertainties that have plagued the concept, no doubt in part because of its very status as a quasi-concept, a look from the other end of the telescope reveals some points of emerging consensus within global social policy communities.

A first is that social cohesion is multidimensional and therefore requires careful attention to operationalization and measurement. It is not a new insight that there is no single attribute that can capture the meaning of social cohesion (see for example the five dimensions identified in Jenson, 1998). What is somewhat newer, however, is the consensus that there can be no stinting of attention to operationalization and measurement tools, no matter the definition adopted or the several dimensions identified. When the quasi-concept re-emerged in the 1990s, there was a tendency to define it with reference to other 'socials' (for example, Levitas, 1996; Jenson, 1998). Social capital and social cohesion were often used as under-operationalized synonyms, as were social cohesion and social inclusion. The inadequacy of the strategy of relying on one quasi-concept to delineate another is now clear. As a recent paper for SALDRU (Southern Africa Labour and Development Research Unit) reminds us:

> As an imprecisely defined term of art, 'social cohesion' is liable to be dismissed as meaningless. It is also vulnerable to various forms of abuse. In particular – and in view of the fact that it is a term much used by governments and influential non-governmental organisations – there is a real danger that it will shift in sense from context to context, acquiring the meaning which suits the interests of the most powerful party. (Burns et al, 2018: 1–2)

In light of such assessments, recent years have brought more systematic attention to operationalization and measurement of the quasi-concept.[19]

A second consensual point upon which the most solid analysis rests is that social cohesion is an attribute of a collectivity; it is not an individual characteristic. The developers of the Social Cohesion Radar, for example, felt it necessary to stress this point because of significant misuse, when some publications suggest that *individuals* can exhibit greater or lesser cohesion. Therefore, to counter this error, Georgi Dragolov and colleagues felt compelled to state explicitly and right upfront: 'We, thus, define social cohesion as the extent of social togetherness in a territorially defined geo-political entity.

Social cohesion is a characteristic of the "collective" residing in this entity, rather than of individual members' (Dragolov et al, 2013: 5). Perhaps one of the reasons for the confusion they saw is that many definitions of social cohesion that include dimensions such as trust or participation actually rely on individual-level data drawn from public opinion or attitudinal surveys. Nonetheless, good analysis aggregates these data to create a measure of the collectivity's cohesion. While some sociologists might quibble that 'the whole is not simply the sum of its parts', careful analysts use only the aggregated data to indicate and measure any group's cohesion.

A third point of consensus is that there is no single scale at which global social policy communities may legitimately deploy the quasi-concept. If at its most general social cohesion means a situation in which a group shares bonds of solidarity and togetherness and demonstrates a willingness to cooperate and collaborate, the group may be any size, from a local community (an urban neighbourhood or refugee camp, for example) to a transnational region (the EU, for example). At the start, there was a tendency to use the national state as the unit of analysis. Very quickly, however, attention also turned to subnational, particularly urban, settings or supranational ones. Currently, global social policy communities use the quasi-concept to assess and compare local groups and areas as much as or even more than national states, and indeed, as noted, are encouraged to do so.

The fourth point of consensus and perhaps that most recently arrived at, is that social cohesion is best understood as part of a process rather than as an end state. The fact that attention to social cohesion has always risen in times of social change and crisis, as noted at the beginning of this chapter, provides a constant reminder that its dimensions are fluid through time. Beyond that, as the previous section laid out, there is increasing recognition of the analytic need to position social cohesion sometimes as cause and sometimes as outcome. While this may initially appear to be a weakness of the concept, the concern disappears when the analysis is of a process. One particular analytic cut into that process may mean the research question is what 'causes social cohesion' while another cut will ask the question 'what does social cohesion cause'. As described, work in global social policy communities has tended towards this processual perspective.

In the end, the ambiguity of the definition of the quasi-concept continues to put it at risk of dismissal as too vague and unmanageable (Burns et al, 2018; Peace and Spoonley, 2019). Nevertheless, continuing academic interest in several disciplines and the possibilities policy makers see for using it as a lens to address multiple problems means that this 'social' continues to garner interest at the same time as provoking controversy in global policy communities.

Notes

[1] For example, the World Development Report 2013 asked 'what is social cohesion' and before citing Durkheim referred to Ibn Khaldun (World Bank, 2012: 128). For an overview of numerous theorists' positions see Norton and de Haan (2012: 5–9).

[2] Other quasi-concepts exist, of course. One garnering enthusiasm in the past years is 'social innovation' (Jenson and Harrisson, 2013: 14–15), while 'social investment' has been another (Jenson, 2010: 71–4). 'Social inclusion' also fits this category.

[3] This European attention eventually gave rise to the major research project by the Bertelsmann Stiftung, the *Social Cohesion Radar*. Among their many publications, see Dragolov et al (2013) or Delhey et al (2018). For another overview of cases see Spoonley and Tolley (2013).

[4] See page 20 at: www.undp.org/content/dam/rbas/doc/SyriaResponse/3RP%20 strategic%20overview%20new%20.pdf.

[5] See the diagram used in this WDR (World Bank, 2012: 8, 75). It is analyzed in Jenson (2019). The key causal factor was 'jobs', both paid and unpaid, formal and informal. This attention to social cohesion and 'work' rather than simply 'employment' is an important innovation for global social policy.

[6] A similar 2014 UNDP project was *Peace Building in Lebanon*, an 'initiative for enhancing social cohesion in Lebanese host communities affected by the Syrian crisis', www.un.org.lb/english/supporting-social-cohesion-by-reducing-tensions.

[7] For a similar comparative assessment of the impact of social capital or institutionalized state policy on reactions to immigrants, see Kessler and Bloemraad (2010).

[8] For example, between 1894 and 1906 France was profoundly divided over the Dreyfus Affair that split Catholics and traditionalist monarchists from republicans, and their values, including *laïcité*. Durkheim intervened on the side of the *dreyfusards*, in the name of reason and a modern moral individualism (Fournier, 2005: 52–3).

[9] The Directorate General of Social Cohesion (DG III) of the Council of Europe (1998–2011) had as its primary task to foster social cohesion and to improve the quality of life in Europe for the genuine enjoyment of fundamental human rights and the respect of human dignity. It defined its work as preserving ethnic and cultural diversity and framing social policies to promote protection of rights, social cohesion and a better quality of life in Europe. A reorganization folded actions on social cohesion into other branches in 2011 (Jenson, 2019: 23–4; see also Farrell and Thirion, 2013).

[10] See the list of publications in the series *Trends in Social Cohesion* that focus predominantly on matters of social and economic inclusion. www.coe.int/t/dg3/ socialpolicies/socialcohesiondev/trends_en.as.

[11] A similar focus, developed in collaboration with the CoE, shaped the joint work undertaken by the Organization for Security and Co-operation in Europe (OSCE) and United Nations Educational, Scientific and Cultural Organization (UNESCO) on educational interventions to counter intolerance and discrimination against Muslims and published in 2011, www.osce.org/odihr/84495?download=true.

[12] http://pm.gc.ca/eng/news/2015/11/26/diversity-canadas-strength#sthash. jdsC4rI6.dpuf.

[13] www.washingtonpost.com/news/worldviews/wp/2015/12/14/angela-merkel-multiculturalism-is-a-sham/.

[14] Almost a decade earlier the CoE was already expressing scepticism about multiculturalism: 'Whilst driven by benign intentions, multiculturalism is now seen by many as having fostered communal segregation and mutual incomprehension, as well as having contributed to the undermining of the rights of individuals – and, in particular, women – within minority communities, perceived as if these were single collective actors. The cultural diversity of contemporary societies has to be acknowledged as an empirical fact. However, a recurrent theme of the consultation was that multiculturalism was a policy with which respondents no longer felt at ease' (CoE, 2008: 19).

[15] See this Recommendation on intercultural integration CM/Rec(2015)1 at: www.coe.int/en/web/culture-and-heritage/-recommendation-on-intercultural-integration.

[16] As early as 1996 Ruth Levitas (1996) had identified the employment-focused definition of social inclusion and cohesion in European and British discourses.

[17] See for example the European Platform against Poverty and Social Exclusion at: http://eur-lex.europa.eu/LexUriServ/LexUriServ.do?uri=COM:2010:0758:FIN:EN:PDF.

[18] http://hdr.undp.org/en/rethinking-work-for-human-development.

[19] See for example the Bertelsmann Siftung's major comparative research initiative generating the Social Cohesion Radar (Dragolov et al, 2013) or the OECD's Social Cohesion Policy Reviews (OECD, 2014). A more recent elaborate example involves incorporation of social cohesion into the SAGE dashboard for assessing comparative wellbeing, an exercise supported by the World Policy Forum (Lima de Miranda and Snower, 2020).

References

Alatas, S. F. (2006) 'A Khaldunian Exemplar for a Historical Sociology for the South', *Current Sociology*, 54(3): 397–411.

Aoun, J. and Zahar, M.-J. (2017) 'Lebanon: Confessionalism, Consociationalism and Social Cohesion', in F. Cox and T. Sisk (eds) *Peacebuilding in Deeply Divided Societies. Rethinking Political Violence*, Cham: Palgrave Macmillan, 103–36.

Banting, K. (2008) *The Models of our Mind: Conceptions of Social Integration and Immigrant Integration*, Ottawa: Global Centre for Pluralism, https://gcp.machinedev.ca/wp-content/uploads/2017/10/banting_paper_pp4.pdf.

Beauvais, C. and Jenson, J. (2002) *Social Cohesion: Updating the State of the Research*, Ottawa: CPRN, http://oaresource.library.carleton.ca/cprn/12949_en.pdf.

Bernard, P. (1999) 'La cohésion sociale: Critique dialectique d'un quasi-concept', *Lien social et Politiques*, 41: 47–59.

Burns, J., Hull, G., Lefko-Everett, K. and Njozela, L. (2018) *Defining Social Cohesion*, SALDRU Working Paper #216, Cape Town: Southern Africa Labour and Development Research Unit and University of Cape Town.

CoE (Council of Europe) (2008) 'Living Together as Equals in Dignity', *White Paper on Intercultural Dialogue*, Strasbourg: CoE, www.coe.int/t/dg4/intercultural/source/white%20paper_final_revised_en.pdf.

Cox, F. and Sisk, T. (2017) *Peacebuilding in Deeply Divided Societies: Toward Social Cohesion*, Cham: Palgrave Macmillan.

CSDH (Commission on Social Determinants of Health) (2008) *Closing the Gap in a Generation: Health Equity through Action on the Social Determinants of Health*, Final Report of the Commission on Social Determinants of Health, Geneva: WHO.

Delhey, J., Boehnke, K., Dragolov, G., Ignácz, Z. S., Larsen, M., Lorenz, J. and Koch, M. (2018) 'Social Cohesion and Its Correlates: A Comparison of Western and Asian Societies', *Comparative Sociology*, 17(3–4): 426–55.

Dragolov, G., Ignácz, Z. Lorenz, J., Delhey, J. and Boehnke, K. (2013) *Social Cohesion Radar Measuring Common Ground: An International Comparison of Social Cohesion Methods Report*, Gütersloh: Bertelsman Siftung.

Durkheim, É. ([1893] 2014) *The Division of Labor in Society*, Edited and with a new introduction by Steven Lukes, Translation by W. D. Halls, New York: Free Press.

Farrell, G. and Thirion, S. (2013) 'Social Cohesion and Well-being: The Council of Europe's View', in P. Spoonley and E. Tolley (eds) *Diverse Nations, Diverse Responses. Approaches to Social Cohesion in Immigrant Societies*, Montreal: McGill-Queen's University Press, 269–88.

Fone, D., Dunstan, F., Lloyd, K., Williams, G., Watkins, J. and Palmer, S. (2007) 'Does Social Cohesion Modify the Association between Area Income Deprivation and Mental Health? A Multilevel Analysis', *International Journal of Epidemiology*, 36(2): 338–45.

Fonseca, X., Lukosch, S. and Brazier, F. (2019) 'Social Cohesion Revisited: A New Definition and How to Characterize It', *Innovation: The European Journal of Social Science Research*, 32(2): 231–53.

Fournier, M. (2005) 'Durkheim's Life and Context: Something New about Durkheim?', in J. Alexander and P. Smith (eds) *The Cambridge Companion to Durkheim*, Cambridge: Cambridge University Press, 41–69.

Government of Jordan (2019) *Jordan Response Platform for the Syrian Crisis 2019*, www.jrpsc.org.

Green, A., Jarmaat, J. G. and Han, C. (2009) *Regimes of Social Cohesion*, LLAKES Research Paper 1, https://dera.ioe.ac.uk//10486/.

Jenson, J. (1998) *Mapping Social Cohesion. The State of Canadian Research*, CPRN F|03, Ottawa: CPRN, http://oaresource.library.carleton.ca/cprn/15723_en.pdf.

Jenson, J. (2010) *Defining and Measuring Social Cohesion*, London: Commonwealth Secretariat and UNRISD, www.files.ethz.ch/isn/151856/Jenson%20ebook.pdf.

Jenson, J. (2019) *Intersections of Pluralism and Social Cohesion*, Ottawa: Global Centre for Pluralism, www.pluralism.ca/intersections-of-pluralism-and-social-cohesion-two-concepts-for-the-practice-of-pluralism/.

Jenson, J. and Harrisson, J. (2013) *Social Innovation Research in the European Union. Approaches, Findings and Future Directions*, Brussels: EC, https://ec.europa.eu/research/social-sciences/pdf/policy_reviews/social_innovation.pdf.

Kawachi, I., Kennedy, B. P., Lochner, K. and Prothrow-Stith, D. (1997) 'Social Capital, Income Inequality, and Mortality', *American Journal of Public Health*, 87(9): 1491–8.

Kessler, C. and Bloemraad, I. (2010) 'Does Immigration Erode Social Capital? The Conditional Effects of Immigration-Generated Diversity on Trust, Membership, and Participation across 19 Countries, 1981–2000', *Canadian Journal of Political Science,* 43(2): 319–47.

Khaldun, I. (1958 [1377]) *The Muqaddimah: An Introduction to History*, New York: Pantheon Books.

King, E. (2013) *A Critical Review of Community-driven Development in Conflict-Affected Contexts*, UK Aid and International Rescue Committee, www.gsdrc.org/go/display&type=Document&id=5326.

King, E. and Samii, C. (2014) 'Fast-Track Institution Building in Conflict-Affected Countries? Insights from Recent Field Experiments', *World Development*, 64: 740–54.

Kushner, H. and Sterk, C. (2005) 'The Limits of Social Capital: Durkheim, Suicide, and Social Cohesion', *American Journal of Public Health*, 95(7): 1139–43.

Kymlicka, W. (2013) 'Neoliberal Multiculturalism?', in P. A. Hall and M. Lamont (eds) *Social Resilience in the Neoliberal Era*, New York: Cambridge University Press, 99–125.

Kymlicka, W. (2015) 'Solidarity in Diverse Societies: Beyond Neoliberal Multiculturalism and Welfare Chauvinism', *Comparative Migration Studies,* 3(17): 1–19.

Levitas, R. (1996) 'The Concept of Social Exclusion and the New Durkheimian Hegemony', *Critical Social Policy*, 46(16): 5–20.

Lima de Miranda, K. and Snower, D. (2020) 'Recoupling Economic and Social Prosperity', *Global Solutions Journal*, 5: 14–23.

Marc, A., Willman, A., Aslam, G., Rebosio, M. with Balasuriya, K. (2013) *Societal Dynamics and Fragility: Engaging Societies in Responding to Fragile Situations*, Washington, DC: World Bank.

Markus, A. and Kirpitchenko, L. (2007) 'Conceptualising Social Cohesion', in J. Jupp and J. Nieuwenhuysen with E. Dawson (eds) *Social Cohesion in Australia,* Melbourne: Cambridge University Press, 21–32.

Muntaner, C. and Lynch, J. (1999) 'Income Inequality, Social Cohesion, and Class Relations: A Critique of Wilkinson's Neo-Durkheimian Research Programme', *International Journal of Health Services*, 29(1): 59–81.

Norton, A. and de Haan, A. (2012) *Social Cohesion: Theoretical Debates and Practical Applications with Respect to Jobs*, Background Paper for the World Development Report 2013, Washington, DC: World Bank.

OECD (Organisation for International Co-operation and Development) (2011) *Perspectives on Global Development 2012: Social Cohesion in a Shifting World*, Paris: OECD Publishing, https://doi.org/10.1787/persp_glob_dev-2012-en.

OECD (2014) *OECD Social Cohesion Policy Reviews – Concept Note*, Paris: OECD Development Centre, www.oecd.org/dev/inclusiveso cietiesanddevelopment/OECD_Social_Cohesion_Policy_Note.pdf.

Peace, R. and Spoonley, N. (2019) 'Social Cohesion and Cohesive Ties: Responses to Diversity', *New Zealand Population Review*, 45: 98–124.

Peace, R., Spoonley, P., Butcher, A. and O'Neill, D. (2005) *Immigration and Social Cohesion: Developing an Indicator Framework for Measuring the Impact of Settlement Policies in New Zealand*, Working Paper 01/05, Wellington, New Zealand: Centre for Social Research and Evaluation/Te Pokapu Rangahau Arotaki Hapori, Ministry of Social Development.

Ritzen, J. and Woolcock, M. (2000) *Social Cohesion, Public Policy, and Economic Growth: Implications for Countries in Transition*, Address prepared for the Annual Bank Conference on Development Economics (Europe), Paris, 26–28 June.

Schiefer, D. and van der Noll, J. (2017) 'The Essentials of Social Cohesion: A Literature Review', *Social Indicators Research*, 132(2): 579–603.

Spoonley, P. and Tolley, E. (eds) (2013) *Diverse Nations, Diverse Responses: Approaches to Social Cohesion in Immigrant Societies*, Montreal: McGill-Queen's University Press.

UNDP (United Nations Development Programme) (2015) *Human Development Report 2015, Work for Human Development*, New York: UNDP, http://hdr.undp.org/sites/default/files/2015_human_development_report.pdf.

Uphoff, E. P., Pickett, K., Cabieses, B., Small, N. and Wright, J. (2013) 'A Systematic Review of the Relationships between Social Capital and Socioeconomic Inequalities in Health: A Contribution to Understanding the Psychosocial Pathway of Health Inequalities', *International Journal of Equity Health*, 12(54): 1–12.

Valli, E., Peterman, A. and Hidrobo, M. (2018) *Economic Transfers and Social Cohesion in a Refugee-hosting Setting*, Innocenti Working Paper WP-2018-10, Florence: UNICEF Office of Research.

Wilkinson, R. (1999) 'Income Inequality, Social Cohesion, and Health: Clarifying the Theory – A Reply to Muntaner and Lynch', *International Journal of Health Services*, 29(3): 525–43.

World Bank (2012) *World Development Report 2013: Jobs*, Washington, DC: World Bank, https://doi.org/10.1596/978-0-8213-9575-2.

12

Putting the global in social justice?

Gary Craig

Introduction

Arguments about the meaning of justice have been central to political philosophy for thousands of years, certainly since the time of key Greek philosophers. The pedigree of the term 'social justice' is much shorter, although considerably longer than many believe to be the case. This chapter briefly addresses the question of how and when 'justice' morphed into 'social justice' and will summarize central elements of current debates about 'social justice' in light of the pressing global social policy imperative, reflected in the United Nations (UN) 2030 Agenda for Sustainable Development, to integrate economic, social and environmental needs for a more just and sustainable world.[1]

A major challenge now facing proponents of social justice in an economically globalized world and where most states are increasingly multicultural, is whether what has been an almost exclusively Eurocentric or Anglo-American, not to say Judaeo-Christian, understanding of the meaning of social justice provides a framework which is recognizable in other religious, ethnic and cultural contexts.[2]

If it does, then paradoxically we might now be able to talk about the concept of 'global social justice' at a time when racism is increasing across the world and social injustice is increasingly being done by majority communities to minorities.

From justice to social justice

Earliest recorded accounts of the nature of justice come from prominent Greek philosophers. In Plato's *Republic*,[3] he sets up a debate between Socrates, his teacher, and Thrasymachus, noted for his sophistry, that is, presenting arguments as truth whilst knowing them to be false. In Thrasymachus' view, justice has only one principle, which was the interest of the stronger, or, representing the centre of power in most states, the government, whether monarchical, dictatorial or democratic.

Plato makes it clear, however, that Socrates thought that justice was an eternal moral concept, challenging the view that 'might is right'. This concept, referred to as natural law, is distinct from the framework of law established in any nation state. Thus killing someone or enslaving them because the law of the land says you should contravenes the precept of natural law; it is unjust. Law does not necessarily deliver justice.

Plato considered his form of justice would be the ideal antidote to what he identified as the excessive individualism characterizing a corrupt, degenerate Athenian society: this individualism finds global expression today in the so-called 'free' market promoted by right-wing political parties. Neither Plato nor his significant contemporaries explicitly discussed the notion of *social* justice although their debates come very close. An individual, in Plato's and others' views, has to acknowledge not just their individualism and personal interests but their place in society as a whole and then to shape their life in relation to both rights and duties, a precursor to formulations of 'rights and responsibilities', propounded by recent UK New Labour governments for example.

Both Plato and Aristotle understood justice as incorporating not just the willingness to obey laws, but as reflecting goodness, a moral, rather than legal duty, incorporating elements of virtue, wisdom, courage, temperance and piety, and a duty which is owed to other community members, that is, social rather than individual. The societal context for the Greek philosophers, and later Roman ones, however, was one which most would now characterize as profoundly unjust, given that notions of fairness and equality could not sensibly be sustained within societies built on slavery, violence and the oppression of women. Social justice could only exist as an abstraction within a society where unjust relationships between different groups were taken as given and reflective of unequal power. This is merely an early, if somewhat extreme, instance where the rhetoric of justice stands apart from the reality: ideal versus real indeed.

The common understanding amongst scholars, politicians and activists is that the concept of social justice emerged in 20th century political philosophy. Jackson (2005: 356) argues that 'Social justice is a crucial ideal in contemporary political thought. Yet the concept ... is a recent addition to our political vocabulary and comparatively little is known about its introduction into political debate'. It is certainly true that as a political philosophy,– and particularly one which translated into political action, it became prominent from the second half of the 20th century onward, prompted most of all by Rawls' path-breaking work, *A Theory of Justice* (1971) – which itself did not discuss social justice as such (although it described justice as a social ideal). However, the concept of social justice actually emerged much earlier.

Hemphill (2015) states that the term social justice originated in Judean literature and in the New Testament, as Hebrew terms *mishpat* and *sedeq*. *Mishpat* referred to the protection of disadvantaged people and *sedeq* to righteousness, that is, a combination of thought and action, which she argues gives the term a strongly historical religious connection. This, in contemporary terms, can be characterized as a moral framework. St Augustine of Hippo, who introduced the concept of the 'just war', wrote explicitly in the *City of God* in the 5th century AD about the nature of social justice when reflecting on the causes of the decline of the Roman Empire; he was opposed, for example, to slavery and trafficking. His writing was strongly theological but influenced many following philosophers, whether Christian or not, including St Thomas Aquinas and, much later, Bertrand Russell.

Hemphill reviews the writings of many of the key subsequent philosophers, political thinkers and activists such as Hobbes, Locke, Hume, Rousseau, Kant, Hegel, Marx and Mill, all of whom addressed the issue of justice without specifically using the term 'social justice'. Thus Paine in *The Rights of Man* argued that persons 'should be given fair and equal rights to all aspects of society.' It was left to a Jesuit priest in the mid-19th century first explicitly to use the term 'social justice'. Taparelli d'Azeglio argued that social justice was 'the habitual inclination to level or balance accounts. Distributive justice equalizes proportions in the common good' (cited in Burke, 2014). By the mid–late 19th century, the term was to be found in many places, not just in the writings of philosophers but in legal and policy discourse.

As noted, Rawls' book was the catalyst for a growing debate, initially amongst those concerned with political philosophy and the law, and, more latterly, those engaged in political action at an individual, governmental and indeed cross-governmental level: for example, the Vienna Declaration and Programme of Action (VDPA) on human rights and education (UN, 1993: para. 80).[4] Rawls saw justice as 'fairness', arguing that the core elements of a good, that is, socially just, society should include freedom of thought, liberty of conscience, political liberties, freedom of association, freedoms necessary for the liberty and integrity of the person, and the rights and liberties covered by the rule of law. Many of these rights and freedoms to which every human being is equally and inalienably entitled became enshrined in the Universal Declaration of Human Rights (UDHR), proclaimed and adopted by the UN General Assembly in 1948 (see Chapter 1 in this volume) in what came to be known as the 'First World' (that is, developed Western economies) coming together under the framework of the UN and associated UN agencies such as the International Labour Organization (ILO), particularly following UN conventions. However, these rights and freedoms were far from secured in many totalitarian or less 'developed' states.

Rawls argued that 'the principal subject of justice is the basic structure of society ... the way in which the major social institutions distribute fundamental rights and duties and determine the division of advantages from *social* co-operation' (Rawls, 1971: 6); that is, he was not concerned with benefits derived for *individuals* from private association. A 'well-ordered society' was one in which 'everyone is presumed to act justly' (Rawls, 1971: 8). Rawls' rejection of the idea of social justice as compatible with a society oriented towards individual gain is echoed by Donnison (1998: 186), arguing that 'standards and values cannot be developed privately', that is, within one institution or in relation to one practice. What, Donnison suggested, 'we apply to others we must apply to ourselves'. These approaches are reflected to varying degrees in modern redistributive welfare states.

Rawls outlines two basic principles:

> 1. each person is to have an equal right to the most extensive scheme of equal basic liberties compatible with a similar scheme of liberties for others ... 2. social and economic inequalities are to be arranged so that they are both (a) reasonably expected to be to everyone's advantage, and (b) attached to positions and offices open to all. (Rawls, 1971: 53)

Social justice thus has a strong interrelationship with the concept of inequality.

These were specific formulations of a more general position, that 'all social values – liberty and opportunity, income and wealth, and the social bases of self-respect – are to be distributed equally unless an unequal distribution of any or all of these values is to everyone's advantage' (Rawls, 1971: 59). The obverse concept, injustice, thus becomes 'simply inequalities that are not to the benefit of all' (Rawls, 1971: 59). This approach highlights distinctions between equality of opportunity, or access, equality of outcome and equality of status. Most contemporary politicians arguing for equality tend to emphasize equality of opportunity (but see later); however, those on the right emphasize equality of rules and processes, the state's role being merely to ensure free market exchanges for all (equally), those broadly on the left for equality of outcome, or at least sufficient equality of outcome to prevent injustice. Rawls observed that if there were to be inequalities, they could only be justified on the basis that everyone had equality of opportunity to compete for the most desirable positions, regardless of class or status. Rawls' famous test of social justice was through what he called the 'veil of ignorance', where people act without any sense of personal advantage.

Rawls' analysis generated a considerable volume of both supportive and hostile comment, some arguing that it could not be defined. It isn't possible adequately to review the range of this commentary here: readers are directed to some of the most significant writers who have challenged, refined or elaborated on Rawls' theory. These include Nozick (1974), Young (1990), Sen (1999), Miller (1999), Dworkin (2000), and Fraser (2001). For summaries and reviews of the range of key debates in the past 50 years, see also Craig and colleagues (2008) and Craig (2018). However, it is worth stating that social justice is still not only a contested theoretical concept but it has been hijacked by politicians of the right to inform political action and put a seemingly 'fair' gloss on what emerged as deeply unfair policies. An extreme example from the UK is that of hard right Conservative politician Iain Duncan-Smith, who, whilst Secretary of State for Social Security and since (through a think tank he established called, outrageously, the Centre for Social Justice) has promoted welfare reforms further immiserating even the poorest in society, especially through the introduction of the much-reviled Universal Credit.[5]

Miller, as one example of critical but broadly supportive comment, argued that social justice, which he regards as interchangeable with the concept of distributive justice, provides the political and philosophical basis for deciding 'how the good and bad things in life should be distributed among the members of a human society' (Miller, 1999: 1). These things incorporate familiar material dimensions of a 'good life': income, wealth, education, housing, health and so on. Miller identifies three key principles underpinning the concept of social justice: desert, need and equality.

In relation to desert, a just society is one 'whose institutions are arranged so that people get the benefits they deserve' (Miller, 1999: 155). This principle must not however become a rigid formulation contingent simply on institutional arrangements within a society, but allow concepts of need into play, that is, resources cannot be committed solely on the basis of desert but also of need. The concept of need is 'not merely idiosyncratic or confined to those who hold a particular view of the good life … it must be capable of being validated on terms that all relevant parties can agree to' (Miller, 1999: 205). This validation is a political process but one from which many parties, such as minorities, have hitherto been excluded because of their lack of power, both in a formal and informal sense; that is, it lacks a participative dimension (we return to this later). In relation to its distributive nature, it 'specifies that benefits of a certain kind – rights, for instance – should be distributed equally because justice requires this' (Miller, 1999: 232). To achieve social justice, we must have

> a political community in which citizens are treated in an equal across-the-board way, in which public policy is geared toward meeting the intrinsic needs of every member, and in which the economy is framed and constrained in such a way that the income and other work-related benefits people receive correspond to their respective deserts. (Miller, 1999: 250)

The concept of social justice thus links closely to other key concepts such as need, to citizenship and to rights. The notion of desert is one linked to need in a moral and not in a punitive sense. Miller's position is highly relevant to multicultural societies although he does not make this explicit.

Social justice and political and social action

The idea of social justice as informing political and social action received prominence in the UK with the work of the Commission for Social Justice established by the Labour Party (CSJ, 1994). In a context of deepening inequality and poverty, it suggested that key elements of social justice were:

- the equal worth of all citizens;
- the equal right to be able to meet their basic needs;
- the need to spread opportunities and life chances as widely as possible; and
- the requirement that we reduce and where possible eliminate unjustified inequalities.

This begged important political questions and the policy programme of New Labour when in power continued to beg some of them; for example, the question of what basic needs are. Social democratic governments provide systems of social assistance but have not effectively defined the adequacy of that assistance to meet basic needs defined by participatory research studies. The UK government's programmes to address social exclusion and reduce poverty were titled *Opportunity for All* but most governments did not go beyond goals related to equality of opportunity to promote equality of outcome, which many would argue was a more robust indicator of a socially just society,

> genuine equality of opportunity and recognition of the equal worth of all our citizens is incompatible with the savagely unequal society we now live in. Equality of opportunity in the context of economic and social structures that remain profoundly unequal is likely to remain a mirage. (Lister cited in NICF, 2001)

So is equality of outcome. Basic needs might also vary in terms of the cultural backgrounds of recipients (Pearce and Paxton, 2005).

Rawls' theory emerged at a time when issues of gender and racial equality had only just begun to emerge within UK policy frameworks (the Equal Opportunities Commission was established in 1975, the Race Equality Commission in 1976) and where the concept of multiculturalism had yet to emerge. Aspects of his theory thus seem overtaken by demographic and political shifts and the issue of cultural rights or how the existence of different cultures within a single polity might impact on understandings of social justice was unexplored. Demographic and attitudinal shifts began to be addressed by Iris Marion Young, who argued that the 'claims of feminist, anti-racist and gay liberation activists that the structural inequalities of gender, race and sexuality did not fit well with the dominant paradigm of equality and inclusion' (Young, 2008: 77). Fraser (1995) advanced arguments for a politics of 'recognition' and 'voice' whereby demands for recognition of difference fuelled struggles of groups mobilized under the banners of nationality, ethnicity, 'race', gender and sexuality (see also Lister, 2008).

Drawing on the debates of the previous 50 or so years, the current author's working definition of social justice as a guide for political and social action follows a framework of objectives, pursued through social, economic, environmental and political policies, based on an acceptance of difference and diversity, informed by values concerned with:

- achieving fairness, equality of outcomes and treatment;
- recognizing the dignity and equal worth and encouraging the self-esteem of all;
- the meeting of basic needs;

- substantially reducing inequalities in wealth, income and life chances; and
- the participation of all, including the most disadvantaged.

This framework adds new elements to the general thrust of what is generally understood to be a left-leaning political consensus: for example, an emphasis on outcomes rather than opportunities, reflecting the findings of much educational research. For example, whilst many Black and Asian minorities enter formal education (that is, apparently enjoying equal opportunities) several points ahead of their white peers, they leave formal education many points behind them, consequent on the institutional racism faced within the school system (Gilborn and Mirza, 2000). There is also an emphasis on a participatory approach to political and social action: this goes beyond the question of voice to incorporate whole populations rather than those highlighted specifically within the new politics of identity. And it emphasizes the issue of environmental justice which has now become an urgent issue.

Social justice, 'race' and multiculturalism: is there a global understanding?

Despite the best attempts of the political right to hijack the concept by linking it to free market economics and individual action, social justice continues to be understood widely as a value system promoting fairness and challenging inequality though collective social and political action. The claims of social justice, however, continue to fall short when translated into actual political and social action and policy making, in terms of outcomes for disadvantaged people, the example of 'race' and ethnicity being a prominent area of failure. Social justice should not be culture-blind any more than it can be gender-blind, yet the overwhelming burden of evidence from the UK shows that public policy, despite the rhetoric of government since large-scale immigration started, has failed to deliver social justice to Britain's minorities in terms of all significant social, economic and political measures. This is not an argument, incidentally, for abandoning the project of multiculturalism, which has been distorted through misrepresentation, facilitating the 'hostile environment' towards migrants promoted by recent Labour and Conservative governments, but for ensuring that it is framed within the values of social justice (Lewis and Craig, 2014).

Elsewhere it is argued in some detail that the British state, under political parties of all persuasions, has signally failed to address the growing racism endemic in British society (Craig, 2007a, 2007b, 2008,

2013; Chattoo et al, 2019) or to offer social justice to its growing minority population, in terms of equal opportunities, equal outcomes, voice, recognition, respect, meeting needs, protecting their status or even, at a most basic level, providing safety and security. The level of racism and racist attacks has recently been growing steadily, boosted both by the 2016 Referendum with its anti-immigrant rhetoric and directly by government policy. Critically, one significant strand of this debate is the argument that the value base of migrant communities has little in common with that of the so-called 'host community', that therefore the notion of a social justice approach relevant to all those resident in the UK is doomed to failure at worst, irrelevance at best. This argument is fallacious but is critical to thinking about a global concept of social justice.

For one thing, almost half of those defined to be an ethnic minority in the UK (often mischaracterized as migrants) were in fact born and raised within the UK, a characteristic of most multicultural societies.

Secondly, in the face of disturbances in UK cities, and, to some degree in relation to violent acts of terror, UK governments argue that a major difficulty facing Britain's minority communities is their failure to 'integrate' and their desire to lead increasingly separate lives, both geographically and culturally, at odds with the traditional values of white Britishness, whatever they are. Government introduced the concept of community cohesion in the early 2000s, displacing 'race relations' in popular policy and political discourse, but this undermined any notion of difference as the basis for policy making (Worley, 2005). Government provided guidance pointing to the meaning of Britishness as a distinct value system to which those migrating to and settling in the UK should aspire (LGA, 2002; Home Office, 2004). The Home Office, whilst acknowledging the continuing presence of racism and discrimination, argued that 'to be British means that we respect the laws, the democratic political structures, and give our allegiance to the State' but also suggested that 'to be British does not mean assimilation into a common culture so that original identities are lost' (Home Office, 2004: 6). It then, even more confusingly, concluded that respect for the law, fairness, tolerance and respect for difference were values shared by all Britons, of whatever ethnic origin (see also Forrest and Kearns, 2000). In reality, what underpins this 'failure to integrate' is the racism embedded in government policies.

The third fallacy is that the presence of substantial minorities in a country necessarily undermines the kind of political solidarity reflected in the development of welfare states. Kymlicka (2008) challenges this view of the impact of increasing ethnic diversity within societies.

He found there is no correlation between the size of the minority population, the strength of multicultural policies and changes in welfare spending over the past 30 years. With minorities now UK Chancellor of the Exchequer, Home Secretary and Mayor of London, one could think this argument might have had its day, despite continuing racism within government.

Thinking about the implications of social and economic globalization, and increasing ethnic diversity, there are more general points to be made. First, culture, a collection of shared values, attitudes and customs amongst a particular group or people, changes over time; so do notions of justice, as political conditions change. This is true whether referring to largely monocultural countries or to multicultural countries where the arrival of migrants bringing different cultures sometimes generates violent political and social contestation, and 'race' hate. Huntington (1996) claims we are witnessing a clash of civilizations where the binary division between capitalism and communism is replaced by that between Islam and the West. War seems to be the logical end of this line of reasoning. We might equally argue, however, that globalization brings with it a requirement for those who have embraced 'Western' values and driven economic globalization to develop a much more nuanced understanding of other cultures and religions, freed from imperial and colonial perspectives, if they are to engage effectively, as Edward Said (2003) argued in respect of Orientalism.

Secondly, linked to this, nationalist sentiments are growing disturbingly in many richer countries as a hostile response to immigration, often again expressed in terms of protecting indigenous (for example, 'British') values. Most serious evidence, however, including a recent study of Muslim clerics, suggests that there is little to differentiate the fundamental values of most cultures and religions: all major religions practised within the UK claim common values: (qualified) freedom of speech, fairness, justice, equality, respect and tolerance, stressing the values of family life. Another recent study showed that the vast majority of migrants, including Muslims, placed the highest value on democracy, fairness, justice and security in Britain. Nevertheless, a report commissioned by the Ahmadiyya Muslim community concluded that half of UK adults felt that Islam was incompatible with British values.[6]

'Western' practice indeed cannot claim the high ground or sole ownership of the concept of social justice although, as with the Judaeo-Christian tradition, many other cultures and religions are the context for internally contested views of the meanings of social justice or of human rights (in relation to Islam, for example, see Saeed, 2018).

Thinking of other cultures, the ideology of individualism and freedom that underpins (unjust) Western corporate capitalism is challenged in Confucianist thought which argues that individuals only exist 'in relation to other human beings'. This view of our interconnectedness is strikingly echoed both in First Nations peoples' collective approaches to rights, perhaps also in the Buddhist notion of compassion, that is, kindness in response to suffering, in Young's idea of relational social justice but also in Desmond Tutu's philosophy of Ubuntu: that we are only human through others; through relationships with others we accord both ourselves and others the socially just values of dignity and respect for difference, as well as meaning. How these values are played out in practice, in political and social action, of course may differ markedly from the theoretical positions espoused by those cultures or religions; but then so too do those of the British majority.

As noted, whatever political theory or religious doctrine may say, there is usually a significant gap between theory and practice: many of these values are observed in reality more in their breach than application and in terms of political practice, Judaism actually argues that actions are far more important than beliefs. Recent research reveals that the values of the British population at large are far from aligning with those of social justice when it comes to the treatment of minorities. For example, A MORI poll for the British Council noted that young people in other countries perceived Britons to be 'arrogant, xenophobic ... racially intolerant ... and frequently drunk' (cited in Craig, 2003). A subsequent poll found that roughly one third of the UK population admitted that they had racist attitudes, a proportion growing substantially in the past few years, in part because of the hostile government and media treatment of asylum-seekers and refugees, increasing Islamophobia generated by the so-called global 'war on terror', and now seemingly legitimized by the 2016 Referendum. Casual observers of British life might indeed argue that Britishness prioritizes alcoholism, sexism, obesity, greed, drunkenness and promiscuity (Ethnos, 2005).

Highlighting another contradiction between theory and practice, whilst the Hindu notion of *dharma* emphasizes the basic moral obligation to treat all others with dignity and respect, the caste system promotes disrespect and undignified treatment for many, consigning millions to poverty. even though Indian law has, in theory, overridden religious practices. Despite claims made by Hinduism and Sikhism to generosity, caste and patriarchy remain stubbornly central in Indian culture. The Universal Declaration of Human Rights, with its emphases on non-discrimination, dignity, respect and equality, may have been endorsed by most countries but clearly this has yet to be reflected in their political practice.

Critically, concepts of social justice generally emerged historically from religious doctrine and theory, but the centrality of religion now varies within and between societies. Over time – some Islamic states being the obvious exception – religious leaders have ceded temporal power to the bureaucrat. Thus, dominant moral values are often driven less by religion and more by increasingly secular political theories, although there are countries such as Turkey where these strands are more in balance. The practice of social justice frequently fails to confront gender discrimination; many women struggle with conflicts between their basic human rights and religious orthodoxy, with governments in multicultural states ambivalent and inconsistent in their stance. Where religious imperatives trump basic human rights, we usually end up with fundamentalist religious states, characterized by sexism, patriarchy, hierarchy and a lack of democratic practice. Even in so-called democratic countries such as the UK, professionals are reluctant to challenge cultural 'rights', such as female genital mutilation (FGM), fearing being labelled as racist even where such 'rights' are clearly oppressive in a wider human rights context.

Most religions are also sites of internal contestation, affecting the search for a common perspective on social justice. Thus Christians argue amongst themselves as to women's place: Catholics deny women the right to priesthood whilst liberation theologians actively promote human rights including for women. Similarly, some Islamic sects are intensely patriarchal, a stance with which the UK government partially colludes; some support oppressive practices such as honour killings, forced marriages and FGM. Women had a much more powerful place in Islamic society 1,000 years ago than they have now, the result of particular readings of the Koran: there is clearly no universal interpretation of Sharia law or of the Islamic meaning of social justice.

Conclusion: can we talk about global social justice?

Amartya Sen (2009: xii–xiii) reminds us that both global democracy and global justice can be seen as eminently understandable ideas that can plausibly inspire and influence practical actions across borders. But there clearly remains some way before one could claim a global consensus about what a theoretical framework of social justice might look like, and, as importantly, a political practice which all mainstream political and cultural groups could accept. There are some positive signs and, of course, international collaborative action has resulted in the frameworks for global social policy and action, such as the eight Millennium Development Goals (MDGs). and the 2030 Agenda for Sustainable Development that includes the 17 Sustainable Development Goals (SDGs). We know, as noted, that there is little evidence supporting the view that in multicultural countries such as the UK, and more widely, as both economies and societies become increasingly open to the forces of globalization and migration, there may well be some common value basis, a global framework of social justice in fact, that is broadly acceptable to the mainstream of different cultures. Unfortunately, at present, our understandings of other cultures remain hugely ill-informed,[7] often with the connivance of right-wing media and politicians. This lack of clarity is demonstrated in everyday debates about aspects of 'othered' cultures: for example, is wearing a hijab about modesty, freedom or oppression? Whilst globalization offers the opportunity for these debates, it simultaneously generates increasing divisions and inequalities both between and within nation states, which feed these misunderstandings (Wilkinson and Pickett, 2009, also writing in Chapter 14).

It remains work in progress to translate research on cultural diversity formally into policy frameworks at a national level but perhaps more importantly to translate policy frameworks into public understanding and political action. At present the most effective cross-national political action is driven by the racist far right, promoting a global, though covert, 'war on terror' on minorities. It is increasingly urgent now not just to consider how the contours of a global framework of social justice might be further developed but to take what we have in terms of a consensus and use that to build a counterargument alongside the processes of globalization and migration. This should not be an impossible task, particularly as we now have a range of international and regional bodies to facilitate this process; indeed, many are already beginning to do so. In Miller's and similar analyses, it was possible to define social justice within the context of a closed political community in which all relevant identifiable actors could be encouraged to engage with debates about social justice. It is clear that the notion of a closed political community is effectively redundant, even at the level of the global.[8] Whilst individual nation states hang on to what remains of their political sovereignty in the face of economic globalization, there is a pressing need to use what theoretical and political consensus we can identify over the concept of social justice to inform joint action. In the field of environmental justice, the melting of the Arctic and the burning of the Amazon rainforest have stimulated that kind of collaboration; why not over social justice and, as a starting point, to challenge the growth of racism globally?

Advancing the claims of social justice at a global level seems an urgent task at a time when economic and cultural conflicts have led to many voicing the fear of wars, particularly over misrepresented cultural differences.[9] The first requirement then is for political thinkers and activists in each nation state to continue to argue the merits of social justice, based on clear understandings of the consensus across cultures, the second is that transnational community institutions can build on this work: most have now become multicultural, multi-ethnic communities where much of the basic thinking about social justice has been done. This would simultaneously challenge the residual notion of a closed political community bringing with it demands for a closed demographic community which, as with Fortress Europe, is simply presented in the context of fears about being overwhelmed by migration (or invasion) by the 'other'. The basic foundation on which this work must be established, paradoxically, is the process of *local* engagement across cultural differences, challenging the myths and fears generated by those who thrive on divisions as a way of promoting their policies of hate.

Notes

[1] The UN 2030 Agenda for Sustainable Development underlines a global commitment to 'achieving sustainable development in its three dimensions, economic, social and environmental in a balanced and integrated manner' (see https://sustainabledevelopment.un.org/post2015/transformingourworld). Social justice is now a fundamental policy objective in this reorientation of global social policy and sustainable development.

[2] A clear example of the Eurocentric nature of current debates can be found in the current author's edited volume, *Global Social Justice* (Craig, 2018), comprising a series of chapters about how a socially just approach can be applied to differing policy areas such as health, transport, the law and the environment. Although the book did not attempt to provide a unifying global perspective and indeed was almost entirely written from a European perspective, the publishers insisted that Global Social Justice would be an appropriate title for the volume.

[3] For a recent discussion see for example Griffith (2000).

[4] The Vienna Declaration of 1993 asserted that democracy and human rights were 'interdependent and mutually reinforcing'. Long-established democracies and human rights are of course continuous processes, formed out of continuous struggle.

[5] See, for example, www.independent.co.uk/voices/editorials/universal-credit-government-failure-national-audit-office-report-alok-sharma-a8400961.html.

[6] Results of the poll carried out on behalf of the Ahmadiyya Muslim Community are available online: www.comresglobal.com/wp-content/uploads/2019/08/ComRes_Ahmadiyya_Muslim_Tables_July2019_Q1.pdf.

⁷ This is despite the multicultural 'settlement' being specific to historical and political conditions in each nation state, most clearly shown in the constitutional position of First Nations peoples in countries such as Aotearoa, Botswana and Canada.

⁸ This is written at a time when the colonization of space has re-emerged onto the global political agenda.

⁹ It seems more likely to this writer that wars may be generated over access to dwindling resources but that these may be disguised with other rationales.

References

Burke, T. P. (2014) *The Origins of Social Justice: Taparelli d'Azeglio*, www.firstprinciplesjournal.com/articles.aspx?article=1760&theme=home&page=loc=b&type=ctbf.

Chattoo, S., Atkin, K., Craig, G. and Flynn, F. (eds) (2019) *Understanding 'Race' and Ethnicity*, Second Edition, Bristol: Policy Press.

Craig, G. (2003) 'Ethnicity, Racism and the Labour Market: a European Perspective', in G. J. Andersen and P. H. Jensen (eds) *Changing Labour Markets, Welfare Policies and Citizenship*, Bristol: Policy Press, 149–81.

Craig, G. (2007a) 'Social Justice in a Multicultural Society: Experience from the UK', *Studies in Social Justice*, 1(1): 93–108.

Craig, G. (2007b) 'Cunning, Unprincipled, Loathsome: The Racist Tail Wags the Welfare Dog', *Journal of Social Policy*, 36(4): 605–24.

Craig, G. (2008) 'The Limits of Compromise', in G. Craig, T. Burchardt and D. Gordon (eds) *Social Justice and Public Policy*, Bristol: Policy Press, 231–50.

Craig, G. (2013) 'Invisibilizing "Race" in Public Policy', *Critical Social Policy*, 33(4): 712–20.

Craig, G. (ed) (2018) *Global Social Justice*, Cheltenham: Edward Elgar.

Craig, G., Burchardt, T. and Gordon, D. (eds) (2008) *Social Justice and Public Policy*, Bristol: Policy Press.

CSJ (Commission on Social Justice) (1994) *Social Justice: Strategies for National Renewal*, London: Verso.

Donnison, D. (1998) *Policies for a Just Society*, Basingstoke: Macmillan.

Dworkin, R. (2000) *Sovereign Virtue: The Theory and Practice of Equality*, Cambridge, MA: Harvard University Press.

Ethnos (2005) *Citizenship and Belonging*, London: Commission for Racial Equality.

Forrest, R. and Kearns, A. (2000) 'Social Cohesion, Social Capital and the Neighbourhood', Paper presented to ESRC Cities Programme Neighbourhood Colloquium, Liverpool, 5 June.

Fraser, N. (1995) 'Dilemmas of Justice in a "Post-Socialist" Age', *New Left Review*, 212: 68–93.

Fraser, N. (2001) 'Recognition without Ethics?', *Theory, Culture and Society*, 8(2–3): 21–42.

Gilborn, D. and Mirza, H. (2000) *Educational Inequality: Mapping Race, Class and Gender*, London: Institute of Education.

Griffith, T. (2000) *Plato: The Republic*, Cambridge: Cambridge University Press.

Hemphill, B. (2015) 'Social Justice as a Moral Imperative', *Open Journal of Occupational Therapy*, 3(2): Article 9.

Home Office (2004) *Strength in Diversity: Towards a Community Cohesion and Race Equality Strategy*, London: Home Office.

Huntington, S. (1996) *The Clash of Civilisations*, London: Simon & Schuster.

Jackson, B. (2005) 'The Conceptual History of Social Justice', *Political Studies Review*, 3(3): 356–73.

Kymlicka, W. (2008) 'Multiculturalism, Social Justice and the Welfare State', in G. Craig, T. Burchardt and D. Gordon (eds) *Social Justice and Public Policy*, Bristol: Policy Press, 53–77.

Lewis, H. and Craig, G. (2014) ' "Multiculturalism Is Never Talked About": Community Cohesion and Local Policy Contradictions in England', *Policy & Politics*, 41(2): 21–38.

LGA (Local Government Association) (2002) *Guidance on Community Cohesion*, London: LGA.

Lister, R. (2008) 'Recognition and Voice: The Challenge for Social Justice', in G. Craig, T. Burchardt and D. Gordon (eds) *Social Justice and Public Policy*, Bristol: Policy Press, 105–23.

Miller, D. (1999) *Principles of Social Justice*, Cambridge, MA: Harvard University Press.

NICF (Northern Ireland Community Foundation) (2001) Annual Report, Belfast: Community Foundation for Northern Ireland.

Nozick, R. (1974) *Anarchy, State and Utopia*, Oxford: Blackwell.

Pearce, N. and Paxton, W. (2005) (eds) *Social Justice: Building a Fairer Britain*, London: IPPR.

Rawls, J. (1971) *A Theory of Justice*, Cambridge, MA: Harvard University Press.

Saeed, A. (2018) *Human Rights and Islam*, Cheltenham: Edward Elgar.

Said, E. (2003) *Orientalism*, Harmondsworth: Penguin.

Scottish Executive (2003) *Social Justice: A Scotland Where Everyone Matters*, Edinburgh: Scottish Executive.

Sen, A. (1999) *Development as Freedom*, Oxford: Oxford University Press.

Sen, A. (2009) *The Idea of Justice*, London: Allen Lane

UN (United Nations) (1993) *Vienna Declaration and Programme of Action on Human Rights Education*, New York: UN.

Wilkinson, R. and Pickett, K. (2009) *The Spirit Level: Why More Equal Societies Almost Always Do Better*, London: Allen Lane.

Worley, C. (2005) ' "It's Not About Race. It's About the Community": New Labour and "community cohesion"', *Critical Social Policy*, 25(4): 483–96.

Young, I. (1990) *Justice and the Politics of Difference*, Princeton, NJ: Princeton University Press.

Young, I. (2008) 'Structural Injustice and the Politics of Difference', in G. Craig, T. Burchardt and D. Gordon (eds) *Social Justice and Public Policy*, Bristol: Policy Press, 77–104.

13

'Go-social'? Inclusive growth and global social governance

Christopher Deeming

Introduction

This chapter addresses the prospects for improved social governance to tackle the global challenges of the 21st century, as humanity moves towards more sustainable patterns of consumption and production, and hopefully a more socially responsible, equitable, inclusive and just world. In particular, the chapter critically examines the emerging social policies being articulated by the Organisation for Economic Co-operation and Development (OECD) in an effort to reform global capitalism. This international organization (a rich-country club) has long been leading and coordinating policy efforts on the global stage, diffusing knowledge to member and non-member states alike with leading expertise to tackle the social, economic and governance challenges of the 21st century (Ougaard, 2010; Clifton and Díaz-Fuentes, 2011; Schmelzer, 2014). It is, at present, in the process of repositioning itself as the international institution responsible for promoting 'global social justice'; although the issues and questions raised by this are complex, arguably much of it may be about representing a particular set of 'Western values' and a particular form of market ideology (see Chapters 6, 8, 11 and 12). Nevertheless, we find the OECD is now shaping important aspects of international governance and global social policy, which is the focus of this chapter, attempting to establish a new global social governance (GSG) architecture in an effort to tackle growing social inequality.

The idea of global social governance

There is no 'world parliament' or 'global government' (a government of the world) as such, at least at present (Monbiot, 2003; Weiss and Thakur, 2010; Leinen and Bummel, 2018), that can enact legislation in order to tackle the pressing global challenges of the 21st century. In this context, social scientists remain divided over whether a truly effective form of world government can realistically exist and how this can function in practice (Beeson, 2019: ch 10). The notions of 'multi-level governance' and 'multilateralism' continue to be most relevant, marred by uncertainty in the struggle for GSG, where the 'economic' and 'social' have long been separate spheres at the international level (O'Brien et al, 2000; Held, 2006; Weiss and Wilkinson, 2019). Governing the 'social' in a global context or GSG, then, as Bob Deacon (2003, 2007) observes, recognizes the multiple institutional levels shaping social policy in individual nation states, local, regional, sub-national to national government, to supra-national levels. Our interest in governance and the social emerges in this disorganized global context (see also Deacon et al, 2010; Deacon, 2014; for a rather different perspective on the social in the global, see Joseph, 2012).

One of the main pressing social regulation issues at the top of the global reform agenda is how to make economic growth inclusive in order to overcome inequality (part of the 2030 Agenda for Sustainable Development).[1] There is, as Bourguignon (2015) argues, a clear need for better regulation of the international economy in order to tackle growing inequality, which has deeply destabilizing social and political consequences (see also Chapter 15).

How then might the GSG reform agenda be advanced to ensure a more equitable world? As Deacon (2003) observed, the social has been absent from GSG reforms for many decades, with the world appearing to be stuck in a neoliberal policy rut. However, things may be changing. The OECD (the warden of the world capitalist economy and longstanding promotor of GDP and the 'growth paradigm', Schmelzer, 2016; Leimgruber and Schmelzer, 2017)[2] is seeking to fashion a new global political economy out of economic liberalization or neoliberalism, with social justice at the centre. It has been putting in place new proposals for social regulation, and working to establish new social governance arrangements and proactive new strategies to ensure growth is inclusive. Inclusive growth (IG), then, is a contender at least for a new emerging global social policy paradigm, as Stephan Klasen (2018) argues.

In it together?

In the early years of free trade and capitalist market development it was thought that the market itself would help to eliminate social equalities within society: 'a rising tide lifts all boats'; and this was certainly Adam Smith's view in *The Wealth of Nations*, as Esping-Andersen (1990) reminds us. Of course, contemporary neoliberals and 'supply-side' economists at the OECD celebrated the deregulated global market emerging towards the end of the 20th century; encompassing welfare states dragged down growth, they claimed, and were out of step with the way the world is or should be governed (Leimgruber, 2013).[3] Today, however, it is now increasingly evident to most that the cold winds of neoliberalism have failed to deliver on the promise of prosperity for all.

During the first decade of the 21st century a wealth of new evidence began to emerge which pointed to the problem of growing inequality and relative poverty amongst the rich countries. Inequality was increasing almost everywhere, even during periods of sustained economic growth. Neoliberal policies associated with 'trickle-down' economics had failed to deliver prosperity for all in the rich nations, as policies sought to limit governmental regulation in order to promote free-market capitalism. In this context shareholders have been able to maximize profits and top incomes have risen as top marginal tax rates were cut. A number of major academic works (for example, Piketty, 2014) have charted the direction and impacts of policy in the rich countries during this period and it is not necessary to rehearse those arguments in detail here.

At the OECD, a series of high-profile reports first rang the alarm bells about rising income inequality in the rich countries (OECD, 2008, 2011a, 2015a). In the inequality reports we can begin to observe a distinct shift in the discourse at the OECD, as the 'growth paradigm' began to be adapted to ensure that, in the future, economic growth will be more fairly distributed and beneficial to all. *Growing Unequal*, the first report, was launched in October 2008, amidst the economic turmoil. Here the OECD (2008) charted the rise of income inequality, a growing trend across the rich nations since the mid-1980s, as the major economic challenge and threat to the global economy. The report also pointed, like Piketty, to the more underlying problem of the widening gap between wages and income from capital. While *Growing Unequal* charted the overall trends, it is clear the OECD did not have a coherent strategy to reverse the trends at this stage. The general conclusion was that 'good government policy can make a difference' (OECD, 2008: 19).

The call to action came in the second report, launched in December 2011. *Divided We Stand* (OECD, 2011a) identifies the root causes of rising inequality and provides specific policy recommendations to tackle inequality through more effective redistribution and social investment social policies. Widening wage disparities were to blame for rising inequality, particularly between skilled and unskilled workers. Technological changes in the global economy favoured skilled workers. But it is also significant that the failings of the 'Golden Age' welfare states were now targeted by the OECD. Welfare systems that had grown over the course of the 20th century were not able to tackle the pressing problems associated with growing inequality, it concluded (OECD, 2011a). Tax and benefit transfer systems were failing to redistribute market income in the rich countries, although the redistributive impact of cash transfers varied significantly across OECD countries in the late 2000s. Here the OECD continued to emphasize the role of 'social investment' (OECD, 1997: 14) to tackle inequality: 'go social' was the message (OECD, 2011a: 19). Workforce upskilling was singled out as one of the most powerful instruments at the disposal of policy makers to counter rising inequality. 'The trend to greater inequality is not inevitable', it concluded, 'governments can and should act' (OECD, 2011b: 1). As the OECD's Secretary-General Angel Gurria remarked in his presentation speech in Paris on 5 December 2011:

> The benefits of economic growth DO NOT trickle down automatically. This study dispels this assumption. Greater inequality DOES NOT foster social mobility. Without a comprehensive strategy for inclusive growth, inequality will continue to rise. There is nothing inevitable about high and growing inequalities. Our policies have created a system that makes them grow and it's time to change these policies. (OECD, 2011c, original emphasis)

While a 'comprehensive strategy' for IG was alluded to here, it is also clear that the OECD had yet to articulate one, at least publicly.

In the subsequent 2015 report, *In It Together*, the OECD (2015a) now focused on the social, political and economic consequences of rising inequality and underscored the pressing need for political action to stem the rising tide of inequality that was seen to be threatening 'social cohesion' in the rich democracies (see Chapter 12 in this volume). In the wake of the global financial crisis, the OECD argued the advanced economies needed to be put back on a path of strong and sustainable growth. Policies that are effective in tackling income inequality and promoting sustained growth are particularly important, the organization noted. Attention focused on four main policy areas to reduce the growing divides between rich and poor: women's participation in economic life, employment promotion and good-quality jobs, skills and education, and tax-and-transfer systems for efficient redistribution of income. The organization noted that, while some may consider the social and political costs of high and rising inequality are in and of themselves sufficient to justify action, the central argument of the

OECD here was very different. High and growing inequality raises major economic concerns, not just for the low-income earners that are left behind but for the wider health and sustainability of the economy. Here the OECD was reflecting the growing research evidence or knowledge-base that suggests income inequality can actually *hinder* GDP growth and its sustainability. The OECD's *Focus on Inequality and Growth* (OECD, 2014a) and *The Productivity-Inclusiveness Nexus* (OECD, 2016a) provide further synthesis of the econometric research evidence.

Acute inequality was now found to be bad for growth, that is, it threatens the 'growth paradigm'. As the *In It Together* report now concluded, 'Put simply: *rising inequality is bad for long-term growth*' (OECD, 2015a: 22, original emphasis). Inequality tends to drag down GDP growth, due to the rising distance of wages at the lower end of the income distribution from the higher end. Today, the wealthiest 1 per cent hold 19 per cent of total wealth compared to just 3 per cent of wealth held by the bottom 40 per cent (OECD, 2017a). The old growth model had failed and neoliberal ideas about 'trickle-down' economics were now discredited, as were the old welfare state safety nets that had been designed to target and alleviate poverty in the 20th century. They were not part of the IG solution. While the evidence was clear, 'inequality is bad for growth' (OECD, 2017a), this did not mean that all policies that reduce inequality are necessarily good for growth, as the OECD maintained. A new 'pro-growth' strategy was clearly required. The challenge now was to identify the appropriate policy packages to tackle inequality in a growth-friendly way. In other words, what was now urgently needed to tackle acute inequality was a comprehensive and coherent strategy for IG. In the process of drawing up the new IG strategy the organization would now lay claim to being the 'world's largest social justice organisation' (Angel Gurria, OECD Secretary-General, OECD, 2013a: 1).

Go-social?

The OECD's 'Inclusive Growth Initiative' (IGI) was launched at the Ministerial Council Meeting held in Paris in May 2012, falling more broadly under the 'New Approaches to Economic Challenges' (NAEC) initiative, established in the aftermath of the global financial crisis (OECD, 2012a, 2019a). While the financial and economic crisis was the key motivating factor behind NAEC, a more coherent inclusive and sustainable growth strategy for the 21st century was now taking shape at the OECD that looked to address the new global challenges, such as 'slow growth' and 'green growth', along with high unemployment and increasing inequality, all in the context of an increasingly interconnected and complex world economy. In doing so, the OECD would draw upon the expertise of member and partner countries, working more closely with other international institutions like the International Labour Organization (ILO), the organizations that comprise the World Bank Group (WBG) and International Monetary Fund (IMF) to ensure a much more coordinated effort to deliver on the 2030 Agenda.

The groundwork for the IGI developed out of a series of events, conferences and workshops organized by the OECD in the early 2010s, held in Paris and New York, which brought together academics, policy makers and practitioners from the advanced, emerging market and developing country contexts (OECD, 2013b). The OECD was keen to broaden its global reach and the consultative process included member and non-member countries, government officials, policy makers and non-policy makers, non-governmental organizations (NGOs), corporate and philanthropic foundations, representatives from civil society, representatives from the other international organizations and regional banks. By now there was a deep realization that action was needed across many different policy domains to ensure pro-growth initiatives to foster inclusiveness (many of the papers discussed at this workshop were published in a collected volume: de Mello and Dutz, 2012).

A second IG workshop 'Changing the Conversation on Growth: Going Inclusive', was held in 2014 in New York (OECD, 2014b, 2014c) and a third in 2016, again in New York, saw the launch of the OECD's IG for cities campaign (OECD, 2016b). Growing unequally was no longer an option. OECD countries were now experiencing slow growth and rising inequality, trapped in a vicious circle of weak economic performance and greater exclusion; the OECD was looking to share more widely its expertise and to set in motion a virtuous circle of growth and inclusiveness, with the message "go inclusive".

While research showed that inequality is likely to be a 'brake on growth', as previously discussed, with lower and middle-income earners falling behind, a new set of policy prescriptions would now be assembled to mark the 'post-neoliberal turn'. As Angel Gurría remarked:

> There is no secret to growing more equal! Our work is beginning to put together the puzzle pieces: there are policies – in education, social, innovation, regulation, health, and so many other domains – that are good for growth and inclusiveness. Where there are trade-offs

between growth and inclusiveness, it is possible to put in place compensatory measures. (OECD, 2014c: 1)

In 2014, the launch of the 'Inclusive Growth Framework' (IGF) (OECD, 2014d, 2014e) signalled a key policy shift, going beyond income, in favour of a multidimensionality assessment of 'wellbeing' and 'living standards' (key pillars of the IGF). Here the OECD was building on the landmark report by the Commission on the Measurement of Economic Performance and Social Progress (CMEPSP), generally referred to as the Stiglitz–Sen–Fitoussi Commission (Stiglitz et al, 2009, 2010), and its work on the measurement of wellbeing, which had identified 11 dimensions of wellbeing, including material and non-material dimensions and both subjective and objective wellbeing outcomes (OECD, 2011d; also Stiglitz et al, 2018).[4] Importantly, GDP growth was no longer to be considered as an end in itself at the OECD. There were also important policy shifts in scale and levels of analysis, capturing the economic system as a whole and the average or typical individual or household income within it, but with more attention to the distribution of income within sub-groups of the population (for example, women, children and older people), and greater attention to income distributions (for example, bottom 10, 20 and 40 per cent). The different dimensions of IG are illustrated in Figure 13.1, clearly showing the relationship between OECD policies and distributional outcomes, along both income and non-income dimensions.

Economic growth (or GDP) is no longer seen as a sufficient indicator of social progress or social wellbeing as Figure 13.1 illustrates. The IGF and its empirical underpinning continues to be developed, in response to the call from government ministers for a more comprehensive evidence-based approach and action plan (OECD, 2017b, 2018a). The latest policy guidance now recommends more attention to ex ante impacts to foster IG (OECD, 2018a). In other words, governments and business leaders should do more to design equality into growth policies from the start, rather than simply relying on redistributive mechanisms afterwards. There is also more attention to investing in people and places (OECD, 2016b), empowering citizens and communities for shared prosperity, supporting businesses and firms (OECD, 2018a), the new 'Business for Inclusive Growth Initiative' (B4IG),[5] and supporting workers with recommendations that wages increase with productivity (OECD, 2018b).

Since IG is now defined as a multidimensional concept, a multifaceted strategy is clearly required to address this most complex of problems: tackling inequality in terms of *income*, *wealth* and

Figure 13.1: Inclusive growth: framework and dimensions

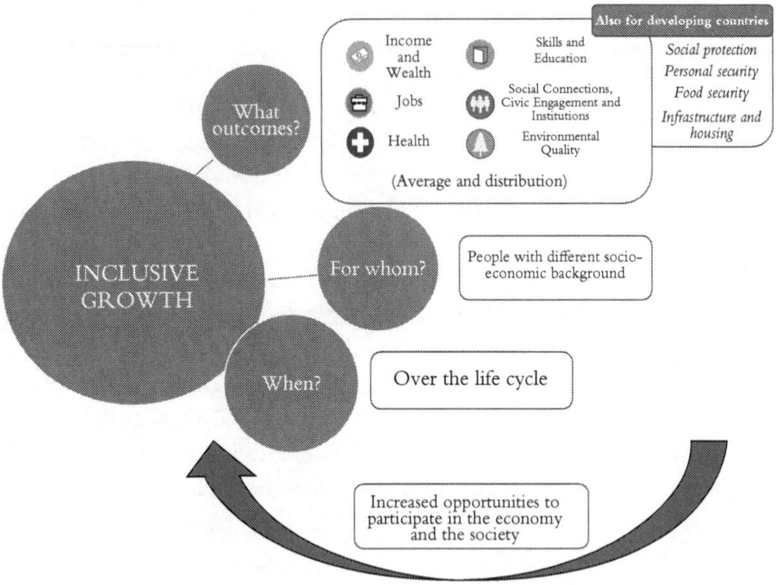

Source: Reproduced from OECD (2013a: 52).
(Reproduced with permission of the OECD.)

opportunities. Experts at the OECD and WBG are now working more closely to understand the key drivers of IG and main policy trade-offs, especially around multidimensional 'growth', and 'whose growth': middle class, bottom 10, 20 or 40 per cent, and growth for different population groups, women, children and older people (OECD/WBG, 2017).

The IGF is evolving and its empirical underpinnings continue to be developed, building on many existing strategies and initiatives, including the 'Jobs Strategy', 'Skills Strategy', 'Innovation Strategy', 'Going for Growth Strategy', 'Going Digital Project', 'Green Growth Strategy' and 'How's Life?'. The IGF is about identifying policies that can deliver improvements across a range of different policy domains:

• inclusive labour market policy proposals developed with the ILO, promoting more and better jobs (OECD, 2012b, 2018c, ILO/OECD, 2018, 2018);
• innovation, education and skills for IG (OECD, 2015b, 2015c);
• the Early Childhood Education and Care (ECEC) social investment agenda now orientating towards IG (OECD, 2016c, 2017c; Deeming and Smyth, 2018);

- fostering diversity for IG, especially for women, family policy and gender equality for IG (OECD, 2014f, 2018d);
- the tax reform agenda for IG, in particular through the OECD/G20 framework on domestic tax *base erosion and profit shifting* (BEPS) that focuses on tax transparency, and improved international cooperation to reduce tax evasion and tax avoidance in the global economy (IMF/OECD, 2017);
- institutions and IG governance (OECD, 2016d, 2016e), and place-based IG initiatives (OECD, 2016b);
- the environmental initiatives for IG, including 'green' and 'sustainable' IG. Action on climate change can generate IG economic growth, the OECD (2017d) claims;
- the emerging corporate and business case, B4IG, aligning business and governmental action.

In sum, we find a vast array of IG social policy designs, situated within the new and evolving IGF. But to what extent does this add up to a new architecture for GSG and what then are the prospects for making IG happen?

Governing the economic and the social

While much has been written about the OECD's role in international governance in the last two decades, this literature pre-dates the 'IG turn' (for example, Mahon and McBride, 2008; Ougaard, 2010; Woodward, 2010). This is significant because so much has changed, in terms of both the arguments and the growing influence of the OECD in GSG. Against this backdrop, there are of course continuities in the mechanisms and modes of governance, in the manner by which the organization looks to influence social governance, largely on the basis of 'soft tools' and the 'better argument' position in social statistics, expert opinions and authoritative reports.

GSG arrangements need further strengthening in order to foster IG, as the OECD maintains (OECD, 2016d, 2016e, 2018a, 2019b). Good, comprehensive governance arrangements include the system of strategic processes and tools, as well as institutions, rules and interactions for effective IG policy making spanning the vast array of policy domains discussed in the last section. The IGF then is perhaps best understood as a meta-framework at the OECD that now informs and frames most new and existing strategies, initiatives and work programmes and ideas for a new model of 'inclusive governance' and 'inclusive policy-making cycle', with more 'inclusive voice'. The stages of the cycle are:

- *Inclusive voice*: engaging with citizens and businesses for more inclusive policies and services.
- *Inclusive design*: innovative policy design for inclusive growth.
- *Inclusive delivery*: improving the delivery of services for and with citizens.
- *Inclusive accountability*: strengthening accountability through better performance management and evaluation (OECD, 2016d, 2016e).

Many policy instruments within the IGF are being designed in collaboration with other international institutions, corporations, NGOs and civil agencies. The OECD is now at the centre of GSG arrangements and IG reforms, involving a series of ongoing collaborations with the IMF designing tax policies for IG (IMF/ OECD, 2017), and labour market policies for IG with the ILO (ILO/ OECD, 2018).

The ILO/OECD collaborations are clearly focused on the challenge of creating more and better jobs in order to accelerate IG. Coordinated under the 'Global Deal for Decent Work and Inclusive Growth' initiative launched in 2016, this increases the overall level of cooperation between the ILO and OECD, and industrial relations engagement between governments, businesses and unions in order to promote decent work and job quality.

There is also the work alongside the WBG (OECD/WBG, 2017) and the IMF (IMF/OECD, 2018) to develop new global labour market strategies for IG, focused on job creation (a key feature of the IG policy paradigm) and improving productivity in the world economy.

While in the context of rising global inequalities adversely impacting growth, the OECD is supporting G20 members in 'injecting' an IG dimension into policy making and policy collaboration through the 'Mutual Assessment Process' (MAP), the foundation of the 'Framework for Strong, Sustainable and Balanced Growth' (FSSBG), adopted at the Pittsburgh G20 Summit in 2009 (OECD, 2012b). The policy focus is centred on improving productivity and encouraging economic growth, with more and better paid jobs.

IG governance should be country-led and context-sensitive, as the OECD notes. It is about fostering local IG solutions and high-quality institutions, as the emerging strategies across world regions and different country contexts demonstrate. Europe has long been pursuing an IG strategy for jobs and social cohesion (EC, 2010, 2014). Also, the regional actors in the UN system have embraced IG policies, for example, in Africa (see recent editions of the Economic Report on Africa (ERA), ECA, 2017, 2019), Asia and the Pacific (the Economic and Social Survey of Asia and the Pacific (ESSAP), ESCAP, 2015, 2016) and Latin America and the Caribbean (ECLAC, 2014, 2015, 2016). Still relatively few countries have formally adopted IG policy frameworks and strategies, at least at present, some clear exceptions here are Scotland, Canada, New Zealand and India (all with remarkably little explicit reference to the work or policy documents of the OECD).[6]

The OECD provides country-specific policy recommendations and assessments (OECD, 2016e), as well as assessments for the G20 as whole (IMF/OECD, 2018), supported by a dashboard of IG indicators (OECD, 2018a) designed to promote 'policy learning' or 'social learning' as it is sometimes called.[7] IG remains elusive however, despite strong economic growth in recent years, and this is the general picture from across the different world regions. The outlook at present is bleak. The coronavirus has triggered a global economic crisis. Global inequality and global poverty are now on the rise at alarming rates.

Conclusion

A number of key conclusions may be drawn.

Boosting faster quantitative growth has long been a priority for the OECD and the rich nations, but while we get a sense of shifting policy perspectives here, we still find ambiguity around the concept of 'growth' itself and the clear absence of any (alternative) strategy for inclusion given prospects for global growth have not been rosy for some time, even before the arrival of COVID-19, as we heard in Chapter 1. On the one hand, the OECD (2018e) is advocating 'beyond GDP', but on the other it is still clearly focused on the pursuit of GDP growth in order to tackle social problems and growing inequality (OECD, 2018c). The IGF is really about creating more and better paid jobs in order to achieve inclusive economic growth (OECD, 2014a). Certainly IG is better than non-IG, as Jackson and Webster (2018: 295) observe, but IG does not question or problematize the goal of growth itself. Thus, the old 'growth paradigm' based on GDP and consumption growth at the OECD is preserved. It has not been replaced with a new post-growth one despite some of the recent policy rhetoric. In many ways, then, the OECD has yet to achieve what it originally set out to do, to change the conversation on growth, even perhaps internally within the organization itself, and the different directorates and bodies. The concern here is primarily with the rate of growth, not its pattern. Economic growth continues to be a gendered process, and gender inequalities are barriers to shared prosperity everywhere (Elson and Seth, 2019).

What about the prospects for the emerging new inclusive social governance architecture designed to foster IG? While there has clearly been a raft of policy documents appearing over the past decade, the implementation of social reforms is still very much work in progress and prosperity is still not being shared very widely. While the IGF is now about a decade old, there is still little evidence of real change in GSG arrangements and inequality levels to conclude the world has now gone social. The OECD has yet to put the brakes firmly on neoliberalism and growing inequality. There are a number of key political economy obstacles and challenges: international tax reform, for example, where progress has been slow (OECD, 2020). While IG strategies at the regional and country level are still very patchy, the IG paradigm change is more apparent than real. The focus on IG has also impacted on global social policy debates in other ways, crowding out important debates about fairness and redistribution in the age of sustainability, as Iris Borowy (2019) argues. More redistributive policy designs are urgently needed to reduce extreme inequality and prevent it in the future, and not just alleviate it.

Finally, it would be easy to overstate the importance and influence of the OECD in the GSG arena. After all, today's global challenges require significant governmental and intergovernmental collaborative efforts at every level, as we heard in Chapter 1. And while the OECD has arguably done much to reform or reinvent itself, moving from the role of neoliberal advisor towards the end of the 20th century to a champion of 'global social justice' in the early part of the 21st century with the IG strategy developed in collaboration with other key international organizations and agencies. However, whether the OECD is now the world's largest social justice organization, as recently claimed, is also doubtful (a mantle long held by the ILO, see Deacon, 2015).

Notes

[1] For example, SDGs 'end poverty' (SDG 1), 'achieve gender equality' (SDG 5), 'reduce inequality within and among countries' (SDG 10), 'promote employment and economic growth' (SDG 8).

[2] The growth goals are clearly stipulated in Article 1 of the OECD Convention, signed on 14 December 1960 in Paris, www.oecd.org/general/conventionontheorganisationforeconomicco-operationanddevelopment.htm.

[3] There are many accounts of Nordic welfare states being at odds with the OECD in the climate of neoliberal ideas. OECD economic surveys for Sweden, Denmark, Norway and Finland warned against strong state involvement in the regulation of

markets and welfare goals. In communications with the OECD, however, national policy makers and government officials strongly defended their Nordic welfare traditions (see Carroll, 2004; Kildal, 2009; Leimgruber, 2013; Kananen, 2014).

[4] Income and wealth, jobs and earnings, housing conditions, health status, work–life balance, education and skills, social connections, civic engagement and governance, environmental quality, personal security, subjective wellbeing.

[5] B4IG comprises of the OECD and a global, CEO-led coalition of companies fighting against inequalities of income and opportunities, see www.oecd.org/industry/oecd-bsr-and-danone-launch-3-year-initiative-to-strengthen-inclusive-growth-through-public-private-collaboration.htm.

[6] India was an early adopter of IG in the Global South, Scotland in the Global North (Government of India, 2008, 2013; Scottish Government, 2015, 2016). Canada and New Zealand have recently adopted IG strategies (Government of Canada, 2017; New Zealand Government, 2019). Country-level approaches are discussed and reviewed by Stephan Klasen (2018) and Brian Nolan (2018). The OECD (2016e) also provides a review of country initiatives.

[7] For example, 'Making Inclusive Growth Happen in the UK', www.oecd.org/about/secretary-general/making-inclusive-growth-happen-in-the-uk.htm. See also the OECD IG website: www.oecd.org/inclusive-growth/.

References

Beeson, M. (2019) *Rethinking Global Governance*, London: Red Globe Press.

Borowy, J. (2019) 'Sustainability and Redistribution', in J. Meadowcroft, D. Banister, E. Holden, O. Langhelle, K. Linnerud and G. Gilpin (eds) *What's Next for Sustainable Development? Our Common Future at Thirty*, Cheltenham: Edward Elgar, 120–37.

Bourguignon, F. (2015) *The Globalization of Inequality*, Princeton, NJ: Princeton University Press.

Carroll, E. (2004) 'International Organisations and Welfare States at Odds? The Case of Sweden', in K. Armingeon and M. Beyeler (eds) *The OECD and European Welfare States*, Cheltenham: Edward Elgar, 75–88.

Clifton, J. and Díaz-Fuentes, D. (2011) 'From "Club of the Rich" to "Globalisation à la Carte"? Evaluating Reform at the OECD', *Global Policy*, 2(3): 300–311.

Deacon, B. (2003) *Global Social Governance: Themes and Prospects*, Helsinki: Ministry of Foreign Affairs of Finland.

Deacon, B. (2007) *Global Social Policy & Governance*, Thousand Oaks, CA: Sage.

Deacon, B. (2014) 'Globalism and Regional Social Governance', in N. Yeates (ed) *Understanding Global Social Policy*, Second Edition, Bristol: Policy Press, 53–76.

Deacon, B. (2015) 'The International Labour Organization and Global Social Governance: The 100 Year Search for Social Justice', in A. Kaasch and K. Martens (eds) *Actors & Agency in Global Social Governance*, Oxford: Oxford University Press, 3–17.

Deacon, B., Macovei, M. C., Van Langenhove, L. and Yeates, N. (eds) (2010) *World-Regional Social Policy and Global Governance: New Research and Policy Agendas in Africa, Asia, Europe and Latin America*, Abingdon and New York: Routledge.

Deeming, C. and Smyth, P. (2018) 'Social Investment, Inclusive Growth That Is Sustainable and the New Global Social Policy', in C. Deeming and P. Smyth (eds) *Reframing Global Social Policy: Social Investment for Sustainable and Inclusive Growth*, Bristol: Policy Press, 11–44.

De Mello, L. and Dutz, M. A. (eds) (2012) *Promoting Inclusive Growth: Challenges and Policies*, Paris: OECD Publishing.

EC (European Commission) (2010) *Europe 2020: A Strategy for Smart, Sustainable and Inclusive Growth*, COM(2010)2020, Brussels: EC, www.eea.europa.eu/policy-documents/com-2010-2020-europe-2020.

EC (2014) *Taking Stock of the Europe 2020 Strategy for Smart, Sustainable and Inclusive Growth*, COM(2014)130, Brussels: EC, https://ec.europa.eu/info/publications/taking-stock-europe-2020-strategy-smart-sustainable-and-inclusive-growth_en.

ECA (United Nations Economic Commission for Africa) (2017) *Economic Report on Africa 2017: Urbanization and Industrialization for Africa's Transformation*, Addis Ababa: UN, https://doi.org/10.18356/5d8e4ec9-en.

ECA (2019) *Economic Report on Africa 2019: Fiscal Policy for Financing Sustainable Development in Africa*, Addis Ababa: UN, https://doi.org/10.18356/7ece2581-en.

ECLAC (United Nations Economic Commission for Latin America and the Caribbean) (2014) *Social Panorama of Latin America 2014*, LC/G.2635-P, Santiago: UN, https://doi.org/10.18356/1e11f104-en.

ECLAC (2015) *Education, Structural Change and Inclusive Growth in Latin America*, LC/L.3974, Santiago: UN, https://digitallibrary.un.org/record/800154?ln=en.

ECLAC (2016) *Time to Tax for Inclusive Growth*, LC/L.4159, Santiago: UN, https://digitallibrary.un.org/record/833428?ln=en.

Elson, D. and Seth, A. (eds) (2019) *Gender Equality and Inclusive Growth: Economic Policies to Achieve Sustainable Development*, New York: UN Women, https://digitallibrary.un.org/record/3813186?ln=en.

Esping-Andersen, G. (1990) *The Three Worlds of Welfare Capitalism*, Princeton, NJ: Princeton University Press.

ESCAP (United Nations Economic and Social Commission for Asia and the Pacific) (2015) *Economic and Social Survey of Asia and the Pacific 2015: Making Growth more Inclusive for Sustainable Development*, Bangkok: UN, https://digitallibrary.un.org/record/828926?ln=en.

ESCAP (2016) *Economic and Social Survey of Asia and the Pacific 2016: Nurturing Productivity for Inclusive Growth and Sustainable Development*, Bangkok: UN, https://digitallibrary.un.org/record/829020?ln=en.

Government of Canada (2017) *Growth That Works for Everyone*, www.international.gc.ca/world-monde/issues_development-enjeux_developpement/inclusive_growth-croissance_inclusive/index.aspx?lang=eng.

Government of India (2008) *11th Five-Year Plan: 2007–2012, Volume 1: Inclusive Growth*, New Delhi: Oxford University Press, https://niti.gov.in/planningcommission.gov.in/docs/plans/planrel/fiveyr/11th/11_v1/11th_vol1.pdf.

Government of India (2013) *Twelfth Five-Year Plan: 2012–2017, Volume I: Faster, More Inclusive and Sustainable Growth*, New Delhi: Sage, https://nhm.gov.in/images/pdf/publication/Planning_Commission/12th_Five_year_plan-Vol-1.pdf.

Held, D. (2006) 'Reframing Global Governance: Apocalypse Soon or Reform!', *New Political Economy*, 11(2): 157–76.

ILO/OECD (International Labour Organization/Organisation for Economic Co-operation and Development) (2018) *Building Trust in a Changing World of Work: The Global Deal for Decent Work and Inclusive Growth Flagship Report 2018*, Global Deal, www.ilo.org/wcmsp5/groups/public/---dgreports/---dcomm/---publ/documents/publication/wcms_629764.pdf.

IMF/OECD (International Monetary Fund/Organisation for Economic Co-operation and Development) (2017) *Tax Certainty*, IMF/OECD Report for the G20 Finance Ministers, www.oecd.org/tax/tax-policy/tax-certainty-report-oecd-imf-report-g20-finance-ministers-march-2017.pdf.

IMF/OECD (2018) *G20 Framework for Strong, Sustainable, Balanced and Inclusive Growth*, www.imf.org/external/np/g20/pdf/2018/111918.pdf.

Jackson, T. and Webster, R. (2018) 'Limits to Growth Revisited', in C. Deeming and P. Smyth (eds) *Reframing Global Social Policy: Social Investment for Sustainable and Inclusive Growth*, Bristol: Policy Press, 295–322.

Joseph J. (2012) *The Social in the Global: Social Theory, Governmentality and Global Politics*, New York: Cambridge University Press.

Kananen, J. (2014) *The Nordic Welfare State in Three Eras: From Emancipation to Discipline*, Aldershot: Ashgate.

Kildal, N. (2009) 'Comparing Social Policy Ideas within the EU and the OECD', in R. Ervik, N. Kildal and E. Nilssen (eds) *The Role of International Organizations in Social Policy*, Cheltenham: Edward Elgar, 20–48.

Klasen, S. (2018) 'Measuring and Monitoring Inclusive Growth in Developing and Advanced Economies: Multiple Definitions, Open Questions and Some Constructive Proposals', in C. Deeming and P. Smyth (eds) *Reframing Global Social Policy: Social Investment for Sustainable and Inclusive Growth*, Bristol: Policy Press: 123–44.

Leimgruber, M. (2013) 'The Embattled Standard-bearer of Social Insurance and Its Challenger: The ILO, The OECD and the "Crisis of the Welfare State", 1975–1985', in S. Kott and J. Droux (eds) *Globalizing Social Rights: The International Labour Organization and Beyond*, Basingstoke: Palgrave Macmillan, 293–309.

Leimgruber, M. and Schmelzer, M. (2017) 'Introduction: Writing Histories of the OECD', in M. Leimgruber and M. Schmelzer (eds) *The OECD and the International Political Economy Since 1948*, Basingstoke: Palgrave Macmillan, 1–22.

Leinen, J. and Bummel, A. (2018) *A World Parliament: Governance and Democracy in the 21st Century*, Translated from German by Ray Cunningham, Berlin: Democracy Without Borders.

Mahon, R. and McBride, S. (2008) 'Introduction', in R. Mahon and S. McBride (eds) *The OECD and Transnational Governance*, Vancouver, BC: University of British Columbia Press, 3–22.

Monbiot, G. (2003) *Manifesto for a New World Order*, New York: The New Press.

New Zealand Government (2019) *Economic Plan: For a Productive, Sustainable and Inclusive Economy*, Wellington: Government of New Zealand, www.mbie.govt.nz/assets/economic-plan.pdf.

Nolan, B. (ed) (2018) *Inequality and Inclusive Growth in Rich Countries: Shared Challenges and Contrasting Fortunes*, Oxford: Oxford University Press.

O'Brien, R., Goetz, A., Scholte, J. and Williams, M. (2000) *Contesting Global Governance: Multilateral Economic Institutions and Global Social Movements*, Cambridge: Cambridge University Press.

OECD (Organisation for Economic Co-operation and Development) (1997) *Societal Cohesion and the Globalising Economy: What Does the Future Hold?*, Paris: OECD.

OECD (2008) *Growing Unequal? Income Distribution and Poverty in OECD Countries*, Paris: OECD Publishing, https://doi.org/10.1787/9789264044197-en.

OECD (2011a) *Divided We Stand: Why Inequality Keeps Rising*, Paris: OECD Publishing, https://doi.org/10.1787/9789264119536-en.

OECD (2011b) *Divided We Stand: Why Inequality Keeps Rising*, www.oecd.org/els/soc/49499779.pdf.

OECD (2011c) *Divided We Stand: Why Inequality Keeps Rising* (Speech), www.oecd.org/els/soc/dividedwestandwhyinequalitykeepsrisingspeech.htm.

OECD (2011d) *How's Life? Measuring Well-being*, Paris: OECD Publishing, https://doi.org/10.1787/9789264121164-en.

OECD (2012a) *New Approaches to Economic Challenges: Framework Paper*, presented at the OECD 2012 Ministerial Council Meeting, Paris, 23–24 May 2012, Paris: OECD Publishing, www.oecd.org/general/50452415.pdf.

OECD (2012b) *Boosting Jobs and Living Standards in G20 Countries: A Joint Report by the ILO, OECD, IMF and the World Bank*, Paris: OECD Publishing, https://elibrary.worldbank.org/doi/abs/10.1596/27112.

OECD (2013a) *OECD Workshop on Inclusive Growth, Proceedings*, 3 April 2013, OECD Conference Centre, www.oecd.org/inclusive-growth/events/Proceedings_Inclusive%20Growth%20for%20Shared%20Prosperity_03.04.13.pdf.

OECD (2013b) *OECD Workshop on Inclusive Growth, Session Notes*, 3 April 2013, OECD Conference Centre, Paris: OECD Publishing.

OECD (2014a) *Focus on Inequality and Growth*, Directorate for Employment, Labour and Social Affairs www.oecd.org/social/Focus-Inequality-and-Growth-2014.pdf.

OECD (2014b) *Changing the Conversation on Growth: Going Inclusive, Background Note*, New York: Ford Foundation, www.oecd.org/inclusive-growth/events/Background%20Notes_IG%20Workshop_27%202%202014__US.pdf.

OECD (2014c) *Changing the Conversation on Growth: Going Inclusive, Proceedings*, New York: Ford Foundation, www.oecd.org/inclusive-growth/events/Proceedings_Going%20Inclusive_27.02.14.pdf.

OECD (2014d) *All on Board: Making Inclusive Growth Happen*, Paris: OECD Publishing, https://doi.org/10.1787/9789264218512-en.

OECD (2014e) *Report on the OECD Framework for Inclusive Growth*, Meeting of the OECD Council at Ministerial Level, Paris, 6–7 May 2014, www.oecd.org/mcm/IG_MCM_ENG.pdf.

OECD (2014f) *Women, Government and Policy Making in OECD Countries: Fostering Diversity for Inclusive Growth*, Paris: OECD Publishing, https://doi.org/10.1787/9789264210745-en.

OECD (2015a) *In It Together: Why Less Inequality Benefits All*, Paris: OECD Publishing, https://doi.org/10.1787/9789264235120-en.

OECD (2015b) *Innovation Policies for Inclusive Growth*, Paris: OECD Publishing, https://doi.org/10.1787/9789264229488-en.

OECD (2015c) *Skills for Social Progress: The Power of Social and Emotional Skills*, OECD Skills Studies, Paris: OECD Publishing, https://doi.org/10.1787/9789264226159-en.

OECD (2016a) *The Productivity–Inclusiveness Nexus*, Paris: OECD Publishing, https://doi.org/10.1787/9789264292932-en.

OECD (2016b) *Inclusive Growth in Cities Campaign: A Roadmap for Action*, The New York Proposal for Inclusive Growth in Cities, Paris: OECD Publishing, www.oecd.org/inclusive-growth/about/inclusive-cities-campaign/NY%20Proposal%20-%20English.pdf.

OECD (2016c) *Enhancing Child Well-Being to Promote Inclusive Growth*, Paris: OECD Publishing, www.oecd.org/officialdocuments/publicdisplaydocumentpdf/?cote=DELSA/ELSA(2016)7/REV1&doclanguage=en.

OECD (2016d) *The Governance of Inclusive Growth*, Paris: OECD Publishing, https://doi.org/10.1787/9789264257993-en.

OECD (2016e) *The Governance of Inclusive Growth: An Overview of Country Initiatives*, Paris: OECD Publishing, https://doi.org/10.1787/9789264265189-en.

OECD (2017a) Ministerial Council Statement 'Making Globalisation Work: Better Lives for All', C/MIN(2017)9/FINAL, Paris: OECD Publishing.

OECD (2017b) *Time to Act: Making Inclusive Growth Happen, Policy Brief*, Paris: OECD Publishing, www.oecd-inclusive.com/champion-mayors-doc/Policy_Brief_Time_to_Act.pdf.

OECD (2017c) *Starting Strong 2017: Key OECD Indicators on Early Childhood Education and Care*, Paris: OECD Publishing, https://doi.org/10.1787/9789264276116-en.

OECD (2017d) *Investing in Climate, Investing in Growth*, Paris: OECD Publishing, https://doi.org/10.1787/9789264273528-en.

OECD (2018a) *Opportunities for All: A Framework for Policy Action on Inclusive Growth*, Meeting of the OECD Council at Ministerial Level Paris, 30–31 May 2018, Paris: OECD Publishing, www.oecd.org/mcm-2018/documents/C-MIN-2018-5-EN.pdf.

OECD (2018b) *Opportunities for All: A Framework for Policy Action on Inclusive Growth*, Inclusive Growth Initiative Policy Brief, Paris: OECD Publishing.

OECD (2018c) *Going for Growth: An Opportunity that Governments Should not Miss*, Paris: OECD Publishing.

OECD (2018d) *Is the Last Mile the Longest? Economic Gains from Gender Equality in Nordic Countries*, Paris: OECD Publishing.

OECD (2018e) *Beyond GDP: Measuring What Counts for Economic and Social Performance*, Paris: OECD Publishing.

OECD (2019a) *Beyond Growth: Towards A New Economic Approach*, SG/NAEC(2019)3, Paris: OECD Publishing.

OECD (2019b) *Policy Coherence for Sustainable Development 2019: Empowering People and Ensuring Inclusiveness and Equality*, Paris: OECD Publishing.

OECD (2020) *Statement by the OECD/G20 Inclusive Framework on BEPS on the Two-Pillar Approach to Address the Tax Challenges Arising from the Digitalisation of the Economy, OECD/G20 Inclusive Framework on BEPS*, Paris: OECD.

OECD/WBG (Organisation for Economic Co-operation and Development/World Bank Group) (2017) *Policy Framework to Help Guide the G20 in Its Development of Policy Options to Foster More Inclusive Growth*, www.oecd.org/g20/topics/framework-strong-sustainable-balanced-growth/OECD-WBG-Policy-Framework-to-help-Gguide-the-G20-in-its-development.pdf.

Ougaard, M. (2010) 'The OECD's Global Role: Agenda Setting and Policy Diffusion', in K. Martens and A. P. Jakobi (eds) *Mechanisms of OECD Governance: International Incentives for National Policy-Making?*, Oxford: Oxford University Press, 26–49.

Piketty, T. (2014) *Capital in the Twenty-First Century*, Translated by Arthur Goldhammer, Cambridge, MA: Harvard University Press.

Schmelzer M. (2014) 'A Club of the Rich to Help the Poor? The OECD, "Development", and the Hegemony of Donor Countries', in M. Frey, S. Kunkel and C. R. Unger (eds) *International Organizations and Development, 1945–1990*, Basingstoke: Palgrave Macmillan.

Schmelzer M. (2016) *The Hegemony of Growth: The OECD and the Making of the Economic Growth Paradigm*, Cambridge: Cambridge University Press.

Scottish Government (2015) *Scotland's Economic Strategy*, Edinburgh: The Scottish Government (especially Section 3: Promoting Inclusive Growth).

Scottish Government (2016) *Scottish Draft Budget 2017–2018: Equality Statement*, Edinburgh: The Scottish Government (especially Chapter 3: Inclusive Growth), www.gov.scot/binaries/content/documents/govscot/publications/speech-statement/2016/12/equality-statement-scottish-draft-budget-2017-18/documents/00511772-pdf/00511772-pdf/govscot%3Adocument/00511772.pdf?forceDownload=true.

Stiglitz, J. E., Sen, A. and Fitoussi, J.-P. (2009) *Report by Commission on the Measurement of Economic Performance and Social Progress*, www.stiglitz-sen-fitoussi.fr.

Stiglitz, J. E., Sen, A. and Fitoussi, J.-P. (2010) *MIS-Measuring Our Lives: Why GDP Doesn't Add Up*, The Report of the Commission on the Measurement of Economic Performance and Social Progress, New York: The New Press.

Stiglitz, J., Fitoussi, J. and Durand, M. (2018) *Beyond GDP: Measuring What Counts for Economic and Social Performance*, Paris: OECD Publishing, https://doi.org/10.1787/9789264307292-en.

Weiss, T. G. and Wilkinson, R. (2019) *Rethinking Global Governance*, Cambridge: Polity.

Weiss, W. G. and Thakur, R. (2010) *Global Governance and the UN: An Unfinished Journey*, Bloomington, IN: Indiana University Press.

Woodward, R. (2010) 'The OECD and Economic Governance: Invisibility and Impotence?', in K. Martens and A. P. Jakobi (eds) *Mechanisms of OECD Governance: International Incentives for National Policy-Making?*, Oxford: Oxford University Press, 53–74.

14

For better or worse?

Richard Wilkinson and Kate Pickett

Introduction

A crucial reason why governments everywhere drag their feet about the transition to environmental sustainability is that it is widely thought to depend primarily on a reduction in living standards. It looks not only as if reducing carbon emissions will mean tightening our belts and consuming less, but also having to make do with substitutes for what we prefer: having to give up eating meat, stop flying, use less plastic and replace private cars with public transport. In the public mind that inevitably makes facing the climate emergency a pretty dismal prospect, to be avoided for as long as possible.

To counter that perspective, some have argued that it is possible to transition to sustainability while at the same time producing higher standards of human wellbeing. This perspective is based primarily on three considerations. First, that in high-income countries, continued increases in material standards no longer lead to higher levels of happiness and life satisfaction. Second, that sustainable societies could satisfy fundamental human social needs very much better than high-income societies do now; for instance, by strengthening community life and reducing status competition. And third, that societies using renewable sources of power and electric public transport systems will be cleaner and quieter and will produce higher health standards. These views link the transition to sustainability to large-scale socioeconomic restructuring. Proposals span everything from replacing economic growth with maximizing human wellbeing as the central objective of government policy, to the much more radical demand for the abolition of capitalism itself.

The demand to replace gross domestic product (GDP) with wellbeing as the main objective of government policy has led to a growing academic industry devoted to developing wellbeing measures. Few of these, however, have been supported by research identifying *determinants* of wellbeing. Even when governments have adopted measures of wellbeing, as a few have, that does not mean that wellbeing will increase, nor does substituting wellbeing for the growth of GDP per head mean that the drivers of growth will lose their force. Not only is economic growth probably propelled by more fundamental forces than government policy, but it is likely that the same is true of wellbeing.

That governments are not in control of the economy is shown by the many examples around the world where governments have failed, despite their best efforts, to achieve desired increases in economic growth rates. For example, Japan has had little or no growth since the early 1990s and successive governments in Britain have not only failed to achieve more than very slow growth but have also failed to halt the business cycle.

Nor is this a superficial issue of getting policy right. It is often said that a minimum requirement for economic growth is a government sufficiently functional to be able to provide stability and enforce the rule of law. In the absence of effective administrative institutions, it might be said that it makes little difference what policy governments aim to implement, whether they are intended to be pro-growth or not. Although there is *cross-sectional* evidence that economic growth is associated with measures of overall government effectiveness, it is less clear which way round that relationship works. A study that looked at changes over time found that government effectiveness is unrelated to *subsequent* rates of economic growth. It concluded that the relationship probably goes from better economic performance to more effective government (Kurtz and Schrank, 2007).

We suspect that, rather than being primarily dependent on policy, growth is more likely to be an expression of the simple fact that most people want to maximize their incomes and consumption and most businesses want to maximize sales and profits. For these and other reasons, many, including Karl Marx, have regarded growth as inherent to capitalism itself. Like these money-making pressures, economic growth preceded explicit government concern for GDP growth (probably by at least two centuries) and is likely to continue even when governments have shifted their focus. Unless we find ways of addressing these income and profit maximizing pressures, they are likely to continue to drive growth even if we persuade governments to abandon growth as an objective.

With the strategic objective of making a sustainable society more attractive, people (ourselves included) have tried to present the transition to sustainability as a transition to a maximally attractive 'good' society. But the slow progress towards reducing world carbon emissions means that it may now be seriously misleading to suggest that we still have the possibility of creating a better world. It looks increasingly likely that the future will be dominated by attempts to respond to a never-ending series of environmental emergencies: floods, storms, droughts, crop failures, food and water shortages as well as increasing numbers of armed conflicts and refugees fleeing these threats. As David Attenborough suggested, it may be too late to make things better; perhaps all we can do is to make them get worse more slowly. A recent warning, signed by 11,000 scientists in 153 different countries, pointed to the continuing increases in world population, in world gross national product (GNP), in meat consumption per head, in deforestation and air travel, all contributing to a continuing rise in greenhouse gas emission, in global temperatures and in sea levels (Ripple et al, 2020). The article warned of 'potential irreversible climate tipping points ... that could lead to a catastrophic "hothouse Earth", well beyond the control of humans' (Ripple et al, 2020: 9), and emphasized that to 'avoid untold suffering' we need 'an immense increase of scale in endeavours to conserve our biosphere' (Ripple et al, 2020: 8). Failing that, temperatures are predicted, on current policies, to rise by around 3°C by the end of this century, with catastrophic consequences. Another report by Future Earth (2020), based on questionnaires sent to 222 scientists in 52 countries, found that more than one third of them thought there was a real danger that interlinked emergencies 'might cascade to create global systemic crises' and 'ecosystem collapse' (Future Earth, 2020: 15).

Under such circumstances, what happens to human wellbeing would have little to do with current attempts to devise new measures of it. Wellbeing might instead be a question of ensuring adequate emergency supplies of food and shelter, of the creation of standing emergency relief teams and systems for evacuating people from danger and providing emergency relief.

A crucial determinant of how populations come through the hazards of climate change would be the extent to which people respond with mutual support rather than simply fending for themselves. The danger is that the rich, and anyone who can afford to, would use their resources to establish themselves in protected safe havens and abandon others to their fate. Recent experience suggests that the political response is likely to be further complicated by hostility to increasing flows of refugees from environmental disasters. The scale of migration we have already seen is small in comparison with what is likely to result from the advancing climate crisis, but the public reaction has, nevertheless, already had a profound effect on politics in many of the recipient countries, contributing to populism, racism and nationalism, and effectively diverting political attention even further from the urgency of policies to counter the climate crisis.

But the future is not set in stone. While it is always inherently unknowable, there are possibilities for the future which might make the picture we have outlined a lot better or worse. For example, the forecast temperature rises do not include the effects of highly plausible major changes in natural feedback effects which could seriously exacerbate climate change, leading to runaway global warming beyond any human means of control. There are also possibilities of major technical developments which would make it much easier to reduce global carbon emissions. For example, as some, including George Monbiot, suggest, current developments of laboratory-grown alternatives to meat may lead to massive reductions in numbers of cattle and their methane production. There might also be major breakthroughs in battery technology, making it easier and cheaper to store electricity and so hastening the conversion to renewable power and electric transport. Nor do we know the longer-term effects on material consumption of the digital and information economy, which may be as profound as Jeremy Rifkin described in his book *The Zero Marginal Cost Society* (Rifkin, 2014).

We cannot, however, rely on these or any other possibilities rescuing us from the disastrous implications of the climate emergency. There can be little doubt that the most predictable part of the picture is that continuing increases in greenhouse gas concentrations in the atmosphere will lead to further environmental destruction.

So where does that leave us? Above all, we need to work out what kind of society will give us the best chance of surviving whatever the future brings. There are four key criteria. First, our societies need to be highly cohesive and adaptable: they must become willing and able to make the almost continuous changes in our way of life necessary to minimize our impact on the environment (changing our diets, reducing our need for transport, developing renewable power sources and changing our technology), in order to achieve the long transition to sustainability. Second, we need to think what kind of societies will best provide the mutual support and aid to areas hit by ever more frequent threats, crises and environmental disasters. The increased level of CO_2 already in the atmosphere means that climate disruption will undoubtedly get much worse even if we cut emissions as fast as possible. Third, we need to find out how to convert the production- and consumption-maximizing leviathan that the market economy has become back into a waste-minimizing system which would enable a sociable human society to live within its planetary boundaries. And fourth and lastly, although with the difficulties they face it is unlikely that our societies will achieve new heights of wellbeing, we can at least remove some of the things which most obviously reduce the wellbeing of large sections of the population, things such as poverty, lack of education and lack of political voice.

There is now very little doubt that the extent of inequality (income and wealth) is much the most powerful determinant of which societies will survive these tests and which will succumb to processes of social breakdown. In the following sections we will show that more equal societies, those with smaller income differences between rich and poor, are more cohesive, more adaptable and perform better in almost all areas of social functioning.

Cohesive and adaptable societies

Many studies show that the larger the income differences in a society, the weaker local community life is. With more inequality, people are less likely to belong to local organizations and voluntary groups, they are less likely to take part in community activities and less likely to know their neighbours. Research also shows that people are not only less likely to feel they can trust others in more unequal societies but also that violence (as measured by homicide rates) becomes very much more common in more unequal societies. Together, the studies confirm what many people have recognized intuitively over the centuries: that inequality increases social divisions and weakens social cohesion. And as inequality increases, the social bonds of reciprocity and sense of community which, in more egalitarian societies, knit neighbourhoods together, give way to self-interest, status competition and a drive for self-advancement.

The causal process seems to be that bigger income differences make the divisions of class and status more powerful, increasing the idea that some people are 'worth' much more than others. As a result, we come to judge each other's personal worth more by status and, at the same time, worry more about how others judge us. Insecurities about our own self-worth increase so we feel more anxious about social comparisons and less at ease with other people. In short, social relationships become increasingly marred by the social awkwardness and fears which accompany considerations of superiority and inferiority. As George Bernard Shaw said, 'Inequality of income takes the broad, safe, and fertile plain of human society and stands it on its edge so that everyone has to cling desperately to her foothold' (Shaw, 1928: 418).

This in turn has serious implications for people's willingness to take action to solve common problems, including environmental ones. It makes people much less able or willing either to act together or even to discuss shared problems. That is nicely described in a book by Edward Banfield (1958) called *The Moral Basis of a Backward Society*, which describes the effects of a lack of social capital on life in a village in southern Italy. He explains how despite the village having obvious needs, such as to repair the road, there was no concept of people coming together to work on projects for the common good. Apart from a nepotistic loyalty to their families, people regarded themselves and each other as motivated only by self-interest. The lack of trust and suspicion of anyone who tried to do anything in the public interest made cooperative activity almost impossible and placed a severe limitation on the possibilities for progress in the village.

Because inequality leads to the decline of community life, self-advancement takes over from concern for the common good. As taking action on the environment is so dependent on how public-spirited people are, more unequal societies tend to do less for the environment. An international survey of business leaders found that those from more unequal countries attached a much lower priority to international environmental agreements. The same tendency can also be seen at the household level: the data shows that people in more unequal countries recycle a smaller proportion of waste materials. They also bicycle less, have higher CO_2 emissions per $100 of GNP per capita and get less of their power from renewables.

For the same reason, in more unequal countries there is likely to be both less pressure from public opinion to get governments to take decisive action on carbon emissions and more danger of public opposition to any such action.

Inequality is relevant to how we adapt to deal with environmental problems because it also increases consumerism, a major obstacle to sustainability. The more that money is seen as a measure of a person's worth and the goods we buy are used to enhance people's appearance of status and success, the more avaricious we become. As a result, studies show that people living in more unequal areas spend more on status goods. Indeed, the pressure to keep up appearances through consumption is so great that borrowing goes up in periods when inequality is high. This means that if we are serious about the transition to sustainability, we must reduce the inequality which ramps up status competition and consumerism.

Given the past lack of far-reaching action to combat climate change, it is hard not to fear that levels of public spiritedness and concern for the common good among the general population are too weak to support the action necessary to combat the climate emergency now.

This dilemma has similarities to one faced by Britain during the Second World War when priorities had to be changed to serve the war effort. In his essay *War and Social Policy*, Richard Titmuss described the thinking that went into the government's approach. He said, 'If the cooperation of the masses was thought to be essential [to the war effort], then inequalities had to be reduced and the pyramid of social stratification had to be flattened' (Titmuss, 1958: 86). As a result, the war was marked by far-reaching policies designed to make people feel the burden of war was equally shared. Income differences were rapidly reduced by taxation, essential goods were subsidized, luxuries were taxed, and rationing was introduced for food. Action on the climate emergency now needs a similar raft of egalitarian policies: without them governments everywhere may face movements analogous to the Gilets Jaunes' opposition to the French government's plan to raise fuel taxes.

Mutual aid

In the future, much will depend on the ability of societies to withstand successive climate emergencies and disasters. Recovery from short-term crises should be much more rapid and less traumatic if we not only have robust and well-prepared systems of support, but also a strong ethos of mutual aid. The decline of community life, the focus on self-advancement, the decline in trust and the rise in violence, all fostered by inequality, take us in the opposite direction. The increasing numbers of homeless people on the streets in more unequal societies are another indication of the decline of mutual aid, but international survey data also show that people in more unequal societies are simply less willing to help each other.

The anti-social effects of inequality can be seen from the top to the bottom of society. At the top, among governments, the level of overseas development aid given by governments of more unequal countries falls further below the UN recommended standard of 0.7 per cent of national income than it does in more equal societies. At the other end of society come the results of studies of bullying among children. Using data from different sources covering children between 8 and 14 years old, research shows a powerful tendency for bullying to be much more common in more unequal countries. Instead of finding their peers 'kind and helpful', conflict becomes much more common. Part of the explanation is likely to be that parents pass on their experience of adversity and conflict to their children, perhaps partly through epigenetic imprinting.

The evidence that inequality has such widespread anti-social effects is too well established to doubt either the basic pattern or the causal processes. The first peer-reviewed research showing that health and violence were worse in more unequal countries came out in the 1970s and there are now hundreds of articles looking at these relationships in different ways, using different methods and controlling for possible 'confounders'. Indeed, in the technical jargon, there are even meta-analyses of multilevel models looking at the effects of changes in inequality over time and studies which show the lag periods between a change in inequality and its effects.

Understanding the causal links between inequality and its effects is fairly straightforward. It starts with our sensitivity to the character of social relations, to friendship on the one hand and social hierarchy on the other. Because individual members of the same species have the same basic needs, there is almost always the possibility for repeated conflict between them, for food, shelter, territories, sexual partners and so on. One way, but not the best, of avoiding endless conflict over access to each thing is simply for members to know who is strongest, to know who would win a fight for access. If you know who is strongest, you can predict the outcome, so the weaker can give way to the stronger without the need for actual conflict. Essentially that is the basis of animal dominance hierarchies: the stronger are recognized as dominant and the weaker as subordinate and the ranking system tends to be a hierarchy graded by strength (sometimes moderated by support from trusted allies). Everyone has to know their position in the ranking system and how to behave in relation to superiors and inferiors: when to give way and when not to. In effect, subordinates eat last. Getting it wrong is likely to result in injuries which may sometimes be life-threatening. Being as far up the hierarchy as possible is a huge advantage, not only in terms of access to food and other necessities, but also for reproductive opportunities and better survival chances for offspring. Hence there have been powerful selective pressures which have shaped our concern for social status. This is the prehuman origin (from our ape ancestors) of our evolved sensitivity to social status. But the dominance hierarchy was essentially a bullying hierarchy, ordered by fear and consequently highly stressful.

That, however, is only half the story. The other half is in sharp contrast with our desire for dominance and is made up of our highly developed ability to be each other's best source of help, cooperation, love, learning and assistance of every kind. In essence, we have the potential not only to be each other's worst rivals and greatest threat, but also to be each other's best source of cooperation, support and security.

How is it that we can contain the potential for two such opposite social characteristics? There is widespread agreement among anthropologists that the hunting and gathering societies of our human pre-history were, with few exceptions, highly egalitarian. They were marked by cooperation, food sharing and reciprocity, with no sign of the pattern, common among animals, for the weakest to eat last or to be excluded when food was scarce. Within these egalitarian societies, people with more pro-social characteristics, who were less selfish, better at sharing and reciprocity, were more likely to get selected as sexual partners and as collaborators for cooperative activities (Boehm, 2012). These societies have been described as not only consciously egalitarian, but sometimes as 'assertively' egalitarian. Indeed, the evidence suggests that people who were implacably anti-social were excluded and cast out of the sharing group, a treatment that amounted almost to a death sentence. And the best way of ensuring that you remained a secure member of the cooperative group was to have skills and to perform tasks which others valued. That propensity has become enshrined as part of our evolved psychology in our capacity to get pleasure from doing things which others appreciate, and in our desire to be valued by others.

In a nutshell, then, while the egalitarian social environment of our hunting and gathering human prehistory selected people for pro-social characteristics, the dominance hierarchies of our *pre*-human existence had selected for the anti-social strategies of self-advancement most consistent with self-preservation in dominance hierarchies. And it is not difficult to imagine how the advantages of cooperation could have become crucial.

We are left then with a psychological legacy containing both of these very different tendencies and we of course use social strategies rooted in both all the time. With friends, who are usually chosen from among our near equals, we use egalitarian social strategies of sharing and reciprocity; we treat them as equals and we are careful not to put people down or give the impression we think we are better than them. But in settings where social status is important, we know how to act snobbishly, to stand on our dignity, to name drop and attempt to set ourselves apart from those we regard as our social inferiors. Indeed, snobbishness has been described as driven by the desire for what divides people rather than for what unites them.

Crucially important, however, is that which strategy we use is strongly influenced by our experience of the social environment. The bigger the differences in income and wealth, the more visible the differences in class and status become, and the more external wealth is seen as if it was a measure of individual worth.

Essentially these are the two opposite ways people can come together. At one extreme, scarce resources are allocated according to power differentials in the service of self-interest, while at the other, the allocation reflects the mutual recognition of each other's needs, sharing and cooperation. People have, of course, lived in every kind of society from the most hierarchical and tyrannical to the most egalitarian, but the contrasting nature of social relationships makes more unequal societies much more stressful.

As these contrasting systems of relationships require such different behavioural strategies, we are very likely to discover that there are epigenetic switches controlling gene expression to prepare our cognitive and emotional development either for a world in which we must fight for what we can get and learn not to trust others because we are all rivals, or for a world where we depend on gaining each other's trust and depend on mutual cooperation and reciprocity.

This interpretation of the effects of inequality fits well with what we know about the extraordinary sensitivity of human beings to the nature of social relationships. It explains why both low social status and wider status differentials are such powerful health-damaging stressors, and why friendship is so highly protective of health.

Sustainable wellbeing

The effects of inequality have, as we have seen, very major implications for the health and wellbeing of populations. They are all the more important because they are a key to redressing the imbalance in high-income countries between the unprecedented material living standards and the threadbare quality of the social fabric.

This contrast has been shown many times. Although higher material standards are needed in low-income countries where many do not yet have access to necessities, in middle- and high-income countries there are sharply diminishing gains to wellbeing associated with economic growth, so much so that among the richest countries further increases in material standards seem to do nothing for health or wellbeing. The predictable implication is that having more and more of everything makes less and less difference. Whether you look at measures of happiness, life satisfaction or life expectancy, the picture is the same. Wellbeing rises rapidly among poorer countries with economic growth but then levels out among the richer countries. The same basic story is told in analyses that use measures of economic wellbeing such as the Genuine Progress Indicator (GPI). Despite the failure to tackle serious relative poverty in high-income countries, those societies have reached what should be recognized as a saturation point in terms of their material development.

This contrasts with the evidence of huge deficits in emotional and psychological wellbeing among the populations of high-income countries. In 2018, the Mental Health Foundation reported that almost three quarters of all adults in the UK felt levels of stress which left them feeling overwhelmed or unable to cope (Mental Health Foundation, 2018). Almost a third of adults had suicidal feelings as a result of stress and half that number had self-harmed. In each case the rates among younger adults (18–24 years) were even higher. Although the available survey measures differ, figures for other rich countries look broadly similar. Almost 80 per cent of Americans feel stressed each day and 57 per cent say they are paralyzed by stress. One in five adult Americans have a mental illness that meets diagnostic criteria.

It is clear that further improvements in the quality of life in high-income countries depend on switching attention from the material to the social environment. As shown in the book *The Inner Level* (Wilkinson and Pickett, 2018), reductions in inequality are key to improvements in psychosocial wellbeing across whole populations. At their core, the causal processes involve the effect of inequality on our worries about how we are seen and judged by others: status anxiety, social comparisons and insecurities about self-worth.

The scale of relative poverty is another very major force that dramatically lowers wellbeing. As it is defined as living on less than 60 per cent of the median income, it would be almost inevitably reduced by greater equality. Relative poverty has particularly serious consequences for children, affecting their education, health and development: it blights their future. The Resolution Foundation has forecast that 37 per cent of British children will, by 2023–24, be growing up in relative poverty.

It is also clear that since 2010 wellbeing has been seriously reduced by cuts in public services resulting from government austerity policies, so much so that death rates in some population groups have risen and life expectancy for the population as a whole has ceased its long historical decline. Worst affected are women over 85 years old, the section of the population most in need of public services. But in the period 2011–16 death rates among the whole population under 50 have ceased to decline and among those in their late 40s they have actually risen. Nor do these adverse trends mean we have reached the limits of human life expectancy: not only does it continue to increase in some countries where it is already several years longer than in the

UK, but the adverse trend in the UK is most marked among the least well off where life expectancy is anyway lowest.

No serious attempt to improve population wellbeing can ignore the injustice of huge differences in life expectancy. People living in the most privileged 10 per cent of areas can expect to live close to 20 years longer in good health than people living in the most deprived decile of areas in the UK.

Measures of wellbeing

Although it is not a lack of wellbeing measures that prevents governments from tackling the most glaring issues that stop people flourishing, new measures may, nevertheless, be helpful: helpful in taking stock of where we have got to, in providing targets and making comparisons between countries easier.

A search engine used by the International Society for Quality of Life Studies has apparently found 894 different measures of aspects of wellbeing, quality of life, happiness and life satisfaction. They include things such as positive and negative affect, emotional wellbeing, self-actualization, a sense of meaning, life satisfaction, satisfaction with different aspects of life, mental health and stress. Key aspects of this large and complex field have been well summarized in a review by Ahuvia (2018). It ends, however, by saying that people's self-reports of happiness do not seem to guide their decisions. That suggests either that their self-reports are mistaken or that people fail to make the decisions which would maximize happiness.

Almost all the measures are self-reports of subjective states. But when it comes to international comparisons, important evidence is often overlooked, suggesting that subjective measures are unreliable. People's reports of their own objective or subjective state are strongly influenced by culture. What makes that particularly important in the present context is that reporting differences vary systematically with inequality. This can make the associations between inequality and national differences in self-reported states highly misleading. Evidence comes from two sources. First, self-reported health, which is usually assessed with a question such as 'in general, would you say that your health is excellent, very good, good, fair, or poor?' Although within a country it is quite a good predictor of mortality and morbidity, it breaks down when you make comparisons between countries. Objectively, a country's death rate may be high or low, but that seems to have no relation to whether or not people say their health is good. Among a group of rich developed countries in one study, the country which had the *highest* life expectancy also had the *lowest* proportion of people who rated their health as good. Overall, there was a weak inverse tendency for countries with the best self-rated health to have lower life expectancy (Dorling and Barford, 2009). So, although life expectancy was better in the countries with smaller income differences, self-reported health was not. The second example comes from a study of what its authors called 'self-enhancement bias' or 'illusory superiority': a tendency to exaggerate your desirable qualities compared to other people (Loughnan et al, 2011). The study showed that there was a much stronger tendency for people in more unequal societies to go in for this kind of narcissistic self-aggrandisement.

Why people in more unequal societies have a greater tendency to exaggerate their positive characteristics is that inequality, as research has shown, increases people's status anxiety. In more unequal societies there is a systematic tendency for people at every income level, from the poorest all the way through to the richest tenth, to worry more about what others think of them than do people in more equal societies (Layte and Whelan, 2014). As a result, they try harder to make a positive impression on others. If you live in a society where some people seem to be regarded as supremely important while others are treated as if they were almost worthless, we end up using status as a measure of worth and worrying more about how others judge us. That has, as we saw earlier, been shown to lead people living in more unequal societies to spend more on status goods, flashy cars and clothes with expensive labels, as a form of self-enhancement. In effect, inequality makes people more narcissistic; and indeed measures using the Narcissistic Personality Inventory have shown that narcissism has risen in the United States while income inequality has increased.

We call this the 'happiness–inequality paradox'. Greater inequality makes people feel they have to hide signs of weakness or vulnerability in favour of projecting an image of success, independence and self-reliance. We suspect that for an American to answer a survey question on happiness by saying they are unhappy, may feel like lowering their guard and an admission of failure, but for someone in a much more equal country to say they are happy might feel almost like complacency or bragging.

If researchers and policy makers are not to be blind to the benefits that greater equality brings to wellbeing, it is crucial that they understand this paradox. Otherwise they could find themselves imagining that reducing inequality had no impact on happiness even though it reduces violence, improves objective measures of physical and mental health, strengthens trust and community life, improves child wellbeing and more.

Although the last decade has seen impressive progress in *recognizing* the importance of reducing inequality, much less progress has been made in actually reducing it. Despite the fact that many international organizations, including the International Monetary Fund (IMF), the World Bank, the World Economic Forum (WEF), Organisation for Economic Co-operation and Development (OECD) and Oxfam, have all emphasized the need for greater equality and it is now enshrined as the tenth of the 17 UN Sustainable Development Goals (SDGs), effective government action has rarely been forthcoming. There are important parallels here with the huge rise in awareness of the climate crisis and yet the lack of adequate action. And although there are clear signs that opinion is beginning to switch to thinking that wellbeing rather than economic growth is the proper focus of government policy, only a tiny group of governments (including Finland, Iceland, New Zealand and the devolved governments of Scotland and Wales) have actually made that switch (Coscieme et al, 2019). Too often academics and policy makers seem to act as if action to improve wellbeing must await better measurements; as if we were unaware of all the components of deprivation, from poverty and inequality to housing shortages, which are overwhelmingly the most important limitations on a population's wellbeing.

Whether or not it would take the end of capitalism to dethrone economic growth, greater equality would at least reduce consumerism and ease the transition to environmental sustainability. And it would do so while also improving the social fabric, physical and mental health, and the quality of our lives.

References

Ahuvia, A. C. (2018) 'Wealth, Consumption and Happiness', in A. Lewis (ed) *The Cambridge Handbook of Psychology and Economic Behaviour*, Cambridge: Cambridge University, 199–226.

Banfield, E. C. (1958) *The Moral Basis of a Backward Society*, New York: Free Press.

Boehm, C. (2012) *Moral Origins: The Evolution of Virtue, Altruism, and Shame*, New York: Basic Books.

Coscieme, L., Sutton, P., Mortensen, L. F., Kubiszewski, I., Costanza, R., Trebeck, K., Pulselli, F. M., Giannetti, B. F. and Fioramonti, L. (2019) 'Overcoming the Myths of Mainstream Economics to Enable a New Wellbeing Economy', *Sustainability*, 11(16): 4374.

Dorling, D. and Barford, A. (2009) 'The Inequality Hypothesis: Thesis, Antithesis, and a Synthesis?', *Health Place*, 15(4): 1166–9; discussion 1163–5.

Future Earth (2020) *Our Future on Earth 2020*, www.futureearth.org/ .

Kurtz, M. J. and Schrank, A. (2007) 'Growth and Governance: Models, Measures, and Mechanisms', *Journal of Politics*, 69(2): 538–54.

Layte, R. and Whelan, C. T. (2014) 'Who Feels Inferior? A Test of the Status Anxiety Hypothesis of Social Inequalities in Health', *European Sociological Review*, 30(4): 525–35.

Loughnan, S., Kuppens, P., Allik, J., Balazs, K., de Lemus, S., Dumont, K., Gargurevich, R., Hidegkuti, I., Leidner, B., Matos, L., Park, J., Realo, A., Shi, J., Sojo, V. E., Tong, Y. Y., Vaes, J., Verduyn, P., Yeung, V. and Haslam, N. (2011) 'Economic Inequality Is Linked to Biased Self-Perception', *Psychological Science*, 22(10): 1254–8.

Mental Health Foundation (2018) *Stress: Are We Coping?*, www. mentalhealth.org.uk/file/3432/download?token=709ABkP8.

Rifkin, J. (2014) *The Zero Marginal Cost Society: The Internet of Things, the Collaborative Commons, and the Eclipse of Capitalism*, New York: St. Martin's Press.

Ripple, W. J, Wolf, C., Newsome, T. M., Barnard, P. and Moomaw, W. R. (2020) 'World Scientists' Warning of a Climate Emergency', *BioScience*, 70(1): 8–12.

Shaw, B. (1928) *The Intelligent Woman's Guide to Socialism, Capitalism, Sovietism, and Fascism*, London: Alma Books.

Titmuss, R. M. (1958) *Essays on 'The Welfare State'* (Chapter 4: War and Social Policy), London: George Allen & Unwin, 75–87.

Wilkinson, R. and Pickett, K. (2018) *The Inner Level: How More Equal Societies Reduce Stress, Restore Sanity and Improve Everyone's Wellbeing*, London: Allen Lane.

15

The struggle for social sustainability

Christopher Deeming

Introduction

This final chapter draws lessons from across the volume, for thinking through the conceptual 'lynchpin' of the 'social' and the seismic shifts in social policy over time and space. Here we return to the different conceptualizations of 'the social' and 'the social question' posed in the different chapters, reflecting further on the 'social' in social policy and the struggle for social sustainability in the 21st century. Emerging global social policy frameworks, and proposed pathways and alternatives for accelerating global social progress, are critically examined, alongside current issues and future challenges.

Internationalizing the social

The 'social question' (German: Soziale Frage, French: *la question sociale*, Danish: *Arbejderspørgsmaalet*, Swedish: *arbetarfrågan*) constituted the dominant social problem, to be addressed by social reforms in the early 19th century, as we heard in Chapters 1 and 3, with the emergence of social policy in Europe.[1] Originally identified with the problem of pauperism that shaped the systems of poor relief in the 19th century (Steinmetz, 1993: ch 3), it then became bound up with 'the workers question' or the 'labour question' (*die Arbeiterfrage*, the question of the workers) associated with unemployment (Walters, 2000), which became 'the international workers question' under the auspices of the International Labour Organization (ILO) from 1919 (Bellucci and Weiss, 2020). The 'social question' was internationalized, key global institutions put 'the social' into international activities and programmes, at the ILO but also the League of Nations from 1923 (Miller, 1995), and in the work of the UN from 1945 (Emmerij et al, 2001). The League of Nations convened an Advisory Committee on Social Questions and the Health and Social Questions Section, known as the 'Social Questions bureau', worked to promote the welfare of women and children. While the ILO has made a key defining contribution to our understanding of social rights, especially workers' rights, and global social justice over the last 100 years, reflected in the ideological struggles and the changing character of work and labour, advancing the rights of homeworkers in the pandemic (see, for example, Standing, 2008; Kaufmann, 2012; Kettunen, 2013; Deacon, 2015; Boris, 2019; Maul, 2019).[2]

In national contexts, social groups and movements coalesced to counteract the dissolution of the social, labour organizations and trade union movements played a vital role in the struggle for economic and social rights (Polanyi, [1944] 2001; Fox Piven and Cloward, 1977; Esping-Andersen, 1990). Social policies varied according to the way in which the social question was originally posed in response to social struggle (Kaufmann, 2013). In other words, the reactions of policy makers to political struggle was not only key to understanding the institutional development of social rights (Marshall, 1950), but also variability in social policy designs, and the continuing evolution of welfare and citizenship regimes in response to social movements and political activism, such as the campaign and struggle for the rights of women (Huber and Stephens, 2001; Jenson and Saint-Martin, 2003). In Sweden, the idea of the 'people's home' originally carried a strong notion of a common social and economic struggle, in the pursuit of national efficiency (Edling et al, 2015). Social policy could be understood as an investment in production factors. 'Productive' or 'prophylactic' social policies were directed at the entire structure of the economy and not at the individual symptoms of social problems. Social-democratic social policy could effectively do away with social problems like social inequality, and social policy was certainly not resigned to the residual role of dealing with the worst effects of capitalism, the problem of poverty, as in the liberal model of welfare capitalism.

As Jenny Andersson (2006) explains, discussions of *productive* social policy bore the stamp of the economic discourse that surrounded the social question from the 19th century onwards, until the closing decades of the 20th century when the social question informing social policy was then challenged by the ideological adaptation to permanent austerity. The so-called 'crisis' related to the sustainability of Western welfare states, amid growing concerns about the affordability of social welfare (*Growth to Limits*, Flora, 1986a, 1986b; Frericks and Maier, 2012, provide a review). However, it also stemmed in part from the changing nature of (post-industrial) capitalist societies, a 'new social question' concerning work and welfare was now clearly visible at the turn of 21st century, relating to 'new social risks' like 'social exclusion' (on the formulation of the 'new' social question see Rosanvallon, [1995] 2000; Castel, [1995] 2003;

and Marx, 2007). The political struggle to reconfigure the social had been building in the 20th century, as policy makers attempted to meet growing equality demands and the social rights of citizenship (Williams, 1992 and writing in Chapter 10 in this volume; Lewis, 1999).

Social planning too was falling short of expectations amid increasing individualization and consumerism, with the logic of market-driven contractual obligations and 'duties' of citizenship appearing to challenge the very notion of the social and social citizenship (see Chapter 2; and Taylor-Gooby, 2009). There was a growing sense that the socially defined welfare state was increasingly being subordinated to the market and privatized risk, amid growing insecurities and rising inequality created by global capitalism. The social did not disappear, however, but was hidden by the dominant political discourses, claiming 'individualization' and 'neoliberalism' in the midst of fundamental change (Chapter 3). Ultimately this would provoke a reaction, and a reappraisal of the social, seen in the stream of influential works by prominent academics, Giddens (1998) and Esping-Andersen (2001, 2002), are notable, and from the international and global institutions (OECD, 1994a, 1997; World Bank, 1997, 2004). In Chapter 4, Jean-Michel Bonvin and Francesco Laruffa nevertheless associate this trend with the growing economization and de-politicization of the social.

The political frameworks of the 20th century, born out of democratic struggle, continue to hold relevance of course. For the liberal, it is 'work, not welfare'; as Goodin (2001) recalls, the corporatist slogan was always 'welfare through work' (that is occupation-based rights) and the social-democratic slogan, 'welfare and work' (citizenship-based rights). However, these are all essentially 'productivist' slogans in one way or another, and increasingly they are being called into question in the age of sustainability. While the *social* foundations of welfare capitalism were excavated in the rich countries of the Global North (Esping-Andersen, 1999), it was claimed the social dimensions of economic development were largely absent in the developing countries of the Global South (Gough, 2008). The enduring welfare regimes frameworks continue to both help and hinder thinking about social policy in a global context, in terms of colonial legacies (Mkandawire, 2011), the gendered structure of 'the social' (Razavi and Hassim, 2006), the fundamental importance of the family as an institution, alongside state and market (UN Women, 2020) and ecosocial policy perspectives (Fitzpatrick, 2001; and Chapter 6 in this volume).

The social question, increasingly framed as the 'global' or 'transnational' social question, brings new but familiar challenges; while continuous struggle shapes and defines social policy, ideas about social investment

(Chapter 4 in this volume) and inclusive growth (Chapter 13), social sustainability (Chapters 5 and 6), social cohesion (Chapter 11) and social justice (Chapter 12), as well as ideas about welfare within and beyond the state (Chapters 7–10 and 14). Taken together, the global policy response to date has largely been about maintaining GDP growth and promoting productivism, jobs, production, consumption, as we heard in earlier chapters (Chapters 5, 6, 13). Capitalist societies are configured to be pro-productive; there is an electoral politics to growth, as Peter Hall (2020) observes. Governments are encouraged to implement more assertive growth policies in order to secure legitimacy and satisfy voter demands for rising living standards. Today's call for sustained high growth continues long-established traditions for organizing economy and society along productivist lines (Commission on Growth and Development, 2008).[3] The latest slogan, 'inclusive growth that benefits all and to which everyone contributes', signals the intensification of paid work (employment) as the route to inclusion and social cohesion but raises many issues, as we heard in Chapter 11.

Strategies for sustaining work and welfare in the 21st century

In summary, there are a number of broadly competing visions for sustaining work and welfare in the 21st century (Box 15.1). Those advocating the right to work, 'full employment' (Schmid, 2008), 'job guarantees' (Murray and Forstater, 2014; 2018) and 'employment insurance' (Schmid, 2015), maintain there are strong ethical arguments that underline the capability to earn one's own living, a basic fundament of human dignity embodied in many constitutions and international conventions (Schmid, 2018). The 1944 ILO Declaration of Philadelphia, for example, affirms a commitment to 'full employment'; the 2008 Declaration on Social Justice for a Fair Globalization speaks of 'decent work for all'; while Article 23 of the Universal Declaration of Human Rights (UDHR) states: 'Everyone has the right to work, to free choice of employment, to just and favourable conditions of work and to protection against unemployment.'

Box 15.1: Strategies for sustaining work and welfare in the 21st century

• **Full employment policy**: policies for 'full employment' and the 'right to work' can take many forms, including public job guarantees, employment guarantee programmes and employment insurance, but essentially the call is for full participation in the labour market, it is about valuing decent work and promoting economic inclusion. Increasingly known as 'inclusive growth', the policy goal to maintain the economy at as close to full employment as possible, this promotes the principle of inclusion, it enhances labour productivity and innovation, generates economic wealth and growth and raises living standards in society.

- **Universal Basic Income (UBI)**: again many different UBI schemes have been proposed, but essentially a basic income is a tax-financed minimum income guarantee granted to all members of a society on an individual basis, unconditionally, as a right without means test or work.

- **Participation income (PI)**: the idea of a participation income is to reward those who make a social contribution to society; as such it is designed to complement existing social protection systems rather than replace them. Compared to UBI, granted unconditionally, the basic income payment here is conditional on participation. As a consequence, participation income draws attention to the various forms of social participation and the different ways in which people contribute to society, which could include, say, education or training, caring roles or undertaking approved forms of voluntary work and other socially valuable activities.

- **Universal Basic Services (UBS)**: the call for UBS is essentially a call for the extension of the welfare state; an encompassing and reformed collective public provisioning system would serve and promote shared human needs. In other words, the state would have a key role in ensuring universal services that are essential and sufficient to enable people to meet their needs basic goods and public services are provided and delivered, in order to address shared human needs in society and the sustainability challenge now facing humanity.

Full employment is seen as the best way to secure redistribution and growth, now termed 'inclusive growth', and can address global poverty and inequality, Target 1.B of the MDGs became Target 8.5 of the SDGs, for example: 'achieve full and productive employment and decent work for all'. Prospects for global employment have been good in recent years, according to the World Development Reports (WDR) focused on 'jobs', and certainly better than many critics would claim, at least prior to the arrival of COVID-19 (World Bank, 2011, 2012, 2019). Active social policy programmes of various kinds have been expanded across the globe in order to promote productive employment and inclusive growth policies (Bonoli, 2018). Social investment and human capital accumulation policy is about equipping workers with the skills needed in the global economy, as we heard in Chapter 4, helping them to manage work transitions and insecurity in the era of labour flexibility. These then are the key defining features of the labourist policy model advocating notions of employment security and the right to work, based on employment entitlements and job guarantees. India, for example, has long been a leader in the implementation of employment guarantee programmes, from the 1970s (Drèze and Sen, 2013). The Mahatma Gandhi National Rural Employment Guarantee Act (MGNREGA) in India is the world's largest public works programme, introduced in 2006, it provides 50 million jobs in rural areas, guaranteeing up to 100 days' work for those in need of social support (Basole, 2019). Ultimately, people have to be protected, not jobs as Schmid (2018) argues. Forms of reduced working times, short-time work, part-time work and job-sharing can help to address decent work deficits in non-standard employment around the world (ILO, 2016, 2019). A shorter working week, for example adopting a four-day rather than a five-day week, as the default model for employment could expand opportunities and limit inequalities, it would help to improve work-life balance and foster sustainability (Coote and Franklin, 2013; Coote et al, 2021). ('Everyone has the right to rest and leisure, including reasonable limitation of working hours and periodic holidays with pay', Article 24 of the UDHR, Box 1.2).

More work, more production and more consumption, and more GDP growth, present challenges in the age of social sustainability, however, as we have heard in earlier chapters. Sustainability beyond growth is now being discussed much more in global policy debates. There is likely to be a need for the Global North to consume less. In this age 'post-productivist' calls for 'welfare without work' are also growing (for example, Van Parijs and Vanderborght, 2015; Downes and Lansley, 2018). Advocates of Universal Basic Income (UBI) are sceptical of the labourist strategy (largely based on the ideals of the Nordic social model belonging to the 20th century), which calls for the intensification of work, not least because the world of work itself is fundamentally changing (see Standing, 1999, and 2009). Importantly, the World Bank (2019) is now calling for a new social contract with the changing nature of work, centred on larger investments in human capital and universal, guaranteed minimum levels of social protection and UBI. The coming of the 'gig' economy brings new challenges; the lack of decent jobs and decent incomes makes the case for UBI more appealing according to proponents (Standing, 2020). Basic income or UBI is a call for security beyond the workplace. Arguably, UBI requires a different attitude towards work and welfare for the 21st century; and while interest in UBI continues to grow, no country has officially adopted UBI in governmental policy (see Standing, 2017; and the major new report by the World Bank considering the feasibility of UBI, Ugo et al, 2020). However desirable, then, or necessary the ecosocial and post-productive economy may be, there appear to be many (insurmountable) obstacles at present that will need to be overcome, as Tony Fitzpatrick concedes. Fortunately, there may be more common ground between pro-productivists and post-productivists than is often thought, offering hope for the future (Chapter 6 in this volume).

Participation income may occupy the middle ground here, since the idea of a PI is to reward those who make a social contribution to society; as such it is designed to complement existing social protection systems rather than offer a replacement to them (Atkinson, 1996, 2015). For Ruth Lister (2018), UBI does not necessarily value or reward caring roles or domestic work in the home. In other words, Lister appears to be making a distinction, suggesting that those who participate in socially valuable activities, who add social value, should be rewarded over and above those who do not make a socially valuable contribution. Indeed, Tony Atkinson was motivated by his opposition to the so-called 'free-riding' problem when everyone in society stands to benefit from UBI. There may be social justice in fair conditionality, as David Piachaud (2018) suggests.

The call for Universal Basic Services (UBS) is essentially a call for the extension of the welfare state, an encompassing and reformed public provisioning system that would serve to promote shared human needs. In other words, the state would have a key role in ensuring UBS, that basic goods and public services (illustrated in Table 15.1) are provided and delivered, in order to address shared human needs in society and the sustainability challenges now facing humanity (Floud et al, 2018; Gough, 2019; Coote and Percy, 2020). Proponents of UBS, however, claim this sort of collective action is now needed on a global scale if we are to address shared human needs in an equitable fashion, build social resilience and meet the sustainability challenges facing humanity now and in the future (see Brundtland Commission, Chapter 5).

Reconciling these different visions for sustainability in the 21st century is certainly challenging. Many conclude that full employment policy and UBI cannot easily coexist, and clearly UBS provides an alternative to UBI by extending the delivery of direct provisioning services to satisfy human needs. If all services are distributed through the public sphere, including adequate food supplies, then presumably there is little need or room left for a basic income approach to sustain livelihoods in a market economy, as the argument implies. Ultimately, then, there could be a contradiction between UBS and UBI, at least in theory as illustrated in Table 15.1, but real world political compromises may be found in practical policies, between universal healthcare and universal incomes for example. UBS is a radical all-encompassing welfare statist approach in the pursuit of equality and sustainability, while UBI is more in tune with market ideology; at least proponents are not seeking to replace market exchange altogether: 'liberty, equality, ecology' are the core founding principles (Van Parijs, 1992).

Those that stand firmly in favour of the right to work dismiss UBI as an unrealistic and disruptive utopia. Those that are advocating UBI defend the right *not* to work; some jobs are exploitative and demeaning. In part, this is why proponents of UBI object to active labour market policies and workfare programmes. Still others claim public job guarantees and basic income might coexist, but if basic income is not universal then it must by its very nature be a form of targeted welfare assistance, which of course is dismissed by advocates of UBI. Perhaps PI sits somewhere in between. It is conceptually different from 'workfare', although what makes for a good or useful contribution to society is not without controversy. Any formalised list of contributions based on notions of fundamental human rights, opportunities and capabilities, would almost certainly benefit from public deliberation and territorial confinement, necessary to achieve acceptability in democratic societies, as Sen (2004, 2005) observes. For many advocates of UBI, then, PI would inevitably lead to UBI anyway, since firm distinctions over the usefulness of a contribution are hard to maintain across time and place.

Proponents of UBI do not accept that UBS is a better or preferable alternative to UBI either. Wanting more and better public services is not the issue, however an all-encompassing provision system like that found in Table 15.1 is simply not feasible or desirable they claim. The idea of UBS seems far too paternalistic, undermining basic freedoms and liberties. Yet the advocates of UBI are themselves grappling with complex issues: how to ensure that any income is decent, meaningful and socially acceptable for example (Torry, 2020). For advocates of UBS, this is the only sure way to secure humanity's growing needs and ensure sustainable consumption and production patterns for the future. Clearly, however, there are issues to do with the word 'universal' in these lively debates, because in practice some people are unlikely to be entitled to UBI or UBS, non-resident citizens perhaps. Territorial confinement is likely to be important for both.

Putting 'the social' into the international

A basic determinant of the world's ability to address the pressing global challenges, achieve the SDGs, ensure the struggle for human rights and freedoms (embedded in the UDHR), will largely depend on how global social policies are formulated and the quality of governance at all levels, as we heard in previous chapters. Present strategies for tackling global social problems such as the plight of refugees and the climate emergency, global poverty and extreme social inequality, ending racial discrimination and protecting human rights are severely challenged, often proving inadequate and ineffective (Pogge, 2008; Stiglitz, 2010; Bourguignon, [2012] 2015; Jackson, 2017; Betts and Collier, 2017, 2018). Understanding how the world is governed is one thing, arguments over how it *ought* to be governed are another. Whether the current multilateral state system provides effective global governance is debatable – while the notion of 'global governance' is not unproblematic itself as we heard in Chapter 13.

Global climate change represents a significant challenge to global social governance (Gough, 2014). Climate policy should respect the human rights of all, both now and in the future, but the global response and climate policy for the world is heavily contested. The Kyoto Protocol, adopted in 1997, provided for emissions reductions by developed countries but not developing ones, even if developing countries have benefited from that economic activity (UN, 1998). Many developed countries did not accept responsibility for past emissions, although present generations have benefited from past emissions associated with economic activity and low- and middle-income countries suffer the burden of environmental harm (Heymann and Barrera, 2014; Oxfam, 2015).[4] The Kyoto Protocol assumed that obligations start now. The 2015 Paris Agreement charted a new course in the global struggle; both developed and developing countries are supposed to now curb emissions, according to national plans and circumstances (UN, 2015a). Many challenges remain. Not only did the US Congress fail to ratify the Kyoto Protocol, but on 4 November 2020 the US became the first nation in the world to formally withdraw from the Paris climate agreement. Donald Trump's withdrawal of the US from the World Health Organization (WHO) threatened US and global health. While claiming to act 'in the national interest', Trump also signed an executive order, titled 'Protecting the Nation', halting refugee admissions and banned people from some Muslim-majority and African countries from entering the USA (Executive Order 13769),[5] these actions gained traction with the resurgence of populism (Chapter 9 in this volume). In 17 executive orders and memorandums, the new Biden administration has moved swiftly to dismantle Trump administration policies, rejoining the WHO, and the Paris climate accord and rescinding Trump's travel bans.

Clearly, however, global institutions are not sufficiently strong or mandated to ensure all countries uphold human rights, including women's rights, child rights, disability rights, indigenous rights and the rights of migrants and refugees and displaced persons to safe asylum (Mertus, 2009; Betts and Collier, 2017, 2018). The UN proclaims human rights but struggles to implement them (UDHR is only a declaration). While it campaigns for their realization around the world, the implementation of the international human rights regime is relatively weak, and in some instances some countries and governments have hitherto been reluctant to concede them (Freeman, 2017). Violations are experienced locally, and unfortunately there are at present many limitations to the domestic implementation of human rights policies; shortcomings and failings are evident at all levels, in the global institutions and the systems for monitoring and enforcement. The lack of respect for human rights often stems from the principles and practices of territorial state sovereignty on the one hand, citizenship regimes (relating to social and economic rights and institutions) shaped by politics and ideology, and, on the other hand, weaknesses in the international human rights regime, consisting of rules and institutions at the global level (Jenson and Levi, 2013).

Government gains legitimacy from respecting the human rights of its citizens, yet avoidable human rights violations are often the direct result of governmental policies. Established human rights should be (legally) enforceable within states but often they are not. They are often social constructions; determination and implementation is a continuing social process, influenced by political factors and the resources of the state, and there is much uncertainty on the conditions under which states have the power, right or duty to intervene in human rights violations. The principle and practice of state sovereignty is therefore a major impediment to the implementation of human rights standards. Often social reforms that violate or challenge human rights are pursued over long periods of time, as in the UK context, undoing or severely eroding the social foundations of welfare capitalism (the damning indictment of British welfare policies by the United Nations (UN) Special Rapporteur on Extreme Poverty and Human Rights leaves little room for doubt: UNHRC, 2019). At the global level, the right to live free from gender-based violence remains a major challenge (UNHRC, 2009, 2018; Human Rights Watch, 2020).[6] The timeless vision of the UNCRC has yet to be realized thirty years on. UNICEF (2019a) is now calling on all UN member states to refresh their commitments to implement the United Nations Convention on the Rights of the Child, or UNCRC. Human rights entail that climate change policy respects the human rights of all, including the human rights of future generations, yet the Intergovernmental Panel on Climate Change (IPCC) negotiations have largely ignored human rights issues (Caney, 2005, 2006). No global institutional order could prevent all human rights violations, but many could be avoided if the global order was made more sustainable and just.

Globalization has sharpened the need for effective international cooperation in the pursuit of global social justice, global social governance and collective action. Much more can and should be done to strengthen global and regional partnerships and social governance arrangements in order to promote social sustainability. This is widely recognized and is reflected in the 2030 Agenda itself, particularly in Goal 17 of the SDGs for example. The message is, global partnerships need to be strengthened in order to meet the SDGs and the ambitious global targets:

> Goal 17 IN ACTION: A successful sustainable development agenda requires partnerships between governments, the private sector and civil society. These inclusive partnerships built upon principles and values, a shared vision, and shared goals that place people and the planet at the centre, are needed at the global, regional, national and local level. To strengthen worldwide partnerships, we all have to take action.[7]

There are signs and indications, presented in earlier chapters, that international institutions, regional offices and social agencies are working more collaboratively to strengthen global social policy and sustainability frameworks in an effort to achieve the UN's SDGs. This does not mean contestation and struggle between global social policy actors and their ideas has is a thing of the past. Divisions and longstanding disagreements continue to hinder social progress, as we heard in Chapter 14. Old ideological divides are still apparent in global social policy debates; the struggle to embed the social in the international market economy has long been an ideological tug-of-war, increasingly waged in a global context where social struggle takes place (Chapter 8). Until relatively recently, powerful international organizations such as the World Bank (1994, 1996), the IMF (1993) and the OECD (1994a, 1994b, 1998a) had all advocated residual social policy perspectives in a series of high-profile reports in order to promote free-market and pro-growth solutions to social problems and issues. Envisaging the minimal role of the (welfare) state, they advocated minimum 'safety nets' and user fees in their desire to promote markets in healthcare, social services, education and pensions and market-based labour market policies (McBride and Williams, 2001; Orenstein, 2008; Park and Vetterlein, 2010; Boughton, 2012; Labonté and Ruckert, 2019).

By contrast, the international institutions and agencies in the UN system have long promoted a human rights-based policy agenda (Cornia et al, 1987; Jolly, 1991; Murphy, 2006). From this perspective, the institutions and agencies of the UN have tended to advocate universalism in health and social protection systems to safeguard human rights (Jolly et al, 2009), including children's rights (Jolly, 2014). Fundamental human rights principles should be universally protected (UDHR, see Box 1.2); these principles and declarations are deeply embedded in the constitutions and mandates of the UN bodies involved in human rights promotion and protection. Human rights principles are thus embodied in the sorts of universalist social policies being advocated by the likes of the UNDP, the United Nations Development Programme (see UNDP, 2014, 2019), UNICEF, the United Nations Children's Fund (see Blank and Handa, 2008; UNICEF, 2017, 2019b), the International Labour Organization (for example, ILO, 2004, 2019) and the World Health Organization (for instance, WHO, 2000, 2007). Can past privatizations of (social) policy be reversed, however, in favour of strengthening universalism and the social foundations of development and global social policy more generally, and if so, how, and to what extent? Such thorny questions are once again at the heart of heated global social policy debates (see Townsend, 2004; Deacon, 2005; Deacon and Macovei, 2010; for key debates over universal social provisions in health and social services see Koivusalo and Ollila, 1998; and Kaasch, 2015; on pensions see Orenstein, 2005, 2008, 2011, 2013; and Ortiz et al, 2018; on changing labour relations see Standing, 2008; and Kott and Droux, 2013).

In addition, there are important differences between the international institutions and the sorts of actions and types of policy instruments that they advocate and pursue in order to achieve the global goals and targets agreed by world leaders. The World Bank and the IMF have long been leading advocates of conditional cash transfers (CCTs) for development (World Bank, 2001; Grosh et al, 2008; Lange et al, 2018). They claim them to be 'pro-poor', and the evidence, according to the World Bank researchers, shows that CCTs promote human capital formation and generally help to reduce national poverty levels overall (Fiszbein et al, 2009; World Bank, 2015a, 2018a). For the World Bank and the IMF, then, these policy instruments help to promote effective global action, necessary for meeting global goals and targets like the SDGs (World Bank, 2015b, 2018b). The international financial institutions hold huge sway over domestic and donor policy agendas, as Hall (2015) and Leisering (2019) suggests. Globally, the spread of CCTs across world regions and developing countries has increased dramatically over the past two decades; hundreds of millions of people are now beneficiaries.[8] The level of World Bank and IMF loans linked to CCTs now comprises a significant share of social protection spending in low-income countries, accounting for about 10 per cent of total lending by both institutions in 2017.

The international institutions in the UN system offer a different perspective, in that they do not actively advocate or promote 'conditionality'. Instead, the ILO and the WHO, UNICEF and other UN bodies are strong advocates of universalism and a rights-based global social policy approach, supported by an architecture of international human rights treaties and protocols (the right to social security, the right to work, the right to asylum, the right to equality before the law, the right to an adequate standard of living, and so on, Box 1.2 and 1.3). These rights apply in all circumstances. State parties

---

Box 15.2: The Social Protection Floor (SPF) recommendation

ILO Recommendation No. 202, adopted on 14 June 2012, provides guidance to UN member states on how to extend and adapt SPFs to national circumstances. The recommendations states that national social protection floors should include at least four essential guarantees:

1. Access to essential healthcare, including maternity care.
2. Basic income security for children, providing access to nutrition, education, care and any other necessary goods and services.
3. Basic income security for persons in active age who are unable to earn sufficient income, in particular in cases of sickness, unemployment, maternity and disability.
4. Basic income security for older persons.

Such guarantees should be provided to all residents and all children, as defined in national laws and regulations, and subject to existing international obligations.

Source: Adapted from OHCHR (2015: 2).
(Reproduced with the permission of the United Nations.)

---

must recognize and guarantee them; they should ensure that human rights are fully realized. The ILO, the WHO, UNICEF and other UN bodies like the UNDP have long been at the forefront of the global campaign for publicly funded rights-based social protection systems (see UNDP, 2000, 2006; ILO/WHO, 2011; UNICEF, 2016, 2019b; ILO, 2017; also Jolly, 2014: ch 6, for a discussion of the human rights approach to child wellbeing and human development at UNICEF). The Social Protection Floor (SPF) initiative for example, driven by the ILO and a coalition of UN agencies (ILO/WHO, 2011), is promoting government-funded minimum (or first level) essential security guarantees in an effort to strengthen social protection systems globally. The aim is to put a social floor under the global economy, focusing on access to essential healthcare and basic income security over the life cycle (the recommendations can be seen in Box 15.2). According to Bob Deacon (2013), the SPF initiative became a rallying point for the struggle for global social policy synergy in the 2000s; that is, for the struggle to try to ensure that all UN agencies, along with the World Bank and the IMF, lined up behind the strategy in order to tackle the shortcomings of market-driven globalization.

While there may be growing synergy in global social policy, important differences remain. Many UN bodies like UNICEF are the leading advocates of Unconditional Cash Transfers (UCTs) in global social policy, maintaining that the evidence on the *added value* of conditions is inconclusive. It is certainly true that rigorous evaluations show the benefits of both CCTs and UCTs, but conditionality is found to limit coverage. To date, there have been few studies directly comparing the benefits of UCTs versus CCTs, and there is much uncertainty in terms of their effects and health and social outcomes (Pega et al, 2017). CCTs and behavioural economics represent the experimental approach to development, and the assessment of social impact according the Nobel Laureates, Abhijit Banerjee and Esther Duflo (2011). Still others point to more practical issues inherent in experimental approaches to social policy and development, associated with the design of randomized controlled trials (RCTs) themselves, for example, Angus Deaton (2010), another Nobel Laureate. In addition, there are strong ethical objections to CCTs and RCTs; involving human subjects in quasi-scientific experiments, the programmes are divisive and many regard them as 'unjust' and 'asocial' (Cookson, 2018; and reviews, Deeming, 2013a, 2017).

Advocates of unconditional transfers, that is UCTs and UBI, claim the moral high ground from a human rights perspective. As Davala and colleagues (2015: 69–70) observe, 'basic income's emancipatory value exceeds the monetary value'. Based on pilot work evaluations in India funded by UNICEF, the researchers show the UCTs are transformative, with clear improvements in individual and family welfare, with reductions in poverty and economic insecurity, and less exposure to lenders, loans and the debt trap. In practice, CCTs curtail human rights, it is claimed. In fact, a right must be unconditional to be a right, as Guy Standing (2011) observes. Everyone has the 'right to have rights' as Hannah Arendt (1951) so eloquently argues (see Somers, 2008), either expressed through the social state (based on citizenship) or through the existence of humanity, the *pre*-social universal human rights possessed by all humans, proclaimed in the UDHR.

The case in favour of 'universalism', 'unconditionality' and rights-based international social policy is certainly growing; meanwhile the use of CCTs continues to spread around the globe, meaning fierce debates are unlikely to subside anytime soon. There are some signs that the policy approach at the World Bank may be shifting. In 2015 for the first time the Bank explicitly endorsed universal social protection as a primary development priority, with the launch of its global partnership with the ILO. For the 2019 WDR, the Bank also gave a commitment to working more collaboratively with government to enhance social protection systems and extend social protection to all, irrespective of the terms on which they work, even if that now means increasing the role and size of government and the tax base, as it inevitably does in many national and regional contexts (World Bank, 2019). These initiatives may help to strengthen partnerships between institutions in the global social policy arena, but to what extent are the different positions reconcilable? The Bank and IMF still appear to favour CCTs and often attach stringent conditions to their development loans, while UN institutions continue to advance universalism and the human rights-based policy paradigm. Many argue that the major institutions of global governance like the World Bank and IMF should now be democratized in order to allow Global South countries (the world's majority) to have a fair and equal representation in these institutions and a say in the formulation of policies that affect them (Townsend, 2004; Stone and Wright, 2007; Weaver, 2008; Momani, 2010; Hickel, 2017). The Western-dominated governance structures at the center of global governance architecture are not only failing to address power and structural imbalances, but they need to be redesigned in order to address issues of poverty and inequality more effectively.

In global society, however, we find the fragility of the social, with increasing global migration, generational and intersectionality struggles and conflicts, amid multiple crises, as we saw in earlier chapters. The

---

Box 15.3: Commission on Social Determinants of Health: recommendations

Health equity through action on the social determinants of health. The Commission's overarching recommendations:

1. Improve daily living conditions

Improve the wellbeing of girls and women and the circumstances in which their children are born; put major emphasis on early child development and education for girls and boys; improve living and working conditions and create social protection policy supportive of all; and create conditions for a flourishing older life. Policies to achieve these goals will involve civil society, governments and global institutions.

2. Tackle the inequitable distribution of power, money and resources

In order to address health inequities, and inequitable conditions of daily living, it is necessary to address inequities, such as those between men and women, in the way society is organized. This requires a strong public sector that is committed, capable and adequately financed. To achieve that requires more than strengthened government; it requires strengthened governance: legitimacy, space and support for civil society, for an accountable private sector, and for people across society to agree public interests and reinvest in the value of collective action. In a globalized world, the need for governance dedicated to equity applies equally from the community level to global institutions.

3. Measure and understand the problem and assess the impact of action

Acknowledging that there is a problem, and ensuring that health inequity is measured, within countries and globally, is a vital platform for action. National governments and international organizations, supported by WHO, should set up national and global health equity surveillance systems for routine monitoring of health inequity and the social determinants of health and should evaluate the health equity impact of policy and action. Creating the organizational space and capacity to act effectively on health inequity requires investment in training of policy makers and health practitioners and public understanding of social determinants of health. It also requires a stronger focus on social determinants in public health research.

Source: Adapted from CSDH (2008: 2).
(Reproduced with permission of the copyright owner.)

Box 15.4: Commission on Social Determinants of Health: action

Health equity through action on the social determinants of health. Three principles of action:

1. Improve the conditions of daily life: the circumstances in which people are born, grow, live, work and age.
2. Tackle the inequitable distribution of power, money and resources: the structural drivers of those conditions of daily life, globally, nationally and locally.
3. Measure the problem, evaluate action, expand the knowledge base, develop a workforce that is trained in the social determinants of health and raise public awareness about the social determinants of health.

Source: Adapted from CSDH (2008: 2).
(Reproduced with permission of the copyright owner.)

---

calls for more transformative collective action are growing and the struggles are becoming more evident on a global scale, long before the 2020 pandemic swept the world.

Action: sustaining the social

In the present climate, it is increasingly accepted that strong social protection floors and universal health and social services offer the best way to promote human flourishing and social sustainability, as recommended by the WHO global Commission on Social Determinants of Health (CSDH, 2008, representing a global network of policy makers, researchers and civil society organizations). Strong (universal) public health and social protection systems are also found to cope better in crises and emergencies: protecting health, reducing human suffering, stabilizing economy and society (Stuckler et al, 2009; Starke et al, 2013; Deeming, 2020). Social justice is a matter of life and death, as the WHO Global Commission observes. In its Final Report, it provides a large number of policy-related recommendations, and actions designed to promote health equity, improve daily living conditions and reduce inequalities (summarized in Box 15.3 and 15.4). The need to focus on the social determinants of health and the need to strengthen social governance at all levels, from the community level to global institutions, are among the key messages in the boxes.

First and foremost, the human right to health and social security is far from a reality for the majority of the world's population. The expansion of social protection coverage has stalled worldwide, and in many parts of the world many people lack even the most basic health and social security rights. The majority of developing countries are unlikely to achieve their targets for universal health coverage (UHC) and the health- and poverty-related SDGs shown in Box 1.1 (Goal 3 includes Target 3.8: 'Achieve universal health coverage' by 2030). Current estimates from the ILO suggest only 45 per cent of the global population are effectively covered by at least one social protection benefit, while the remaining 55 per cent, some 4 billion people, have limited or no social protection according to the ILO flagship report World Social Protection Report (WSPR) ((ILO, 2017).[9] Coverage gaps are particularly evident in Africa, Asia and the Arab States, where there is significant underinvestment in social protection. At the same time, half of the world's population do not have access to the healthcare they need, according to the World Health Organization (WHO, 2019).[10] Urgent action is required to strengthen health and social protection systems in many parts of the world, particularly in developing countries. The case for long-term sustainable public financing has been growing; however, prospects for increased state investment in health and social protection systems are now diminishing in many countries, as COVID-19 is inflicting the deepest global recession in decades on a global economy that was already suffering since the global financial crises, the poorest and most vulnerable populations are always hardest hit (UNIATF, 2019; WBG, 2019; World Bank, 2020, 2021).

In global social policy terms, the experience with the eight international development goals, the MDGs (Box 1.1), was positive and is certainly encouraging (UN, 2015b), offering hope for a global multilateral response and a sustainable recovery from the pandemic (UNCTAD, 2020a, 2020b, 2020c). Shared goals agreed by world leaders are shown to be critical for global mobilization; in order to help beat COVID-19 and accelerate action on the SDGs, a vaccine should be considered a global public good, another common goal according to the UN (Sachs, 2015; Browne, 2017; Polonenko and Besada, 2017; UNIATF, 2020).[11] However, while Agenda 2030 and the 17 SDGs represent a global social policy framework for concerted action and multilateral cooperation, it also contains many potentially diverging policy goals that challenge the social. The tensions and trade-offs are especially evident if we consider the economic, social and environmental interlinkages that may hinder social progress, as we saw in earlier chapters. The achievement of Agenda 2030 may depend on whether humankind can maximize synergies and resolve existing trade-offs, particularly balancing environmental sustainability and climate action (SDG 13) on the one hand, and economic growth and productive employment on the other (SDG 8). More jobs are said to be needed to end poverty and reduce all forms of inequality (SDGs 1, 5 and 10).[12] However, there is growing evidence of a widespread and alarming inability to overcome such trade-offs, as we saw in Chapter 5 (for more on SDG interactions, see Kroll et al, 2019).

Many claim that more transformative action is now urgently required in order to promote social sustainability, and to ensure the obligations of states are met. Values and freedoms, of the sort advocated by Martha Nussbaum (1999, 2003, shown in Box 15.5), that belong to all of us must be upheld. We must at the very least create and ensure that everyone has the opportunity and capability to live a good life in harmony with the planet, as Nussbaum argues.

Box 15.5: Martha Nussbaum on central human functional capabilities

1. **Life**: being able to live to the end of a normal human life.
2. **Bodily health**: being able to have good health.
3. **Bodily integrity**: being able to move freely from place to place and be secure against assault.
4. **Senses, imagination, and thought**: being able to use the senses, to imagine, think and reason in a way informed and cultivated by an adequate education along with freedom of political, artistic and religious expression.
5. **Emotions**: being able to have attachments to things and people, to love and to grieve and to experience and express justified anger.
6. **Practical reason**: being able to form a conception of the good and to engage in critical reflection.
7. **Affiliation**: being able to live and engage in various forms of social interaction and to be treated with respect and dignity.

8. **Other species**: being able to live with concern for animals, plants and the world of nature.
9. **Play**: being able to laugh and play and enjoy recreational activities.
10. **Control over one's environment**: being able to participate effectively in political choices with the right to freedom of opinion and the expression of free speech; having equal property and employment rights; having the freedom from unwarranted search and seizure; being able to work as a human being and entering into meaningful relationships of mutual recognition with other workers.

Source: Adapted from Warner (2014: 460–61).
(Reproduced with permission of the copyright owner.)

Box 15.6: Guy Standing's proposals for a Precariat Charter

Article 1. Redefine work as productive and reproductive activity.
Article 2. Reform labour statistics.
Article 3. Make recruitment practices brief encounters.
Article 4. Regulate flexible labour.
Article 5. Promote associational freedom.
Articles 6–10. Reconstruct occupational communities.
Articles 11–15. Stop class-based migration policy.
Article 16. Ensure due process for all.
Article 17. Remove poverty traps and precarity traps.
Article 18. Make a bonfire of benefit assessment tests.
Article 19. Stop demonizing the disabled.
Article 20. Stop workfare now!
Article 21. Regulate payday loans and student loans.
Article 22. Institute a right to financial knowledge and advice.
Article 23. Decommodify education.
Article 24. Make a bonfire of subsidies.
Article 25. Move towards a basic income.
Article 26. Share capital via sovereign wealth funds.
Article 27. Revive the commons.
Article 28. Revive deliberative democracy.
Article 29. Re-marginalize charities.

Source: Adapted from Standing (2014: 151–379).
(Reproduced with permission of the copyright owner and author.)

So how might humankind address human needs and universal human rights beyond borders, the transnational social question. There are no easy answers, no simple fixes, no one clear strategy, but the need to develop international human rights and social welfare systems beyond the state seems to be growing. However, while calls for an international welfare state (see Townsend and Donkor, 1996; Townsend, 2002) appear to have largely gone unanswered, the case for strengthening social governance and social protection on a global scale is now overwhelming. Guy Standing (2014), for example, has been calling for a new global Charter of Rights (Box 15.6), enshrining social security beyond the (welfare) state in the face of growing pressures from global market capitalism. All citizens have a right to socially inherited wealth, 'the commons', he claims, to promote freedom, fraternity and equality (Standing, 2014, 2019). Standing advocates building up a 'Commons Fund' from levies on the (commercial) use of the commons, that is our public wealth that creates private wealth, in order to ensure the payment of 'Commons Dividends' to all. At the global level, the philosopher Thomas Pogge proposes a 'Global Resources Dividend' (the GRD) in order to tackle global poverty, with echoes of the original 'Tobin tax' idea put forward by Nobel prize-winning American economist James Tobin in 1972; Tobin suggested a tax on foreign currency exchanges to raise funds to be used as aid for developing countries (Pogge, 2008). Globally, the top 1 per cent of earners have captured twice as much of global income growth since the 1980s as the bottom 50 per cent of the poorest individuals (Alvaredo et al, 2017). Oxfam also recently reported that the richest 1 per cent now have more wealth than the rest of the world combined (Hardoon et al, 2016).

Tony Atkinson (2015) and Thomas Piketty (2014, 2020) have also put forward concrete proposals for tackling high levels of inequality. Atkinson and Piketty both recommend ambitious new policies and proposals to reorganize the global economy and help transform the inequality regimes of the 20th century. Atkinson's detailed proposals are reproduced in Appendix 15.1, Piketty's are summarized in chapter 17 of *Capital and Ideology*. Both recommend more progressive taxation on income and wealth and greater redistribution to reduce inequality between rich and poor in society. Atkinson, like François Bourguignon ([2012] 2015: ch 5), also recommends more development aid to reduce inequality between rich and poor countries (development aid is the only true instrument of international redistribution). There is also the struggle of citizens against tax avoidance and tax evasion, and the increasing amount of the world's money held in tax havens, which requires better and more coordinated global action. Financial systems and financial registers need to be overhauled, taxing across borders and at source would help, along with well-enforced and comprehensive wealth taxes that can act against the rise of inequality (Zucman, 2015; Pogge and Mehta, 2016). Atkinson and Piketty both also recommend universal capital endowments for young adults, so that they can study, for example. There are key differences, however, Atkinson favours minimum wage guarantees by the state (#3) and a participation income (#13). While Piketty supports 'universal basic incomes', minimum guaranteed income systems should become more automatic and universal, he argues, to help homeless people for example, along with 'activity bonuses' and in-work supplements for low-waged workers. Piketty is also in favour of transcending private ownership in favour of what he calls 'participatory socialism' (social ownership), involving workers and unions in corporate governance (drawing inspiration from social democratic thought, and the Nordic and Rhine models of coordinated capitalism).

Table 15.1: Ian Gough on Universal Basic Services, linking needs and provisioning systems

Universal needs	Contemporary need satisfiers	Provisioning systems
Nutrition	Adequate nutritious diets; food security	Agriculture, food processing and food retailing systems: 'from field to fork'
Shelter	Adequate, secure, affordable housing	Housing: land, building, owning, letting
	Energy	Utilities
	Water and sanitation	Utilities
Social participation: Education/ information Communication	Schooling and adult education	Education and training systems
	Phone, computer and internet connection	Telecommunications
	Access to effective and healthy means of transport	Road, rail, infrastructure Public transport services
Health: prevention, cure, care	Public health Medical services Social care	Public health services National health services Social care services
Physical security	Emergency services	Emergency services
Income security	Employment	Decent, secure job
	Income maintenance	Social security; private insurance
	Money/payment systems	Retail banking

Source: Gough (2019: 537).

(Reproduced with permission of the copyright owner and author.)

By contrast, there are also more transformative agendas to promote sustainability that are attracting interest given the nature and severity of the global social crises: anti-neoliberal (Smith and Max-Neef, 2011) and anti- or post-capitalist (Harvey, 2014). Philip Smith and Manfred Max-Neef propose that change has to start with the 'non-toxic' teaching of economics within university education systems, the place where dominant neoliberal ideology is reproduced. Similarly, David Harvey has long been a leading critic of contemporary capitalist society and a campaigner for anti-capitalist change. An open global assembly is needed, he claims in *Seventeen Contradictions and the End of Capitalism*, to take incisive action and chart a post-capitalist future (Harvey, 2014). Here Harvey sketches out an agenda for a post-capitalist future, with capitalism plunging deeper into crisis, proposing 17 strategies for a political praxis for a post-capitalist future (Appendix 15.2). In so doing, Harvey is provoking further deliberation and discussion, inviting us to consider the possibilities and alternatives for a post-capitalist future, ultimately he is an advocate for wholesale transformative action. His call for the direct provision of adequate 'use values' (#1) or UBS is nothing new in socialist thought: under socialism, production and provision would be regulated to ensure needs are satisfied.[13] In the growing struggle for sustainability the case for UBS becomes more compelling, as we heard (UBS exemplified in Table 15.1).

At the same time, small actions can create transformative social change. The International Panel on Social Progress (IPSP, 2018), chaired by Amartya Sen, emphasizes the importance of transformative local actions (see Box 15.7 and Box 15.8). The slogan 'think global, act local' encourages local initiatives for social and environmental sustainability. If we all take the sorts of steps described by Marc Fleurbaey and colleagues in Box 15.7 then we can all play a vital role in securing change and social sustainability (Fleurbaey et al, 2018). The social institution of the family can engender major change, and can advance important aspects of social justice; 'bring change through your family' is the first recommendation in Box 15.7. If families are places of equality and justice, then economies and societies thrive, as UN Women's (2020) flagship report *Progress of the World's Women* (PWW) shows. The Equality Trust, founded in the UK in 2009, also advises on the sorts of things we can all do to help tackle inequality (Box 15.8).

Box 15.7: Marc Fleurbaey and colleagues with five ideas that can change your life, and the world

1. **Bring change through your family**: the family shapes the deepest social injustices, in terms of the education of girls, the health of women and task

sharing. Family members should be open minded and respectful of difference, sexual orientation, gender identity, romantic relations across religions or races.

2. **Bring change through your work**: work also shapes the deepest social injustices, especially with the downward trend in unionization; a just workplace would treat everyone as a partner, as a contributor to the collective venture.

3. **Bring change through your consumption and savings choices**: you can also change workplaces in your consumer decisions; consume products that have been made in good conditions, this makes you a contributor to the general good and incentivizes companies and firms to improve their social and environmental performance. Information tools will expand and improve.

4. **Bring change through your community**: the 'think global, act local' slogan remains valid; community life can be improved, neighbourhoods can be revitalized. Participating in local clubs, groups and associations contributes to maintaining community life and cohesion, for example, but also local decisions and planning to shape neighbourhood life and facilities.

5. **Be a torchbearer**: by choosing the type and contents of education and news for oneself and one's children, education and qualifications but also education for civic and cultural competence that responsible citizens need in order to be able to understand how the world is going and where the common good lies. Be an active citizen, be open and adaptive.

Source: Adapted from Fleurbaey et al (2018: 201–10).

Box 15.8: The Equality Trust on ten things you can do to tackle inequality

We can all do our bit to help reduce inequality. Here are TEN actions you can take:

1. **As a voter**: vote for parties that pledge to tackle inequality. Read their manifestos and choose the party that you think has the best policies to reduce inequality.

2. **As a citizen**: hold your elected representatives to account: be an active citizen and challenge decisions that will worsen inequality, and lobby for changes that will improve it.

3. **As a worker**: join a trade union. Countries with large and strong trade unions have lower inequality.

4. **As an activist**: join or start a local equality group.

5. **As a consumer**: favour good businesses that pay the real Living Wage, pay their taxes and treat their workforces well – and shun those that don't wherever possible.
6. **As a saver**: move your money to ethical banks or building societies. Mutuals (owned by their customers) tend to be more egalitarian than shareholder-owned banks.
7. **As a parent**: send your children to your local state schools and always favour non-selective schools wherever possible. Educational inequality is a key driver of overall inequality.
8. **As a road-user**: if you own a car or motorbike, drive slowly (up to 20mph in the UK) in residential areas. Road safety is an inequality issue. People in poorer areas suffer road accidents more frequently.
9. **As a neighbour**: get involved in your community: meet your neighbours and set up 'Play Streets'. Inequality erodes trust and reduces social interaction but you can change this.
10. **As a taxpayer**: pay all the taxes you owe, in the spirit not just the letter of the law. Erosion of our tax base leads to less money for public services and this hits poorer people harder.

Source: The Equality Trust.[14]
(Reproduced with permission from the Equality Trust.)

Box 15.9: High-impact actions to reduce annual personal emissions

High-impact (that is, low emissions) actions with the potential to contribute to systemic change and substantially reduce annual personal emissions.

1. Having smaller families, having one fewer child on average for developed countries provides 58.6 tonnes CO_2-equivalent (tCO_2e) reductions in emission per year.
2. Living car-free means 2.4 tCO_2e saved per year.
3. Avoiding airplane travel means 1.6 tCO_2e saved per roundtrip transatlantic flight.
4. Eating a plant-based diet means 0.8 tCO_2e saved per year.
5. Purchase green energy
6. Other more moderate-impact actions include: buy energy efficient products, conserve energy, reduce food waste, eat less meat, reduce consumption, reuse, recycle and eat local.

Source: Adapted from Wynes and Nicholas (2017: 4).

Box 15.10: The Framework for Strategic Sustainable Development

In a sustainable society, nature is not subject to systematically increasing:

1. Concentrations of substances extracted from the Earth's crust, for example, heavy metals and fossil fuels.
2. Concentrations of substances produced by society, for example, plastics, dioxins, PCBs and DDT (polychlorinated biphenyls are synthetic human-made chemicals used in electrical equipment and machinery and dichloro-diphenyl-trichloroethane is an insecticide).
3. Degradation by physical means and, in that society, for example, over-harvesting forests, destroying habitat and overfishing.
4. People are not subject to conditions that systematically undermine their capacity to meet their basic human needs, for example, unsafe working conditions and not enough pay to live on.

Source: Adapted from Smith and Max-Neef (2011: 182–3).[15]

Importantly, we can influence social sustainability by our own actions, as the research by Wynes and Nicholas (2017) demonstrates (key high-impact actions are summarized in Box 15.9). Want to fight climate change? Have fewer children. It is also the case, as we heard in Chapter 7, that prospects for smaller families are much better in more equitable societies, where people tend not to have to think of having more children in future in order to help pay for their own old age. The research evidence appears incontrovertible: equality is not only better for everyone in society but for the planet as a whole, as Richard Wilkinson and Kate Pickett (2009, 2010) maintain in Chapter 14. With a shrinking world population we may well see social inequalities rapidly diminishing in the future, as Danny Dorling maintains in Chapter 7, but the urgent need for equality can't wait and neither should it.

It is true: if we want to build a better society, it is essential we all take action, and the recommendations in Boxes 15.7–15.9 provide a good place to start. The growing eco-municipality movement emerged out of grassroots struggle for sustainability in Sweden in the 1980s. Its ideas continue to spread rapidly around the globe, encouraging a vibrant civil society and infusing local politics. The movement is in favour of more respectful social relations and eco-municipalities, where members of the community actively engage and work together with local government representatives to implement local sustainable development initiatives. The four key principles that the movement draws on to define a sustainable society are shown in Box 15.10.

The number of social movements, civil society organizations and transnational advocacy networks and coalitions mobilizing for change continues to grow, after the decades lost to neoliberalism, market-fundamentalism and a world obsessed with economic growth (Castells, 2010; 2015; Tilly et al, 2019). School climate strikes soon became an environmental and social movement for change, youth climate strikes for example (Thunberg, 2019). Extinction Rebellion, the global environmental movement founded in 2018, is compelling governments to take urgent action to avoid social and ecological collapse, in the face of the unprecedented global climate emergency, while Black Lives Matter (BLM) is now a rallying cry against systematic racism across the globe (Chapters 1 and 10).[16] Other global environmental groups, international NGOs and social justice movements such as the World Wide Fund for Nature (WWF, 2020), Friends of the Earth, Amnesty International, Oxfam and Greenpeace predate the new environmentalisms and social justice movements and networks but they are constantly adapting to changing circumstances (Atkinson and Scurrah, 2009).

Academics and academic institutions and research centres can play a key role in securing change: the likes of Pierre Bourdieu, Jacques Derrida, Michel Foucault, Jürgen Habermas, Alain Touraine and Alva Myrdal at the UN Department of Social Welfare were all interventionists, strong defenders of the social and society (Sluga, 2014). Today, the Institute of Health Equity (IHE), established in 2011, led by Michael Marmot, is a world-leading academic institution mobilizing public health expertise and campaigning for fairer, healthier societies (Marmot et al, 2020). The Centre for Sustainable Development (CSD) at the Earth Institute, Columbia University is another, directed by Jeffrey Sachs (2015). CSD helps to mobilize scientific expertise to address the challenges of sustainable development; it also assembles the World Happiness Report (WHR) (see Table 15.2).[17]

Active engagement at major (global) conferences, global forums and global networks can bring about change; by bringing together representatives from global institutions and corporations, policy makers, scientists and academics, NGOs and unions, think tanks and civil society, as we heard in Chapter 13. Drawing inspiration from South Africa's anti-apartheid struggle, the United Nations World Conference Against Racism, Racial Discrimination, Xenophobia and Related Intolerance (WCAR) was held in Durban in September 2001. Some 10,000 delegates from around the world, women in the majority, brought multi-issue frameworks, learning about each other's political struggles. It was here intersectionality (Chapter 10) gained a political platform for global social reform. More recently, the International Conference for Ecological Sustainability (ICES), held at the University of Leipzig in September 2014, brought together 3,000 delegates from around the world, academics and activists involved in ecological and social justice struggles. The conference marked a significant step forward for the international degrowth movement.[18]

Finally, new networks are being established to mobilize for change. The likes of the Basic Income Earth Network (BIEN) is a network of academics, politicians and activists campaigning for basic income. The Equality Trust, founded in the UK in 2009, is attempting to build a social movement for change, in order to tackle social inequality; while the Equality Can't Wait campaign, launched in 2012, is seeking to accelerate progress towards gender equality in the USA. In addition, the People's Health Movement (PHM) is a growing global network of grassroots activists calling on the people of the world to support all attempts to implement the right to health, under a People's Charter for Health (Labonté and Ruckert, 2019). The United Nations Sustainable Development Solutions Network (SDSN) initiative was launched in 2012 by then UN Secretary-General Ban Ki-moon in order to help localize and mobilize support for the SDGs. Today, it has 38 national and regional networks worldwide; while SDSN Youth has established 20 regional and national networks empowering young people globally, seeking sustainable solutions.[19]

Prophecy and progress in the age of sustainability development

Social progress globally has been slow, as we heard in Chapter 14. For far too long we have been governed by economic growth objectives and metrics. As Martha Nussbaum (2011) suggests, policy makers have long told us a story that has distorted the human experience; the growth model asserted that quality of life in a nation was improving when, and only when, GDP per capita (per person) was increasing.

As Dale (2017) writes, the obsession with growth became increasingly identified with social progress and the material standard of living over many centuries. After the Second World War, GDP became the monetary measure of economic growth, as the market value of all goods and services, used for calculating a country's economy. The general acceptance of 'growthism' meant preserving, maintaining and promoting the idea and policy goal of growth, in the discourses and policy advocacy work of international institutions like the OECD (Schmelzer, 2016) and at the World Bank (Allan, 2019). As well as identifying opportunities and the conditions for fostering economic growth, international organizations also mobilize against any perceived threats to growth in the global economy, as we heard in Chapter 13.[20]

GDP, however, 'measures everything in short, except that which makes life worthwhile', as Robert Kennedy observed in 1968, counting as it does car manufacturing and nuclear warheads, for example, rising with crime, pollution and catastrophes.[21] Production carries social and environmental 'costs', not just the 'benefits' counted in the GDP calculations (Fioramonti, 2013). GDP also fails to take into account other essential goods and services that have social and economic value, such as unpaid work in the home (Nussbaum, 2011). Around the world, women do the vast majority of the unpaid work, including childcare that sustains families, cooking and cleaning, and farming in many developing countries. The current patterns of family life limit women's opportunities and the economic paradigm that is meant to serve society does little to value the social.

GDP then has little relevance to moral principles such as equity, social justice and redistribution and the general quality of life. More recently, policy makers have started to consider more holistic measures of social progress, incorporating social welfare and sustainability metrics across its social, economic and environmental dimensions (Fleurbaey, 2009; Stiglitz et al, 2018a, 2018b). The problems associated with economic growth became much more visible from the 1970s onwards. Humanity was drawing on the world's resources faster than they could be restored, there are planetary and environmental boundaries to exponential growth (Meadows et al, 1972, 1992, 2004). The world now needed to face up to a sustainable future. At the same time, the idea that exponential growth in affluent economies raises happiness was also now called into question, the so-called 'Easterlin Paradox' (Easterlin, 1974); along with the 'paradox of affluence' proposed by Fred Hirsch (1977: 1–2). In the *Social Limits to Growth*, Hirsch argued that economic growth in affluent economies undermined the social foundations of society. Individual competition for consumer goods, 'status symbols' and 'positional goods', undermines collective societal goals (Chapters 7 and 8).

From the early 1970s onwards, alternative measures to GDP were also conceived, like Gross National Happiness (GNH) in Bhutan,[22] the Measure of Economic Welfare (MEW) (Nordhaus and Tobin, 1972), the Index of Sustainable Economic Welfare (ISEW) (Daly and Cobb, 1989) and the Genuine Progress Indicator (GPI) (Cobb et al, 1995; Kubiszewski

Table 15.2: Charting social progress

1934	Simon Kuznets produces a new system to measure national income, commissioned by the US government to capture productivity and help restore prosperity to Americans during the Great Depression. Increasingly GDP becomes the preferred metric for measuring the economy.
1968	Robert Kennedy's historic speech on the limitations of the GDP: 'it measures everything in short, except that which makes life worthwhile'.
1972	Gross National Happiness (GNH) proposed by Bhutan's fourth Dragon King, Jigme Singye Wangchuck, as a measure of the collective happiness in a nation. Measure of Economic Welfare (MEW) developed by William Nordhaus and James Tobin as an alternative to crude GDP.
1983	The UN established the World Commission on Environment and Development (WCED), and *Our Common Future* was published in 1987, known as the 'Brutland Report' after the chair (see Chapter 5).
1989	Index of Sustainable Economic Welfare (ISEW) developed by Herman Daly and John Cobb to replace GDP.
1990	UNDP published the first annual *Human Development Report* (HDR) and first Human Development Index (HDI).
1992	UN Conference on Environment and Development (UNCED), known as the 'Rio Earth Summit' (see Chapter 5).
1995	Genuine Progress Indicator (GPI) proposed by Clifford Cobb, Ted Halstead and Jonathan Rowe, another alternative macroeconomic indicator of progress to replace GDP.
1997	Kyoto Protocol to the United Nations Framework Convention on Climate Change (UNFCCC) was adopted in 1997 and became enforceable law in 2005 (UN, 1998).
2000	UN adopts Resolution A/RES/55/2 and the 8 Millennium Development Goals (MDGs), part of the UN Millennium Declaration agreed by world leaders at the United Nations General Assembly (UNGA) in September 2000 (UNGA, 2000). UN member states agreed to try to achieve the goals by the year 2015. First issue of the *Journal of Happiness Studies* is published, founding editors Ed Diener, Alex Michalos and Ruut Veenhoven.
2002	UK Prime Minister's Strategy Unit publishes its report, *Life Satisfaction: The State of Knowledge and Implication for Government.*
2007	Scottish government publishes details of the National Performance Framework (NPF) 14 November. The NPF provides broad measures of national wellbeing covering a range of economic, health, social and environmental indicators and targets. Refreshed in 2011 and 2016, it now includes 50 National Indicators. European Commission hosted the high-level conference 'Beyond GDP' 19–20 November to clarify which indices are most appropriate to measure progress. In August 2009 the EC in a communication outlines details of the EU roadmap ahead.

(Continued)

Table 15.2: Charting social progress

2008 President Sarkozy creates the Commission on the Measurement of Economic Performance and Social Progress (CMEPSP) in February to overcome the limitations of GDP economics. Generally referred to as the Stiglitz–Sen–Fitoussi (SSF) Commission, the Final Report published 14 September 2009 expanded the focus to wellbeing.

US legislation proposes Key National Indicators, Act of 2008, signed into law in March 2010, part of the Patient Protection and Affordable Care Act. The Commission on Key National Indicators is established with oversight and reporting responsibilities.

2010 The UK Measuring National Wellbeing programme was established in November to measure and monitor national wellbeing. MNW now includes an interactive web-application and dashboard with international comparisons against EU and OECD member states.

2011 The *OECD Better Life Initiative* launched 24 May; this work programme was originally mandated by ministers in 2001. The *How's Life?* report includes internationally comparable indicators of wellbeing and there is also an interactive web application, the *Better Life Index*: www.oecdbetterlifeindex.org/. Other publications focus on the local-level distribution of wellbeing in *How's Life in Your Region*, and historical trends in wellbeing from 1820 in *How Was Life?*

UN adopts Resolution 65/309 on 19 July *Happiness: Towards a Holistic Definition of Development* (UNGA, 2011), inviting member countries to measure the happiness of their people and to use the data to help guide public policy, placing 'happiness' on the global development agenda.

2012 The first World Happiness Report (WHR) was published on 1 April (Helliwell et al, 2012), bringing together the available global data on national happiness, assembled at the CSD, Earth Institute, Columbia University.

UN High Level Meeting 2 April, Wellbeing and Happiness: Defining a New Economic Paradigm, at the UN Headquarters in New York, convened by the Royal Government of Bhutan.

The Oxfam Humankind Index launched 24 April, offers a new way of measuring what makes a good life in and for Scotland, produced by Oxfam Scotland.

2013 The OECD establishes the High Level Expert Group on the Measurement of Economic and Social Progress, HLEG is co-chaired by Joseph Stiglitz, Jean-Paul Fitoussi and Martine Durand, announced on 28 May, to continue the work of the SSF Commission.

The US National Research Council publishes its report on 18 December, *Subjective Well-Being: Measuring Happiness, Suffering, and Other Dimensions of Experience*, commissioned by the US National Institute on Aging and the UK ESRC jointly, to assess and report on whether measuring experienced wellbeing has value for informing policy.

2014 OECD hosts the first meeting of the HLEG on 16–17 January at the OECD Headquarters in Paris.

(Continued)

Table 15.2: Charting social progress (continued)

2015	UN adopts Resolution A/RES/70/1 *Transforming Our World: The 2030 Agenda for Sustainable Development* and the 17 Sustainable Development Goals (SDGs) that form part of the 2030 Agenda for Sustainable Development adopted by world leaders at the UNGA meeting at the UN Headquarters in New York on 25–27 September 2015 (UNGA, 2015), officially the SDGs came into force on 1 January 2016 and are intended to be achieved by the year 2030.
	At the twenty-first session of the Conference of the Parties (COP 21) in Paris, on 12 December 2015, parties to the UNFCCC reached a landmark agreement, the Paris Agreement (UN, 2015a). The central aim of the 2015 Paris Agreement is to strengthen the global response to the threat of climate change by keeping a global temperature rise this century well below 2 degrees Celsius above pre-industrial levels and preferably to 1.5 degrees Celsius. To date, 189 of the 197 Parties have ratified the Convention (the current number of ratifications can be found here: https://unfccc.int/process/the-paris-agreement/status-of-ratification).
2018	The New Zealand government delivered the 'wellbeing budget' 30 May, declaring it the first in the world to measure success by its people's wellbeing.
	HLEG issues its final reports, *Beyond GDP* (Stiglitz et al, 2018a) and *For Good Measure* (Stiglitz et al, 2018b) presenting the latest thinking on measuring people's wellbeing and societies' progress, they were published on 27 November and launched at the 6th OECD World Forum on Statistics, Knowledge and Policy in Incheon, Korea.

et al, 2013) for example (shown in Table 15.2). Today, policy makers in some contexts at least are increasingly trying to move the policy agenda beyond GDP, in order to reflect real social progress, where life can keep improving without the need for growth. In 2007, the Scottish government launched the National Performance Framework (NPF) to help monitor progress, supported by a dashboard of indicators and measures of national wellbeing. While Oxfam (2012, 2013) developed the Humankind Index for Scotland, a new way of measuring what makes a good life based on what people living in Scotland say is important to them. In New Zealand, the government introduced the 'wellbeing budget', declaring it the first in the world to measure success by its people's wellbeing (New Zealand Government, 2018). Economies are now being organized around life, rather than GDP growth. Health and life satisfaction are the new metrics by which New Zealand's progress is to be measured and judged, rather than wealth or economic growth. At the global level, there is the growing array of measures and indices that are being updated annually to track social progress. The objective indicators such as the UN's Human Development Index (HDI) (UNDP,

2019), the OECD's Better Life Index, in *How's Life?* (OECD, 2020), as well as subjective wellbeing (SWB) measures and indicators that are used to produce country league tables and rankings. The World Happiness Report (WHR) for example, first published in 2012, ranks countries by how happy their citizens perceive themselves to be, happiness is a measure of SWB (Helliwell et al, 2012, 2020).

Arguably, the 'social' remains stubbornly subordinate to the economic sphere in the early part of the 21st century; society is disrupted by the market, as we have heard throughout this volume. Economic growth is still the macroeconomic goal for policy makers, rather than sustainability, cohesion and social justice, as is evident in the institutional ideas, discourses and narratives of many powerful global policy actors, this despite a slowdown well underway before COVID-19 arrived and the growing concern about environmental limits to growth (Jackson, 2017; Dorling, 2020).[23] Worryingly, there is also a lack of attention to the *social* determinants of *social* wellbeing in national policy agendas (Deeming, 2013b), and in global social policy more generally (CSDH, 2008; Marmot et al, 2020). Things need to change, as Richard Wilkinson and Kate Pickett argued in Chapter 14. Over the next decade, all of this *is* supposed to change as (more) countries look to move beyond GDP to focus on the things that really matter in the age of sustainability. The goal, to end unjustifiable social problems and human inequalities, is forcing policy makers to think, not just about 'how much is enough' (minimum living standards) but also more about 'how much is too much' (income ceilings to tackle inequality) to promote social justice and sustainable living (Deeming, 2020).

Consequently, challenging and contesting the arguments of international institutions and policy makers, global social governance arrangements and shortcomings, concerning the *social* of social policy will be important in the continuing struggle for social sustainability and justice on a global scale in the 21st century.

Appendix 15.1: Tony Atkinson's 15 proposals for tackling inequality

1. The direction of technological change should be an explicit concern of policy makers, encouraging innovation in a form that increases the employability of workers and emphasizes the human dimension of service provision.
2. Public policy should aim at a proper balance of power among stakeholders, and to this end should (a) introduce an explicitly distributional dimension into competition policy; (b) ensure a legal framework that allows trade unions to represent workers on level terms; and (c) establish, where it does not already exist, a Social and Economic Council involving the social partners and other non-governmental bodies.

3. The government should adopt an explicit target for preventing and reducing unemployment and underpin this ambition by offering guaranteed public employment at the minimum wage to those who seek it.
4. There should be a national pay policy, consisting of two elements: a statutory minimum wage set at a living wage, and a code of practice for pay above the minimum, agreed as part of a 'national conversation' involving the Social and Economic Council.
5. The government should offer via national savings bonds a guaranteed positive real rate of interest on savings, with a maximum holding per person.
6. There should be a capital endowment (minimum inheritance) paid to all at adulthood.
7. A public Investment Authority should be created, operating a sovereign wealth fund with the aim of building up the net worth of the state by holding investments in companies and in property.
8. We should return to a more progressive rate structure for the personal income tax, with marginal rates of tax increasing by ranges of taxable income, up to a top rate of 65 per cent, accompanied by a broadening of the tax base.
9. The government should introduce into the personal income tax an Earned Income Discount, limited to the first band of earnings.
10. Receipts of inheritance and gifts inter vivos should be taxed under a progressive lifetime capital receipts tax.
11. There should be a proportional, or progressive, property tax based on up-to-date property assessments.
12. Child Benefit should be paid for all children at a substantial rate and should be taxed as income.
13. A participation income should be introduced at a national level, complementing existing social protection, with the prospect of an EU-wide child basic income.
14. (alternative to 13): There should be a renewal of social insurance, raising the level of benefits and extending their coverage.
15. Rich countries should raise their target for Overseas Development Assistance (ODA) to 1 per cent of Gross National Income (GNI).*

Alongside these proposals are several possibilities and ideas to explore further:
- A thoroughgoing review of the access of households to the credit market for borrowing not secured on housing.
- Examination of the case for an 'income-tax-based' treatment of contributions to private pensions, along the lines of present 'privileged' savings schemes, which would bring forward the payment of tax.
- A re-examination of the case for an annual wealth tax and the prerequisites for its successful introduction.
- A global tax regime for personal taxpayers, based on total wealth.
- A minimum tax for corporations.

Note: *UK ODA stood at 0.7 per cent of GNI in 2019 (DFID, 2020). The 0.7 per cent aid target is a target for donor countries to contribute 0.7 per cent of their GNI as ODA. It was adopted as a target by a resolution of the UN General Assembly in 1970.

Source: Adapted from Atkinson (2015: 302–5). Also available online: www.tony-atkinson.com/the-15-proposals-from-tony-atkinsons-inequality-what-can-be-done/.

(Reproduced with permission of the copyright owner.)

Appendix 15.2: David Harvey's 17 strategies for a political praxis for a post-capitalist future

1. The direct provision of adequate use values for all (housing, education, food security and so on) takes precedence over their provision through a profit-maximizing market system that concentrates exchange values in a few private hands and allocates goods on the basis of ability to pay.

2. A means of exchange is created that facilitates the circulation of goods and services but limits or excludes the capacity of private individuals to accumulate money as a form of social power.

3. The opposition between private property and state power is displaced as far as possible by common rights regimes (with particular emphasis upon human knowledge and the land as the most crucial commons we have), the creation, management and protection of which lie in the hands of popular assemblies and associations.

4. The appropriation of social power by private persons is not only inhibited by economic and social barriers but becomes universally frowned upon as a pathological deviancy.

5. The class opposition between capital and labour is dissolved into associated producers freely deciding on what, how and when they will produce in collaboration with other associations regarding the fulfilment of common social needs.

6. Daily life is slowed down (locomotion shall be leisurely and slow) to maximize time for free activities conducted in a stable and well-maintained environment protected from dramatic episodes of creative destruction.

7. Associated populations assess and communicate their mutual social needs to each other to furnish the basis for their production decisions; in the short run, realization considerations dominate production decisions.

8. New technologies and organizational forms are created that lighten the load of all forms of social labour, dissolve unnecessary distinctions in technical divisions of labour, liberate time for free individual and collective activities, and diminish the ecological footprint of human activities.

9. Technical divisions of labour are reduced through the use of automation, robotization and artificial intelligence. Those residual technical divisions of labour deemed essential are dissociated from social divisions of labour as far as possible. Administrative, leadership and policing functions should be rotated among individuals within the population at large. We are liberated from the rule of experts.

10. Monopoly and centralized power over the use of the means of production is vested in popular associations through which the decentralized competitive capacities of individuals and social groups are mobilized to produce differentiations in technical, social, cultural and lifestyle innovations.

11. The greatest possible diversification exists in ways of living and being, of social relations and relations to nature, and of cultural habits and beliefs within territorial associations, communes and collectives. Free and uninhibited but orderly geographical movement of individuals within territories and between communes is guaranteed. Representatives of the associations regularly come together to assess, plan and undertake common tasks and deal with common problems at different scales: bioregional, continental and global.

12. All inequalities in material provision are abolished other than those entailed in the principle of from each according to his, her or their capacities and to each according to his, her, or their needs.

13. The distinction between necessary labour done for distant others and work undertaken in the reproduction of self, household and commune is gradually erased, such that social labour becomes embedded in household and communal work and household and communal work becomes the primary form of unalienated and non-monetized social labour.

14. Everyone should have equal entitlements to education, healthcare, housing, food security, basic goods and open access to transportation to ensure the material basis for freedom from want and for freedom of action and movement.

15. The economy converges on zero growth (though with room for uneven geographical developments) in a world in which the greatest possible development of both individual and collective human capacities and powers and the perpetual search for novelty prevail as social norms to displace the mania for perpetual compound growth.

16. The appropriation and production of natural forces for human needs should proceed apace but with the maximum regard for the protection of ecosystems, maximum attention paid to the recycling of nutrients, energy and physical matter to the sites from whence they came, and an overwhelming sense of re-enchantment with the beauty of the natural world, of which we are a part and to which we can and do contribute through our works.

17. Unalienated human beings and unalienated creative personas emerge armed with a new and confident sense of self and collective being. Born out of the experience of freely contracted intimate social relations and empathy for different modes of living and producing, a world will emerge where everyone is considered equally worthy of dignity and respect, even as conflict rages over the appropriate definition of the good life. This social world will continuously evolve through permanent and ongoing revolutions in human capacities and powers. The perpetual search for novelty continues.

Source: Adapted from Harvey (2014: 294–7).

Notes

1 The geopolitical social questions have been wide-ranging across populations and spatial scales (global, national, regional, local, communal); the 'German question' on unification for example, or the 'Southern question' in Italy after unification (relating to the living conditions of the south that occupied Antonio Gramsci), or the so-called 'Irish Question' and 'Scottish Question' and struggle for home rule (Mitchell, 2014; Ferrera, 2018). Chapter 1 also considered the so-called social questions relating to 'race' and 'women'. While historically embedded in the context of the culturally and linguistically defined nation states, and the socially defined welfare state, increasingly the social question is cast as the 'transnational question' in global times (see Chapters 1 and 3).

2 Founded in 1919, the ILO marked 100 years of advancing social justice in 2019. The ILO is the longest established international organization concerned with social questions. It has long promoted tax-financed and contributions-based social security systems, including health, pension and unemployment protection.

3 As *The Growth Report* notes, sustained economic growth enables and is essential for many of the things that people care about, such as poverty reduction, education, health and, importantly, productive employment and the opportunity to be creative.

4 While low- and middle-income countries constitute 80 per cent of the world's population, they have contributed only 23 per cent of cumulative global emmissions since the mid-18th century.

5 Executive Order 13769 of 27 January 2017, https://www.federalregister.gov/documents/2017/02/01/2017-02281/protecting-the-nation-from-foreign-terrorist-entry-into-the-united-states.

6 UNHRC is an intergovernmental body within the United Nations system responsible for strengthening the promotion and protection of human rights around the globe and for addressing situations of human rights violations and make recommendations on them, see www.ohchr.org/EN/HRBodies/HRC/Pages/Home.aspx. Human Rights Watch is an international NGO that investigates and reports on abuses happening in all corners of the world, see www.hrw.org/.

7 See www.un.org/sustainabledevelopment/globalpartnerships/; www.globalgoals.org/17-partnerships-for-the-goals.

8 CCTs increased dramatically, from 2 countries in 1997 to 27 in 2008 and 64 in 2014. UCTs are the most prevalent type of transfer, present in 131 countries.

9 Only 29 per cent of the global population is covered by comprehensive social security systems that include the full range of benefits, from child and family benefits to old-age pensions. Yet the large majority, 71 per cent or 5.2 billion people, are either not protected or are only partially protected.

10 Health is a fundamental human right and the WHO is committed to ensuring the highest attainable level of health for all. The WHO's 1946 Constitution declared that 'the enjoyment of the highest attainable standard of health is one of the fundamental rights of every human being'. This mandate, that came into force in 1948, has framed the organization's work to advance human rights in global health over the past 70 years, see www.who.int/about/who-we-are/constitution. All UN member states have pledged agreement to UHC by 2030.

11 'Challenging World – Change Needed in Right Direction: UN chief on the United Nations at 75', https://www.globalpeaceandprosperityforum.com/news/challenging-world.

12 The relationship between GDP and employment is well known. Okun's law suggests that for every two or three percentage point increase in GDP, unemployment falls

one percentage point. Arthur Okun was an economist and advisor to President John F. Kennedy. The theory dating from 1962 informs monetary policy, keep growing the economy, and everything will be fine, the thinking goes.

[13] The vision for society where needs prevail has a long history in socialist thinking that pre-dates Marx, who promoted the old socialist slogan or maxim 'to each according to his needs'. The 'basic needs' approaches to development were influential in the development discourses of the 1970s and 1980s, promoted by the ILO and World Bank alike (see Max-Neef, 1992). Attention is once again firmly on needs and satisfiers to protect all forms of life on earth in the struggle for social sustainability (see Doyal and Gough, 1991; Smith and Max-Neef, 2011: ch 10).

[14] www.equalitytrust.org.uk/sites/default/files/resource/attachments/FINAL_Individual_Manifesto.pdf.

[15] Broman and Robèrt (2017) also discuss the methodology underpinning the Framework for Strategic Sustainable Development (FSSD); see also the Natural Step Framework (NSF) and four system conditions for a sustainable society, www.naturalstep.ca/four-system-conditions.

[16] The BLM Global Network is now a global movement in the fight for freedom, liberation and justice, seehttps://blacklivesmatter.com/. For more on Extinction Rebellion see https://extinctionrebellion.uk/.

[17] For information about IHE see www.instituteofhealthequity.org/home; for CSD see https://csd.columbia.edu/.

[18] WACR is series of international conference events organized by the United Nations Educational, Scientific and Cultural Organisation (UNESCO), see www.un.org/WCAR/. For information about Degrowth and ICED, see www.degrowth.info/en/.

[19] For information about BIEN see https://basicincome.org/; for the Equality Trust see www.equalitytrust.org.uk/; for Equality Can't Wait see www.equalitycantwait.com/. For information about the PHM see https://phmovement.org/. The People's Charter for Health can be downloaded online: https://phmovement.org/the-peoples-charter-for-health/. For information on SDSN, a global initiative for the UN, see www.unsdsn.org/; and for SDSN Youth see https://sdsnyouth.org/.

[20] While it is true that growth defined progress through much of the 20th century, it is also true that the OECD and other organizations began to invest in developing alternative measures of social progress, from the 1970s onwards (for example, OECD, 1977, 1998b).

[21] Remarks at the University of Kansas, 18 March 1968: www.jfklibrary.org/learn/about-jfk/the-kennedy-family/robert-f-kennedy/robert-f-kennedy-speeches/remarks-at-the-university-of-kansas-march-18-1968.

[22] In 1972, the 4th King of Bhutan, King Jigme Singye Wangchuck, declared, 'Gross National Happiness is more important than Gross Domestic Product', see https://ophi.org.uk/ophi-measure-used-in-creating-the-bhutan-gross-national-happiness-index/

[23] Many like Tim Jackson argue we need to get out of the current crises and transition to a sustainable economy; but there are different competing narratives and solutions, from 'green growth' to 'de-growth'. For example, 'green growthers' like Nicholas Stern (2019) argue that a transition to a low- or zero-carbon economy offers an alternative and dynamic growth economy, trust 'high tech solutions' they say. From this perspective, capitalism can solve the climate emergency. By contrast, 'de-growthers' propose the need for radical solutions given the scale of the problem. This involves rolling back growth, or 'de-growth', and overhauling the way society is organized. From this perspective capitalism is the problem; a future-blind system.

The old 'growth paradigm' is in need of a radical overhaul, to be replaced by a new 'de-growth paradigm'.

References

Allan, B. B. (2019) 'Paradigm and Nexus: Neoclassical Economics and the Growth Imperative in the World Bank, 1948–2000', *Review of International Political Economy*, 26(1): 183–206.

Alvaredo, F., Chancel, L., Piketty, T., Saez, E. and Zucman, G. (2017) *World Inequality Report 2018*, Cambridge, MA: Belknap Press.

Andersson, J. (2006) *Between Growth and Security: Swedish Social Democracy from a Strong Society to a Third Way*, Manchester: Manchester University Press.

Arendt, H. (1951) *The Origins of Totalitarianism*, New York: Harcourt, Brace & Company.

Atkinson, A. B. (1996) 'The Case for a Participation Income', *Political Quarterly*, 67(1): 67–70.

Atkinson, A. B. (2015) *Inequality: What Can Be Done?*, Cambridge, MA: Harvard University Press.

Atkinson, J. and Scurrah, M. (2009) *Globalizing Social Justice: The Role of Non-Government Organizations in Bringing about Social Change*, Basingstoke: Palgrave Macmillan.

Banerjee, A. V. and Duflo, E. (2011) *Poor Economics: A Radical Rethinking of the Way to Fight Global Poverty*, New York: Public Affairs.

Basole, A. (2019) *State of Working India 2019*, Centre for Sustainable Employment, Bengaluru: Azim Premji University.

Bellucci, S. and Weiss, H. (2020) '1919 and the Century of the Labour Internationalisation', in S. Bellucci and H. Weiss (eds) *The Internationalisation of the Labour Question: Ideological Antagonism, Workers' Movements and the ILO since 1919*, Cham: Palgrave Macmillan, 1–19.

Betts, A. and Collier, P. (2017) *Refuge: Rethinking Refugee Policy in a Changing World*, New York: Oxford University Press.

Betts, A. and Collier, P. (2018) *Refuge: Transforming a Broken Refugee System*, London: Penguin.

Blank, L. and Handa, S. (2008) *Social Protection in Eastern and Southern Africa: A Framework and Strategy for UNICEF*, Nairobi: UNICEF Eastern and Southern Africa Regional Office.

Bonoli, G. (2018) 'Active Labour Market Policies for an Inclusive Growth', in C. Deeming and P. Smyth (eds) *Reframing Global Social Policy: Social Investment for Sustainable and Inclusive Growth*, Bristol: Policy Press, 169–87.

Boris, E. (2019) *Making the Woman Worker Precarious Labor and the Fight for Global Standards, 1919–2019*, New York: Oxford University Press.

Boughton, J. M. (2012) *Tearing Down Walls: The International Monetary Fund 1990–1999*, Washington, DC: IMF.

Bourguignon, F. ([2012] 2015) *The Globalization of Inequality*, Princeton, NJ: Princeton University Press.

Broman, G. I. and Karl-Henrik Robèrt, K.-H. (2017) 'A Framework for Strategic Sustainable Development', *Journal of Cleaner Production*, 140(1): 17–31.

Browne, S. (2017) *Sustainable Development: Goals and UN Goal-setting*, Abingdon: Routledge.

Caney, S. (2005) 'Cosmopolitan Justice, Responsibility, and Global Climate Change', *Leiden Journal of International Law*, 18(4): 747–75.

Caney, S. (2006) 'Cosmopolitan Justice, Rights and Global Climate Change', *Canadian Journal of Law & Jurisprudence*, 19(2): 255–78.

Castel, R. ([1995] 2003) *From Manual Workers to Wage Laborers: Transformation of the Social Question*, Translated and edited by Richard Boyd, New Brunswick, NJ: Transaction Publishers.

Castells, M. (2010) *The Power of Identity*, Second Edition, Oxford: Wiley-Blackwell.

Castells, M. (2015) *Networks of Outrage and Hope: Social Movements in the Internet Age*, Second Edition, Cambridge: Polity.

Cobb, C., Halstead, T. and Rowe, J. (1995) *The Genuine Progress Indicator: Summary of Data and Methodology*, Washington, DC: Redefining Progress.

Commission on Growth and Development (2008) *The Growth Report: Strategies for Sustained Growth and Inclusive Development*, Washington, DC: WBG, https://doi.org/10.1596/978-0-8213-7491-7.

Cookson, T. (2018) *Unjust Conditions: Women's Work and the Hidden Cost of Cash Transfer Programs*, Oakland, CA: University of California Press.

Coote, A. and Franklin, J. (eds) (2013) *Time on Our Side: Why We All Need a Shorter Working Week*, London: nef.

Coote, A. and Percy, A. (2020) *The Case for Universal Basic Services*, Cambridge: Polity.

Coote, A., Harper, A. and Stirling, A. (2021) *The Case for a Four Day Week*, Cambridge: Polity.

Cornia, G. A., Jolly, R. and Stewart, F. (1987) *Adjustment with a Human Face. A Study by Unicef*, Volume 1: *Protecting the Vulnerable and Promoting Growth*, Oxford: Clarendon Press.

CSDH (Commission on Social Determinants of Health) (2008) *Closing the Gap in a Generation: Health Equity through Action on the Social Determinants of Health*, Final Report of the Commission on Social Determinants of Health, Geneva: WHO.

Dale, G. (2017) 'Seventeenth-Century Origins of the Growth Paradigm', in I. Borowy and M. Schmelzer (eds) *History of the Future of Economic Growth: Historical Roots of Current Debates on Sustainable Degrowth*, Abingdon: Routledge, 27–51.

Daly, H. E. and Cobb, J. (1989) *For the Common Good: Redirecting the Economy Toward Community, the Environment, and a Sustainable Future*, Boston, MA: Beacon Press.

Davala, S., Jhabvala, R., Standing, G. and Mehta, S. K. (2015) *Basic Income: A Transformative Policy for India*, London and New Delhi: Bloomsbury.

Deacon, B. (2005) 'From "Safety Nets" Back to "Universal Social Provision": Is the Global Tide Turning?', *Global Social Policy*, 5(1): 19–28.

Deacon, B. (2013) *Global Social Policy in the Making: The Foundations of the Social Protection Floor*, Bristol: Policy Press.

Deacon, B. (2015) 'The International Labour Organization and Global Social Governance: The 100 Year Search for Social Justice', in A. Kaasch and K. Martens (eds) *Actors & Agency in Global Social Governance*, Oxford: Oxford University Press, 3–17.

Deacon, B. and Macovei, M. (2010) 'Regional Social Policy from Above: International Organisations and Regional Social Policy', in B. Deacon, M. Macovei, L. van Langenhove and N. Yeates (eds) *World-Regional Social Policy and Global Governance: New Research and Policy Agendas in Africa, Asia, Europe and Latin America*, Abingdon: Routledge, 41–62.

Deaton, A. (2010) 'Instruments, Randomization, and Learning about Development', *Journal of Economic Literature*, 48(2): 424–55.

Deeming, C. (2013a) 'Trials and Tribulations: The "Use" (and "Misuse") of Evidence in Public Policy', *Social Policy & Administration*, 47(4): 359–81.

Deeming, C. (2013b) 'Addressing the Social Determinants of Subjective Wellbeing: The Latest Challenge for Social Policy', *Journal of Social Policy*, 42(3): 541–65.

Deeming, C. (2017) 'Use and Misuse of Evaluation in Social Policy', in B. Greve (ed) *Handbook of Social Policy Evaluation*, Cheltenham: Edward Elgar, 161–82.

Deeming, C. (ed) (2020) *Minimum Income Standards and Reference Budgets: International and Comparative Policy Perspectives*, Bristol: Policy Press.

DFID (Department for International Development) (2020) *Statistics on International Development: Provisional UK Aid Spend 2019*, April 2020, London: DFID.

Dorling, D. (2020) *Slowdown: The End of the Great Acceleration – and Why It's Good for the Planet, the Economy, and Our Lives*, New Haven, CT: Yale University Press.

Downes, A. and Lansley, S. (eds) (2018) *It's Basic Income: The Global Debate*, Bristol: Policy Press.

Doyal, L. and Gough, I. (1991) *A Theory of Human Need*, Basingstoke: Macmillan.

Drèze, J. and Sen, A. (2013) *An Uncertain Glory: India and its Contradictions*, London: Allen Lane.

Easterlin, R. (1974) 'Does Economic Growth Improve the Human Lot? Some Empirical Evidence', in P. A. David and M. W. Reder (eds) *Nations and Households in Economic Growth: Essays in Honor of Moses Abramovitz*, New York: Academic Press, 89–125.

Edling, N., Henrik, J., Petersen, J. and Petersen, K. (2015) 'Social Policy Language in Denmark and Sweden', in D. Béland and K. Petersen (eds) *Analysing Social Policy Concepts and Language: Comparative and Transnational Perspectives*, Bristol: Policy Press, 13–34.

Emmerij, L., Jolly, R. and Weiss, T. G. (2001) *Ahead of the Curve? UN Ideas and Global Challenges*, Bloomington, IN: Indiana University Press.

Esping-Andersen, G. (1990) *The Three Worlds of Welfare Capitalism*, Princeton, NJ: Princeton University Press.

Esping-Andersen, G. (1999) *Social Foundations of Postindustrial Economies*, Oxford: Oxford University Press.

Esping-Andersen, G. (2001) 'A Welfare State for the 21st Century', in A. Giddens (ed) *The Global Third Way Debate*, Cambridge: Polity, 134–56.

Esping-Andersen, G. (ed) (2002) *Why We Need a New Welfare State*, Oxford: Oxford University.

Ferrera, M. (2018) 'Italy: Wars, Political Extremism, and the Constraints to Welfare Reform', in H. Obinger, K. Petersen and P. Starke (eds) *Warfare & Welfare: Military Conflict and Welfare State Development in Western Countries*, Oxford: Oxford University Press, 99–126.

Fioramonti, L. (2013) *Gross Domestic Problem*, London: Zed Books.

Fiszbein, A., Schady, N., Ferreira, F. H. G., Grosh, M., Keleher, N., Olinto, P. and Skoufias, E. (2009) *Conditional Cash Transfers: Reducing Present and Future Poverty*, Washington, DC: World Bank.

Fitzpatrick, T. (2001) 'Making Welfare for Future Generations', *Social Policy & Administration*, 35(5): 506–20.

Fleurbaey, M. (2009) 'Beyond GDP: The Quest for a Measure of Social Welfare', *Journal of Economic Literature*, 47(4): 1029–75.

Fleurbaey, M., Bouin, O., Salles-Djelic, M., Kanbur, R., Nowotny, H. and Reis, E. (2018) *A Manifesto for Social Progress: Ideas for a Better Society*, Cambridge: Cambridge University Press.

Flora, P. (ed) (1986a) *Growth to Limits: The Western European Welfare States Since World War II*, Volume 1: *Sweden, Norway, Finland, Denmark*, Berlin and New York: Walter de Gruyter.

Flora, P. (ed) (1986b) *Growth to Limits: The Western European Welfare States Since World War II*, Volume 2: *Germany, United Kingdom, Ireland, Italy*, Berlin and New York: Walter de Gruyter.

Floud, J., Moran, M., Johal, S., Salento, A. and Williams, K. (2018) *Foundational Economy: The Infrastructure of Everyday Life*, Manchester: Manchester University Press.

Fox Piven, F. and Cloward, R. A. (1977) *Poor People's Movements: Why They Succeed, How They Fail*, New York: Pantheon.

Freeman, M. (2017) *Human Rights*, Third Edition, Cambridge: Polity.

Frericks, P. and Maier, R. (2012) *European Capitalist Welfare Societies: The Challenge of Sustainability*, Basingstoke: Palgrave Macmillan.

Giddens, A. (1998) *The Third Way: The Renewal of Social Democracy*, Cambridge: Polity.

Goodin, R. (2001) 'Work and Welfare: Towards a Post-Productivist Welfare Regime', *British Journal of Political Science*, 31(1): 13–39.

Gough, I. (2008) 'European Welfare States: Explanations and Lessons for Developing Countries', in A. A. Dani and A. de Haan (eds) *Inclusive States: Social Policy and Structural Inequalities*, Washington, DC: World Bank, 3–38.

Gough I. (2014) 'Climate Change, Social Policy, and Global Governance', in A. Kaasch and P. Stubbs (eds) *Transformations in Global and Regional Social Policies*, Basingstoke: Palgrave Macmillan, 108–33.

Gough, I. (2019) 'Universal Basic Services: A Theoretical and Moral Framework', *Political Quarterly*, 90(3): 534–42.

Grosh, M., del Ninno, C., Tesliuc, E. and Ouerghi, A. (2008) *For Protection and Promotion: The Design and Implementation of Effective Safety Nets*, Washington, DC: World Bank, http://hdl.handle.net/10986/6582.

Hall, A. (2015) 'It Takes Two to Tango: Conditional Cash Transfers, Social Policy, and the Globalizing Role of the World Bank', in S. McBride, G. Boychuk and R. Mahon (eds) *After 08: Social Policy and the Global Financial Crisis*, Vancouver: UBC Press, 140–58.

Hall, P. (2020) 'The Electoral Politics of Growth Regimes', *Perspectives on Politics*, 18(1): 185–99.

Hardoon, D., Fuentes-Nieva, R. and Ayele, S. (2016) *An Economy For The 1%: How Privilege and Power in the Economy Drive Extreme Inequality and How this can be Stopped*, Oxford: Oxfam International, http://oxf.am/ZniS.

Harvey, D. (2014) *Seventeen Contradictions and the End of Capitalism*, London: Profile Books.

Helliwell, J., Layard, R. and Sachs, J. (2012) *World Happiness Report 2012*, New York: SDSN, https://worldhappiness.report/ed/2012/.

Helliwell, J. F., Layard, R., Sachs, J. D. and De Neve, J.-D. (2020) *World Happiness Report 2020*, New York: SDSN, https://worldhappiness.report/ed/2020/.

Heymann, J. and Barrera, M. (2014) *Ensuring a Sustainable Future: Making Progress on Environment and Equity*, New York: Oxford University Press.

Hickel, J. (2017) *The Divide: A Brief Guide to Global Inequality and Its Solutions*, London: Heinemann.

Hirsch, F. (1977) *Social Limits to Growth*, London: Routledge & Kegan Paul.

Huber, E. and Stephens, J. (2001) *Development and Crisis of the Welfare State: Parties and Policies in Global Markets*, Chicago, IL: University of Chicago Press.

Human Rights Watch (2020) *Submission to the UN Special Rapporteur on Violence Against Women, Its Causes and Consequences Regarding COVID-19 and the Increase of Domestic Violence Against Women*, www.hrw.org/news/2020/07/03/submission-un-special-rapporteur-violence-against-women-its-causes-and-consequences.

ILO (International Labour Office) (2004) *Economic Security for a Better World*, Geneva: ILO, www.social-protection.org/gimi/gess/RessourcePDF.action?ressource.ressourceId=8670.

ILO (2016) *Non-Standard Employment Around the World: Understanding Challenges, Shaping Prospects*, Geneva: ILO.

ILO (2017) *World Social Protection Report 2017–19: Universal Social Protection to Achieve the Sustainable Development Goals*, Geneva: ILO, www.ilo.org/wcmsp5/groups/public/---dgreports/---dcomm/---publ/documents/publication/wcms_604882.pdf.

ILO (2019) *Work for a Brighter Future: Global Commission on the Future of Work*, Geneva: ILO, https://digitallibrary.un.org/record/3827525?ln=en.

ILO/WHO (International Labour Office/World Health Organization) (2011) *Social Protection Floor for a Fair and Inclusive Globalization: Report of the Advisory Group chaired by Michelle Bachelet convened by the ILO with the collaboration of the WHO*, Geneva: ILO, www.ilo.org/wcmsp5/groups/public/---dgreports/---dcomm/---publ/documents/publication/wcms_165750.pdf.

IMF (International Monetary Fund) (1993) *Social Safety Nets in Economic Reform*, EBS/93/34, Washington, DC: IMF.

IPSP (International Panel on Social Progress) (2018) *Rethinking Society for the 21st Century. Report of the International Panel on Social Progress*, Volume 1: *Socio-Economic Transformations*, Volume 2: *Political Regulation, Governance, and Societal Transformations*, Volume 3: *Transformations in Values, Norms, Cultures*, Cambridge: Cambridge University Press.

Jackson, T. (2017) *Prosperity without Growth: Foundations for the Economy of Tomorrow*, Second Edition, Abingdon and New York: Routledge.

Jenson, J. and Levi, R. (2013) 'Narratives and Regimes of Social and Human Rights: The Jack Pines of the Neoliberal Era', in P. A. Hall and M. Lamont (eds) *Social Resilience in the Neoliberal Era*, New York: Cambridge University Press, 69–98.

Jenson, J. and Saint-Martin, D. (2003) 'New Routes to Social Cohesion? Citizenship and the Social Investment State', *Canadian Journal of Sociology/Cahiers Canadiens De Sociologie*, 28(1): 77–99.

Jolly, R. (1991) 'Adjustment with a Human Face: A UNICEF Record and Perspective on the 1980s', *World Development*, 19(12): 1807–21.

Jolly, R. (2014) *UNICEF (United Nations Children's Fund): Global Governance that Works*, Abingdon: Routledge.

Jolly, R., Emmerij, L. and Weiss, T. G. (2009) *UN Ideas that Changed the World*, Bloomington, IN: Indiana University Press.

Kaasch, A. (2015) *Shaping Global Health Policy: Global Social Policy Actors and Ideas about Health Care Systems*, Basingstoke: Palgrave Macmillan.

Kaufmann, F.-X. (2012) *European Foundations of the Welfare State*, Translated from the German by John Veit-Wilson, New York: Berghahn Books.

Kaufmann, F.-X. (2013) *Variations of the Welfare State: Great Britain, Sweden, France and Germany Between Capitalism and Socialism*, German Social Policy 5, Translated from the German by Thomas Dunlap, Edited and introduced by Lutz Leisering, Heidelberg: Springer.

Kettunen, P. (2013) 'The ILO as a Forum for Developing and Demonstrating a Nordic Model', in S. Kott and J. Droux (eds) *Globalizing Social Rights: The International Labour Organization and Beyond*, Basingstoke: Palgrave Macmillan, 210-30.

Koivusalo, M. and Ollila, E. (1998) *Making a Healthy World: Agencies, Actors and Policies in International Health*, London and New York: Zed Books.

Kott, S. and Droux, J. (eds) (2013) *Globalizing Social Rights: The International Labour Organization and Beyond*, Basingstoke: Palgrave Macmillan.

Kroll, C., Warchold, A. and Pradhan, P. (2019) 'Sustainable Development Goals (SDGs): Are We Successful in Turning Trade-Offs into Synergies?', *Palgrave Commun*, 5: 140, https://doi.org/10.1057/s41599-019-0335-5.

Kubiszewski, I., Costanza, R., Franco, C., Lawn, P., Talberth, J., Jackson, T. and Aylmer, C. (2013) 'Beyond GDP: Measuring and Achieving Global Genuine Progress', *Ecological Economics*, 93: 57–68.

Labonté, R. and Ruckert, A. (2019) *Health Equity in a Globalizing Era: Past Challenges, Future Prospects*, Oxford: Oxford University Press.

Lange, G.-M., Wodon, Q. and Carey, K. (2018) *The Changing Wealth of Nations 2018: Building a Sustainable Future*, Washington, DC: World Bank.

Leisering, L. (2019) *The Global Rise of Social Cash Transfers: How States and International Organizations Constructed a New Instrument for Combating Poverty*, Oxford: Oxford University Press.

Lewis, J. (1999) *Rethinking Social Policy: Gender and Welfare Regimes*, IWM Working Paper No 6/1999, Vienna: IWM, https://cdn.atria.nl/epublications/1999/RethinkingSocialPolicy.pdf.

Lister, R. (2018) 'Coming Off the Fence on Universal Basic Income', in A. Downes and S. Lansley (eds) *It's Basic Income: The Global Debate*, Bristol: Policy Press, 54-7.

Marmot, M., Allen, J., Boyce, T., Goldblatt, P. and Morrison, J. (2020) *Health Equity in England: The Marmot Review 10 Years On*, London: IHE.

Marshall, T. H. (1950) *Citizenship and Social Class, and Other Essays*, Cambridge: Cambridge University Press.

Marx, I. (2007) *A New Social Question? On Minimum Income Protection in the Postindustrial Era*, Amsterdam: Amsterdam University Press.

Maul, D. (2019) *The International Labour Organization: 100 Years of Global Social Policy*, Berlin: De Gruyter Oldenbourg.

Max-Neef, M. (1992) 'Development and Human Needs', in P. Ekins and M. Max-Neef (eds) *Real Life Economics: Understanding Wealth Creation*, London: Routledge, 197–214.

McBride, S. and Williams, R. A. (2001) 'Globalization, the Restructuring of Labour Markets and Policy Convergence: The OECD "Jobs Strategy"', *Global Social Policy*, 1(3): 281–309.

Meadows, D. H., Meadows, D. L., Randers, J. and Behrens III, W. W. (1972) *The Limits to Growth: A Report for the Club of Rome's Project on the Predicament of Mankind*, Washington, DC: Potomac Associates.

Meadows, D. H., Meadows, D. L. and Randers, J. (1992) *Beyond the Limits: Global Collapse or a Sustainable Future*, Post Mills, VT: Chelsea Green.

Meadows, D., Randers, J. and Meadows, D. (2004) *Limits to Growth: The 30-Year Update*, White River Junction, VT: Chelsea Green.

Mertus, J. A. (2009) *The United Nations and Human Rights: A Guide for a New Era*, Second Edition, Abingdon: Routledge.

Miller, C. (1995) 'The Social Section and Advisory Committee on Social Questions of the League of Nations', in P. Weindling (ed) *International Health Organisations and Movements, 1918–1939*, Cambridge: Cambridge University Press, 154–75.

Mitchell, J. (2014) *The Scottish Question*, Oxford: Oxford University Press.

Mkandawire, T. (2011) 'Welfare Regimes and Economic Development: Bridging the Conceptual Gap', in V. FitzGerald, J. Heyer and R. Thorp (eds) *Overcoming the Persistence of Inequality and Poverty*, Basingstoke: Palgrave Macmillan, 149–71.

Momani. B. (2010) 'IMF Rhetoric on Reducing Poverty and Inequality', in J. Clapp and R. Wilkinson (eds) *Global Governance, Poverty and Inequality*, Abingdon: Routledge, 71–89.

Murray, M. J. and Forstater, M. (eds) (2014) *The Job Guarantee: Toward True Full Employment*, Basingstoke: Palgrave Macmillan.

Murray, M. and Forstater, M. (eds) (2018) *Full Employment and Social Justice: Solidarity and Sustainability*, Cham: Palgrave Macmillan.

New Zealand Government (2018) *The Wellbeing Budget, Budget 2019*, Wellington: New Zealand Treasury, https://treasury.govt.nz/sites/default/files/2019-05/b19-wellbeing-budget.pdf.

Nordhaus, W. and Tobin, J. (1972) 'Is Growth Obsolete?', in National Bureau of Economic Research, *Economic Growth: Fifth Anniversary Colloquium*, New York: Columbia University Press, 509–64.

Nussbaum, M. C. (1999) *Sex and Social Justice*, New York: Oxford University Press.

Nussbaum, M. C. (2003) 'Capabilities as Fundamental Entitlements: Sen and Social Justice', *Feminist Economics*, 9(2–3): 33–59.

Nussbaum, M. C. (2011) *Creating Capabilities: The Human Development Approach*, Cambridge, MA: Belknap Press.

OECD (Organisation for Economic Co-operation and Development) (1977) *Measuring Social Well-being: A Progress Report on the Development of Social Indicators*, OECD Social Indicator Development Programme No 3, Paris: OECD.

OECD (1994a) *New Orientations for Social Policy*, Paris: OECD.

OECD (1994b) *The Jobs Study: Facts, Analysis, Strategy*, Paris: OECD.

OECD (1997) *Societal Cohesion and the Globalising Economy: What Does the Future Hold?*, Paris: OECD Publishing, https://doi.org/10.1787/9789264163874-en.

OECD (1998a) *Maintaining Prosperity in an Ageing Society*, Paris: OECD Publishing, https://doi.org/10.1787/9789264163133-en.

OECD (1998b) *Towards Sustainable Development: Environmental Indicators*, Paris: OECD Publishing, https://doi.org/10.1787/9789264163201-en.

OECD (2020) *How's Life? 2020: Measuring Well-being*, Paris: OECD Publishing.

OHCHR (Office of the United Nations High Commissioner for Human Rights) (2015) *Report on Social Protection Floors and Economic and Social Rights*, www.ohchr.org/Documents/Issues/SocialSecurity/ReportSocialProtectionFloors.pdf.

Orenstein, M. A. (2005) 'The New Pension Reform as Global Policy', *Global Social Policy*, 5(2): 175–202.

Orenstein, M. A. (2008) *Privatizing Pensions: The Transnational Campaign for Social Security Reform*, Princeton, NJ: Princeton University Press.

Orenstein, M. A. (2011) 'Pension Privatization in Crisis: Death or Rebirth of a Global Policy Trend?', *International Social Security Review*, 64(3): 65–80.

Orenstein, M. A. (2013) 'Pension Privatization: Evolution of a Paradigm', *Governance*, 26(2): 259-81.

Ortiz, I., Durán-Valverde, F., Urban, S. and Wodsak, V. (2018) *Reversing Pension Privatizations: Rebuilding Public Pension Systems in Eastern Europe and Latin America*, Geneva: ILO.

Oxfam (2012) *Oxfam Humankind Index: The New Measure of Scotland's Prosperity*, Oxford: Oxfam.

Oxfam (2013) *Oxfam Humankind Index: The New Measure of Scotland's Prosperity*, second results, Oxford: Oxfam, https://policy-practice.oxfam.org/resources/oxfam-humankind-index-the-new-measure-of-scotlands-prosperity-second-results-293743/.

Oxfam (2015) *Extreme Carbon Inequality: Why the Paris Climate Deal Must Put the Poorest, Lowest Emitting and Most Vulnerable People First*, 2 December, www-cdn.oxfam.org/s3fs-public/file_attachments/mb-extreme-carbon-inequality-021215-en.pdf.

Park, S. and Vetterlein, A. (2010) *Owning Development: Creating Policy Norms in the IMF and the World Bank*, New York: Cambridge University Press.

Pega, F., Liu, S. Y., Walter, S., Pabayo, R., Saith, R., Lhachimi, S. K. (2017) 'Unconditional Cash Transfers for Reducing Poverty and Vulnerabilities: Effect on Use of Health Services and Health Outcomes in Low- and Middle-Income Countries', *Cochrane Database of Systematic Reviews*, 11: CD011135.

Piachaud, D. (2018) 'Basic Income: Confusion, Claims and Choices', *Journal of Poverty and Social Justice*, 26(3): 299–314.

Piketty, T. (2014) *Capital in the Twenty-First Century*, Translated by Arthur Goldhammer, Cambridge, MA: Harvard University Press.

Piketty, T. (2020) *Capital and Ideology*, Translated by Arthur Goldhammer, Cambridge, MA: Harvard University Press.

Polanyi, K. ([1944] 2001) *The Great Transformation: The Political and Economic Origins of Our Time*, foreword by Joseph E. Stiglitz, with a new introduction by Fred Block, Boston: Beacon Press.

Polonenko, L. M. and Besada, H. (2017) 'Introduction: Meeting Future Challenges with Past Lessons', in H. Besada, L. M. Polonenko and M. Agarwal (eds) *Did the Millennium Development Goals Work? Meeting Future Challenges with Past Lessons*, Bristol: Policy Press, 1–12.

Pogge, T. (2008) *World Poverty and Human Rights: Cosmopolitan Responsibilities and Reforms*, Second Edition, Cambridge: Polity.

Pogge, T. and Mehta, K. (eds) (2016) *Global Tax Fairness*, Oxford: Oxford University Press.

Razavi, S. and Hassim, S. (eds) (2006) *Gender and Social Policy in a Global Context: Uncovering the Gendered Structure of 'the Social'*, UNRISD, Basingstoke: Palgrave Macmillan.

Rosanvallon, P. (2000) *The New Social Question: Rethinking the Welfare State*, Translated by Barbara Harshav, Princeton, NJ: Princeton University Press.

Sachs, J. D. (2015) *The Age of Sustainable Development*, New York: Columbia University Press.

Schmid, G. (2008) *Full Employment in Europe: Managing Labour Market Transitions and Risks*, Cheltenham: Edward Elgar.

Schmid, G. (2015) 'Sharing Risks of Labour Market Transitions: Towards a System of Employment Insurance', *British Journal of Industrial Relations*, 53(1): 70–93.

Schmid, G. (2018) 'Towards an Employment Strategy of Inclusive Growth', in C. Deeming and P. Smyth (eds) *Reframing Global Social Policy: Social Investment for Sustainable and Inclusive Growth*, Bristol: Bristol University Press, 145–67.

Schmelzer, M. (2016) *The Hegemony of Growth: The OECD and the Making of the Economic Growth Paradigm*, Cambridge: Cambridge University Press.

Sen, A. (2004) 'Elements of a Theory of Human Rights', *Philosophy & Public Affairs*, 32(4): 315–56.

Sen, A. (2005) 'Human Rights and Capabilities', *Journal of Human Development*, 6(2): 151–66.

Sluga, G. (2014) 'The Human Story of Development: Alva Myrdal at the UN, 1949–1955', in M. Frey, S. Kunkel and C. R. Unger (eds) *International Organizations and Development, 1945–1990*, Basingstoke: Palgrave Macmillan, 46–74.

Smith, P. B. and Max-Neef, M. (2011) *Economics Unmasked: From Power and Greed to Compassion and the Common Good*, Darlington: Green Books.

Somers, M. R. (2008) *Genealogies of Citizenship: Markets, Statelessness and the Right to Have Rights*, New York: Cambridge University Press.

Standing, G. (1999) *Global Labour Flexibility: Seeking Distributive Justice*, Basingstoke: Macmillan.

Standing, G. (2008) 'The ILO: An Agency for Globalization?', *Development and Change*, 39(3): 355–84.

Standing, G. (2009) *Work After Globalization: Building Occupational Citizenship*, Cheltenham: Edward Elgar.

Standing, G. (2011) 'Behavioural Conditionality: Why the Nudges Must be Stopped – An Opinion Piece', *Journal of Poverty and Social Justice*, 19(1): 27–38.

Standing, G. (2014) *A Precariat Charter: From Denizens to Citizens*, London and New York: Bloomsbury.

Standing, G. (2017) *Basic Income: And How We Can Make It Happen*, London: Pelican.

Standing, G. (2019) *Plunder of the Commons: A Manifesto for Sharing Public Wealth*, London: Pelican.

Standing, G. (2020) *Battling Eight Giants: Basic Income Now*, London: Bloomsbury.

Starke, P., Kaasch. A. and van Hooren, F. (2013) *Explaining the Diversity of Policy Responses to Economic Crisis*, Basingstoke: Palgrave Macmillan.

Steinmetz, G. (1993) *Regulating the Social: The Welfare State and Local Politics in Imperial Germany*, Princeton, NJ: Princeton University Press.

Stern, N. (2019) 'Afterword: Poverty and Climate Change', in A. B. Atkinson, *Measuring Poverty Around the World*, Princeton, NJ: Princeton University Press, 232–46.

Stiglitz, J. (2010) *The Stiglitz Report: Reforming the International Monetary and Financial Systems in the Wake of the Global Crisis*, New York: The New Press.

Stiglitz, J., Fitoussi, J. and Durand, M. (2018a) *Beyond GDP: Measuring What Counts for Economic and Social Performance*, Paris: OECD Publishing, https://doi.org/10.1787/9789264307292-en.

Stiglitz, J., Fitoussi, J. and Durand, M. (eds) (2018b) *For Good Measure: Advancing Research on Well-being Metrics Beyond GDP*, Paris: OECD Publishing, https://doi.org/10.1787/9789264307278-en.

Stone, D. and Wright, C. (eds) (2007) *The World Bank and Governance: A Decade of Reform and Reaction*, Abingdon: Routledge.

Stuckler, D., Basu, S., Suhrcke, M., Coutts, A. and McKee, M. (2009) 'The Public Health Effect of Economic Crises and Alternative Policy Responses in Europe: An Empirical Analysis', *The Lancet*, 374(9686): 315–23.

Taylor-Gooby, P. (2009) *Reframing Social Citizenship*, Oxford: Oxford University Press.

Thunberg, G. (2019) *No One Is Too Small To Make A Difference*, London: Penguin.

Tilly, C., Castañeda, E. and Wood, L. (2019) *Social Movements, 1768–2018*, Fourth Edition, New York: Routledge.

Townsend, P. (2002) 'Poverty, Social Exclusion and Social Polarisation: The Need to Construct an International Welfare State', in P. Townsend and D. Gordon (eds) *World Poverty: New Policies to Defeat an Old Enemy*, Bristol: Policy Press, 3–24.

Townsend, P. (2004) 'From Universalism to Safety Nets: The Rise and Fall of Keynesian Influence on Social Development', in T. Mkandawire (ed) *Social Policy in a Development Context*, Basingstoke: Palgrave Macmillan, 37–62.

Townsend, P. with Donkor, K. (1996) *Global Restructuring and Social Policy: The Need to Establish an International Welfare State*, Bristol: Policy Press.

Torry, M. (2020) 'Minimum Income Standards in the Basic Income Debate', in C. Deeming (ed) *Minimum Income Standards and Reference Budgets: International and Comparative Policy Perspectives*, Bristol: Policy Press, 319–29.

Ugo, G., Grosh, M., Rigolini, J. and Yemtsov, R. (2020) *Exploring Universal Basic Income: A Guide to Navigating Concepts, Evidence, and Practices*, Washington, DC: World Bank, http://hdl.handle.net/10986/32677.

UN (United Nations) (1998) *Kyoto Protocol to the United Nations Framework Convention on Climate Change*, New York: UN.

UN (2015a) *The Millennium Development Goals Report 2015*, New York: UN, https://doi.org/10.18356/6cd11401-en.

UN (2015b) *The Paris Agreement*, New York: UN.

UN Women (2020) *Progress of The World's Women 2019–2020: Families in a Changing World*, New York, NY: UN Women, https://doi.org/10.18356/696a9392-en.

UNCTAD (United Nations Conference on Trade and Development) (2020a) *Trade and Development Report 2020: From Global Pandemic to Prosperity for All: Avoiding Another Lost Decade*, Geneva: UN, https://doi.org/10.18356/aea7b3b9-en.

UNCTAD (2020b) *Transforming Trade and Development in a Fractured, Post-Pandemic World*, Geneva: UN, https://unctad.org/system/files/official-document/osg2020d2_en.pdf.

UNCTAD (2020c) *Impact of the COVID-19 Pandemic on Trade and Development: Transitioning to a New Normal*, New York: UN, https://unctad.org/system/files/official-document/osg2020d1_en.pdf.

UNDP (United Nations Development Programme) (2000) *Human Development Report 2000: Human Development and Human Rights*, New York: UNDP.

UNDP (2006) *Social Protection: The Role of Cash Transfers*, United Nations Development Programme, Brasilia: International Poverty Centre.

UNDP (2014) *Human Development Report 2014: Sustaining Human Progress: Reducing Vulnerabilities and Building Resilience*, New York: UNDP.

UNDP (2019) *Human Development Report 2019: Beyond Income, Beyond Averages, Beyond Today: Inequalities in Human Development in the 21st Century*, New York: UNDP.

UNGA (United Nations General Assembly) (2000) *United Nations Millennium Declaration*, A/RES/55/2, https://digitallibrary.un.org/record/422015?ln=en.

UNGA (2011) *Happiness: Towards a Holistic Definition of Development*, A/RES/65/309, https://digitallibrary.un.org/record/715187?ln=en.

UNGA (2015) *Transforming Our World: The 2030 Agenda for Sustainable Development*, A/RES/70/1, https://digitallibrary.un.org/record/808134?ln=en.

UNHRC (United Nations Human Rights Council) (2009) *15 Years of the United Nations Special Rapporteur on Violence Against Women, Its Causes and Consequences (1994–2009): A Critical Review*, https://digitallibrary.un.org/record/1641160?ln=en.

UNHRC (2018) *Report of the Special Rapporteur on Violence Against Women, Its Causes and Consequences on Online Violence Against Women and Girls from a Human Rights Perspective*, A/HRC/38/47, https://digitallibrary.un.org/record/1641160?ln=en.

UNHRC (2019) *Visit to the United Kingdom of Great Britain and Northern Ireland: Report of the Special Rapporteur on Extreme Poverty and Human Rights*, Human Rights Council, Forty-first session, A/HRC/41/39/Add.1, https://digitallibrary.un.org/record/3806308?ln=en.

UNIATF (United Nations Inter-agency Task Force on Financing for Development) (2019) *Financing for Sustainable Development Report 2019*, New York: UN, https://doi.org/10.18356/9444edd5-en.

UNIATF (2020) *Financing for Sustainable Development Report 2020*, New York: UN, https://doi.org/10.18356/6fab9229-en.

UNICEF (United Nations Children's Fund) (2016) *Conditionality in Cash Transfers: UNICEF's Approach*, New York: UNICEF, https://socialprotection.org/discover/publications/conditionality-cash-transfers-unicef%E2%80%99s-approach.

UNICEF (2017) *Making Cash Transfers Work for Children and Families*, New York: UNICEF, www.unicef.org/lac/sites/unicef.org.lac/files/2019-11/Making%20cash%20transfers%20work%20for%20children%20and%20families.pdf.

UNICEF (2019a) *National Commitments for CRC30*, www.unicef.org/sites/default/files/2019-07/National-commitments-for-CRC30.pdf.

UNICEF (2019b) *UNICEF's Global Social Protection Programme Framework*, New York: UNICEF.

Van Parijs, P. (ed) (1992) *Arguing for Basic Income: Ethical Foundations for a Radical Reform*, London and New York: Verso.

Van Parijs, P. and Vanderborght, Y. (2015) 'Basic Income in a Globalised Economy', in R. Hasmath (ed) *Inclusive Growth, Development and Welfare Policy: A Critical Assessment*, New York: Routledge, 229–49.

Walters, W. (2000) *Unemployment and Government: Genealogies of the Social*, New York: Cambridge University Press.

Warner, J. (2014) 'God and Martha C. Nussbaum: Towards a Reformed Christian View of Capabilities', in F. Comim and M. C. Nussbaum (eds) *Capabilities, Gender, Equality: Towards Fundamental Entitlements*, Cambridge: Cambridge University Press, 437–63.

WBG (World Bank Group) (2019) *High-Performance Health Financing for Universal Health Coverage*, Washington, DC: WBG, https://doi.org/10.1596/31930.

Weaver, C. (2008) *Hypocrisy Trap: The World Bank and the Poverty of Reform*, Princeton, NJ: Princeton University Press.

WHO (World Health Organization) (2000) *The World Health Report 2000: Health Systems: Improving Performance*, Geneva: WHO, https://apps.who.int/iris/handle/10665/42281.

WHO (2007) *Everybody Business – Strengthening Health Systems to Improve Health Outcomes: WHO's Framework for Action*, Geneva: WHO, https://apps.who.int/iris/handle/10665/43918.

WHO (2019) *Universal Health Coverage (UHC)*, Fact sheet, 24 January, www.who.int/news-room/fact-sheets/detail/universal-health-coverage-(uhc).

Wilkinson, R. and Pickett, K. (2009) *The Spirit Level: Why More Equal Societies Almost Always Do Better*, London: Allen Lane.

Wilkinson, R. and Pickett, K. (2010) *The Spirit Level: Why Equality Is Better for Everyone*, London: Penguin.

Williams, F. (1992) 'Somewhere Over the Rainbow: Universality and Diversity in Social Policy', in N. Manning and R. Page (eds) *Social Policy Review 4*, Canterbury: Social Policy Association, 200–219.

World Bank (1994) *Averting the Old Age Crisis: Policies to Protect the Old and Promote Growth*, New York: World Bank, https://doi.org/10.1596/0-8213-2970-7.

World Bank (1996) *World Development Report 1996: From Plan to Market*, Washington, DC: World Bank, https://doi.org/10.1596/978-0-1952-1107-8.

World Bank (1997) *World Development Report 1997: The State in a Changing World*, Washington, DC: World Bank, https://doi.org/10.1596/978-0-1952-1114-6.

World Bank (2001) *Social Protection Sector Strategy: From Safety Net to Springboard*, Washington, DC: World Bank, http://documents1.worldbank.org/curated/en/299921468765558913/pdf/multi-page.pdf.

World Bank (2004) *World Development Report 2005: A Better Investment Climate for Everyone*, Washington, DC: World Bank, https://doi.org/10.1596/0-8213-5682-8.

World Bank (2011) *World Development Report 2011: Conflict, Security, and Development*, Washington, DC: World Bank, https://doi.org/10.1596/978-0-8213-8439-8.

World Bank (2012) *World Development Report 2013: Jobs*, Washington, DC: World Bank, https://doi.org/10.1596/978-0-8213-9575-2.

World Bank (2015a) *The State of the Social Safety Nets 2015*, Washington, DC: World Bank, https://doi.org/10.1596/978-1-4648-0543-1.

World Bank (2015b) *Global Monitoring Report 2014/2015: Ending Poverty and Sharing Prosperity*, Washington, DC: World Bank, https://doi.org/10.1596/978-1-4648-0336-9.

World Bank (2018a) *Poverty and Shared Prosperity 2018: Piecing Together the Poverty Puzzle*, Washington, DC: World Bank, https://doi.org/10.1596/978-1-4648-1330-6.

World Bank (2018b) *The State of Social Safety Nets 2018*, Washington, DC: World Bank, https://doi.org/10.1596/978-1-4648-1254-5.

World Bank (2019) *World Development Report 2019: The Changing Nature of Work*, Washington, DC: World Bank, https://doi.org/10.1596/978-1-4648-1328-3.

World Bank (2020) *Global Economic Prospects, June 2020*, Washington, DC: World Bank, http://hdl.handle.net/10986/33748.

World Bank (2021) *Global Economic Prospects, January 2021*, Washington, DC: World Bank, https://doi.org/10.1596/978-1-4648-1612-3.

WWF (World Wide Fund for Nature) (2020) *Living Planet Report 2020: Bending the Curve of Biodiversity Loss*, Gland: WWF.

Wynes, S. and Nicholas, K. A. (2017) 'The Climate Mitigation Gap: Education and Government Recommendations Miss the Most Effective Individual Actions', *Environmental Research Letters*, 12(7): 12074024.

Zucman, G. (2015) *The Hidden Wealth of Nations: The Scourge of Tax Havens*, Chicago, IL: University of Chicago Press.

Index

Burns, J. 229, 230
Bush, George 99
Business for Inclusive Growth Initiative
(B4IG) 261, 263

C

Canada 68n7, 182–3, 190, 192, 219,
226, 265
Cantat, C. 50
capability approach (CA) 73, 74–81,
82–4, 309
capitalism
affordability of social policies 292
alternatives to 312–13
boom-bust cycles 55
and Epicurean ethics 112
and the future of labour markets 113
global social governance 255
and inequality 293
inherently crisis-prone 21n4
intersecting global crises 199–207
intersectionality 195–215
markets 11, 40–1, 56, 65, 94, 164,
200, 203, 205, 278, 293, 298
versus participatory socialism 312
post-productivism 111–25, 296,
297, 313
profit motives 116, 117, 119, 122,
200, 202, 276
pro-productivity 294
social justice 247
and the 'social' question 38, 45,
55–71
see also neoliberalism
Capitalocene 204
carbon dioxide emissions 102, 110,
112, 170, 204, 276–8, 280, 315
Card, D. 66
caring work 202–4, 209, 297, 319
cash transfers 302–3, 304, 305
CEDAW (Convention on the
Elimination of All Forms of
Discrimination against Women) 8
Centre for Social Justice 241
Centre for Sustainable Development
(CSD) 317
Charter of Rights 310, 311
Chattoo, S. 197, 245
Chiappero- Martinetti, E.C. 77
childhood deprivation 165–6
children's rights 302
China 104, 119, 130, 157
chronic conditions 165, 167, 169
citizenship
duties 293
global citizenship 119
intersectionality 207–8
participatory democracy 209

post-productivism 118
social cohesion 221, 224–5
social investment 75, 78–80
social justice 242
social policy as a political-democratic
matter 81–3
civic agora 118
civil society 83, 119, 228, 301, 317
'clap for carers' 6
Clarke, J. 7, 11, 41, 47, 74
class 9–10, 52, 60, 120, 202, 203, 220
climate change
carbon dioxide emissions 102, 110,
112, 170, 204, 276–8, 280, 315
central human functional
capabilities 309
climate debt trap 5
dominating the future 277–8
and economic policy 66
global social governance 299
inclusive growth 263
inequality 122–3
intersectionality 204–5, 208
job creation 66–7
migration 204, 208
mutual support/aid 281
Sustainable Development Goals
(SDGs) 3–4, 103
youth climate movements 317
see also environment
CMEPSP (Commission on the
Measurement of Economic
Performance and Social
Progress) 261
collective action problem (CAP)
116–17, 124
collective social provision 45, 99, 209
collectivity in global social policy
229–30, 247
Collins, P. H. 9, 196, 198
colonialism 39, 196, 202, 246, 293
commercialization 119
Commission for Social Justice
(CSJ) 242
Commission on Growth and
Development 294
Commission on the Social
Determinants of Health
(CSDH) 223, 306–7, 308, 323
Committee of Ministers to Member
States on Intercultural
Integration 227
commodification 119, 200–1, 202
commoditization of individuals 74
commons 49, 97, 209
commons dividends 311
Commons Fund 311

The 'social' in the age of sustainability 5